Large-Scale Land Acquisitions

International Development Policy

Editor-in-Chief

Gilles Carbonnier (*Professor of Development Economics, The Graduate Institute, Geneva*)

Guest Editors

Christophe Gironde (*Senior Lecturer, The Graduate Institute, Geneva*)
Christophe Golay (*Coordinator of the Project on Economic, Social and Cultural Rights, Geneva Academy of International Humanitarian Law and Human Rights*)
Peter Messerli (*Director of the Centre for Development and Environment (CDE), University of Bern*)

VOLUME 6

The titles published in this series are listed at *brill.com/idp*

Cover photo courtesy Amaury Peeters.

Library of Congress Cataloging-in-Publication Data

Large-scale land acquisitions : focus on South-East Asia / edited by Christophe Gironde, Christophe Golay, and Peter Messerli.
    pages cm. — (International development policy ; volume 6)
    Includes bibliographical references and index.
    ISBN 978-90-04-30474-1 (pbk. : alk. paper) — ISBN 978-90-04-30475-8 (e-book) 1. Land tenure—Law and legislation—Southeast Asia. 2. Eminent domain—Southeast Asia. 3. Land use—Law and legislation—Southeast Asia. 4. Real estate development—Law and legislation—Southeast Asia. 5. Law and economic development. I. Gironde, Christophe, editor. II. Golay, Christophe, editor. III. Messerli, Peter, editor.

KNC772.L37 2015
333.330959—dc23

2015026735

This publication has been typeset in the multilingual 'Brill' typeface. With over 5,100 characters covering Latin, IPA, Greek, and Cyrillic, this typeface is especially suitable for use in the humanities.
For more information, please see www.brill.com/brill-typeface.

ISSN 1663-9383
ISBN 978-90-04-30474-1 (hardback)
ISBN 978-90-04-30475-8 (e-book)

This book is printed on acid-free paper.

Printed by Printforce, the Netherlands

Large-Scale Land Acquisitions

Focus on South-East Asia

Edited by

Christophe Gironde, Christophe Golay, and Peter Messerli

BRILL

NIJHOFF

LEIDEN | BOSTON

Contents

PART 3

Human Rights and Large-Scale Land Acquisitions

Conclusion

Foreword

Gilles Carbonnier, Editor-in-Chief

The crisis that hit the financial, energy, and food sectors with booming prices in the mid-2000s gave rise to a new wave of transnational, large-scale land acquisitions (LSLAs) in developing countries. Energy and food price hikes accompanied by export restrictions on rice and other staples raised food security concerns worldwide, and in particular among net food importing countries. Both foreign and domestic investors from the private and public sectors have since sought to acquire ownership rights and long-term leases over large portions of land in low-income countries.

This spurred renewed research interest in agrarian change and 'land grabbing', as reflected in a series of special issues dealing with the topic in major development and agrarian studies journals. On the policy side, social mobilisation against large-scale land acquisitions encouraged intergovernmental organisations and governments to elaborate regulatory frameworks and voluntary guidelines meant to protect the interests of local communities and other stakeholders affected by the new land rush.

Notwithstanding a rapidly growing body of knowledge on LSLAs, there remain various gaps, for example between specific insights from case studies performed at the community level and studies that look at land acquisition dynamics at the macro level. There remains much scope to better grasp how land deal plans are effectively implemented on the ground and how they impact the livelihood of community members over the mid to long run, including in terms of human rights.

In 2014, the editorial board of International Development Policy invited three guest editors for a special issue on the LSLA phenomenon. We asked Christophe Gironde (Senior Lecturer, the Graduate Institute, Geneva), Christophe Golay (Coordinator of the Project on Economic, Social and Cultural Rights, Geneva Academy of International Humanitarian Law and Human Rights) and Peter Messerli (Director of the Centre for Development and Environment, University of Bern) to fill specific gaps in our understanding of LSLAs. I wish to commend the guest editors for bringing major innovative features to this Special Issue, which—in the context of a rapidly growing literature on LSLAs—stands out in four respects.

First, the Issue brings a broad range of disciplines to bear in a coherent framework, thus providing a rich interdisciplinary perspective on LSLAs that includes history, sociology, economics, geography, and law, alongside significant expertise in the fields of agrarian and development studies. Second, this Issue strikes a delicate balance between theoretical, critical reflections and detailed analysis of actual practice and field reality, looking not only at global actors, but also at the role of political and economic elites at the national and local levels. Third, the Issue offers the first major collection of articles on LSLAs with a focus on South-East Asia, a region that has attracted relatively little attention thus far. It looks at actual processes and practices of land acquisitions and agrarian change in Cambodia and Laos in particular. Fourth, this Special Issue stands out by analysing the impact of land acquisition and agrarian change from a human rights perspective: several contributions examine LSLA dynamics through human rights instruments and frameworks.

A series of chapters draw on a collaborative, North-South research project funded by the Swiss Network for International Studies (SNIS).[1] This project—entitled 'Large Scale Land Acquisitions in Southeast Asia: Rural Transformations between Global Agendas and Peoples' Right to Food'—was carried out between 2012 and 2014 under the leadership of the guest editors. For other papers, we invited authors unrelated to the research project to offer additional historical and global perspectives, and provide the views of public and private investors, as well as of multilateral organisations. The draft papers were first examined and debated during an international workshop held in Geneva in September 2014. This was followed by intense exchanges between the authors and the editors as well as external experts who participated in the workshop. The volume was then submitted to an anonymous peer review process. I wish to thank in particular Ben White and an anonymous reviewer who provided insightful remarks, constructive critique, and numerous suggestions for improvements on the whole Issue.

The volume is organised in three parts. Part 1 sets the scene by providing a historical perspective on contemporary LSLAs, situating this phenomenon within global agro-food dynamics and land policies. Part 2 discusses a rich collection of case studies from South-East Asia. Part 3 examines critical questions on the influence and relevance of human rights instruments. I hope that our readers will enjoy this collection of papers that shed novel light on a phenomenon that lies at the intersection between development and agrarian policies, involving complex social, economic, political and environmental dynamics that affect people's livelihoods, food security, and social dynamics in many parts of the developing world.

---

1   See 'Large-Scale Land Acquisitions in Southeast Asia: Rural Transformations between Global Agendas and Peoples' Right to Food project', SNIS website: http://www.snis.ch/project_large-scale-land-acquisitions-southeast-asia-rural-transformations-between-global-agendas (accessed on 4 June 2015).

Preface

International Development Policy is a critical source of analysis focusing on development policy and international cooperation. The target audience includes scholars, policy-makers, development professionals, and others interested in international development.

International Development Policy is edited by the Graduate Institute of International and Development Studies, an institution of research and higher education dedicated to advancing world affairs.

http://graduateinstitute.ch/publications
http://devpol.org | http://debate.devpol.org

We extend our thanks to the Swiss Agency for Development and Cooperation (SDC) for financial support.

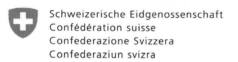

Schweizerische Eidgenossenschaft
Confédération suisse
Confederazione Svizzera
Confederaziun svizra

List of Figures

List of Tables

List of Acronyms and Abbreviations

AAAID	Arab Authority for Agricultural Investment and Development
ABCDS	Archers Daniels Midlands, Bunge, Cargill, Louis Dreyfus
ADHOC	Cambodian Human Rights and Development Association
ADLI	Agricultural Development Led Industrialisation
ADM	Archers Daniels Midlands (US)
AOAD	Arab Organisation for Agricultural Development
APHR	ASEAN Parliamentarians for Human Rights
AR	active ratio
AS	active sum
ASEAN	Association of Southeast Asian Nations
BABC	Bridges across Borders Cambodia
CBNRM	community-based natural resource management paradigm
CC	Cadastral Commission (Cambodia)
CDE	Centre for Development and Environment, University of Bern (Switzerland)
CEDAW	Convention on the Elimination of All Forms of Discrimination against Women
CERD	Committee on the Elimination of Racial Discrimination
CESCR	UN Committee on Economic, Social and Cultural Rights (OHCHR)
CLEC	Community Legal Education Center (Cambodia)
CLEP	Commission for the Legal Empowerment of the Poor
CEO	chief executive officer
CIC	China Investment Corporation
COFCO	China National Cereals, Oils and Foodstuffs Corporation
COHRE	Centre on Housing Rights and Evictions (NGO, Geneva)
CRC	Convention on the Rights of the Child
CRPD	Convention on the Rights of Persons with Disabilities
CSR	corporate social responsibility
ELCS	economic land concessions (Cambodia)
EMP	environmental management plans
ESIA	Environmental and Social Impact Assessment
EU	European Union
FAO	Food and Agriculture Organization of the United Nations
FDI	foreign direct investment
FEAICO	Far East Agricultural Investment Corporation
FSC	Forest Stewardship Council
GAM	Gerakan Aceh Merdeka (Free Aceh Movement, Indonesia)

GCC	Gulf Cooperation Council
GIZ	Gesellschaft für Internationale Zusammenarbeit (Germany)
ha	hectare
HOPU	name of a private equity investment firm (China)
ICCPR	International Covenant on Civil and Political Rights
ICERD	International Convention on the Elimination of All Forms of Racial Discrimination
ICESCR	International Covenant on Economic, Social and Cultural Rights
IFAD	International Fund for Agricultural Development
IFOAM	International Foundation for Organic Agriculture
IISD	International Institute for Sustainable Development
ILD	Institute for Liberty and Democracy (Peru)
ILO	International Labour Organization
IMF	International Monetary Fund
INDIGENOUS	International Network for Diplomacy Indigenous Governance Engaging in Nonviolence Organizing for Understanding and Self-Determination
INDOCERT	Indian Organic Certification Agency
IPO	initial public offering
IR	total strength of interaction
LAK	Laotian kip (currency)
LECS	Lao Expenditure and Consumption Survey (Laos)
LFA	Land and Forest Allocation Programme (Laos)
LICADHO	Cambodian League for the Promotion and Defense of Human Rights
LMAP	land management and administration project (Cambodia)
LSLAS	large-scale land acquisitions
MEC	Minerals Energy Commodities Holding (UAE)
MENA	Middle East and North Africa
MESC	Middle East Supply Center
MLMUPC	Ministry of Land Management, Urban Planning and Construction (Cambodia)
MoU	memorandum of understanding
MRICOP	Mong Reththy Investment Cambodia Oil Palm Company (Cambodia, Preah Sihanouk province)
NEP	new economic policy (USSR)
NGO	non-governmental organisation
NLMA	National Land Management Authority (Laos)
NTFPS	non-timber forest products

OECD	Organisation for Economic Co-operation and Development
OPEC	Organization of the Petroleum Exporting Countries
OREC	Organisation of Rice Exporting Countries
PL	Public Law (US)
PS	passive sum
QNFSP	Qatar National Food Security Programme
RSPO	Roundtable on Sustainable Palm Oil (Cambodia)
SEIAS	social and environmental impact assessments
SLCS	social land concessions (Cambodia)
SNIS	Swiss Network for International Studies
SWF	sovereign wealth fund
TCD	tonnes of cane per day
TNCS	transnational corporations
UAE	United Arab Emirates
UGC	United Grain Company (Russia)
UK	United Kingdom
UN	United Nations
UNCFS	United Nations Committee on World Food Security
UNCTAD	United Nations Conference on Trade and Development
UNDP	United Nations Development Programme
UNPO	Unrepresented Nations and Peoples Organization
US	United States of America
USAID	United States Agency for International Development
USD	United States dollar (currency)
USSR	Union of Soviet Socialist Republics
WTO	World Trade Organization

Notes on Contributors

Maria Lisa Alano
is a PhD candidate at the University of Amsterdam. She has extensive experience in development work in Mindanao, Philippines. Her past and current research includes land policies, indigenous peoples and women's land rights, gender and agrarian change in the Philippines.

Ioana Cismas
is Lecturer in Law at the University of Stirling, Scotland, UK. She has undertaken research and provided legal and policy advice to UN experts, governments, and NGOs in the areas of international law, human rights, transitional justice, and law and religion. Ioana Cismas holds a PhD in International Law (summa cum laude) from the Graduate Institute, Geneva.

Michael B. Dwyer
is postdoctoral fellow in the Governance Program of the Center for International Forestry Research, Bogor (Indonesia). He has studied natural resource development and regulation in South-East Asia since 2004, focusing on property as a meeting point for multi-scalar and historical questions related to agrarian change, state formation, and international relations.

Christophe Gironde
is a political economist who works as a lecturer in development studies and researcher at the Graduate Institute, Geneva. His research interests are agrarian change, sustainable livelihoods and human development, in particular in continental South-East Asia.

Christophe Golay
is research fellow and coordinator of the Project on Economic, Social and Cultural Rights at the Geneva Academy of International Humanitarian Law and Human Rights. He is also a lecturer at the Geneva Centre for Research and Education in Humanitarian Action.

Andreas Heinimann
is a senior research scientist and lecturer at the Centre for Development and Environment (CDE) and the Institute of Geography of the University of Bern. He holds a PhD in Geography from the University of Bern. He is also a member of the Scientific Steering Committee of the Global Land Project (GLP) of International Geosphere Biosphere Programme (IGBP) and Future Earth.

Martin Keulertz

is a post-doctoral research associate at the Department of Agricultural and Biological Engineering, Purdue University. He specialises in global water and food resource management, the water-energy-food nexus, international virtual water 'trade', and food politics. He is Lead Editor of the *Handbook of Land and Water Grabs in Africa: Foreign Direct Investment and Food and Water Security* (Routledge, 2013).

Marcel Mazoyer

is Honorary Professor of Comparative Agriculture and Agricultural Development at AgroParisTech, and Visiting Professor at the University of Paris XI. He has piloted numerous studies and research programmes in Africa, Latin America, Asia, and Europe and was previously research director at the Institut national de la recherche agronomique.

Peter Messerli

is Director of the CDE at the University of Bern. He is a human geographer who focuses on human–environmental systems in developing countries and is hence specifically interested in processes of rural transformation where land decisions are increasingly driven by globalised and distant decision-making processes.

Hafiz Mirza

is Chief of Investment Issues Research at UNCTAD. Besides contributing to the *World Investment Report,* he works on areas such as FDI impact and development, responsible agricultural investment, multinationals in developing countries, and global value chains/investment-trade nexus.

Vong Nanhthavong

is a research fellow at CDE office in Laos. His current work focuses on rural development and governance in the framework of foreign direct investment in natural resources in Laos. He has worked in these fields in Laos for more than eight years.

Gerben Nooteboom

is a lecturer and researcher at the University of Amsterdam's Department of Anthropology and Sociology/Asian Studies. Via fieldwork, mainly in Java and East Kalimantan, his research principally offers anthropological perspectives on, and critiques of, development, risk, rural transformation, and social science in South-East Asia.

Patricia Paramita

is a research assistant at the Programme on Gender and Global Change (PGGC) of the Graduate Institute, Geneva, and has worked intensively on land grab issues in Cambodia for the past two years. Prior to that she worked for Human Rights Watch and the secretariat of the ASEAN. She holds a master's degree in Development Studies and a master's degree in Anthropology from the Graduate Institute, Geneva.

Amaury Peeters

is a bioengineer specialised in land use planning. He holds a PhD in Agricultural Sciences from the Université catholique de Louvain. Based in Cambodia, his recent research activities include the spatial analysis of LSLA and the socio-economic consequences of the related agrarian transformations on farmers.

Emily Polack

is a researcher in the Natural Resources Group at the International Institute for Environment and Development, London. Her research focus is on land rights and legal empowerment with regard to agricultural and other natural resource investments.

Laurence Roudart

is Professor of Agricultural Development at the Université Libre de Bruxelles, where she occupies the chair devoted to 'The agrarian issue in developing countries'. Her research focuses on matters relating to agricultural policies, land policies, and food security policies in developing countries.

Oliver Schoenweger

is PhD student at the CDE. During this research, he also was responsible for the implementation of a nationwide land concession inventory—now considered an example of collecting and processing data on such issues. Prior to his PhD studies he has worked as a land management adviser for a mining company in Laos, and for GIZ and UNDP in the fields of sustainable development and responsible investment in land.

Olivier De Schutter

is the former UN Special Rapporteur on the right to food (2008–2014) and a Member of the UN Committee on Economic, Social and Cultural Rights. A Professor at the Catholic University of Louvain and at Sciences Po (Paris), he has frequently advised the EU and the Council of Europe on fundamental rights issues.

Gilda Senties Portilla

is a PhD candidate in Anthropology and Sociology at the Graduate Institute, Geneva. She is writing her thesis on the changing livelihoods of farming households amidst land concessions in Lao PDR. Her research interests include the aspirations of rural youth and livelihood trajectories, and more broadly agrarian transitions.

Mohamad Shohibuddin

is a PhD candidate at the University of Amsterdam and a lecturer at Bogor Agricultural University, Indonesia. He did mainly research in Central Sulawesi, Java and Aceh, focusing on agrarian dimensions of social change, violent conflict and peace processes.

Sokbunthoeun So

was a postdoctoral fellow at the Faculty of Social Science of VU University Amsterdam and Senior Research Fellow at the Cambodia Development Resource Institute when this article was first drafted. His research focus is on state-society relations, land governance, decentralisation, and public sector governance.

William Speller

is an economist in the Division on Investment and Enterprise at UNCTAD. His research focus is on the role and impact of foreign direct investment and multinationals on social and economic development.

Eckart Woertz

is Senior Research Fellow at the Barcelona Centre for International Affairs (CIDOB). He specialises in the political economy of the Middle East, food security, energy, sovereign wealth funds, and financial markets. Eckart Woertz is the author of *Oil for Food* (Oxford University Press, 2013).

James Zhan

is Director of Investment and Enterprise at the UNCTAD and Editor-in-Chief of the *World Investment Report*. He has decades of experience in international consensus-building and has provided technical assistance to more than 160 governments.

PART 1

Setting the Scene: History, State, and Law

∵

CHAPTER 1

Large-Scale Land Acquisitions: A Historical Perspective

Laurence Roudart and Marcel Mazoyer

Abstract

Large-scale land acquisitions have been a recurrent historical phenomenon since ancient times. This article analyses four of these historical processes: the *latifundia* of ancient Rome, enclosures in Britain, *latifundia* in the Spanish and Portuguese colonies of the Americas, and Soviet collectivisation. The article then compares these historical occurrences with the current wave of acquisitions in order to better understand the latter and to shed light on certain important debates in the areas of public policy and research that have once again come to the fore. Both the historical and current experiences share a set of economic and social characteristics: a small number of beneficiaries and a large number of dispossessed, exploitation of all or part of the land and the labour of those dispossessed of their land—some of them being excluded in certain cases—resistance, armed violence, laws favouring acquisitions, the decisive role of governments, and legitimising discourse. At the same time, the current wave of acquisitions has some specific characteristics of its own: its global scale, the context of public policy liberalisation, the facilitating role played by governments and international organisations, and the risk of wholesale exclusion. All of these features run counter to the main economic and social objectives of sustained development, namely, to reduce poverty, generate jobs and livelihoods for the greatest possible number, promote growth, ensure food security for all, and narrow income disparities.

1   Introduction

Following the surge in agricultural prices in 2007–2008, the increasingly frequent acquisitions of land rights, whether through purchase, lease, concession, or de facto occupation, has raised many questions. Can such a trend lead to the global expansion of wage-based, capitalist agriculture, and to what extent will this form of agriculture replace family holdings in developing countries, or indeed in developed countries? What are the potential economic, environmental, social, cultural, and political consequences of such upheavals?

What might the effects be on production, employment, poverty, and food security?

Far from being a new movement or one unique to the capitalist system, the large-scale acquisition of vast areas for the benefit of their new owners, and to the detriment of previous rights holders and users who have been dispossessed of some or all of their rights, is in fact a recurrent event in history. Tombstone inscriptions and papyrus writings indicate that there were already large public estates under the Old Kingdom of Egypt during the third millennium BC, where several villages were often obliged to provide unpaid labour to the state. Some of these estates were granted to the clergy or to officials of the royal court. Royal estates possibly existed even before the unification of Egypt and the establishment of the First Pharaonic Dynasty (Moreno García, 2008).

The first aim of this article is to analyse four historical instances of large-scale land dispossession in order to single out their shared economic and social features. We have selected the following cases: the *latifundia* of the Roman Republic and Empire, as an experience of ancient colonisation that existed well before the development of capitalism; the enclosures in Britain, as an endogenous dynamic linked to the dissolution of the feudal regime and the emergence of capitalism; the large Spanish and Portuguese colonial estates in the Americas as a product of colonisation by external powers, which itself was linked to the expansion of mercantile capitalism; and collectivisation in the Union of Soviet Socialist Republics (USSR), as an endogenous dynamic linked to the wish to establish a sort of state capitalism within a managed economy. Our approach is fundamentally inductive in nature. It is aimed at bringing to the fore the traits common to historical experiences that each fall within a given economic and social dynamic. Nevertheless, this approach is also inspired by existing analytical frameworks, in particular concepts pertaining to agrarian political economy and the issues that this raises: who were the original possessors and users of land? What other social categories were concerned? What social relations existed between these various categories? Through what processes did these acquisitions and dispossessions of land take place? Were they sanctioned by legal and judicial mechanisms? Were they legitimised by a particular type of discourse? What social categories were involved in the newly-established production structures? What relations existed between them? What was being produced? Under what working conditions? How was the wealth thus created then distributed? For what purpose was it used? What were the consequences of these developments for the former users of the land? Did they become richer or poorer (Fairbairn et al., 2014; White et al., 2012; White and Dasgupta, 2010)?

The second aim of this article is to analyse the current trend of acquisitions and dispossessions in the light of the common features identified from past experiences, so as to determine the extent to which the current trend is similar to or different from past instances of large-scale land acquisitions and thus shed light on a number of public policy and research issues that are currently being examined: what agricultural production structures are best suited to encouraging sustained human development—large-scale, wage-labour farm holdings *or* family-owned operations? What are the prospects for a political project based on an alternative conception of agricultural and general development?

Sections 2 to 6 of this chapter are each devoted to one of the four historical instances of land acquisition mentioned earlier, with Section 5 reviewing several others. Section 7 will present their common features. Section 8 analyses the current trend of large-scale acquisitions and dispossessions of land in the light of these common features while also pointing out their specific characteristics. Section 9 summarises the main findings of our analysis and correlates these with a number of important ongoing public policy and research debates.

2   The *latifundia* of the Roman Republic and Empire

In the fifth century BC, Rome was only a small republic whose peasant soldiers could barely hold out against attacks from neighbouring cities. By the end of the third century, a thoroughly battle-hardened Rome had already conquered the entire Italian peninsula, Sicily, Sardinia, Corsica and the southern part of Hispania. In the process, it had expropriated a large part of these territories, generally the best land, declaring it to be *ager publicus*—that is to say, agricultural land belonging to the Roman people. The Romans also confiscated mines, salt works, and the treasures of the conquered peoples, enslaving hundreds of thousands of prisoners of war.

Governed by its Senate, the Roman State rented out the greater part of this *ager publicus* in the form of large estates to rich individuals, most of whom were already landowners, senators or knights. As the state had fallen heavily into debt to support its wars and always needed further money to continue waging them, it sold whole sections of *ager publicus* at reduced rates or ceded full ownership by way of repayments. Roman property rights were individual, exclusive and fairly unrestricted. Large agricultural estates called *latifundia* were thus created, most often through the seizure of conquered land, which was leased out or sold as property (Nicolet, 1967). There came into existence a highly influential landed oligarchy, which put constant pressure on the state to make new conquests for the sake of increasing its wealth further.

Over the following centuries, thanks to military conquest, the *ager publicus* and *latifundia* greatly increased in area. Under the Empire, rich citizens started to occupy plots of *ager publicus* that had not been allocated by the state, initially upon payment of a modest amount of tax, and then without paying any tax at all as, over time, they came to regard themselves as owners of these plots. Large estate holders used other methods, legal or otherwise, to extend their holdings, by purchasing or usurping land belonging to peasants who had died in battle, who had been ruined, or who had given up farming, and by appropriating unregistered land and common pasture.

A single individual could control dozens, hundreds, or even thousands of hectares of land, perhaps divided into multiple different holdings of a few dozen or a few hundred hectares, which might be spread across different regions. Most owners of *latifundia* estates did not live on them, except occasionally for leisure purposes, and delegated the task of supervision to stewards. The necessary labour was generally provided by slaves or, failing that, by poorly-paid free peasants or by colonists, who were a category of tenant farmers allocated a plot of land in exchange for a share of their harvest, possibly reaching as much as two-thirds (Garnsey, 1988; Jones, 1974).

Over the course of various conquests, the extent of these colonial *latifundia* increased. As they were using very cheap land and labour, their grain, wine, and olive oil were shipped for sale at low prices in Rome and certain provincial cities, or to the military (CNRS, 1995). They gained market share at the expense of small and medium-sized holdings, which could not survive the competition. In the area around Rome, *latifundia* specialised in horticulture or extensive livestock breeding, the products of which faced less competition from imports (Aymard and Auboyer, 1995; Roux, 1910).

As a consequence, the Italian countryside became depopulated. A large number of peasants were at war or had been killed; many others, impoverished by the competition they faced, abandoned the land and became plebs in Rome. By the second century BC, the recruitment of legionnaires from among the ranks of peasant landowners had declined significantly. The army was becoming professional, and Italy's food dependency on the provinces was becoming chronic (White, 1970).

In the first century BC, several well-known Latin writers were sharply critical of the *latifundia*. In *De Re Rustica*, Varro admonished the absentee owners of large estates living idly in Rome and voiced concern regarding Italy's food dependency. In the *Georgics*, Virgil (1982) lyrically sang the praises of mixed-crop and livestock farming as practised by the owners of small farms, an increasingly rare breed. In the first century AD, in his *Natural History* (book

XVIII), Pliny the Elder felt that 'large estates have been the ruin of Italy, and are slowly proving to be the ruin of the provinces too', and reminded the reader that, '[i]n old times it was thought that to observe moderation in the size of a farm was of primary importance, for the maxim was: sow less, plough better' (Pliny the Elder, 1848).

Yet at the start of the second century BC, an agrarian law had been passed with the aim of addressing this problem, by limiting the amount of *ager publicus* that could be leased to 125 hectares (500 *jugera*) per individual, capping the number of animals grazing there (100 head of large livestock, 500 head of small livestock), and placing an obligation on the tenants of large estates to employ a given proportion of free men rather than just slaves, all of which was enforceable by fines. However, this law was only very rarely applied and, in 133 BC, Tiberius Sempronius Gracchus, a Tribune of the Plebs, had a new agrarian law passed, which sought to return some urban plebs to the land, increase army recruitment, and restore the grandeur of Rome. This law was concerned exclusively with the *ager publicus*, rather than land held as property, which was not subject to any limitation. It confirmed the state's repossession of *ager publicus* above the maximum 125 hectares per person, permitting the ownership of an additional 62.5 hectares per male child, up to a limit of two children. In exchange, the holders of *ager publicus* obtained the land that remained to them as their full property. The land taken back by the state was supposed to be redistributed to poor citizens in 7.5 hectare lots, which was perceived as a truly revolutionary step. The law provoked strong opposition from senators and other owners of significant quantities of land, such that it sparked a civil war against the plebs who supported the law, and resulted in the assassination of Gracchus. Some years later, his brother Gaius picked up the baton of reform, and this set off a fresh wave of terror and massacres. Yet, despite this ferocious opposition, the law, as the expression of the people's will, was partly applied, albeit with numerous amendments. In particular, there was a growing tendency for plots of land to be allocated only in the provinces, and only to war veterans. The allocation of land to poor citizens would be resumed only under the consulship of Julius Caesar (Earl, 1963; Stockton, 1979).

These land allocations were however insufficient to stem the rural exodus and the swelling of Rome's plebeian population. By the early second century AD, the population of the city had reached about 1 million. As the food offered by the rich became less and less adequate to feed the poor, a whole series of *wheat distribution laws*, providing for the distribution of free or inexpensive grain to Roman citizens, were adopted (Duncan-Jones, 1974).

However, as the Empire slowly sank into a military and economic impasse because of the expansion of its frontiers, the growing strength of its external enemies, and the increasing number of domestic uprisings (by slaves and plebs), the Roman State no longer had the means to plunder new territories, with all their riches and their fresh manpower, by which it supported itself and its slave-based economy. Agricultural production collapsed on the Italian peninsula, despite numerous attempts by the state to remedy the situation (Finley, 1976).

During the highly-troubled times at the end of the Roman Empire, an increasing number of large landowners took refuge in their country villas. They organised by themselves the defence of their estates against attacks from disbanded legions, barbarians, and looters. They also arranged for their land to be farmed by a new kind of colonists, or serfs: these were former slaves, peasants, city dwellers or deserting soldiers, to whom the property owners allocated a plot of land in exchange for a share of the harvest and a significant amount of unpaid labour on the land they set aside for themselves (Bloch, 1947). This was the starting point for the gradual emergence of a new political, economic, and social order, which would take centuries to establish itself in the West, namely, feudalism.

3   Enclosures in Britain

As a result of the agricultural, food and health crisis of the fourteenth century, which culminated in the Black Death (1347–1350), Europe had lost around half its population. Land was once again plentiful but labour was in short supply (Mazoyer and Roudart, 2006). In early fifteenth century England, the feudal system found itself in difficulty. After two centuries of social conflict, the unpaid tasks that the serfs had to carry out on manorial land had become less arduous, and had been partly replaced by paid work, whose price was on the rise. Manorial estates had become difficult to manage. At the same time, a class of enriched serfs had come into being. They farmed more land on their own account, owned more livestock than others, and had control over the use of common pasture and forests. They even fulfilled certain judicial roles and helped maintain law and order. Given this situation, in the first half of the fifteenth century, almost all the landlords opted to lease their estates to these richer peasants, rather than to continue managing them by themselves (Byres, 2009).

The archetypal large structure of agricultural production that thus emerged would become the point of reference for the founding fathers of classical political economy (including Smith, Ricardo, Malthus, and Marx), in which the landlord rents out his land in exchange for payment of a land rent; the tenant farmer uses this land with the aim of turning a profit and pays this land rent;

while agricultural labourers sell their labour to the tenant farmer in exchange for a wage.

Nevertheless, many peasant families who had been freed from serfdom continued to farm the plot of land to which they had been attached. Small and medium-sized farm holdings thus developed on the ruins of the feudal system, run by independent freeholders called *yeomen*, who cultivated their land on a more or less individual basis. They made use of common grazing rights on the fields after they had been harvested, and had access to common forests and pastures.

However, in the sixteenth century, the landlords formed alliances with their tenant farmers and began forcibly to take possession of common land as well as that being farmed by independent peasants. They demarcated the new boundaries of their estates, closing them off by means of hedges or low stone walls, hence the term *enclosure* given to this process of appropriation/dispossession. These appropriations grew in scale under the Protestant Reformation, when the royal authorities confiscated part of the estates of the Catholic Church, which until that time had been the largest landowner in the country, and granted this land to their clients, either free of charge or against payment. Many peasants were then driven out, and individual houses or even whole villages were razed to the ground. Many other peasants lost all or part of their access to common or individual land, and were therefore deprived of a large part of their livelihoods. A whole series of peasant revolts prompted the royal authorities to promulgate laws restricting these abusive practices. In the end, however, these laws had only a limited effect (Land, 1977).

Many of these newly-enlarged units specialised in raising sheep in response to the strong demand for wool from the rapidly-developing cloth manufacturing industries in Flanders and England. Sir Thomas More described the situation as follows: 'sheep, which are naturally mild, and easily kept in order may be said now to devour men and unpeople, not only villages, but towns, [...] there the nobility and gentry, and even those holy men [...] stop the course of agriculture, destroying houses and towns, reserving only the churches, and enclose grounds that they may lodge their sheep in them. [...] for when an insatiable wretch [...] resolves to enclose many thousand acres of ground, the owners, as well as tenants, are turned out of their possessions [...] are all forced to change their seats, not knowing whither to go; [...] what is left for them to do but either to steal, and so to be hanged (God knows how justly!), or to go about and beg and if they do this they are put in prison as idle vagabonds, while they would willingly work but can find none that will hire them; [...] One shepherd can look after a flock, which will stock an extent of ground that would require many hands if it were to be ploughed and reaped' (More, 1978).

The policy of enclosure was pursued until the eighteenth and nineteenth centuries, and was furthered by a succession of Acts of Parliament, which sought to promote the first agricultural revolution of modern times by replacing fallow land with feed crops so as to increase livestock production, improve soil fertility, and boost crop production (Mazoyer and Roudart, 2006). These laws abolished common grazing rights, provided for common land to be shared and obliged owners to enclose their consolidated areas of land (Mingay, 2014; Slater, 1907). Though the application of the laws did not lead to dispossession everywhere (Hunt and Leuilliot, 1956), it undermined the economic position of those smallholders who lacked the means to enclose their land and lost their communal rights, to the extent that the worst off amongst them finally had to sell their land. As a result, whereas peasant land had still made up almost a third of agricultural land in England at the end of the seventeenth century, it accounted for only a fifth of it by the end of the nineteenth century (Beckett, 1999).

The enclosures caused many peasant holdings to disappear in favour of a small number of farming businesses employing only the minimum number of workers required to satisfy industrial and urban demand. This contributed to release many more unemployed onto the labour market than the number of jobs available in industry and in the cities. Therefore, enclosures were largely responsible for the development of a poor unemployed underclass in England, and more widely in Great Britain and the United Kingdom, which led the authorities to put in place a series of Poor Laws from 1536 to 1930 (Polanyi, 1971). According to E. Hobsbawm (1977, 188), 'the *Poor Law* of 1834 was designed to make life so intolerable for the rural paupers as to force them to migrate to any jobs that offered. [...] From 1850 land-flight became general'.

In Book One of *Das Kapital*, Karl Marx was already speaking about 'land grabbing' in relation to enclosures (Marx, 1965). He interpreted them as the founding event of the capitalist regime, prompting the formation of a class of individuals who owned the means of production, in this case land that had largely been stolen, and a class of footloose workers who had to sell their labour in order to survive, even if it meant working under the most unfavourable conditions.

Hoping for better times, many of the poor and unemployed emigrated to the settlements of North America, Australasia, and southern Africa, where vast territories were being seized by force from the native inhabitants. Enjoying access to vast lands that were usually cheaper than in the United Kingdom, and, from the nineteenth century onwards, being well-equipped with industrial machinery, these colonial farmers became more competitive than their European counterparts, to the extent that British industrialists, concerned to lower their costs of production as much as possible, concluded that it would be more beneficial for them if Britain imported agricultural produce at low prices (American wheat to feed the workers, Australian and New Zealand wool to supply the textile mills), rather than producing it locally. After much heated debate, they secured the repeal in 1846 of the protectionist grain legislation known as the Corn Laws (Schonhardt-Bailey, 2006), which led to the ruin of many British farmers. By an ironic twist of history, the landlords and tenant farmers had to concede defeat to those who were mostly descendants of the peasants that their ancestors had driven off their land at the time of the enclosures (Mazoyer and Roudart, 2006).

4   *Haciendas* and *Fazendas*: Spanish and Portuguese Colonies in the Americas

In January 1492, the armies of the Catholic Monarchs of Spain completed the reconquest of the Iberian Peninsula from the Muslims. A few months later, Christopher Columbus landed in the Bahamas, opening up the New World to the Spanish Crown.

The Spaniards who set out to conquer the Americas from this time onwards were mostly penniless nobles who had borrowed the necessary capital from merchants and bankers to fund their arms, travel to, and settlement in America, as well as the costs of the servants with which they surrounded themselves. There were also royal officials, soldiers, and clerics. In debt and greedy for profit, they began by pillaging the treasures of the defeated indigenous societies. Then, they set about exploiting the gold and silver mines. From the outset of the conquest, the royal authorities confiscated the conquered territories and distributed them as *encomiendas*—immense feudal fiefdoms—to expedition leaders, soldiers, royal officials and clerics, as well as compliant dignitaries from among the indigenous peoples. For example, Hernán Cortés, who defeated the Aztec Empire, received around four million hectares (Piel, 2013). These allocations usually applied for one or two generations. The *encomenderos* were responsible for exploiting the wealth of these fiefdoms while protecting, civilising, and evangelising the resident native populations. Taking advantage of what was in practice their absolute power, the *encomenderos* kept a large share of the best land for themselves, forcing the indigenous inhabitants onto marginal land. The *encomenderos* subjected them to large-scale unpaid labour on their own estates, to forced labour in the mines, to deductions from their harvests in order to supply the towns and the mines, and to all sorts of ill-treatment or even massacres in response to any revolt.

The consequences were disastrous. On the territory of the former Inca Empire, the indigenous population, which had been around 10 million in 1530, fell to 2.5 million in 1560 and to 1.4 million by 1590, a level at which it remained unchanged until the early nineteenth century (Wachtel, 1977).

In response to the fervent denunciations of the *encomienda* system by clerics and royal officials, for both moral and economic reasons, the Crown undertook in the late sixteenth century gradually to replace this system with *haciendas*. These very large estates could cover several tens of thousands of hectares, with the *hacendado* enjoying sole ownership of the soil and the subsoil, as under ancient Roman law. This form of land tenure was a fundamentally alien notion to the native American societies, for whom possession of the land could only be collective.

A number of these *haciendas* were based on the old *encomiendas*, to which some territories purchased from the Spanish Crown had been added, while others were created from scratch, granted by the Crown for services rendered or sold, to conquistadors or compliant native chiefs. The Catholic Church, which benefited from large numbers of donations, became the biggest land-owner. The fate of the indigenous populations was little different from before: they were confined to restricted areas, known as *reducciones*, where each family farmed its own plot and made use of common forests and pastures while being collectively subject to the payment of tribute to the *haciendas*, in labour or in kind (Kay, 1974). Tribute in kind was gradually replaced by taxation in cash, which obliged the farmers to work even harder for their sole employ-ers, the *hacendados*, for a paltry wage. There were many revolts against these taxes and the endless expansion of the *haciendas* for the benefit of whites and mestizos (those of mixed race) to the detriment of the indigenous peoples, especially in the eighteenth century. These revolts were put down, however, and did not hinder the process (Luna, 2013).

Large-scale land grabbing also took place in Brazil, the vast territory that fell to the Portuguese Crown by the terms of the Treaty of Tordesillas (1494) between Spain and Portugal. Initially, the territory was divided into 15 heredi-tary captaincies allocated to nobles, who were responsible for exploring, exploiting, and administering them. The Portuguese Crown then conceded vast tracts of land, called *seismarias*, to individuals on long leases. Large plan-tations were set up, with a labour force consisting of slaves captured from amongst the indigenous populations, to produce sugar cane, cotton, coffee, cocoa beans, tobacco, etc. in function of the demand from Portugal and else-where in Europe. Over time, however, slave labour became scarcer and more expensive as the indigenous population had collapsed and survivors had fled to the interior or taken refuge in missions. Slaves then began to be imported from Africa to replace them, until the abolition of slavery towards the end of the nineteenth century. Thereafter, the masters of the large agricultural estates employed 'free' workers who were either ill-paid labourers, hired on a daily or seasonal basis, or tenant farmers or sharecroppers, often in debt to their masters and therefore at their mercy, or else resident former slaves who would be allotted a plot of land in exchange for their labour—effectively, they were a kind of serf (Bauer, 1979; Monbeig, 1984).

Independence was far from heralding an end to land grabbing. In the former Spanish colonies, constitutional decrees made changes to the conditions for accessing land, presenting new opportunities for setting up or enlarging *haciendas*. When the economic climate was favourable to exports (in 1850–1873 and 1890–1920, for example), the *haciendas* were further expanded, to the detriment of the indigenous peoples, either through the military conquest of new territories, with populations that resisted being exterminated, or by confiscating grazing land that had been declared to be surplus (Piel, 1988).

All in all, these large-scale land grabs gave rise to very significant transfers of wealth to Spain and Portugal, including to their respective Crowns. In addition, they formed the basis of the *minifundia-latifundia* land system that has endured in most countries of Latin America to this day, since subsequent agrarian reforms have in the main not been sufficient to supplant these dualist structures (Chonchol, 1970; Graziano Neto, 1991; Kay, 1998; 2014).

5   Other Cases of Colonial and Postcolonial Dispossession

Following the Age of Discovery, colonisation greatly accelerated, and took on different forms. Aside from the Spanish and Portuguese colonies in the Americas, it was above all in the *colonies of settlement*, set up in temperate zones, that land grabs at the expense of the native populations were most significant. These took place in the British colonies of North America, Australasia, and east and southern Africa; in the French colonies in North America and northern Africa; and in the Dutch colonies of South Africa. In different locations and at different periods, the indigenous people were either exterminated, driven out, or resettled in reserves, where the scarcity of good quality land forced them to work on the farms or plantations, or in the mines of the colonists (Bernstein, 2010).

In *colonies of exploitation*, the colonists exploited the land, the workforce, and other resources by forcing the indigenous populations to grow specific crops or to pay tax in cash, which obliged them either to produce and sell agricultural produce to be shipped to the home nation, or to carry out paid work in the mines or on the plantations. This was the case, for example, in the French colonies of sub-Saharan Africa, in the British colonies of South Asia and in the Dutch colonies of the East Indies (now Indonesia). At the same time, however, with the support of the colonial powers, vast tracts of land were also appropriated to be used by either companies or wealthy settlers to establish large plantations (of sugar cane, rubber trees, oil palms, cotton, bananas, tea, cloves, sisal, etc.) or to create areas for large-scale rice cultivation. These plantations developed most of all during periods of economic growth and expansion in international trade, especially following the two world wars (Bagchi, 2009; Beckford, 1999).

In sub-Saharan Africa, many newly independent states decided to nationalise their land, thus appropriating the rights to its use, in particular so that they could allocate vast tracts of land to be used for major agricultural projects by state or parastatal agencies, public or private companies, and even individuals. Millions of hectares were thus perfectly legally confiscated from local populations (Alden Wily, 2012).

6   Collectivisation in the USSR

In 1929, when the Communist Party decided to launch its collectivisation programme, the Russian peasantry still had memories of the terrible struggles for land and freedom that it had previously been compelled to wage.

To be sure, the Tsar had decided to abolish serfdom in 1861 and to redistribute some of the land owned by the nobility to peasant communities (*mirs*). This agrarian reform was rendered largely inoperative, but the idea itself became widespread at the end of the nineteenth century and after the Revolution of 1905. During the summer of 1917, after the Tsar had been deposed and many nobles had taken flight, peasants occupied their estates and undertook to distribute the land amongst themselves. After the Bolsheviks seized power, the decree on land of October 1917 endorsed this state of affairs, proclaiming the confiscation of large estates, and making them freely available to local agrarian committees (Méquet, 1930). In issuing this decree, Lenin and the Bolshevik Party, anxious to rally the peasantry to the revolution, conveniently shelved the ideas of *nationalising* all the land in the country and *collectivising* the large estates in order to set up model farms, as advocated in Lenin's *April Theses* and approved by the Bolshevik Party (Sorlin, 1964).

In 1921, to put an end to the peasant revolts and workers' strikes caused by the ambient economic chaos, the Bolshevik Party also agreed to adopt the more liberal 'New Economic Policy' (NEP). In 1928, however, to resolve problems with grain supply, the party launched the 'battle for grain'. Party emissaries were sent into the countryside to collect grain by whatever means necessary. This sparked a great many revolts, giving rise to fears that the first five-year plan of 1928–1932 might fail. To salvage the plan, and the revolution, a number of Politburo members, in particular Stalin, decided to implement a new policy, *collectivisation*, which came into effect in 1929 (Lewin, 1971).

The main objective of collectivisation was to oblige the peasantry to produce and deliver enough foodstuffs to supply the cities and permit the rapid industrialisation of the country (Nove and Morrison, 1982; Sapir, 1990). Furthermore, many Party members, inspired by Marx and Lenin, believed that family holdings were much less economically efficient than larger farms. But the official line went much further: according to Stalin (1930) it was imperative to 'eliminate the kulaks as a class', which meant that it 'must be deprived of the productive resources that make its existence and development possible (free use of land, ownership of the means of production, land-renting, right to hire labour, etc.).'

In a return to the Bolshevik Party programme of 1917, collectivisation involved nationalising all the land in the country, dissolving the *mirs* and replacing them with agricultural production cooperatives, or *kolkhozes*. The state made available land that had been nationalised, while villagers had to give over most of their means of production and pay to be admitted into the cooperative. Each family was meant to enjoy individual use of their dwelling, their vegetable garden, their gardening tools, and a small amount of livestock intended for domestic consumption (Stalin, 1930). Collectivisation also gave rise to the large state farms known as *sovkhozes*, along with machine and tractor stations that carried out work for the collective farms. In essence, the Soviet Union's land, workers, and farming activity were all controlled by the managers of the *kolkhozes* and *sovkhozes*, who were themselves under the orders of the Party.

Collectivisation got under way in the summer of 1929 and by March 1930 had already been applied to nearly 60 per cent of peasant families, or around 15 million families (Lewin, 1971). Supposedly voluntary, collectivisation was in fact imposed by force, often with acts of unheard-of violence being perpetrated by armed militia. There was mass destruction of livestock and agricultural equipment, both by peasants who refused to give them up to the *kolkhozes* and by the militias. The 'liquidation of the kulaks as a class' and of other opponents in general took the form of outright murder and mass deportation (Viola et al., 2005).

Fearing that this violence might eventually lead to failure, the Party's Central Committee allowed peasant families to leave the *kolkhozes*, which 9 million of them did in the spring of 1930, despite all the obstacles put in their way. This policy reversal did not last long, however, for in the autumn of 1930, collectivisation had resumed and would continue for nearly four years. By 1935, upwards of 90 per cent of agricultural land in the USSR was collectivised, with 4 per cent being set aside for family plots (Conquest, 1986).

Under Stalin, each *kolkhoz* was obliged to supply the state with large volumes of agricultural produce at low prices and to pay high taxes, either in cash or in kind. Agricultural labourers were organised into brigades. The pay for this work did not even cover the workers' basic needs, and the family plots only partly made up for the shortfall. The *kolkhozniks* lived in such deplorable conditions that many fled to the cities, leading the authorities to prohibit them from moving without formal permission (Danilov, 1988). With insufficient land for themselves, and now obliged to stay in their villages to work for almost nothing on large estates run by the state to supply industry and the cities, Russian peasants found themselves reduced to a situation of virtual state serfdom.

7   Common Characteristics

Although these past instances of large-scale land acquisitions are far removed from one another in both time and place, and are different in their social contexts and applications, they nonetheless share a set of common basic features.

Each of them benefited a very small number of individuals who, at little expense to themselves, became owners, tenants, de facto owners or stewards of large estates, whether the beneficiaries were foreign, like the Roman senators and knights, the Spanish *hacendados* or the Portuguese *fazendeiros*, or whether they originated from amongst the indigenous population, like the British landlords and tenant farmers or the Soviet hierarchs. These acquisitions were detrimental to a great number of previous rights holders and users of the land, who were completely or partially dispossessed of their land and livelihoods.

The beneficiaries were able to exploit not only the land, which was generally chosen from amongst the best available, but also, depending on the situation, all or part of the workforce formed by the dispossessed. In some cases, the dispossessors enlisted almost the entire workforce. In the Roman colonies, most of the able-bodied dispossessed were reduced to the condition of captive slave workers, or serfs paying a double tribute in the form of work and benefits in kind, or sharecroppers compelled to surrender a proportion of their harvest. In the Spanish and Portuguese colonies, they were reduced to being slaves or serfs, and then sharecroppers or small-scale tenant farmers or paid workers earning barely enough to live. In the Soviet Union at the time of collectivisation, dispossessed peasants became virtual state serfs. In other cases, the dispossessors employed only some of the labour of the dispossessed. At the time of the enclosures in Britain, landlords and tenant farmers employed only a fraction of those who had been dispossessed, as sharecroppers or agricultural labourers. Everyone else had to seek gruelling, low-paid employment, in the mines or in the burgeoning industrial sector, or had to settle for life as a vagabond or beggar, taking refuge in workhouses or poorhouses, or else emigrating to the colonies of settlement.

These large-scale acquisitions of land allowed a small number of dispossessors to derive unparalleled comparative advantages from their cheap land and workforce in responding to demand from more or less distant markets, or to orders from the state: wheat, wine and olive oil for Rome and its army; sugar, cotton, hides, meat, coffee, cocoa beans and tobacco for the European colonial powers; foodstuffs and raw materials for the expanding British cities and industries, and also for Soviet cities and industries under a regime of planned growth.

In every case, elements within the populations affected openly resisted the appropriation, and the consequent exploitation and marginalisation. There were instances of resistance to colonisation by 'barbarians' and native American populations, and there were escapes and revolts by slaves, serfs, and peasants who were maltreated or excluded, or who refused to accept collectivisation. All of these victims put up clandestine resistance to the domination of the oppressors on an everyday basis (Kerkvliet, 2009; Scott, 1987). Occasionally, these resistance movements managed to halt, locally and temporarily, and had the overall effect of slowing down the drive towards acquisition and dispossession. However, the lack of a broad alliance with the dispossessed of other regions and with other victims of the established order meant that the balance of power between the dispossesors and the dispossessed was not reversed and the acquisitions/dispossessions continued.

For the most part, land acquisitions were extended and perpetuated through the exercise of armed force that was greatly superior to that of the dispossessed: Roman, Spanish, and Portuguese armies; private militias imposing de facto the enclosures in sixteenth century Britain, or the seizures by Spanish and Portuguese conquerors; police forces applying the Enclosure Acts from the eighteenth century onwards; and—in Russia—Party militia, police, and the army imposing collectivisation. Those who resisted were pursued and killed as an example to others, or tortured before being put back to work, either in situ or in deportation camps.

Acquisitions were generally reinforced by an arsenal of formal legal and regulatory measures that established and protected the rights of the new possessors, without regard to the previous rights of the dispossessed. These statutory provisions either predated the appropriations—as was the case with Roman law for example—or they were imposed on an ad hoc basis, as was the case with the 'Indian Laws' of Spain, the Enclosure Acts, and the decrees on the nationalisation or collectivisation of agricultural land in the USSR.

Furthermore, the beneficiaries developed a narrative to legitimise their actions: Rome's 'preventive' conquests to stave off supposed threats of attack (Castignani, 2012); the civilisation and evangelisation of indigenous peoples; the rational exploitation of resources and growth in productivity justifying the enclosures from the eighteenth century onwards; and the economic development and the construction of socialism during collectivisation in the USSR. At the same time, a derogatory discourse, depicting the dispossessed as inferior, developed: to the Romans they were uncivilised barbarians; to the Iberian conquistadors the Indians were inhuman savages; to the British nobles they were vile peasants; and to the Bolsheviks they were peasants with bourgeois aspirations.

Finally, by contributing to this discourse legitimising acquisitions of land rights, by adopting laws and regulations legalising these acquired land rights, and by the use of public force to impose and enforce these laws, states and governments, acting in concert with the beneficiaries, played a decisive role in these acquisitions (Lewin, 1971; Nicolet, 1967; Piel, 2013; Slater, 1907).

8   Acquisitions Today

Although the current wave of land acquisitions has given rise to a great many publications, the information that they convey is often unreliable and fragmentary (Scoones et al., 2013). They nevertheless allow us to consider that these current acquisitions share, in their own way, the general features described above, while differing from previous waves of acquisitions in terms of their context and some of their methods.

Their first particularity, from a geopolitical standpoint, is that such acquisitions are developing throughout the world, in virtual defiance of national borders, whereas they previously occurred in national or colonial territories that, while they might be vast, were under the control of a single state.

Since the 1980s, acquisitions have been greatly facilitated by the liberalisation of public policies. Indeed, the liberalisation of agricultural policies in developing countries, implemented as part of stabilisation and structural adjustment programmes, has deprived farmers of the technical, economic, and financial support that had enabled them to invest and progress, insofar as this support existed. Moreover, liberalisation in the international trade of agricultural produce, albeit incomplete, combined with the use of increasingly powerful and inexpensive methods of transportation and trade, has brought an ever-increasing number of farmers from all regions into competition with the world's most competitive agricultural producers, who in some cases receive subsidies from their governments. This has impoverished or ruined hundreds of millions of farmers (Mazoyer and Roudart, 2006). Finally, financial liberalisation has made it possible for major investors to enjoy easy access to cheap, large-scale credit.

Besides, the land policies implemented in many countries since the 1990s have facilitated large-scale land acquisitions (Gironde and Senties Portilla, this volume) and have encouraged the concentration of land ownership rather than its redistribution (Borras Jr. and Franco, 2012). Governments and administrative authorities in the countries in which recent acquisitions have taken place play a considerable role, on the one hand by acting as intermediaries between national or foreign investors and local political authorities, and on the other by acquiring land themselves (Wolford et al., 2013). Meanwhile, some governments of the investors' countries of origin actively support these acquisitions (Woertz and Keulertz, this volume).

Another specific feature of the current wave of acquisitions is the major role played by international organisations. The International Monetary Fund (IMF), the World Bank, the Organisation for Economic Co-operation and Development (OECD), and the World Trade Organization (WTO) have greatly contributed to putting in place today's liberal economic rules. Furthermore, the Multilateral Investment Guarantee Agency (an agency of the World Bank) provides investors with guarantees against risks, while the World Bank and other development banks fund the infrastructures enabling such investments to become profitable. In addition, several international organisations have begun to draft non-binding principles to guide investors in their strategies (Borras Jr. and Franco, 2010).

Where land currently being acquired is effectively used for agricultural purposes, it is generally exploited by large, highly-capitalised farming units employing extremely productive mechanical, chemical, and biological means of production. These means are much more productive than those used by the vast majority of the world's farmers, most of whom work with manual tools and little or no agricultural inputs. The gap in productivity between the world's most productive and least productive farmers has never been as wide as it is today (Mazoyer and Roudart, 2006). It follows that production costs are far lower for the most productive farmers than for the others. And, within the

current context of globalised trade, large, highly-capitalised farms are expanding over vast swathes of the globe and gaining increased market share to the
detriment of many farmers in other regions.

The current wave of acquisitions and its consequences are therefore global
in their implications. If it continued to grow, it could have a negative impact on
hundreds of millions of individuals, either indirectly through competition on
markets or directly through partial or complete dispossession. In today's world,
land is an essential means of existence for many populations: when dispossessed, or excluded, they find themselves incapable of meeting their essential
needs because they are surplus to labour requirements in other sectors of the
economy (Li, 2011), without new continents available to colonise as a potential
outlet. Over time, such a development would pose colossal political risks.

In order to combat these acquisitions, peasant organisations, some of which
have an international outreach, have been engaging in campaigns of resistance.
They are attempting to attract the attention of the press, public opinion, and
political authorities, while mobilising other civil society organisations across
the world (Borras Jr. et al., 2008; Edelman, 2003; McMichael, 2006). Some of
these efforts have been successful: in 2009, the mobilisation against a project
in Madagascar to lease more than one million hectares to the South Korean
company Daewoo led to the resignation of the country's President and the
abandonment of the project (Petric, 2011).

These particular features aside, the current wave of land acquisitions shares,
in its own way, the characteristics common to past waves of acquisitions analysed above. Existing studies, although far from being exhaustive, show that
these current acquisitions are of actual benefit to a small number of actors—a
few thousand individual entrepreneurs, company shareholders, and managers
or investors in public or private investment funds. In the meantime, on the
ground, a great many individuals have already lost all or part of their livelihoods (Anseeuw et al., 2012; Gironde and Senties Portilla, this volume).

Just like the landlords and tenant farmers at the time of the enclosures, the
new acquirers of land do not employ all the manpower offered by the dispossessed, partly because new holdings, when they are developed, are equipped
with powerful machinery and require little labour (Li, 2011). It is also because
a large portion of the newly-acquired land remains uncultivated (Land Matrix,
2014). In fact, many acquirers keep land in reserve, probably in anticipation of
its increasing value or of a new surge in agricultural prices, or alternatively for
reasons of environmental conservation. Others are slow to develop their land
because of a wide range of technical, financial, and organisational difficulties
(Boche, 2014).

The working conditions of labourers on large agricultural estates are usually
very harsh. Permanent jobs are rare, while casual employment, of a daily or

seasonal nature, is common. Working hours are variable and often unfair. Pay is often on a piecework basis, and is rarely adequate to cover the costs of supporting a family and even the labourer himself. Social security and accident prevention measures are practically non-existent (Hervieu and Purseigle, 2013; Hurst et al., 2005; IFAD, 2010; Jacques-Jouvenot and Laplante, 2009). Despite this, these jobs are sought after by the dispossessed, who are compelled to undertake any sort of casual work, legal or otherwise, or else end up as beggars or vagrants (Anseeuw et al., 2012). Being of no use to the economic or social system as either workers or consumers, these surplus populations are in practice excluded (Castells, 1998).

In fact, whenever investors develop newly acquired land, it is obviously to derive a profit by producing foodstuffs for which there exists a solvent demand. This corresponds to diverse, more or less distant markets (Borras Jr. and Franco, 2012), but the aim is not to satisfy non-commercial domestic needs.

Open acts of resistance by the dispossessed have taken place. As was the case in the past, they trigger a response from the forces of law and order, the army, paramilitary groups or private militias (Grajales, 2011). To forestall or stamp out such resistance, the dispossessors and the authorities resort to various forms of pressure including intimidation, threats, the withholding of information and the presenting of situations as faits accomplis. They claim that the transfer of land rights is necessary for the country's development, and equate any resistance with political opposition to the regime or the governing authorities (Cismas and Paramita, this volume; Jacob and Le Meur, 2010).

The neo-liberal-inspired legal and regulatory measures that have been put in place in many developing countries since the 1980s (bilateral or multilateral investment treaties, and laws or codes governing investment and land) considerably benefit major acquirers of land rights, whereas the rights of the previous users, with no formal title that they can assert, are generally not taken into consideration (Alden Wily, 2012). In addition, the dispossessed have hardly any prospect of judicial redress (Golay, this volume). In this regard, the processes which formalise and commodify land rights have often had damaging effects on the poor (De Schutter, this volume).

The arguments of those who legitimise current land acquisitions emphasise what is considered to be the relatively unproductive, or even non-existent, use of the land in question, and the need to invest to increase agricultural production so as to feed a rapidly-growing human population and to supply biofuels, textile fibres, wood and other products. This discourse of legitimisation also asserts that 'large' farms (employing wage-earning manpower) are more productive than 'small' (family) farms, and that no significant progress can be expected from the latter (Collier, 2008). Finally, some new landowners claim to be acting in the name of environmental conservation (Fairhead et al., 2012).

9   Key Findings and Implications for Public Policy and
       Research Debates

In the preceding pages, we have analysed the current wave of large-scale land acquisitions in the light of similar historical experiences. Given the limited space available, we have selected only four historical cases amongst many others. Our analysis is therefore incomplete and no claim is made here that the features identified as being common to these four cases would prove valid for all others. We nevertheless feel that this study permits a better understanding of current acquisitions and sheds light on the public policy and research debates that they have reopened.

One such debate concerns the structures of agricultural production and seeks to answer the following question: which production structures (family-owned farms or wage-based farms) are better capable of encouraging sustained development, primarily aimed at reducing poverty, generating jobs and livelihoods for hundreds of millions of people, promoting growth, providing food security for all and reducing income disparities while enhancing the environment (Byerlee et al., 2009; Thematic Group on Sustainable Agriculture and Food Systems, 2013)?

Our analysis shows that the current wave of acquisitions is driven, as were several past waves, by the search for cheap land and labour, for the purpose of creating large competitive units able to generate a profit by producing agricultural goods cheaply and by selling these goods to populations enjoying a degree of purchasing power. Like the previous waves, the current one is largely predicated on the dispossession of local populations, which directly impoverishes and excludes certain of their members. And, insofar as present land acquisitions are followed by the creation of large-scale, highly-equipped, productive and competitive farms, this current wave, like several previous waves, results indirectly in the impoverishment and exclusion of rural populations in other parts of the world through competition on the international market.

All of these effects run counter to the above-mentioned aims of sustained development.

Our analysis also suggests that the present acquisitions, promoted by many governments and major investors, reflect a broad consensus amongst the leading decision-makers, and that the negatively-affected social categories, and their various potential allies, appear unable to organise an effective political force putting up resistance and putting forward alternative proposals at the international, national, and sometimes local levels. Therefore, the current wave of large-scale land acquisitions leads researchers in the field of agrarian political economy to reflect on the parameters of an alternative agricultural development model to replace that which has held sway over the past few decades. Admittedly, this dominant model has created a great deal of wealth but it has also caused major environmental damage and much poverty and exclusion (McIntyre et al., 2009; MEA, 2005). And it has generated the current wave of large-scale land acquisitions, which leads researchers to consider also how an alternative agricultural development model could harness widespread political support.

10   Conclusion

On a planet where there is practically no more unused arable or grazing land left, it is more or less impossible to acquire the right to exploit large tracts of land without directly acting against the interests and living conditions of dispossessed rights holders and their descendants. And, in a global economy where solvent demand is already limited by enormous poverty, there are no more opportunities for large-scale investment in agriculture without indirectly reducing the market shares, incomes, or jobs of less competitive family farmers.

The current wave of large-scale land acquisitions, since it knows no boundaries, would, if it continued, have consequences on an unprecedented scale. Who would then house, feed and occupy the billions of people living in slums? Which authority would regulate the hundreds of millions of beggars, homeless people and migrants flocking towards those islands of prosperity that still remained? What army would contain the endless, pointless global civil war that would ensue?

Fortunately, however, we can never be certain that the worst will happen. At the beginning of the twentieth century, many democratic liberal governments concluded that large agricultural estates with paid workers were less conducive to economic development and social harmony than family farms, and accordingly adopted policies to further the development of the latter. And several of these governments even made agrarian reform the first step in their economic and social development policy. In the aftermath of the Second World War, the victorious liberal democracies, drawing lessons from the two major economic crises, totalitarian regimes, and two World Wars of the long preceding half-century, were anxious to provide full employment and an adequate level of well-being. They adopted policies to encourage widespread economic and social development, with close links between large-scale industry and family farming. They imposed agrarian reforms in several of the defeated countries, where the landed oligarchy had clearly been in league with the dictatorships.

All of this with evident success! As the world attempts to steer a path towards sustained development on a global scale, it is a point worth remembering.

References

Alden Wily, L. (2012) 'Looking Back to See Forward: The Legal Niceties of Land Theft in Land Rushes', *Journal of Peasant Studies*, 39 (3–4), pp. 751–775, DOI: 10.1080/ 03066150.2012.674033.

Anseeuw, W., L. Alden Wily, L. Cotula and M. Taylor (2012) *Land Rights and the Rush for Land: Findings of the Global Commercial Pressures on Land Research Project* (Rome: International Land Coalition), http://www.landcoalition.org/sites/default/files/ publication/1205/ILC GSRreport_ENG.pdf (accessed on 4 June 2015).

Aymard, A. and J. Auboyer (1995[1954]) *Rome et son Empire* (Paris: Presses Universitaires de France/Quadrige).

Bagchi, A.K. (2009) 'Nineteenth Century Imperialism and Structural Transformation in Colonized Countries' in Akram-Lodhi, A.H. and C. Kay (eds.) *Peasants and Globalization: Political Economy, Rural Transformation and the Agrarian Question* (London and New York: Routledge) pp. 83–110.

Bauer, A.J. (1979) 'Rural Workers in Spanish America: Problems of Peonage and Oppression', *Hispanic American Historical Review*, 59(1), pp. 34–63, DOI: 10.2307/ 2514135.

Beckett, J.V. (1999) 'La propriété foncière en Angleterre aux XVIIᵉ et XVIIIᵉ siècles', *Histoire, Economie et Société*, 18(1), pp. 25–41, http://www.persee.fr/web/revues/ home/prescript/article/hes_0752-5702_1999_num_18_1_2016 (accessed on 4 June 2015).

Beckford, G. (1999[1972]) *Persistent Poverty: Underdevelopment in Plantation Economies of the Third World* (Kingston, Jamaica: University of the West Indies Press).

Bernstein, H. (2010) *Class Dynamics of Agrarian Change. Agrarian Change & Peasant Studies* (Sterling, VA: Kumarian Press).

Bloch, M. (1947) 'Comment et pourquoi finit l'esclavage antique', *Annales. Histoire, Sciences Sociales*, 2(1), pp. 30–44, http://www.jstor.org/stable/27578330 (accessed on 4 June 2015).

Boche, M. (2014) *Contrôle du foncier, agricultures d'entreprise et restructurations agraires: une perspective critique des investissements fonciers à grande échelle. Le cas de la partie centrale du Mozambique*, unpublished PhD thesis (Paris: Université de Paris-Sud), https://tel.archives-ouvertes.fr/tel-01126967/ (accessed on 4 June 2015).

Borras Jr., S.M. and J.C. Franco (2012) 'Global Land Grabbing and Trajectories of Agrarian Change: A Preliminary Analysis', *Journal of Agrarian Change*, 12(1), pp. 34–59, DOI: 10.1111/j.1471-0366.2011.00339.x.

———— (2010) 'From Threat to Opportunity? Problems with the Idea of a "Code of Conduct" for Land-Grabbing', *Yale Human Rights and Development Law Journal*, 13, pp. 507–523.

Borras Jr., S.M., M. Edelman and C. Kay (2008) 'Transnational Agrarian Movements: Origins and Politics, Campaigns and Impact', *Journal of Agrarian Change*, 8(2–3), pp. 169–204, DOI: 10.1111/j.1471-0366.2008.00167.x.

Byerlee, D., A. De Janvry and E. Sadoulet (2009) 'Agriculture for Development: Toward a New Paradigm', *Annual Review of Resource Economics*, 1(1), pp. 15–31, DOI: 10.1146/annurev.resource.050708.144239.

Byres, T.J. (2009) 'The Landlord Class, Peasant Differentiation, Class Struggle and the Transition to Capitalism: England, France and Prussia Compared', *The Journal of Peasant Studies*, 36(1), pp. 33–54, DOI: 10.1080/03066150902820453.

Castells, M. (1998) *End of Millennium* (Malden, MA: Wiley-Blackwell).

Castignani, H. (2012) 'L'impérialisme défensif existe-t-il? Sur la théorie romaine de la guerre juste et sa postérité', *Raisons politiques*, No. 45, pp. 35–57, DOI: 10.3917/rai.045.0035.

CNRS (Centre national de la recherche scientifique) (1995) *Du latifundium au latifondo: un héritage de Rome, une création médiévale ou moderne?* (Paris: Centre Pierre Paris).

Chonchol, J. (1970) 'Eight Fundamental Conditions of Agrarian Reform in Latin America', in Stavenhagen, R. (ed.) *Agrarian Problems and Peasant Movements in Latin America* (Garden City, NY: Doubleday), pp. 159–172.

Collier, P. (2008) 'The Politics of Hunger: How Illusion and Greed Fan the Food Crisis', *Foreign Affairs*, 87(6), pp. 67–79, http://www.jstor.org/stable/20699372 (accessed on 4 June 2015).

Conquest, R. (1986) *The Harvest of Sorrow: Soviet Collectivization and the Terror-Famine* (New York: Oxford University Press).

Danilov, V.P. (1988) *Rural Russia under the New Regime* (Bloomington: Indiana University Press).

Duncan-Jones, R. (1974) *The Economy of the Roman Empire: Quantitative Studies* (Cambridge: Cambridge University Press).

Earl, D.C. (1963) *Tiberius Gracchus: A Study in Politics* (Bruxelles: Latomus).

Edelman, M. (2003) 'Transnational Peasant and Farmer Movements and Networks', in Kaldor, M., H. Anheier and M. Glasius (eds.) *Global Civil Society Yearbook 2003* (London: Sage), pp. 185–220.

Fairbairn, M., J. Fox, S.R. Isakson, M. Levien, N. Peluso, S. Razavi, I. Scoones and K. Sivaramakrishnan (2014) 'Introduction: New Directions in Agrarian Political Economy', *Journal of Peasant Studies*, 41(5), pp. 653–666, DOI: 10.1080/03066150.2014.953490.

Fairhead, J., M. Leach and I. Scoones (2012) 'Green Grabbing: A New Appropriation of Nature?', *Journal of Peasant Studies*, 39(2), pp. 237–261, DOI: 10.1080/03066150.2012.671770.

Finley, M.I. (ed.) (1976) *Studies in Roman Property* (Cambridge: Cambridge University Press).

Garnsey, P. (1988) *Famine and Food Supply in the Graeco-Roman World: Responses to Risk and Crisis* (Cambridge: Cambridge University Press).

Grajales, J. (2011) 'The Rifle and the Title: Paramilitary Violence, Land Grab and Land Control in Colombia', *Journal of Peasant Studies*, 38(4), pp. 771–792, DOI: 10.1080/03066150.2011.607701.

Graziano Neto, F. (1991) *A tragédia da terra: o fracasso da reforma agrária no Brasil* (São Paulo: IGLU–FUNEP–UNESP).

Hervieu, B. and F. Purseigle (2013) *Sociologie des mondes agricoles* (Paris: Armand Colin).

Hobsbawm, E.J. (1977[1962]) *The Age of Revolution: Europe 1789–1848* (London: Abacus).

Hunt, H.G. and P. Leuilliot (1956) 'Vers une revision critique et statistique: aspects de la révolution agraire en Angleterre au XVIIIe siècle', *Annales. Histoire, Sciences Sociales*, 11(1), pp. 29–41, http://www.jstor.org/stable/27579767 (accessed on 4 June 2015).

Hurst, P., P. Termine and M. Karl (2005) *Agricultural Workers and Their Contribution to Sustainable Agriculture and Rural Development* (Rome and Geneva: FAO–ILO–IUF), http://www.fao-ilo.org/fileadmin/user_upload/fao_ilo/pdf/engl_agricultureC4163.pdf (accessed on 4 June 2015).

IFAD (International Fund for Agricultural Development) (2010) *Rural Poverty Report 2011* (Rome: IFAD), http://www.ifad.org/rpr2011/report/e/overview.pdf (accessed on 4 June 2015).

Jacob, J.P. and P.Y. Le Meur (2010) 'Introduction', in Jacob, J.P. and P.Y. Le Meur (eds.) *Politique de la terre et de l'appartenance: droits fonciers et citoyenneté dans les sociétés du Sud* (Paris: Karthala) pp. 5–57.

Jacques-Jouvenot, D. and J.J. Laplante (2009) *Les maux de la terre: regards croisés sur la santé au travail en agriculture* (La Tour-d'Aigues: Editions de l'Aube).

Jones, A.H.M. (1974) *The Roman Economy: Studies in Ancient Economic and Administrative History* (Oxford: Brunt P.A).

Kay, C. (2014) 'Rural Livelihoods and Peasant Futures', in Gwynne, R.N. and C. Kay (eds.) *Latin America Transformed: Globalization and Modernity*, 2nd ed. (London: Routledge) pp. 232–250.

———— (1998) 'Latin America's Agrarian Reform: Lights and Shadows', *Journal of Land Reform, Land Settlement and Cooperatives* (FAO), No. 2, pp. 8–31.

———— (1974) 'Comparative Development of the European Manorial System and the Latin American Hacienda System', *Journal of Peasant Studies*, 2(1), pp. 69–98, DOI: 10.1080/03066157408437916.

Kerkvliet, B. (2009) 'Everyday Politics in Peasant Societies (and Ours)', *Journal of Peasant Studies*, 36(1), pp. 227–243, DOI: 10.1080/03066150902820487.

Land, S.K. (1977) *Kett's Rebellion: The Norfolk Rising of 1549* (Ipswich, UK, and Totowa, NJ: Boydell Press—Rowman and Littlefield).

Land Matrix (2014) *Newsletter*, various issues.

Lewin, M. (1971[1968]) *Russian Peasants and Soviet Power* (Evanston, IL, and London: Allen & Unwin).

Li, T.M. (2011) 'Centering Labor in the Land Grab Debate', *Journal of Peasant Studies*, 38(2), pp. 281–298, DOI: 10.1080/03066150.2011.559009.

Luna, P.F. (2013) 'Latifundia, haciendas et landgrabbing, en perspective historique', *HISTOIRE(S) de l'Amérique latine*, 8, http://www.hisal.org/revue/article/Luna2013-8b (accessed on 4 June 2015).

Marx, K. (1965[1867]) 'Le Capital, livre premier', in Marx, K., Œuvres: I, *Economie* (Paris: Gallimard).

Mazoyer, M. and L. Roudart (2006) *A History of World Agriculture: From the Neolithic Age to the Current Crisis* (London: Earthscan Publications).

McIntyre, B.D., H.R. Herren, J. Wakhungu and R.T. Watson (eds.) (2009) *Agriculture at a Crossroads: Global Report* (Washington, D.C.: International Assessment of Agricultural Knowledge, Science and Technology for Development), http://apps.unep.org/publications/pmtdocuments/Agriculture_at_a_Crossroads_Global_Report.pdf (accessed on 4 June 2015).

McMichael, P. (2006) 'Reframing Development: Global Peasant Movements and the New Agrarian Question', *Canadian Journal of Development Studies/Revue canadienne d'études du développement*, 27(4), pp. 471–483, DOI: 10.1080/02255189.2006.9669169.

MEA (Millennium Ecosystem Assessment) (2005) *Ecosystems and Human Well-Being* (Washington, D.C.: World Resources Institute), http://www.millenniumassessment.org/documents/document.356.aspx.pdf (accessed on 4 June 2015).

Méquet, G. (1930) 'Le problème agraire dans la Révolution russe', *Annales d'histoire économique et sociale*, 2(6), pp. 161–192, http://www.jstor.org/stable/27572184 (accessed on 4 June 2015).

Mingay, G.E. (2014[1997]) *Parliamentary Enclosure in England: An Introduction to Its Causes, Incidence and Impact, 1750–1850* (London and New York: Routledge).

Monbeig, P. (1984) *Pioneiros e fazendeiros de São Paulo* (São Paulo: Hucitec).

More, T. (1978) *L'Utopie de Thomas More* (C edition, Bâle, 1518), edited by Prévost, A. (Paris: Mame).

Moreno García, J.C. (2008) 'Estates (Old Kingdom)', in Frood, E. and W. Wendrich (eds.) *UCLA Encyclopedia of Egyptology* (Los Angeles: University of California), https://escholarship.org/uc/item/1b3342c2 (accessed on 4 June 2015).

Nicolet, C. (1967) *Les Gracques: crise agraire et révolution à Rome* (Paris: Julliard).

Nove, A. and D. Morrison (1982) 'The Contribution of Agriculture to Accumulation in the 1930s', in Bettelheim, C. (ed.) *L'industrialisation de l'URSS dans les années trente* (Paris: Editions de l'Ecole des hautes études en sciences sociales), pp. 47–64.

Petric, B. (2011) 'La ruée vers la terre', *Transcontinentales*, No. 10/11, http://transcontinentales.revues.org/1060 (accessed on 4 June 2015).

Piel, J. (2013) 'L'expropriation des terres et la formation du latifundium en Amérique espagnole et latine', *HISTOIRE(S) de l'Amérique latine*, 8, http://www.hisal.org/revue/article/Piel2013-8 (accessed on 4 June 2015).

———— (1988) *Capitalisme agraire au Pérou* (Paris: Economica), http://books.openedition.org/ifea/1332 (accessed on 4 June 2015).

Pliny the Elder (1848) *Histoire naturelle: Livre XVIII, traitant des céréales*, edited by Littré, E. (Paris: Dubochet).

Polanyi, K. (1971[1944]) *The Great Transformation: The Political and Economic Origins of Our Time* (Boston: Beacon Press).

Roux, P. (1910) *La question agraire en Italie: le latifundium romain* (Paris: Félix Alcan).

Sapir, J. (1990) *L'économie mobilisée* (Paris: La Découverte).

Schonhardt-Bailey, C. (2006) *From the Corn Laws to Free Trade: Interests, Ideas, and Institutions in Historical Perspective* (Cambridge, MA: The MIT Press).

Scoones, I., R. Hall, S.M. Borras Jr., B. White and W. Wolford (2013) 'The Politics of Evidence: Methodologies for Understanding the Global Land Rush', *Journal of Peasant Studies*, 40(3), pp. 469–483, DOI: 10.1080/03066150.2013.801341.

Scott, J.C. (1987) *Weapons of the Weak: Everyday Forms of Peasant Resistance* (New Haven: Yale University Press).

Slater, G. (1907) *The English Peasantry and the Enclosure of Common Fields* (London: A. Constable and Co.).

Sorlin, P. (1964) 'Lénine et le problème paysan en 1917', *Annales. Histoire, Sciences Sociales*, 19(2), pp. 250–280, http://www.jstor.org/stable/27576148 (accessed on 4 June 2015).

Stalin, J. (1930) *La collectivisation du village* (Paris: Bureau d'Editions).

Stockton, D. (1979) *The Gracchi* (Oxford and New York: Oxford University Press).

Thematic Group on Sustainable Agriculture and Food Systems (2013) *Solutions for Sustainable Agriculture and Food Systems*, Technical Report for the Post-2015 Development Agenda (New York: United Nations–Sustainable Development Solutions Network).

Viola, L., V.P. Danilov, N.A. Ivnitskii, D. Kozlov and S. Shabad (2005) *The War against the Peasantry, 1927–1930: The Tragedy of the Soviet Countryside* (New Haven, CT: Yale University Press).

Virgil (1982) *Géorgiques*, edited by de Saint-Denis, E. (Paris: Les Belles Lettres).

Wachtel, N. (1977) *The Vision of the Vanquished: The Spanish Conquest of Peru through Indian Eyes, 1530–1570* (New York: Barnes & Noble).

White, B., S.M. Borras Jr., R. Hall, I. Scoones and W. Wolford (2012) 'The New Enclosures: Critical Perspectives on Corporate Land Deals', *Journal of Peasant Studies*, 39(3–4), pp. 619–647, DOI: 10.1080/03066150.2012.691879.

White, B. and A. Dasgupta (2010) 'Agrofuels Capitalism: A View from Political Economy', *Journal of Peasant Studies*, 37(4), pp. 593–607, DOI: 10.1080/03066150.2010.512449.

White, K.D. (1970) *Roman Farming* (Ithaca, NY: Cornell University Press).

Wolford, W., S.M. Borras Jr., R. Hall, I. Scoones and B. White (2013) 'Governing Global Land Deals: The Role of the State in the Rush for Land', *Development and Change*, 44(2), pp. 189–210, DOI: 10.1111/dech.12017.

CHAPTER 2

States as Actors in International Agro-Investments

Martin Keulertz and Eckart Woertz

Abstract

Since the global food crisis of 2008 states have encouraged international agro-investments by their respective private sectors or have undertaken them directly via state-owned companies and sovereign wealth funds. This chapter analyses the crucial role played by national governments with the help of three case studies: the Gulf countries, China, and potential host countries. It thus shows the varying constraints experienced by these three cases and the strategies pursued to overcome them. States in the Gulf are heavily dependent on food imports and are concerned that export restrictions could undermine their food security. For the same reason, China has pursued a strategy of grain self-sufficiency, which is now being modified in the light of recent changes to diet and rises in demand. Governments in potential host countries and regions, like South-East Asia, Russia, and Brazil, on the other hand, have sought to keep their agricultural export industries national, maximise their revenue streams, and leverage them for geopolitical purposes. While much of the literature has focused on 'land grabbing' by foreign states in developing countries, this chapter offers a different perspective by placing the interests of states into the context of twenty-first century food politics. It concludes that: the focus of investments has been on value chains downstream rather than on farmland in the upstream sector; that 'security mercantilism' is far more complex than the land acquisition processes themselves; and that emerging economies in Asia seek to challenge the Western world in its hegemony over food production and virtual water trade.

1 Introduction

Food and agriculture have been intertwined with national interests historically. Initially these interests focused on food provision for armies; later, local populations were ruthlessly subjugated to serve development agendas, be it during the famines in the colonial tropical belts in the second half of the nineteenth century or during the brutal modernization of communist regimes in the twentieth century (Davis, 2001). The idea that affordable food should be an inalienable right entered the vocabulary of political legitimacy only in the recent past. It did so in a context of proliferating support for farms and of nutrition programmes in the US in the 1930s that became closely intertwined with a development model of intensive growth. Labour was no longer a mere cost factor, as seen in the extensive growth model of the nineteenth century; it was also an important source of demand in growing consumer markets, such as those for white goods and cars. The Right to Food was enshrined in international treaties, like the Universal Declaration of Human Rights in 1948, and the International Covenant on Economic, Social and Cultural Rights in 1966.

Agricultural overproduction became a permanent feature of the post-war decades, first in North America and then in Western Europe. Countries were eager to dispose of their structural surpluses via subsidised food aid and used the allocation and withdrawal of such aid to further their foreign policy agendas during the Cold War. Governments in the developing world in turn used such subsidised food imports to feed their growing urban populations and as an input factor for their import-substituting industrialisation strategies, which were prevalent at the time.

The global food crisis of 2008, with its price hikes and export restrictions, has raised doubts over whether global agricultural trade flows will remain as readily available as in the past. Food importers in the Middle East and Asia have reacted by announcing agro-investments in developing countries, which have been identified as a 'new frontier' of agriculture as they have supposedly unused or underutilised land that could produce more food if yield gaps were closed by introducing modern management and production technologies (Deininger and Byerlee, 2011). These investments have met with a critical reception as they could threaten the land rights of smallholders and pastoralists, especially if such rights are not registered and are only customary in nature. Although there is a large implementation gap and media reports have often been inaccurate, the interests of these governments illustrate a growing concern about global food production and trade. Their role in international foreign direct investment (FDI) flows has increased over the last decade. While sovereign wealth funds predominantly pursue portfolio investments, some of them have a more proactive private equity orientation. The roughly 550 state-owned transnational corporations (TNC) make up only 1 per cent of global TNCs, but a substantial 10 per cent of global FDI (UNCTAD, 2009; UNCTAD, 2014). The relative share of agriculture in these FDI flows is miniscule, but still substantial in absolute terms. Often governments try to provide framework conditions for their respective private sectors, rather than investing themselves. Ownership also does not necessarily mean managerial control, which often follows commercial prerogatives at the state-owned entities. Yet the direct and indirect investment initiatives clearly point to a heightened interest on the part of states.

This article analyses the role of states in international agro-investments with the help of three case studies. Countries located in the Gulf are heavily dependent on food imports and are concerned that export restrictions could undermine their food security. For the same reason China has pursued a strategy of grain self-sufficiency, which is now being modified in the light of recent changes to diet and rises in demand. Governments in potential host countries and regions, like South-East Asia, Russia, and Brazil on the other hand have sought to keep their agricultural export industries national, maximise their revenue streams, and leverage them for geopolitical purposes.

While much of the literature has focused on 'land grabbing' by foreign states in developing countries, this article offers a different perspective by placing the interests of states into the context of twenty-first century food politics. The focus of investments has been on value chains downstream rather than on farmland in the upstream sector. 'Security mercantilism' is far more complex than the land acquisition processes themselves. Emerging economies in Asia seek to brace themselves and to challenge the Western world in its hegemony over food production and virtual water trade.

2   Food Importers in the Second Food Regime

While the long-distance trade in grains played only a limited role in the Roman Empire, by the nineteenth century it had become a cornerstone of food supplies and food security strategies. In 1846 the British abolished the protectionist Corn Laws after a long struggle between the landed aristocracy, which had an interest in high grain prices, and the nascent industrial bourgeoisie, which wanted lower grain prices in order to moderate the wages of urban workers. From a position of maritime supremacy the United Kingdom (UK), by 1880, imported the majority of its grain from colonial settler states like North America and Australia, but also from India and Russia. Fuelled by railways and steam ships, the grain trade fed Britain's workers and facilitated its industrial revolution in a first food regime that lasted from the 1870s to the 1930s. Exports of tropical commodities—such as sugar, cotton, and rubber—from the colonies were a second pillar of this first food regime (McMichael, 2009b).

After a period of crisis and reconfiguration, the first food regime was superseded by a second food regime in the aftermath of the Second World War. This new regime was characterised by subsidised grain production in core states and surplus disposal in the developing world via export promotion programmes like the Public Law (PL) 480 programme in the US that was renamed the Food for Peace programme during the Kennedy administration. Diets underwent a process of 'meatification' in the developed world, and one of 'wheatification' in the developing world. The market for packaged, durable foods expanded in industrialised countries. Domestically produced input factors like soy oil, corn syrup, and synthetic fibres increasingly substituted colonial export crops like sugar and cotton.

There is an ongoing debate regarding whether we can speak of a third food regime today in which nation states have been superseded as main actors by transnational companies and the World Trade Organization (WTO), due to these increasingly influential actors' dominant roles in value chains and trade liberalisation (McMichael, 2009b; McMichael, 2009a; Friedmann, 2009; Pritchard, 2009; Burch and Lawrence, 2009). Many emerging markets are now also undergoing the same processes undergone by the developed world in earlier decades, such as the 'meatification' of diets and the 'supermarketisation' of distribution systems. As a result, new actors have emerged and new relationships have been forged. Thailand and Vietnam have developed into major rice exporters. Brazil is now a soybean superpower and an indispensable feedstock supplier to the Chinese livestock industry. Russia has become a large cereal exporter again akin to its nineteenth and early twentieth century role. The Soviet days—when the union was one of the largest grain importers in support of the ambitious livestock programme of the 1970s and 1980s—are gone. Yet these changes notwithstanding, the geography of food trade that was drawn after the Second World War still looms large.

The picture of the global net trade in cereals is telling: with 88 million tons in 2013–14, North America is by far the largest net exporter, followed by the former Soviet Union economies (57 million tons), Oceania (24 million tons), Europe (17 million tons) and South America (14 million tons). South Asia has also had a significant export surplus over the last three years, with its net exports currently standing at 16 million tons. On the other side of this equation, Middle East and North African (MENA) countries are the largest net importers of cereals globally (92 million tons), although their population size is relatively small with about 500 million people. East Asia and South-East Asia with over two billion people have less cereal net imports than the MENA (66 and 11 million tons respectively). Central America and the Caribbean are net importers too, at 10 million tons. So is sub-Saharan Africa with 29 million tons, a figure that is expected to increase in the future (USDA, 2014).

Of course, there are other important agricultural commodities, like soybeans or palm oil, which are dominated by other producer countries such as

Brazil, Indonesia and Malaysia. But the focus on cereals is warranted; corn and barley are important feedstocks for livestock and wheat and rice alone constitute roughly 40 per cent of human calorie intake globally (FAOSTAT, 2013). Hence, cereals are of particular strategic significance. The cereal trade—especially that in wheat, as rice, corn, and barley are traded less across borders—also constitutes about 15 per cent of global virtual water trade, surpassed only by water-intensive cotton (25 per cent) and followed by soybeans (9 per cent) (Sojamo et al., 2012). Virtual water is the water, in food and fibres, that is used to produce a given commodity. It cannot be pumped like blue water, but is accessible via trade. As 70 per cent of global crops are produced by rain-fed agriculture, the focus of the global debate on blue water and the conflicts over surface water sharing can be misleading because water scarcity can be mitigated by virtual water 'imports' (Allan, 2011). Accessing foreign rainfalls via food, and therefore the virtual water trade, is of paramount strategic importance for food importers.

The food question also reveals the power of North America and Europe in the global economy. Over a period of 150 years, vertical integration in the food supply chain enabled and fostered the establishment of the agribusiness industry. Aided by subsidies of up to USD 1 billion per day, Western agribusiness corporations permeated the global food trade (Peterson, 2009). In 2003, Archer Daniels Midlands (ADM), Bunge, Cargill, and Louis Dreyfus (the ABCDs) were estimated to be trading 73 per cent of global bulk cereal commodities (Murphy et al., 2012). This estimation did not even include the Swiss energy and food commodity trader Glencore, which has grown and ranks now as the fifth largest market participant from Organisation for Economic Co-operation and Development (OECD) countries. The upstream and downstream management of the food supply chain has been strategically transferred to the private sector since the 1980s, which has enabled the West to control global food trade. By making use of economic power, Western agribusiness companies do not rely solely on domestic agriculture for trade. The companies are also strategically present in water-endowed regions such as Latin America and Asia. The resulting dependence on companies in the West for food imports and virtual water 'provision' has developed into a concern for emerging economies seeking to define the twenty-first century politically and economically.

This dependence has implications for the three case studies in question, for the reaction of the respective states to the global food crisis of 2008, and for these states' role in international agro-investments. The Gulf countries' dependence on food imports will increase. Domestic agriculture is being scaled down due to a lack of water, and population growth will only peter out after 2050. The Gulf Cooperation Council (GCC) governments have announced a flurry of agro-investments since 2008; these have so far been largely unsuccessful and are conspicuously reminiscent of the failed Sudan breadbasket strategy of the 1970s. China has traditionally followed a policy of self-sufficiency, supported by its agrarian society model. However, China's rapid industrialisation has led to a moderation of the self-sufficiency paradigm. Beijing now seeks to accommodate changing diets and subsequent rising demand with additional imports made possible by strategic investments in supply chains throughout the world. Meanwhile, the new agro-exporters that have emerged over recent decades, like Brazil, Russia, and the rice exporters of South-East Asia, try to strengthen their positions in the new geo-economic landscape of food trade.

The agricultural investment policy choices made by the GCC countries and China illustrate the importance of food in the current world order. While theorists in international relations have focused on military capacity or economic power as a key determinant of state power, the role of control over agricultural commodities is often a neglected area of analysis. However, food and water security have always played a strategically important role for people charged with state power. State interests in agricultural investment reveal a new 'security mercantilism' seeking to repatriate agricultural products to investing states (McMichael, 2013). The contemporary multipolar order represents a new phase of 'inverse globalisation' by which new actors in the global political order, such as the GCC countries and China, start to become investors instead of being the beneficiaries of investment (Allan et al., 2013; Sojamo et al., 2012). This chapter will return to this issue in its conclusion. First, the objectives and strategies, and the preliminary results of state actors' involvement in agricultural investment will be analysed in the following sections.

3 Of Self-Sufficiency and Breadbasket Illusions: The Gulf Countries

Beside Asian countries, like China and South Korea, and western financial investors, Gulf countries constitute a third grouping in the wave of agro-investment announcements triggered by the global food crisis of 2008. Like the former two, Gulf countries share a specific set of motivations and concerns and a historical background all of which drives their actions. All are net food importers with a severe water shortage, and during the Second World War and in the 1970s all experienced the risk of geopolitical food supply disruptions. As oil exporters, Gulf countries were able to digest the concomitant food price hikes of the commodities boom of the 2000's, but they have been unnerved by the temporary export restrictions that food exporters like Russia, Argentina, Vietnam, and India announced in 2008. Affordable food is part of the social contract of Gulf countries, which are ruled in an authoritarian manner and buy off possible dissent over a lack of participation by using welfare payments and the offer of public sector jobs. Beside fuel and electricity, food and water are subsidised to varying degrees, at least for the local population. There are also differences between individual Gulf countries' approaches to agro-investments; Qatar and Saudi Arabia have the most institutionalised approach with the United Arab Emirates (UAE) as a distant third, while Kuwait and Bahrain lag behind. While Saudi Arabia only aims at providing favourable framework conditions for its private sector, Qatar has established Hassad Food, a bespoke sovereign wealth fund (SWF) for agro-investments. Oman is yet to announce any agro-investments, but has the most advanced strategy in terms of strategic storage and other relevant domestic factors (Woertz, 2013).

These states' sense of vulnerability is heightened by a lack of water and a need to downsize domestic agriculture. Gulf countries have one of the world's highest domestic per capita water consumption rates. Agriculture accounts for the lion's share of water withdrawal at about 80 per cent. While residential supplies are largely satisfied by desalinated seawater, farming has exploited fossil water aquifers at unsustainable rates, and these are drawn down and suffer from salt-water intrusion. Governments have started to react. Saudi Arabia has begun to phase out its subsidised wheat production and plans to end it in 2016 and the UAE is doing the same with Rhodes grass. However, livestock production continues to expand. As a result alfalfa is in high demand and farmers have switched from wheat to the latter crop, the cultivation of which consumes more water than wheat as it is planted all year round, and not only in the winter months. Saudi Arabia imports an enormous 40–45 per cent of globally traded barley as feedstock. As it will need to decrease its domestic alfalfa production it is expected to become the largest alfalfa importer in the world, importing either as hay or pellets, surpassing other major importers like the UAE, Japan, South Korea, and Taiwan (Personal interviews, Kuwait, November 2013).

The Qatar National Food Security Programme (QNFSP) raised eyebrows in 2009 with its cornucopian plan to raise self-sufficiency from its current level of 10 per cent to 70 per cent in 2023, with the help of futuristic farming designs and solar-based desalination. This figure was reduced to a more conservative 40–60 per cent in a later version of the programme's food security 'Master Plan' (Kanady, 2013). Even that target is unlikely to be met. QNFSP has been downgraded after internal restructurings and food security issues have been handed over to an inter-ministerial committee. The QNFSP website no longer exists. For a state with a small population and large amounts of capital at its disposal QNFSP's plans might have been possible in theory, but they hardly made ecological or economic sense. While some fruits and vegetables could be produced in greenhouses with sufficient water efficiency, this is not the case with cereals and other water intensive crops that would be better imported. Yet, like other Gulf countries, Qatar has been interested in self-sufficiency out of fear of supply disruptions. During the Second World War famines in the region were only averted by food supplies from the Allied Middle East Supply Center (MESC) in Cairo and in the 1970s the US threatened a food boycott in retaliation for the Arab oil embargo (Woertz, 2013: ch. 2 and 4).

At the time of that threatened boycott, the Gulf countries devised an ambitious plan to develop Sudan as an Arab breadbasket to reduce such exposure to geopolitical risk. New institutions were founded in Khartoum, like the Arab Authority for Agricultural Investment and Development (AAAID) or the Arab Organization for Agricultural Development (AOAD), and private Gulf capital appeared on the scene. The Saudi arms trader Adnan Khashoggi and the Kuwaiti royal Sabah al-Ahmad al-Jaber engaged closely with the Nimeiri regime, which engineered an ecologically questionable expansion of mechanised, rain-fed farming, and had an infatuation with large-scale project designs that it tried to satisfy by increasing foreign and domestic indebtedness. Fears of land grabs mounted and displacements occurred (O'Brien, 1985), but the role of the Gulf countries remained subdued. Mostly they did not follow up on their ambitious announcements, and were anxious about lacking infrastructure and the notorious corruption and cronyism of Nimeiri's regime. They dragged their feet and rarely moved beyond feasibility studies. When they did, many projects—like the Faisal scheme—proved to be failures. The Kenana Sugar Company is the only surviving signature project of that era. It received sumptuous investment guarantees from the Sudanese government and is half-owned by Kuwait and Saudi Arabia (Woertz, 2013: ch. 6). Meanwhile Sudan went through an epic famine in 1984–5, which must also be ascribed to Nimeiri's breadbasket plans, which neglected and disenfranchised traditional smallholders and pastoralists while being unable to create viable commercial farming ventures (Verhoeven, 2015).

With the reversal of the food price hikes of the 1970s and reduced US politicisation of the food trade, the Gulf countries' interest in foreign agro-investments faded in the 1980s and 1990s. Instead, their focus turned inwards. Saudi Arabia launched its subsidised wheat schemes, which now have to be phased out for lack of water. It reached self-sufficiency and even became the sixth largest wheat *exporter* in the early 1990s. Yet the boom was not sustainable. Due to the global food crisis of 2008 the Gulf countries are, once again, engaged. Now, as in the past, they have announced agro-investments on an epic scale against the backdrop of rising food prices and a global commodities boom. Their interest is in staple foods, not in biofuels that have constituted a majority of announced foreign agro-investments globally. Sudan has again been at the top of the list, followed by Pakistan, the Philippines, Ethiopia, and Egypt, mostly countries that are geographically and politically close, but have food security and water issues of their own. There has also been considerable interest in other countries along the East African coast, like Kenya, Tanzania, and Mozambique (Woertz, 2013). Cash-strapped developing countries have shown an interest in attracting Gulf funds. Sudan, in particular, launched a large dam-building programme in the 2000's and rolled out project designs that make Nimeiri's earlier breadbasket dreams pale by comparison. Gulf and Chinese funds financed the Merowe dam 350 km (220 miles) north of Khartoum, which was finished in 2009. Its construction led to the displacement of over 50,000 people and to violent protests. Other dams are to be built this decade (Verhoeven, 2015).

However, Merowe and a few other projects apart, there has been a huge disconnect between media reports of land grabs and the reality on the ground. Like in the 1970s, Gulf investors have rarely followed up on their announcements. Political instability, poor infrastructure, and a lack of commercial viability have discouraged them. If they have put money on the table, it has been in developed agro-markets rather than in the developing countries in which most announcements have been made. Qatar-based Hassad Food's investments in Australia or Saudi Al Marai's in Argentina are cases in point. In the developing world most of the projects have either not got off the ground at all or only on a fraction of the announced scale. Often they have run into difficulties and are threatened by failure, as is the case of Saudi billionaire Mohamed al-Amoudi's Saudi Star project in Ethiopia's Gambela province (Woertz, 2013; Verhoeven, 2015).

This implementation gap has been particularly pronounced for projects in South-East Asia, which is far away from the Gulf countries and does not have the advantage of geographical proximity like East Africa (Woertz, 2013). The Saudi Bin Ladin group cancelled a USD 4.3 billion project for basmati rice cultivation in Indonesia citing funding problems in the wake of the global financial crisis. Nothing more has been heard about an agricultural project for over 100,000 hectares in East Kalimantan, which UAE based Minerals Energy Commodities Holding (MEC) announced as part of a larger investment in a coal mine, a railway, and an aluminium smelter. Kuwait sent a reconnaissance mission to Cambodia, Thailand, Laos, and Myanmar in 2008 to investigate the potential for Kuwaiti agro-investments in these countries. Although Kuwaiti announcements were interpreted by the press as a sign that investment decisions were imminent and those announcements are still widely quoted to this day, the overall conclusion of the delegation was to 'do nothing' and carefully assess both Kuwait's needs and conditions in target countries first (Interview with a Kuwaiti executive, 20 November 2013, Kuwait City). Political risk, under-developed infrastructure, and the non-existent export capacities of dispersed smallholdings were among the mission's concerns. The sticky white rice that is produced in South-East Asia also does not match the pronounced consumption preference in the Gulf for basmati rice, which is mainly produced in Pakistan and India. The plans of the Saudi Al-Rajhi Group in the Philippines have been more concrete. It has established the Far East Agricultural Investment Corporation (FEAICO) to produce food on 78,000 ha in Mindanao, along with its local partner Aztropex. Its efforts to consolidate landholdings by leasing parcels from smallholders are controversial and it remains to be seen whether the corporation will be able to set up larger farming operations (Salerno, 2010; Revelli, 2012).

Gulf countries lack capacities to implement projects of this scale, espe-cially in foreign ecologies and investment environments. Some of the sover-eign wealth funds that have announced investments in hundreds of thousands of hectares have not had a single agro-engineer among their ranks. If there is implementation, Gulf countries tend to mimic the practice at home of running large-scale agro-projects with Western operating companies; at times even the manual workers are expatriates, at least on the foreman level (Woertz, 2013).

Seven years after the aforementioned wave of announcements, a new sense of reality has set in on the part of investors, target countries, and observers from academia and advocacy groups. The first version of the Land Matrix, a joint research effort of several think tanks to compile and verify media reports about land grabs, still contained numerous on-paper foreign agro-investor projects that had not seen any implementation at all, thus painting an exag-gerated picture. That picture, and the project's database, was used by academ-ics in peer-reviewed journals (Rulli et al., 2013). The media, in turn, picked up these presumably authoritative scientific works, which were in fact based on unreliable media reports, and the news cycle came full circle (Rural Modernity, 2012; Brautigam, 2012; Woertz, 2012b). Revised versions of the Land Matrix have been considerably improved and provide a more accurate picture. Some on-paper projects have been removed from the database and information has been introduced that allows projects to be differentiated according to their implementation status. In academia, there is a growing perception that instead of a quantitative fixation more qualitative case studies are needed to give the topic a differentiated treatment without belittling the many problems that exist (Allan et al., 2013; Edelman, 2013; Oya, 2013). Target countries, like Sudan or Ethiopia, have voiced their frustration with projects that have not been realised and Ethiopia has started withdrawing concessions from companies whose projects are delayed (Edelman, 2013; Davison, 2013; Bekele, 2013). Gulf countries, on the other hand, have lost a great degree of interest in greenfield investments in the developing world in a manner not dissimilar to the events of the 1970s. Beside brownfield investments in developed agro-markets, attention has focused increasingly on food trade and logistics. All Gulf countries have increased their strategic storage capacities. Saudi and Qatari investors participated in the initial public offering (IPO) of commodity trader Glencore, which has expanded its presence in global grain markets with the takeover of Viterra, the largest wheat handler in Canada and South Australia. Port facilities have expanded and emergency plans have been drawn up. If Gulf countries have built pipelines in order to have alternative outlets for their oil exports in case of a closure of the Strait of Hormuz, similar considerations are at work for food. For such an emergency, Kuwait has an agreement in place to land food at the port of Fujairah on the UAE's eastern coast, send it by truck to Jebel Ali in Dubai, and then ship it from there up the Gulf to Kuwait (Interview with a Kuwaiti executive, 20 November 2013, Kuwait City).

4   Food, Development, and Strategic Joint Ventures: China

China's food security challenges are arguably more formidable than those of the Gulf countries. It has only 9 per cent of the world's arable land, but needs to feed 20 per cent of the world's population (Brautigam, 2009). Satisfying most food requirements with imports is an option for the Gulf countries, but not for a country of over 1.3 billion people. Such an enterprise would overwhelm exportable surplus capacities on world markets. This is particularly true for rice, China's main staple food. Only a small proportion, 7–8 per cent, of global rice production is traded across borders. The respective figure for wheat stands at around 20–21 per cent (Timmer, 2013; FAO, 2014). As a result of this lack of liquidity it is difficult to balance rice supply shortages via trade and rice markets are prone to volatility. Rice production and consumption is also heavily concentrated in Asia; India and China alone produce half of the global harvest, mostly for domestic purposes.

Hence, self-sufficiency concerns are of great strategic significance to China. Notwithstanding brutal policy blunders like the 'Great Leap Forward' famine (1959–61) that cost the lives of 30–45 million people, agricultural development issues have been deeply engrained in the mindset of the Communist Party since it built its support base in rural areas that suffered from famines, in the 1930s and 1940s. China has managed to increase agricultural production significantly since the reform era of 1978, yet it became a net importer of food in 2004. Rapid economic development and rising incomes have caused a dietary change towards favouring meat consumption and dairy products. Population growth has decreased due to the one-child policy, but it is still occurring and in a country like China small relative increments still result in large absolute numbers of additional mouths to feed. Further domestic production growth proves challenging, as the north of the country suffers from water shortage and land is lost to urban sprawl and ecological damage.

Demand for animal feedstock is now met to a large extent by imports. In the case of soybeans the figure stands at over 70 per cent, mostly from the US and Brazil (Sharma, 2014). In contrast, the Chinese government has been anxious to maintain a high degree of self-sufficiency in grain production for human consumption. It long regarded 95 per cent self-sufficiency and 120 million ha of cultivated land as an absolute minimum. In 2008, China underlined this self-sufficiency goal in its 20-year food security strategy, in which it ordained that staple crops should be produced at home and outsourcing should be confined to commercial crops like cotton and animal feedstock, similar to the aforementioned soybean imports (Cotula et al., 2009: 55). Cracks in this stance appeared in 2014, when China maintained the self-sufficiency goal in principle, but for the first time set grain production targets well below consumption levels, eyeing a 'stabilisation' of production in 2020 at roughly 10 per cent below the harvest of 2013. Instead, China now places greater emphasis on issues of food safety and quality and the production of higher-value-added foods like meat, vegetables, and fruit (Hornby, 2014).

Whilst China will always need to maintain a high level of self-sufficiency, it has now braced itself for greater reliance on imported food. Due to its size, a marginal increase in its demand has a considerable impact on world markets. This was demonstrated in the global corn markets of 2010–11, when China caused a price hike after becoming a large buyer following a drought. China holds the largest wheat stocks in the world, 31 per cent of the total. It has considerable means to balance price fluctuations and to smooth its increased engagement with world markets. In comparison, the US holds only 12 per cent of global wheat stocks, India 8 per cent, and the Arab world, as the largest cereal-importing region, a relatively low 10 per cent (World Bank and FAO, 2012).

China's 'going global' policy has had two decisive moments. First, policy measures have been put in place—since 1999—to secure raw material supplies for the country's rapid industrialisation. Investments have focused on energy and mining. Second, the introduction of agricultural subsidies in 2004 laid the foundations for increasingly profitable agribusiness. Responding to growing fears of political instability, due to a widening gap between the countryside and China's booming urban centres, the central government in Beijing reversed the practice of taxing agriculture shortly after 1 January 2006. China's transformation from an agricultural to an industrial economy has gone hand in hand with the decreasing economic (yet not strategic) importance of agriculture (Gale et al., 2005).

Although the stimulus of 2004 only marginally affected agricultural output, it offered new opportunities for the private sector. For example, the past ten years has seen the rapid ascension of the Hong Kong-headquartered Noble Group to its position as one of the world's largest agribusiness companies. Founded through a British businessman's investment of USD 100,000 in 1987, the company also trades energy and minerals and currently has similar revenues to the US agribusiness multinational Archer Daniels Midlands (ADM). The growth pace of Noble is breathtaking. While its revenues were only USD 15 billion in 2007, they sextupled within six years to USD 98 billion in 2013 (Forbes, 2014; Stevens, 2007; South China Morning Post, 2012). China's sovereign wealth fund, China Investment Corporation (CIC), holds 15 per cent of shares in—what is referred to as—'the company' (Koons and Venkat, 2014). However, yet another strategic public–private partnership was announced in April 2014. Channelled through the state-owned China National Cereals, Oils and Foodstuffs Corporation (COFCO) and private equity investment firm HOPU Investment, a new joint venture between China's public food companies and Noble will see the establishment of Noble Agri JV, giving COFCO and HOPU, collectively, 51 per cent of the shares while Noble retains 49 per cent. HOPU Investment is owned by the infamous Chinese business tycoon Fang Fenglei, who was previously Goldman Sachs's Asia chief executive officer (CEO). The rationale of this joint venture is to provide Noble with capital and COFCO with Noble's downstream supply-chain knowledge and operations to establish what, in due course, may become the world's biggest global agribusiness company. The new company intends to increase China's access to agricultural production regions and countries, such as Latin America and Russia, as a first step. Other takeovers by Chinese companies in the food processing and trading sector have included Tnuva, the Israeli cheese and consumer foods supplier, US pork producer Smithfield Foods, the UK breakfast brand Weetabix, and Australian winemaker Hollick. China is preparing to compete with the Cargills and Nestlés of this world rather than just gobbling up farmland in the upstream sector.

China has understood that strategic agricultural investments are necessary to maintain its transition from an agrarian society to the potentially biggest economy in the world. To this end, Africa has played a prominent role as a potential target region for supplies of agricultural imports.[1] Mostly state-owned companies have made foreign agro-investments as part of this strategy; focusing on industrial input factors such as, rubber, palm oil, or cotton but avoiding investments in food crops. Insofar as they have aimed at food crops in Africa, they have done so for local markets, not for export to China, since the long distances, underdeveloped infrastructure, and lack of expertise amongst Chinese state investors in downstream supply would make such exports prohibitively expensive. For the stated strategic reasons, China has a preference for domestic production of staple crops. However, this preference may have to be modified in the coming years due to growing prosperity and China's new economic expansion policy.

China regards Africa as an important export market for corn and rice hybrid seeds. In 2006, the Forum on China–Africa Cooperation in Beijing propagated a spirit of 'win-win cooperation' in the field of agriculture and China pledged to set up agricultural demonstration centres in Africa. It has also used agro-investments as an instrument in its competition with Taiwan for diplomatic recognition and as an ancillary tool for soothing concerns about Chinese infrastructure and mining projects with high environmental impacts. Yet, China has remained a minor investor, thus far taking a cautious approach to the 'last frontier' in global agriculture: sub-Saharan Africa. Apart from research and development cooperation, China has not made great efforts to utilize the continent's potential 'food bowls'. Beside Africa and Latin America, South-East Asia has, for China, developed into an important procurement source for industrial input factors such as rubber. Corresponding investments, whether foreign or domestic, have led to a deep restructuring of land tenure systems.[2]

In general, Chinese foreign investments have been blamed for relying on imported labour from China and on large-scale project designs, and for undermining environmental standards and offering limited benefits to target countries. While these reproaches may have merit in many cases, in others they do not accurately reflect economic dynamics, which have been stimulated by Chinese investments, and one is hard pressed to find differences with competing Western investment practices (Asongu and Aminkeng, 2013). Justified criticism of such practices notwithstanding, some Chinese projects have a genuine development motivation. China already undertook rice projects in Africa in the 1960s that had a dedicated smallholder orientation. While the systems

---

1 This is not the case for China alone; Africa has played a similar role for other emerging economies.
2 See Messerli et al., and Gironde and Senties Portilla in this volume.

created by these projects fell into disrepair after the Chinese left, as relative complexity and labour intensity affected project continuity, China is now trying to breathe new life into such schemes.

In addition to the variety of qualitative aspects of Chinese investments, it should be pointed out that a considerable discrepancy exists between media reports on such investments and their quantitative extent in reality. This is strikingly similar to the case of the Gulf countries, outlined above. By 2012 only a few Chinese agro-investments in Africa above 5,000 ha had been implemented and none at all in the large scale bracket above 10,000 ha (Brautigam, 2013). However, the advent of 'China Ag Corporation' triggered by a new growth strategy implemented through strategic investments in 'the company' (Noble) may alter this approach in the coming years.

5   Policies of Host Country States

If governments in the Gulf and China have tried to foster investments in foreign agricultural value chains, governments of host countries have also enacted policies that affect this investment drive. Three different investment targets have been discussed in this article: a) companies in developed markets that focus on upstream value chains like input procurement, food processing, and trading; b) greenfield investments in agricultural land in developing countries; and c) agricultural investments in developed markets, often brownfield. Depending on the nature of the investment, policies in host countries vary.

Value chain investments in developed markets are less emotionally charged than land investments in developing countries. Often they have taken the form of smooth ownership transfers like the aforementioned Chinese acquisitions of Tnuva, Weetabix, and Smithfield. On other occasions they have raised strategic concerns, even though food processing and trading companies are less likely to be identified as strategic industries than are energy or high tech companies. The Australian government blocked a takeover of the grain trader GrainCorp by US based ADM in 2013 citing national interest and food security concerns (Scott and Behrmann, 2013). Australian BHP Billiton's attempted hostile takeover of Canadian fertiliser producer Potash Corp. in 2010 and a potential counter bid from Chinese state-owned Sinochem stirred protectionist sentiments in Canada (Massot, 2011). How SWFs and state-owned TNCs are perceived has changed since the mid-2000s when Western countries were concerned about the political influence of foreign governments on their economies. Since then, SWFs have subscribed to the Santiago Principles, an IMF-sponsored public outreach exercise that aims to alleviate concerns over transparency issues.

SWFs also have become welcome providers of capital in the wake of the global financial crisis of 2008. Currently they are rather perceived as normal market participants, but a renewed wave of protectionist sentiment cannot be ruled out given the shifts in global food markets and the magnitude of global financial imbalances, where government-owned entities in the Middle East and Asia hold large assets in OECD countries (Woertz, 2012a).

Land investments in developing countries are the most controversial of the three types of investments. Cash-strapped governments in host countries have tried to attract them as they are in need of capital imports and have hoped for agricultural development-led industrialisation (ADLI) (ECOSOC, 2007). Ethiopia and Cambodia for example have tried to lure foreign investors with the use of bespoke investment agencies, and favourable laws and taxation regimes (Shepherd, 2012; Shepherd, 2013). However, large-scale greenfield projects have often met with bottom-up resistance from small-scale farmers and holders of customary land rights who stand to lose from such initiatives. Together with political instability in many target countries, this has affected the calculations of potential investors and has contributed to a pronounced implementation gap in this investment category.

Land investments in developed agro-markets, the third category, have met with a different set of challenges. Governments of these host countries are also keen to foster agricultural exports, but on their own terms by leveraging their market position and limiting foreign ownership of land. Thailand only allows agricultural investments if there is a Thai majority partner, Brazil has limited large-scale landownership by foreigners out of fear of Chinese acquisitions, and Australian politicians have mulled over similar steps (Woertz, 2013). Such assertiveness is also reflected in the politics of agro-exporters—like Brazil, Thailand, Canada, South Africa, and Australia—at the WTO, where they have formed the Cairns groups in order to lobby against agricultural subsidies in the US and the EU, which they regard as elements of unfair competition (Weis, 2007).

Russia and the South-East Asian rice exporters provide examples of how newly emerging agro-exporters are trying to leverage their market positions, which could prove to be to the detriment of importer nations. Russia is an importer of fruit, vegetables, meat, and dairy products, but it has become a major grain exporter again, as it was in the nineteenth and early twentieth centuries. At the turn of the millennium, Russia's global wheat market share was still as low as 0.5 per cent. Within only ten years, Russia increased its market share to 13.8 per cent and some expect it to become the largest wheat exporter worldwide by 2019 (Pall et al., 2011). Yet, there is uncertainty about these estimates because rain-fed harvests have been volatile and Russia's agricultural sector continues to be hampered by inefficiencies resulting from poor governance. Similar to China, yet differently conceived, Russia has begun to strategically subsidise and de-tax its agricultural sector. To this end the Russian government has adopted the State Program for Development of Agriculture and Regulation of Agricultural Commodities Markets for the period 2013–2020 (Vassilieva, 2012b).

The Russian government has sought cooperation with neighbours Ukraine and Kazakhstan on grain marketing, which has caused concerns about cartel-like price fixing. On the other hand, Russia has offered Egypt and Algeria subsidised wheat below world market prices (Pall et al., 2011). These political moves echo Russia's plans to use food as a bargaining chip to expand its geopolitical sphere of influence. Through Russian presidential decree no. 290 of March 20, 2009, the United Grain Company (UGC) was established to strategically handle food trade logistics. UGC has since acted as the intermediary agent between the state's interests in domestic and international agricultural relations (Vassilieva, 2012a). In 2010, President Medvedev decided that UGC would have to be partly privatised by 2012 in order to inject more capital. Despite widespread Western interest in purchasing shares of the company, the investment group Summa, owned by the business tycoon Ziyavudin Magomedov, acquired 51 per cent of the shares of UCG to take over the company. As a strategic objective, UCG has formed joint ventures with companies in East Asia to increase its market share there, namely in China, Taiwan, and Japan (Bloomberg Business, 2015). Similar to its energy giant Gazprom and with the core objective to 'look east', Russia's agricultural expansion plans eye Eurasian investments aided by strategic public–private joint ventures.

At the height of the global food crisis of 2008 five rice producers in South-East Asia—Thailand, Vietnam, Cambodia, Laos, and Myanmar—contemplated forming the Organisation of Rice Exporting Countries (OREC). Although Thai prime minister Samak said, 'We don't aspire to be like Organization of the Petroleum Exporting Countries (OPEC),' the mere contemplation of OREC sent shockwaves through rice importing countries like the Philippines and Indonesia, which feared cartel-like price fixing. Thailand and Vietnam alone accounted for half of globally traded rice exports at that time (Brummer, 2011). Cartels usually struggle with internal discipline and can overpower market forces only for a limited time. So far no formal organisation has been established. The website of OREC appears rudimentary[3] and there have been no new posts since early 2013, which would hint at limited activity. In contrast to 2008, rice markets are now well supplied. Thailand grapples with

---

3   Available at http://www.orecinternational.org/ (accessed on 2 April 2015).

overcapacities that go back to a subsidy programme launched in 2011 that paid farmers above world market prices. It was terminated in 2014 after losses of more than $18 billion and widespread accusations of corruption. If a future OREC served as an intergovernmental rice traders' association, as a lobbying arm to reduce rice trade restrictions in Asia, or as a coordinator of regional buffer-stocks instead of as a cartel, it might have a beneficial impact (Brummer, 2011). Yet the mind games surrounding its attempted formation show how food exporters seek to benefit from the changing global food system and the growing interest from food importer nations in their production capacities.

6 Conclusion

States as actors in global food supply-chain investments and trade is a topic that has attracted increasing interest in the past few years. 'Security mercantilism' is far more complex than land acquisition processes. While much of the literature has focused on 'land grabbing' by foreign states in developing countries, this chapter offers a different perspective by placing the interests of states into the context of twenty-first century food politics. It sheds light on a new, and as yet under-researched, period of globalisation. Emerging economies in Asia seek to brace themselves and to challenge the Western world in its hegemony over food production and virtual water trade. These strategies involve sophisticated public–private joint ventures in the respective national interests. The economies analysed differ substantially in their approach to 'security mercantilism'. The defining moment for policy changes was the food price spikes of 2007–08, after which new strategies were conceived in order to gain independence from Western food trade. While the GCC opted for the unsuccessful revival of the 'dream' of a Sudanese 'breadbasket', China strategically channelled capital into the agro-industry to copy the model of the West. New agro-exporters like Brazil, Russia, and Thailand on the other hand sought to influence the changing landscape of food trade to their advantage, by leveraging pricing power and putting ceilings on foreign ownership. Asia will be the most crucial area for the demand side of food politics in the twenty-first century both due to its dominant share of future economic growth and because of the changing diet of its citizens. It will rival the MENA region, which is currently still the largest net-importer of cereals globally. While it remains an ongoing process, Asian economies have begun to prepare themselves to inverse power relations within the food globalisation process. Therefore, it can be concluded that the politics of food will define the first half of the twenty-first century in no minor way.

References

Allan, T. (2011) *Virtual Water: Tackling the Threat to Our Planet's Most Precious Resource* (London: I. B. Tauris).

Allan, T., J. Warner, S. Sojamo and M. Keulertz (eds.) (2013) *Handbook of Land and Water Grabs in Africa: Foreign Direct Investments and Food and Water Security* (London and New York: Routledge).

Asongu, S.A. and G.A.A. Aminkeng (2013) 'The Economic Consequences of China–Africa Relations: Debunking Myths in the Debate', *Journal of Chinese Economic and Business Studies*, 11(4), pp. 261–277, DOI: 10.1080/14765284.2013.838384.

Bekele, K. (2013) 'Saudi Star Rice Project Feels the Pinch', *The Reporter*, 23 November, http://www.thereporterethiopia.com/index.php/news-headlines/item/1282-saudi-star-rice-project-feels-the-pinch (accessed on 17 February 2015).

Bloomberg Business (2015) *Company Overview of JSC United Grain Company*, http://investing.businessweek.com/research/stocks/private/snapshot.asp?privcapId=99331238 (accessed on 17 February 2015).

Brautigam, D. (2013) 'Chinese Engagement in African Agriculture: Fiction and Fact', in Allan, J.A., M. Keulertz, S. Sojamo and J. Warner (eds.) *Handbook of Land and Water Grabs: Foreign Direct Investment and Food and Water Security* (Abingdon: Routledge).

——— (2012) *"Zombie" Chinese Land Grabs in Africa Rise Again in New Database!*, http://www.chinaafricarealstory.com/2012/04/zombie-chinese-land-grabs-in-africa.html (accessed on 30 April 2012).

——— (2009) *The Dragon's Gift: The Real Story of China in Africa* (Oxford and New York: Oxford University Press).

Brummer, M. (2011) 'The Cartel of Good Intentions? OREC and Food Security in Asia', *Asian Journal of Public Affairs*, 4(1), pp. 27–41.

Burch, D. and G. Lawrence (2009) 'Towards a Third Food Regime: Behind the Transformation', *Agriculture and Human Values*, 26(4), pp. 267–279, DOI: 10.1007/s10460-009-9219-4.

Cotula, L., S. Vermeulen, R. Leonard and J. Keeley (2009) *Land Grab or Development Opportunity? Agricultural Investments and International Land Deals in Africa* (London and Rome: IIED–FAO–IFAD).

Davis, M. (2001) *Late Victorian Holocausts: El Niño Famines and the Making of the Third World* (London and New York: Verso).

Davison, W. (2013) 'Ethiopia's Farm Investment Plans Falter on Flood Plain', *Bloomberg Business*, 25 November, http://www.bloomberg.com/news/articles/2013-11-24/ethiopian-drive-to-lure-farm-investment-founders-on-flood-plain (accessed on 2 February 2015).

Deininger, K. and D. Byerlee (2011) *Rising Global Interest in Farmland. Can It Yield Sustainable and Equitable Benefits?* (Washington, D.C.: World Bank–International

Bank for Reconstruction and Development), http://siteresources.worldbank.org/DEC/Resources/Rising-Global-Interest-in-Farmland.pdf (accessed on 26 May 2015).

ECOSOC (United Nations Economic and Social Council) (2007) *The Agricultural Development Led Industrialization (ADLI) Strategy, Ethiopia 2007* (New York: ECOSOC), http://webapps01.un.org/nvp/indpolicy.action?id=124 (accessed on 17 February 2015).

Edelman, M. (2013) 'Messy Hectares: Questions About the Epistemology of Land Grabbing Data', *The Journal of Peasant Studies*, 40(3), pp. 485–501, DOI: 10.1080/03066150.2013.801340.

FAO (Food and Agriculture Organization) (2014) FAO *Cereal Supply and Demand Brief* (Rome: FAO) http://www.fao.org/worldfoodsituation/csdb/en/ (accessed on 16 January 2015).

FAOSTAT (2013) *FAOSTAT* (Rome: FAO), http://faostat.fao.org/ (accessed on 2 November 2014).

Forbes (2014) *Noble Group*, http://www.forbes.com/companies/noble-group/ (accessed on 4 November 2014).

Friedmann, H. (2009) 'Discussion: Moving Food Regimes Forward: Reflections on Symposium Essays', *Agriculture and Human Values*, 26(4), pp. 335–344, DOI: 10.1007/s10460-009-9225-6.

Gale, F., B. Lohmar and F. Tuan (2005) *China's New Farm Subsidies*, WRS-05-01, February (Washington, D.C.: United States Department for Agriculture), http://www.ers.usda.gov/media/872040/wrs0501_002.pdf (accessed on 2 April 2015).

Hornby, L. (2014) 'China Scythes Grain Self-Sufficiency Policy', *Financial Times*, 11 February, http://www.ft.com/intl/cms/s/0/6025b7c8-92ff-11e3-8ea7-00144feab7de.html—axzz2wsaVogtd (accessed on 17 Feburary 2015).

Kanady, S. (2013) 'Food Security Plan Getting Final Touches', *The Peninsula*, 30 June, http://thepeninsulaqatar.com/news/qatar/243335/food-security-plan-getting-final-touches (accessed on 2 November 2014).

Koons, C. and P.R. Venkat (2014) 'China's Cofco, Hopu to Buy 51% Stake in Noble Agriculture Unit', *Wall Street Journal*, 2 April, http://online.wsj.com/news/articles/SB10001424052702304157204579476073967321180 (accessed on 19 April 2014).

Massot, P. (2011) 'Chinese State Investments in Canada: Lessons from the Potash Saga', *Canada-Asia Agenda*, No. 16, 21 January, http://www.asiapacific.ca/sites/default/files/filefield/chinese_state_investments_in_canada_v4.pdf (accessed on 2 April 2015).

McMichael, P. (2013) 'Land Grabbing as Security Mercantilism in International Relations', *Globalizations*, 10(1), pp. 47–64, DOI: 10.1080/14747731.2013.760925.

——— (2009a) 'A Food Regime Analysis of the "World Food Crisis"', *Agriculture and Human Values*, 26(4), pp. 281–295, DOI: 10.1007/s10460-009-9218-5.

———— (2009b) 'A Food Regime Genealogy', *Journal of Peasant Studies*, 36(1), pp. 139–169, DOI: 10.1080/03066150902820354.

Murphy, S., D. Burch and J. Clapp (2012) *Cereal Secrets: The World's Largest Grain Traders and Global Agriculture*, Oxfam Research Reports (Oxford: Oxfam), https://www.oxfam.org/sites/www.oxfam.org/files/rr-cereal-secrets-grain-traders-agriculture-30082012-en.pdf (accessed on 2 April 2015).

O'Brien, J. (1985) 'Sowing the Seeds of Famine: The Political Economy of Food Deficits in Sudan', *Review of African Political Economy*, 12(33), pp. 23–32, DOI: 10.1080/03056248508703630.

Oya, C. (2013) 'Methodological Reflections on "Land Grab" Databases and the "Land Grab" Literature "Rush"', *The Journal of Peasant Studies*, 40(3), pp. 503–520, DOI: 10.1080/03066150.2013.799465.

Pall, Z., O. Perekhozhuk, R. Teuber and T. Glauben (2011) *Wheat Trade—Does Russia Price Discriminate across Export Destinations?*, paper presented at the IAMO Forum 2011, 23–24 June, http://econstor.eu/bitstream/10419/50794/1/670792926.pdf (accessed on 26 May 2015).

Peterson, E.W.F. (2009) *A Billion Dollars a Day: The Economics and Politics of Agricultural Subsidies* (Hoboken: Wiley-Blackwell).

Pritchard, B. (2009) 'The Long Hangover from the Second Food Regime: A World-Historical Interpretation of the Collapse of the WTO Doha Round', *Agriculture and Human Values*, 26(4), pp. 297–307, DOI: 10.1007/s10460-009-9216-7.

Revelli, P. (2012) 'Wie Der Zucker Nach Luzon Kam', *Le Monde Diplomatique*, 12 October, http://www.monde-diplomatique.de/pm/2012/10/12.mondeText.artikel,a0044.idx,14 (accessed on 17 Feburary 2015).

Rulli, M.C., A. Saviori and P. D'Odorico (2013) 'Global Land and Water Grabbing', *Proceedings of the National Academy of Sciences*, 110(3), pp. 892–897, DOI: 10.1073/pnas.1213163110.

Rural Modernity (2012) *The Land Matrix: Much Ado About Nothing*, http://ruralmodernity.wordpress.com/2012/04/27/the-land-matrix-much-ado-about-nothing/ (accessed on 27 April 2012).

Salerno, T. (2010) *Land Deals, Joint Investments and Peasants in Mindanao, Philippines*, unpublished MA Thesis (The Hague: Institute of Social Studies, Graduate School of Development Studies).

Scott, J. and E. Behrmann (2013) 'Adm's $2 Billion Graincorp Bid Blocked by Australia', *Bloomberg Business*, 29 November, http://www.bloomberg.com/news/2013-11-28/australian-treasurer-hockey-rejects-adm-takeover-of-graincorp.html (accessed on 3 November 2014).

Sharma, S. (2014) *The Need for Feed. China's Demand for Industrialized Meat and Its Impacts*, (Minnesota and Washington, D.C.: Institute for Agriculture and Trade Policy) http://www.iatp.org/files/2014_03_26_FeedReport_f_web.pdf (accessed on 2 April 2015).

Shepherd, B. (2013) *GCC States' Land Investments Abroad. The Case of Ethiopia*, Summary Report No. 8 (Doha: Center for International and Regional Studies, Georgetown University School of Foreign Service in Qatar), https://repository.library.george town.edu/bitstream/handle/10822/558319/CIRSSummaryReport8TheCaseof Ethiopia2013.pdf?sequence=5 (accessed on 2 April 2015).

———— (2012) *GCC States' Land Investments Abroad. The Case of Cambodia*, Summary Report No. 5 (Doha: Center for International and Regional Studies, Georgetown University School of Foreign Service in Qatar), https://repository.library.george town.edu/bitstream/handle/10822/558540/CIRSSummaryReport5TheCaseof Cambodia2013.pdf?sequence=5 (accessed on 2 April 2015).

Sojamo, S., M. Keulertz, J. Warner and J.A. Allan (2012) 'Virtual Water Hegemony: The Role of Agribusiness in Global Water Governance', *Water International*, 37(2), pp. 169–182, DOI: 10.1080/02508060.2012.662734.

South China Morning Post (2012) 'Richard Elman Finds Noble Group Successor', *South China Morning Post*, 10 November, http://www.scmp.com/business/commodities/article/1078987/richard-elman-finds-noble-group-successor (accessed on 19 April 2014).

Stevens, A. (2007) 'The Boardroom: Richard Elman, Founder and Ceo, Noble Group', *CNN*, 24 September, http://edition.cnn.com/2007/BUSINESS/09/21/boardroom. elman/index.html (accessed on 19 April 2014).

Timmer, C.P. (2013) 'Food Security in Asia and the Pacific: The Rapidly Changing Role of Rice', *Asia & the Pacific Policy Studies*, 1(1), pp. 73–90, DOI: 10.1002/app5.6.

UNCTAD (United Nations Conference on Trade and Development) (2014) *World Investment Report 2014. Investing in the SDGs: An Action Plan* (New York and Geneva: United Nations), http://unctad.org/en/PublicationsLibrary/wir2014_en. pdf (accessed on 2 April 2015).

———— (2009) *World Investment Report 2009. Transnational Corporations, Agricultural Production and Development* (New York and Geneva: United Nations), http://unctad .org/sections/diae_dir/docs/tdb09_wir_zhan_en.pdf (accessed on 2 April 2015).

USDA (United States Department of Agriculture) (2014) *Foreign Agricultural Service Database. Production, Supply and Distribution (PSD)* (Washington, D.C.: USDA) http://www.fas.usda.gov/psdonline/psdQuery.aspx (accessed on 23 May 2014).

Vassilieva, Y. (2012a) *Privatization of the United Grain Company*, GAIN Report No. RS1240 (Moscow: USDA), http://gain.fas.usda.gov/Recent GAIN Publications/ Privatization of the United Grain Company_Moscow_Russian Federation_6-8-2012. pdf (accessed on 2 April 2015).

———— (2012b) *Russia: Agriculture Development Program 2013–2020*, GAIN Report No. 1270 (Moscow: USDA), http://gain.fas.usda.gov/Recent GAIN Publications/ Agriculture Development Program 2013–2020_Moscow_Russian Federation_ 11-6-2012.pdf (accessed on 2 April 2015).

Verhoeven, H. (2015) *Water, Civilisation and Power in Sudan. The Political Economy of Military-Islamist State-Building* (Cambridge: Cambridge University Press).

Weis, T. (2007) *The Global Food Economy: The Battle for the Future of Farming* (London and New York: Zed Books).

Woertz, E. (2013) *Oil for Food. The Global Food Crisis and the Middle East* (Oxford and New York: Oxford University Press).

———— (2012a) 'Gulf Sovereign Wealth Funds in International Comparison', in Woertz, E. (ed.) GCC *Financial Markets: The World's New Money Centers* (Berlin and London: Gerlach).

———— (2012b) *To Be Expected: Faulty Land Matrix Database Goes Academic . . .*, http://oilforfood.info/?p=423 (accessed on 23 May 2014).

World Bank and FAO (2012) *The Grain Chain. Food Security and Managing Wheat Imports in Arab Countries* (Rome and Washington, D.C.: FAO–World Bank).

CHAPTER 3

The Role of Property Rights in the Debate on Large-Scale Land Acquisitions

Olivier De Schutter

Abstract

The initial reaction to the sudden increase in large-scale leases and acquisitions of farmland in developing countries has been to promote titling schemes, allowing land-users, often poorly protected under customary forms of tenure, to be recognised as fully fledged owners of their land—allowing them to decide whether to sell, to whom, and under which conditions. This chapter places this transformation in a historical and global perspective. It recalls why titling was advocated in the 1990s as a development tool, and why—during the mid-2000s—doubts began to emerge with regard to such an approach. It then reviews alternatives to the simple transposition of Western conceptions of property rights; alternatives that may better serve the needs of rural households currently facing the threat of eviction and displacement, as a result of the race for farmland that we have witnessed in recent years. The chapter notes the importance of avoiding confusion between the need to ensure security of tenure, on the one hand, and the creation of markets for land rights on the other, the latter of which processes—when considered in a dynamic perspective—may not be advantageous to the poorest rural households. For these households, which depend on agriculture for their livelihoods, true security of tenure ultimately should be understood as the right to live decently from the agricultural activities that feed them.

1   Introduction

We have witnessed in recent years an unprecedented rise in the sale or lease of large areas of farmland, particularly in developing countries. The regions concerned are those where both land suitable for cultivation and water are abundant, the workforce is cheap, and access to global markets relatively easy. The investors are either the local elites or, increasingly, foreign investment funds or agribusiness corporations. But they also include the governments of cash-rich but resource-poor countries seeking to outsource food production

© Graduate Institute of International and Development Studies, 2016 | DOI 10.1163/9789004304758_004

in order to ensure a stable and reliable supply of food for their populations (Haralambous et al., 2009; Cotula et al., 2009; Deininger and Byerlee, 2010; Kugelman and Levenstein, 2009; Center for Human Rights and Global Justice, 2010). Of course, the recent wave of large-scale acquisitions or leasing of farmland is not entirely unprecedented. But the speed at which the phenomenon has been developing recently and its overall scope are. In addition, the significance of this current surge is different from what was seen in the past: in many cases, rather than investing in countries that present certain comparative advantages in agriculture in order to supply international markets at the most competitive conditions, the buyers or lessees of land seek to ensure access to a stable supply of agricultural commodities in order to circumvent international markets, which have become increasingly unreliable. A global market for land and water rights is thus rapidly taking shape (Mann and Smaller, 2010).

The main problem, as many commentators see it, is that in many of the regions targeted by these new investments, the rights of land users are not properly secured. As a result of systems of tenure inherited from colonial rule, much of the land in rural areas is formally owned by the government, and land users have no property titles on the land they cultivate. This situation creates legal uncertainty. It also implies that land users will not have access to legal remedies, and will not receive adequate compensation if they are evicted from the land they cultivate, for instance after their government has agreed that foreign investors may take possession of the land.

The answer to the threat of 'land grabs', it would seem then to follow, is to strengthen property rights, or to transform informal use rights into formalised property rights. Titling schemes could be implemented in order to protect land users from the risks of unjustified eviction or eviction without fair compensation. Titling their property would allow land users to decide under which conditions they want to sell, and to whom, and would ensure that if their land is taken by the government for reasons of public interest, they will have access to courts in order to challenge the conditions under which this expropriation has taken place. This is the approach that characterised the 2001 Land Law (No. 197/C) in Cambodia, for instance, which allowed for the registration of property rights that had been enjoyed in peaceful, uncontested circumstances for a period of at least five years, while at the same time defining 'state public' and 'state private' property and imposing a prohibition on the sale or exchange of the former—that is, state property that serves a public purpose (Art. 15) (Special Rapporteur on Adequate Housing, 2006).

We now understand that such an approach underestimates the challenges associated with the commodification of land rights: the rolling out of rural property titles in Cambodia launched in 2012, combined with the 'Leopard-skin strategy' in the country (in which smallholder farming is supported along-side economic land concessions), testifies to the shift that is now taking place (Müller, 2012; Dwyer, 2013 and 2015). This chapter places this transformation in a historical and global perspective. Section 2 recalls why titling was advo-cated in the 1990s, initially to accelerate the transition to market economies in Eastern Europe, but also as a development instrument, and why—a decade later—doubts began to emerge. Section 3 reviews the debate on the pros and cons of titling, illustrating why some of the hopes that were raised about this approach led only to disappointment. Section 4 turns to alternatives to the simple transposition of Western conceptions of property rights; alternatives that may better serve the needs of rural households that are currently facing the threat of eviction and displacement due to the race for farmland that we have witnessed in recent years. Section 5 provides a brief conclusion.

2   A Brief History of Titling: Its Rise and Fall

Though land registration processes have a long history (Place, 2009; Colin and Woodhouse, 2010), the belief that such processes can form the central compo-nent of development strategies is more recent. It emerged first with the large-scale and rapid privatisation of the formerly socialist economies of Central and Eastern Europe. In 1993, the World Bank presented a report entitled *Housing: Enabling Markets to Work*, in which—while it warned against costly titling programmes—it underscored the importance of 'systems of property registration and titling and workable systems of foreclosure and eviction', as these were considered 'necessary to ensure the collateral security of mortgage loans' (Mayo and Angel, 1993, 46). The emphasis in that report was more on ensuring security of tenure than on titling as one means of achieving it, but it did include a strong recommendation for the removal of any restrictions on the emergence of a market in property rights over land (Mayo and Angel, 1993, 117; and see Feder and Feeny, 1991). USAID first supported programmes for the privatisation of land and titling in Russia in 1994, with the purpose of sup-porting the Russian authorities in creating real estate and land registries and clarifying ownership rights, first in a number of 'hub' cities and then in larger areas, including the rural areas. Then, in 1998, a major titling programme was launched in Peru, with Hernando de Soto's Institute for Liberty and Democracy (ILD) in the leading role. That programme inspired de Soto to publish his most important book, *The Mystery of Capital*, in which he attributes the failure of developing countries to grow to undeveloped property regimes (de Soto, 2000).

The book also placed the ILD on the map as the most effective advocacy organisation for titling and the clarification of property rights.

The promoters of titling programmes and land registration schemes see them as presenting a number of advantages. First, and perhaps of most direct relevance here, the security of tenure favoured through titling should encourage individual landowners to make the necessary investments in their land, thus improving their living conditions and, in rural areas, enhancing the productivity of the cultivated plot: the occupants, it is supposed, shall not invest in their land unless they are certain to be protected from the risk of losing it. In addition, as emphasised by de Soto, titling of their property allows the owners to mortgage their land, and thus to obtain access to credit, allowing them to make such investments. Thailand was seen as proof of this process: up to 50 per cent of rural households, having benefited from registration of their property rights, were able to obtain access to credit, leading to what de Soto calls the 'capitalisation process' (Feder et al., 1988). This process transforms 'dead (physical) assets'—'where assets can not be readily turned into capital, can not be traded outside narrow local circles where people know and trust each other, can not be used as collateral for a loan, and can not be used as a share against an investment'—into live capital, which can be mobilised for investment (de Soto, 2000, 6). The World Bank notes, referring to a study by the McKinsey Global Institute on the conditions of growth in India:

> With fewer assets in the formal sector, more entrepreneurs are excluded from using property as a collateral, and less credit is allocated. The possibility of getting loans is the only reason to take on the daunting task of registering in some countries [...] But when it is too difficult, few bother. Entrepreneurs will invest less if their property rights are less secure. Inefficient registration is associated with lower rates of private investment. And it leads to lower productivity, since it is harder for property to be transferred from less to more productive uses. The result is slower growth. One study estimates that restrictive land market regulations cost 1.3% of annual economic growth in India. (World Bank, 2004a, 40; see also World Bank, 2004b, 78)

The contribution of titling to access to capital can operate directly, as registered property can be used as collateral to obtain credit. But it can also operate *indirectly*, as a signalling device that provides information about the trustworthiness of the borrower: recent research in Indonesia illustrates this by relating titling to the practice of local banks, who tend to see titling of property as proof that the household will be able to repay the loan, independently of the use of the property as collateral (Castañeda Dower and Potamites, 2012).

Second, the clarification of property rights should encourage the emergence of efficient land markets: lowering transaction costs, it is supposed, shall result in the land going to the most productive user, thus maximising the productivity of land as an economic asset (Feder and Noronha, 1987). The World Bank notes, thus, that 'secure and unambiguous property rights [...] allow markets to transfer land to more productive uses and users' (World Bank, 2007, 138). The intellectual roots of this argument can be found in the work of Ronald H. Coase, according to which if transaction costs are low enough (and, ideally, reduced to zero), the freedom of transactions shall result in solutions that are most economically efficient (Coase, 1960). The basic reasoning is simple enough: buyers of property will pay the price they considers reasonable, taking into consideration the streams of income that are expected to flow from making productive use of the assets acquired; therefore, if such assets are transferred to the highest bidder, as an efficiently functioning market for property rights should allow, they should ultimately be captured by the economic actors who can use them most productively, thus contributing to general economic growth.

Third, the clarification of property rights and the development of markets for land rights should attract foreign investors. This is why the *Doing Business* rankings of the World Bank, which use a series of indicators to measure the quality of the 'investment climate' of the countries surveyed, include among their criteria the time and cost of transferring a property title from one seller to the buyer—from the moment the buyer has a copy of the seller's title to the moment when the transfer is opposable to third parties, so that the property can be resold or used as collateral when approaching a bank (Chavez Sanchez et al., 2014). The 2014 edition of the *Doing Business* annual report—the eleventh of the series—found that over the period 2008–2013, 90 economies undertook 124 reforms increasing the efficiency of property transfer procedures, though some regions remain far behind. The easier it is to register property rights, the faster and the cheaper the procedures are for transferring property rights, and the more investors will be willing to enter the country concerned and thus, it is hoped, to contribute to its development (although the automaticity of this relationship has of course been questioned; see De Schutter et al., 2012).

Fourth, the formalisation of property rights over land allows public authorities to increase their tax revenues, and where necessary to deliver certain public services that depend on fees being paid by the users. As de Soto remarks, once they are formally registered, assets provide 'an accountable address for the collection of debts and taxes' as well as 'the basis for a creation of reliable and universal public utilities' (de Soto, 2000, 6). The two arguments are combined where public services are provided against the payment of users' fees: only where users have registered property can they be taxed (preferably, at a rate that will depend on the value of the property that they own) in order to finance the provision of water, telephone lines or electricity to the areas in which they live. For cash-strapped countries, struggling to provide basic infrastructure to their populations in large part due to their inability to collect taxes efficiently, this is not of minor significance.

Yet despite these apparently powerful arguments in favour of titling programmes, doubts have emerged in recent years. As more lessons could be drawn from a series of titling programmes implemented in the developing world during the 1990s, a number of ambiguities gradually came to the surface. A turning point was the establishment, in 2005, of the Commission for the Legal Empowerment of the Poor (CLEP). Launched at the initiative of a range of governments from different regions, working together with the United Nations Development Programme (UNDP) and the United Nations Economic Commission for Europe, the CLEP was established under the co-chairmanship of Hernando de Soto and Madeleine Albright. It was tasked with studying the relationship between 'informality' and poverty. The concept note presenting the initiative states:

> One of the staggering facts about poverty, which is not addressed explicitly in the MDGs, is that the vast majority of the world's poor live their daily lives in what is often referred to as the *informal* or *extralegal* sector, often excluded from the benefits of a legal order. [The work of Hernando de Soto shows that] legal exclusion, in the sense that the assets and transactions of the poor are not legally protected and recognised, produces and reproduces poverty throughout the developing world and in former communist societies (CLEP, 2005, 3–4).

The process of 'capitalisation', through which 'dead capital' is brought to life, was central to the inquiry of the commission. Indeed, to many, the CLEP was seen as an opportunity to validate the findings of Hernando de Soto and his conclusion that underdevelopment had much to do with the failure to establish reliable systems for property rights through the registration of assets, especially immovable assets. It therefore came as a surprise to most that, when it presented its final report in June 2008, the CLEP felt compelled to note a number of problems associated with titling schemes. The CLEP referred to the risks associated with 'elite capture': '[i]n many countries,' it noted, 'speculators pre-empt prospective titling programmes by buying up land from squatters at prices slightly higher than prevailing informal ones. Squatters benefit in the short term, but miss out on the main benefits of the titling programme, which accrue to the people with deeper pockets' (CLEP, 2008, 80, citing Platteau, 2000, 68; on the risks of elite capture, see also Firmin-Sellers and Sellers, 1999). The commission also identified, as one of the failures of titling programmes as they had been implemented in the past, that these programmes tended to neglect the role of collective rights and of customary forms of tenure: such forms of tenure, the commission conceded, could be highly legitimate and effective in guaranteeing security of tenure (CLEP, 2008, 52).

The CLEP concluded that the benefits of titling schemes may have been exaggerated in the past, and that it may be inappropriate to simply transplant the Western concept of property rights into the legal systems of developing countries, the legal traditions and needs of which may be markedly different:

> Promoting a truly inclusive property-rights system that incorporates measures to strengthen tenure security requires learning from the mixed experience with past individual titling programmes. To ensure protection and inclusion of the poorest, a broad range of policy measures should be considered. These include formal recognition, adequate representation, and integration of a variety of forms of land tenure such as customary rights, indigenous peoples' rights, group rights, and certificates. Success depends greatly upon comprehensively reforming the governance system surrounding property rights [...] These systems need to be accessible, affordable, transparent, and free from unnecessary complexity. Above all, the poor must be protected from arbitrary eviction by due process and full compensation (CLEP, 2008, 65).

These statements are significant, both because the initial bias of the CLEP clearly was in favour of following de Soto in his optimistic views about the virtues of titling, and of course because—although not a member of the working group on property—he was the co-chair of the commission. But the conclusions of the CLEP were foreshadowed by a number of studies published in the interim, after the first large-scale titling programmes had been launched (Firmin-Sellers and Sellers, 1999; von Benda-Beckmann, 2003; Unruh, 2002). Indeed, the World Bank itself noted in 2006 that 'most policy analysts now no longer simply assume that formalization in a given context necessarily increases tenure security, and leads to collateralized lending. The original assumptions have now become questions for empirical research' (cited in Payne et al., 2007, 3). The next section summarises some of these findings that instilled doubt about titling programmes being the magic bullet they once were thought to be.

3   Why Titling Isn't a Magic Bullet

Why might titling programmes fail? And why is it that, after ten years during which such programmes were actively promoted and supported by all development actors, they now are heavily contested and have become a battleground for a highly ideological debate?

3.1   *The Two Faces of the Commodification of Land*

A major factor explaining this development is that the arguments that are put forward in defence of land registration and titling have been, from the very start, inherently contradictory (Table 3.1). These arguments have been summarised above. They follow two separate logics that run in opposite directions. On the one hand, the clarification of property rights was to provide security of tenure: to allow slum dwellers to be recognised as owners of their home in the informal settlement where they are staying, or to allow those operating small farms to be protected from eviction from the land which they cultivate. On the other hand, however, the clarification of property rights was justified by the need to establish a market for land rights, allowing a more fluid transfer of property rights—a lowering of transaction costs increasing the liquidity of these markets. The expansion from the former conception of 'security of tenure' to include the latter appears in a 1987 study by two authors from the World Bank, where they note that 'the ability of an occupant to undertake land transactions that would best suit his interests' should be considered part of 'security of tenure' (Feder and Noronha, 1987, 159). Yet, the contradiction between these two objectives becomes clear once we realise that the commodification of property rights can be a source of exclusion and increase insecurity of tenure.

Such exclusion may occur by means of any of four mechanisms. First, as already noted, the process of titling itself may be captured by the elites—in addition to the risk of 'pre-emptive speculation' noted by the Commission on the Legal Empowerment of the Poor, titling schemes may be manipulated or tainted by corruption; or the formalisation of property may be too costly or complex for the poorest segment of the population to benefit. Second, once property has been formalised and land demarcated, taxes may be imposed, and more easily collected, by public authorities. This may present an opportunity to better finance public services, as noted above. But it may also have exclusionary effects: it may occur that the poorest are not able to pay those taxes and are forced to sell off their land as a result. Third, whether to pay those taxes or to make the necessary investments in their houses or on their cultivated lands, the poor (who by definition have no capital of their own) shall be tempted to mortgage their land in order to have access to credit. But even if this works—even if, that is, lenders are willing to provide loans—the risk is that the debts will accumulate, and that the land will finally be seized by the lender: the commodification of land, in such a case, shall have made the loss of land possible, rather than protecting the land user from such a risk. Fourth, the rural poor may be tempted to sell off land in order to overcome temporary economic hardship such as a bad harvest or a fall in the 'farm gate prices' received for their crops. In its 2003 report on land rights, the World Bank clearly recognised that land markets could encourage such 'distress sales', thus potentially increasing insecurity of tenure, rather than reducing it (Deininger, 2003, 96–98; see also Cousins et al., 2005, 3).

This risk, it is worth noting, should not be seen as *failure* of the system, or as a problem that should be remedied in order for the system to proceed more smoothly. Instead, it is *inherent in the very process of commodification of property rights* that gives property its value. It has been written that, in de Soto's view, the problem of informal forms of tenure is not so much too little security of tenure, but instead *too much*: the problem of 'dead capital' is that is cannot be lost, because it cannot be sold or mortgaged (Mitchell, 2006, 7). Indeed, de Soto is explicit about this, noting that one of the benefits of formal property systems is that they make people 'accountable', encouraging people 'in advanced countries' to 'respect titles, honor contracts, and obey the law', because of 'the possibility of forfeiture' (de Soto, 2000, 55–56). In other terms, the counterpart of the improved security of tenure that formalisation of property allowed was the insecurity resulting from the possibility of losing property—whether because the household finds itself unable to reimburse the lender after having mortgaged the land, because the level of taxes makes paying those taxes unaffordable and forces the family to leave, or (where rural farming households are concerned) because the household finds it impossible to expand its property following the speculation fuelled by the titling process, and thus cannot achieve the economies of scale required to be competitive on the markets.

Nor was this permanent balancing between providing more security and introducing insecurity the only ambiguity inherent in titling programmes. Another results from the fact that the prescriptions were designed for urban populations (de Soto mostly wrote with the slum dwellers of Lima in mind), yet were transposed, with rather little reflection, to the registration of property in rural areas. The relationship to landed property is very different for each of these groups, however. Real property, for the urban poor, primarily ensures adequate housing. For the rural poor, land is a factor of production: the most important input to the farming upon which they depend for their livelihoods. The stakes are thus much higher for the rural poor. For urban dwellers, being priced out of certain gentrified neighborhoods means having to move to places

TABLE 3.1   *Contradictory arguments in favour of titling programmes*

Titling as a means of ensuring security of tenure	Titling as commodification of property rights
– Protect land users from eviction	– Ensure land goes to the highest bidder, presumed to be the most efficient user
– Encourage land users to invest in their property to increase its long-term value	– Ensure registered owners can be taxed to finance public services—if they can afford it
– Allow land users to use land as collateral in order to have access to credit, bringing 'dead capital' to life	

SOURCE: AUTHOR.

that are located further from employment opportunities or less well covered by public services. But for smallholders who lose the land that they cultivate and lack the education and training necessary to take up jobs in industry or the service sector (provided such jobs exist) this means losing everything: what threatens them if they lose land is a fall into the most extreme poverty. Like the urban poor, rural farming households may benefit from the improved security of tenure that is allowed by the registration of property; but the costs of the insecurity referred to above may also be particularly high for them.

One way of framing this discussion is to distinguish between a static analysis (attentive to the immediate or short-term impacts of the formalisation of property rights) and a dynamic perspective (attentive to the longer-term impacts). The commodification of land rights, which is often seen as being an inherent quality of registration processes, may benefit land users in the short run, as the assets they 'own' (and shall henceforth be recognised as owning) can be transformed into capital, increasing their value. But whether or not they benefit in the long run will depend on the range of conditions that will either allow them to seize the opportunities this creates for them, or instead increase their marginalisation further. Why this possibility of marginalisation should exist becomes clear when we consider the consequences of treating land as a tradeable asset.

3.2   *Land as a Tradeable Asset in a Dynamic Perspective*
Will the registration of land allow small-scale farmers to have access to credit, and thus to improve their productivity? The short answer is that it will

only do so under a specific set of circumstances, including the existence of a network of credit institutions that can provide loans suited to their needs (Bruce and Migot-Adholla, 1994; for a literature review see Place, 2009). But establishing such institutions shall not suffice, unless complementary measures are adopted. Lenders typically will have no interest in accepting as collateral a parcel of land that is too small in size to be of interest to commercial investors, or that cannot be easily resold because of the resistance of the community to the arrival of an outsider (Smith, 2003, 214); and smallholders themselves may be too risk-averse to take loans, particularly if the consequence is that they may loose their land through foreclosure (Platteau, 2000, 59; Shipton and Goheen, 1992, 317).

Even more troubling is the fact that where titling schemes have been implemented, they have often led to increased inequalities, making the poorest even worse off. More than a decade ago, Berry already noted that 'in country after country, when land has become valuable enough, the powerful have pushed the weak off what land they had' (Berry, 2001, 130). This is true to the extent that the national elites, who have superior purchasing power, may emerge victorious from the auctioning of land that titling schemes in fact lead to. As noted by Geoffrey Payne et al. (2007, 9), 'the provision of titles may actually reduce security for both tenants and newly titled owners, given the attraction of the suddenly enhanced values of their assets to higher income groups or others with the motives and ability to take advantage of the changed tenure status'. Because land in general cannot be used twice as collateral, first in order to purchase and then to acquire the working capital required, access to credit by mortgaging land is in fact only a means of improving the productivity of relatively large plots of land or of those who have access to other forms of capital beyond land; it hardly benefits those who have nothing but a small parcel of land that increases in value. Inequalities may increase, rather than be reduced, as a result.

This effect may be further strengthened where investors from abroad seek to acquire large areas of land in order to develop agriculture for export, and are encouraged in their quest by the creation of a market for land rights. As such markets develop, speculation over land increases, and so does land concentration: foreign investors are mostly interested in developing large-scale plantations that are relatively non-labour-intensive and contribute relatively little to rural development (De Schutter, 2011); and conflicts over land increase as land becomes a valuable asset (Amanor, 2012). This is particularly problematic in contexts where the distribution of land is already unequal, because in such contexts access to land—and not merely security of tenure, which in itself may in fact simply confirm existing inequalities—should be a priority for the landless or quasi-landless rural poor. Yet, as acknowleged by Klaus Deininger, a lead economist at the World Bank, in the absence of outside support, 'the purchase market does not operate as a mechanism of land access for labour-abundant, capital-constrained households' (Deininger, 2003, 114).

The further markets for land rights develop, the more there is a risk that the price of land shall increase as a result of speculation. Speculation means that capital that could be put to productive uses, for instance for creating employment, will be immobilised. Even if we hypothesise that the 'speculative' part of price-setting can be separated from the 'market' price, the price of land following titling shall increase, by at least 25 per cent according to most studies available (Payne et al., 2007, 15–16). In principle, that represents a benefit for those who can register their land. But things look quite different when examined in a dynamic perspective: the poorest households may in fact be tempted to sell their land either to overcome a temporary shock or to profit from the opportunity resulting from sudden increases in the price of land, only to discover that the prices of other parcels too have become unaffordable, as the increased price of titled land creates ripple effects making all land more expensive (Payne et al., 2007, 16).

The speculation on land that follows registration processes, leading to inflated prices for land, leads one to question not only the de Soto hypothesis according to which such processes should benefit the poor by allowing them to use their (until then 'dead') assets as capital, but also the Coase hypothesis, which anticipates that, as markets for land rights develop, land will go to the most 'productive' users. As we have seen, these two narratives to a certain extent contradict each other: whereas the latter emphasises the benefits to the poor of the formalisation of property rights, the former emphasises property's contribution to economic growth when in the hands of the most efficient actors. Yet, remarkably, both these narratives fail to take into account the impacts that result from the highly unequal distribution of purchasing power in many of the societies where such formalisation processes take place. One implication of speculation over land is that the poorest landowners will be priced out of land markets, and that even those who manage to register their property may soon lose it, as a result of incurring unsustainable debts or because they seek to benefit from the 'windfall' effect that follows. Another implication is that where land is transferred it does not necessarily go to the most productive user, thus leading to efficiency gains and improving average productivity; rather, it goes to those who have the strongest purchasing power. Indeed, as interest for agricultural land has been rising significantly in recent years, the risk of the poorest being priced out of increasingly speculative land markets is higher now even than in the past.

3.3   The Opportunity Costs of the Registration of Land Rights

A different set of questions arises once we examine the impacts of the formalisation of property rights and land registration for the rural dwellers who have no access to land before the titling process, and are therefore entirely dependent on their labour as a source of income. Titling is generally defended on the grounds that it will support the poor, and small-scale farmers in particular, since the registration of the property that they own de facto shall allow them to unlock their productivity potential (Deininger and Binswanger, 1999; Platteau, 2000, 51–74). What generally fails to be mentioned, however, is that registration also gives a premium to those who already occupy land, making entry into land markets more difficult for the landless. Land registration may benefit the relatively better-off, who have some land and may hope to improve its productivity by making the necessary investments; it is not a means of ensuring access to land for those who have none, who should instead be supported by grants (Deininger, 2003, 96). In that sense, titling may be said to constitute a transfer of wealth from the landless to those who occupy land, and from the next generation to the present one: as titling increases the market value of land, land will become less affordable for the poorest part of the population or for new entrants to the land markets, for whom *access* to land—not just the *consolidation* of unrecognised property rights—is vital. This consequence is, of course, particularly disturbing where inequality in the distribution of land is greatest, and where the population comprises a large number of landless rural workers, or small-scale farmers who must rent the land that they till and may not be able to afford higher rents (Payne, 1997, 46).

3.4   'Clarifying' Property Rights and Competing with Customary Forms of Tenure

A final ambiguity stems from the terms 'clarification' and 'formalization', which are used to refer to the improvements to property rights regimes that titling should allow. The purpose is, ostensibly, to confirm existing use rights. But these use rights are often complex. It is not unusual for conflicting claims to exist over any piece of land. And there are various types of land users, not all of who are 'dormant landowners' awaiting an opportunity to register the land they occupy.

Moreover, prior to the formalisation of property rights through titling, tenure generally is regulated by custom, which is often highly legitimate and, as recognised by an influential report authored in 2003 by Klaus Deininger for the World Bank, can ensure a high level of security of tenure (Deininger, 2003, 53) and deliver the same services as formalised property rights, including by favouring in certain cases efficiency-enhancing exchanges (Deininger, 2003, 31–32). Research has highlighted that, in fact, traditional (or customary) systems of tenure in many cases allow for the individualisation of ownership, and that even where communal ownership subsists, such systems allow for cultivation and possession to remain with individual households (Feder and Noronha, 1987). The superimposition of titling on these pre-existing, customary forms of tenure may result in more conflicts rather than in more clarity, and in less security rather than in improved security (Toulmin and Quan, 2000). In addition, customary forms of property may provide security for those depending on the commons—such as pastoralists, artisanal fishers, or those with small herds—for whom classic property rights are generally not an appropriate solution.

Though they present many advantages, customary forms of tenure tend to exclude certain members of the community and outsiders, however, and are often a tool which traditional elites use to maintain their dominant position within communities. Women in particular may be discriminated against under existing customs. Though the phenomenon is by no means limited to that region (Yngstrom, 2002; Whitehead and Tsikata, 2003), discrimination against women in access to land is particularly pronounced in some parts of Asia. In much of rural China, for instance, though the Marriage Law gave women the right to land within the household unit and the Agrarian Reform Law granted men and women equal right to land in general, customary practices still prevail, and sons rather than widows or daughters continue to be considered the natural heirs of land (OECD, 2010, 25).[1] It is therefore hardly surprising that women's land rights are seldom reflected in the land certificates issued to households: a study published ten years ago concluded that only 7 per cent of certificates were in the name of the woman, while 5 per cent of the certificates were issued to a man and a woman jointly; the remaining land-use certificates were in the name of the husband, father, or father-in-law (Zongmin and Bruce, 2005, 276). In India, to give another example, even after the amendments introduced in 2005 to the Hindu Succession Act, giving women equal rights in their natal family assets,[2] women inheriting property is rare. Women also often tend to renounce their claim to natal property that they are entitled to in order to

---

1 This is particularly troublesome since, in large part due to migratory patterns in which men, more frequently than women, seek employment outside agriculture, women account for between 60 and 70 per cent of all farm labour (de Brauw et al., 2012).

2 A first reform of the Hindu Succession Act, in 1956, had guaranteed equal inheritance rights for sons and daughters, but exempted agricultural land (Ramachandran, 2006, 4).

maintain good social relations with their brothers: in particular, women may accept a lump sum payment in lieu of their property rights, in order to preserve visitation rights to the parental home. Customary forms of tenure should therefore not be idealised: it would be wrong to think of them as inherently equitable and inclusive (Feder and Noronha, 1987).

4 Alternatives to the Commodification of Land through the Globalisation of Property Rights

The recent wave of large-scale land acquisitions has undoubtedly increased the risks of eviction of land users who lack adequate legal protections, and has made the prospects of landless or quasi-landless rural households even more dire. However, it does not follow that the rolling out of titling schemes shall produce the magical outcomes they are sometimes touted for. Rather, the remarks above suggest that we may have to make a clear distinction between protecting the rights of land users against the risks of eviction, which we must, and transplanting Western concepts of property rights into contexts for which they may be ill-suited. At a minimum, protecting the rights of poor rural households requires ensuring security of tenure by the registration of land-use rights and by the adoption of anti-eviction legislation, combined with the provision of tools—such as legal aid, legal literacy training, and access to legal advisors—to ensure that formally recognised rights can be effectively vindicated (Cotula and Mathieu, 2008); and by strengthening the capacity of land administrations and fighting against corruption in these administrations. However, as illustrated for instance by the certification process that took place in Cambodia in 1989—in preparation for the withdrawal of the Vietnamese army from the country, a process during which farmers were granted land certificates confirming that they had applied for title (Dwyer, 2015)—neither certification (or registration of use rights) nor anti-eviction laws require that land be commodified; neither require that fully fledged property rights should be granted as if this were the single institutional means by which security of tenure could be ensured.

Anti-eviction laws should be conceived as the domestic implementation of the international standards set by the Committee on Economic, Social and Cultural Rights in its work on evictions (CESCR, 1998) and by the Special Rapporteur on the right to adequate housing when he presented the Basic Principles and Guidelines on Development-Based Evictions and Displacement to the Human Rights Council (Special Rapporteur on Adequate Housing, 2007).

The main purpose of such laws is to impose on public authorities or on private landowners the condition that, when they seek to evict land users from land that they occupy—provided at least that the land users have been occupying the land for a certain length of time—certain procedures are complied with. Classic examples among these requirements are that the occupiers are given due notice, that no eviction can take place without a negotiation, that the occupants must have options for relocation, and that, in order for their resettlement to be possible, they are provided with financial support (UN-Habitat, 2003). Of course, as illustrated by Chapter 10 (Cismas and Paramita) of this volume, for such laws to be effective the beneficiaries should have access to remedies in cases of violation, including access to legal aid, which in many developing countries is weak or non-existent. Provided the institutional support is adequate, however, anti-eviction laws can ensure a certain security of tenure without requiring the attribution of full property rights as would occur through a classic titling process (Santiago, 1998).

But other instruments may also be used. The adoption of tenancy laws could protect tenants from eviction and from excessive levels of rent or crop-sharing. Thus, for example, the tenancy laws in the Indian state of West Bengal, which a left-wing administration revived in 1977 in what was known as Operation Barga, provide that if tenants register with the Department of Land Revenue, they are entitled to permanent and inheritable tenure on the land they have sharecropped against payment to the landlord of at least 25 per cent of the output as rent (Banerjee, 1999; Banerjee et al., 2002). Such laws may also allow the heirs of the tenant to occupy the land if the tenant dies, and provide the tenant with a right to preemption if the landowner wishes to sell (ideally, at lower than market prices); they may provide for joint titling, as tenants, of both husband and wife in order to protect widows from the risk of eviction; and they could ensure that the tenant will be allowed to remain on the land if the property changes hands. Tenancy laws are often circumvented by unscrupulous landowners who tend not to register their tenants in order to avoid having to recognise their rights. Where such laws have been effectively enforced, however, they have been shown to increase productivity, both because they improve the crop-share of tenants and thus are an incentive to produce, and because they encourage productivity-enhancing investments in land, because of the increased security of tenure that benefits the tenant: in the 2002 study cited above, Banerjee et al. (2002) estimate that the revival of tenancy laws in West Bengal led to a 28 per cent increase in agricultural productivity.

Finally, where landlessness or near-landlessness are strongly correlated with extreme poverty, access to land should be improved by agrarian reform schemes. The international community has acknowledged the importance of agrarian reform 'mainly in areas with strong social disparities, poverty and food insecurity, as a means to broaden sustainable access to and control over land and related resources' (ICARRD, 2006). A more equitable distribution of land can have strong poverty-reducing impacts: cross-country comparisons show that 'a decrease of one-third in the land distribution inequality index results in a reduction in the poverty level of one-half in about 12–14 years', a level of poverty reduction which could only be achieved after 60 years of 3 per cent annual agricultural growth in the absence of changes in land distri-bution (El-Ghonemy, 2003). Progress in the reduction of rural poverty in the Asian region has benefited largely from this approach: post-World War II land reforms in Asia have resulted in a 30 per cent increase in the incomes of the bottom 80 per cent of households while leading to an 80 per cent decline in the income of the top 4 per cent (Penciakova, 2010, 8). This was what led those drawing up the Cambodian 2001 Land Law to include a provision for 'social' land concessions intended to benefit the landless rural poor, though this part of the law remained essentially a dead letter (Dwyer, 2015; Müller, 2012, 3).

In addition to its economic function in stimulating growth and reducing rural poverty, a more equitable access to land for the rural poor contributes to social inclusion and economic empowerment (Quan, 2006, 3). It improves food security, since it makes food more easily and cheaply available, provid-ing a buffer against external shocks (Carter, 2003): as illustrated by the case of China, access to even a small plot of land provides an almost complete insur-ance against malnutrition at the household level (Deininger and Binswanger, 1999, 256). Land distribution schemes also support the growth of small, family-owned farms, which often can use the land in more sustainable way, and con-tribute to rural development because they are more labour-intensive. More equitable distribution of land and the development of owner-operated fam-ily farms is thus desirable on both efficiency and equity grounds (Deininger and Binswanger, 1999, 248). Where rural areas face high unemployment and under-employment of labour and relative scarcity of land, it is sensible both from an economic perspective and from a social justice perspective to raise land productivity rather than to try to increase labour productivity. Such land redistribution schemes will fail to produce such impacts, however, unless the beneficiaries are supported in their ability to use the land productively, and to achieve decent incomes through farming. Indeed, Michael Lipton warns of the risk that land redistribution schemes may benefit primarily those operating larger farms since they can more easily obtain bank loans and thus use land productively, whereas those operating smaller farms may be led into distress sales or be tempted to sell off land (Lipton, 2009, 25). Others have estimated that improving access to credit, access to markets, and rural extension, can account for 60–70 per cent of the total costs of a land reform, thus exceeding the costs of acquiring and transferring the land (Palmer et al., 2009, 31).

A final comment relates to the framing of the debate on land redistribution schemes. In the past, the discussion of land reform was discouraged by a strong ideological divide between the proponents of market-led land reforms and those advocating state-led land reforms. In general, the arguments of the former are based on the principle of a willing seller and a willing buyer negotiating transfers of land at market prices, a relationship in which the role of the state is primarily to provide a regulatory and institutional framework ensuring a fluid market for land rights and to support the access of the poor to credit in order to allow them to enter such markets (Deininger and Binswanger, 1999; World Bank, 2007, 141–147). In contrast, state-led land reforms generally include compulsory expropriations from the owners of large quantities of land in the name of social justice objectives, in principle against a compensation that may or may not correspond to the actual market value of the land concerned. While market-led land reforms are defended as more economically efficient—as land, it is supposed, shall go to the most efficient users, who can use it most productively—state-led reforms are sometimes seen as the only realistic possibility in the face of social inequalities so marked that the state cannot compensate for them; but they also have been associated with authoritarian regimes, and they are seen as exacerbating social and political conflict to such an extent that they may ultimately prove counter-productive. In fact, however, this opposition is misleading. There are many ways in which the state may promote a more equitable access to land, ranging from the taxation of land left unproductive by the owners of large quantities of land to progressive inheritance laws, and from subsidies to smaller production units to ceiling laws that impose limits on how much land can be owned by a single individual (El-Ghonemy, 2003). Classifying the various instruments that can be used into two groups unnecessarily transforms what should be a pragmatic search for the most optimal mix in specific contexts into an ideological discussion in which participants adopt postures that make the emergence of a consensus less likely (Borras Jr. and McKinley, 2006; Borras Jr. et al., 2007).

5   Conclusion

Although the formalisation of property rights has been widely promoted as a safeguard against the threat of expropriation in the current wave of large-scale acquisitions and leases of land, it is important not to confuse security of tenure, which is certainly of considerable importance to rural households, and the creation of markets for land rights, which in a dynamic perspective may not be advantageous to them. The role of property rights in the debate on 'land grabs' has therefore been highly ambiguous: while such rights are seen by some as a key to avoiding massive disruptions, they have also been denounced as legitimising increased land concentration in the hands of the elites or potential buyers with the highest purchasing power. As seen in Section 4 of this paper, there is nothing inevitable in this trade-off. Security of tenure may be protected using a number of tools, without necessarily having to result to fully fledged property rights.

For rural households that depend on agriculture for their livelihoods, security of tenure ultimately should be understood as the right to live decently from farming. This presupposes access to land, and protection from eviction; but it includes much else in addition. Indeed, policies that promote a more equitable access to land are futile, and may in some scenarios render a disservice even to their intended beneficiairies, unless they fit under broader schemes for rural development. Even in regions where the pattern of land distribution is highly unequal and where hunger and malnutrition are closely correlated with landlessness or quasi-landlesness, simply redistributing land will not suffice. In order for such a reform scheme to be sustainable, the beneficiaries must also be supported by comprehensive rural development policies supporting smallholders and improving their ability to compete against larger farms, or the positive redistributive impacts may be significantly eroded.

References

Amanor, K.S. (2012) 'Global Resource Grabs, Agribusiness Concentration and the Smallholder: Two West African Case Studies', *Journal of Peasant Studies*, 39(3–4), pp. 731–749, DOI: 10.1080/03066150.2012.676543.

Banerjee, A.V. (1999) *Land Reforms: Prospects and Strategies*, Department of Economics Working Paper Series, Working Paper No. 99–24, October (Cambridge, MA: Massachusetts Institute of Technology).

Banerjee, A.V., P.J. Gertler and M. Ghatak (2002) 'Empowerment and Efficiency: Tenancy Reform in West Bengal', *Journal of Political Economy*, 110(2), pp. 239–280, DOI: 10.1086/338744.

Berry, A. (2001) 'When Do Agricultural Exports Help the Rural Poor? A Political Economy Approach', *Oxford Development Studies*, 29(2), pp. 125–44, DOI: 10.1080/13600810120059770.

Borras Jr., S.M. and T. McKinley (2006) *The Unresolved Land Reform Debate: Beyond State-Led or Market-Led Models*, UNDP Policy Research Brief No. 2/2006, November

(New York: UNDP), http://www.ipc-undp.org/pub/IPCPolicyResearchBrief2.pdf (accessed on 14 April 2015).

Borras Jr., S.M., C. Kay and A. Haroon Akram Lodhi (2007) *Agrarian reform and Rural Development: Historical Overview and Current Issues*, ISS/UNDP Land, Poverty and Public Action Policy paper No. 1 (The Hague: Institute for Social Studies–UNDP), http://hubrural.org/IMG/pdf/iss_pnud_overview.pdf (accessed on 14 April 2015).

Bruce, W. and S. Migot-Adholla (eds.) (1994) *Searching for Land Tenure Security in Africa* (Washington, D.C.: World Bank).

Carter, M.R. (2003) 'Designing Land and Property Rights Reform for Poverty Alleviation and Food Security', *Land Reform, Land Settlement and Cooperatives*, 2003/2, pp. 44–57, ftp://ftp.fao.org/docrep/fao/006/j0415T/j0415T00.pdf (accessed on 14 April 2015).

Castañeda Dower, P. and E. Potamites (2012) *Signaling Credit-Worthiness: Land Titles, Banking Practices and Formal Credit in Indonesia*, Centre for Economic and Financial Research, New Economic School, Working Paper Series No. 186 (Moscow: CEFIR/NES), http://www.cefir.ru/papers/WP186.pdf (accessed on 14 April 2015).

Center for Human Rights and Global Justice (2010) *Foreign Land Deals and Human Rights: Case Studies on Agricultural and Biofuel Investment* (New York: New York University School of Law), http://chrgj.org/wp-content/uploads/2012/07/landreport.pdf (accessed on 14 April 2015).

CESCR (Committee on Economic, Social and Cultural Rights) (1998) *General Comment 7. The Right to Adequate Housing (article 11.1): Forced Evictions*, UN doc. E/1998/22, annex IV.

Chavez Sanchez, E., L. Diniz, F. Meunier and P. Rakhimova (2014) 'Registering Property', in World Bank, *Doing Business 2014, Understanding Regulations for Small and Medium-Sized Enterprises* (Washington, D.C.: International Bank for Reconstruction and Development–World Bank) pp. 86–89, http://www.doingbusiness.org/reports/global-reports/~/media/GIAWB/Doing%20Business/Documents/Annual-Reports/English/DB14-Chapters/DB14-Registering-property.pdf (accessed on 9 September 2014).

CLEP (High-Level Commission on the Legal Empowerment of the Poor) (2008) *Final report* (New York: United Nations).

———— (2005) *Poverty Reduction through Improved Asset Security, Formalisation of Property Rights and the Rule of Law*, Concept Paper, 6 September (New York: United Nations).

Coase, R.H. (1960) 'The Problem of Social Cost', *Journal of Law and Economics*, 3, pp. 1–44.

Colin, J.-P. and P. Woodhouse (2010) 'Interpreting Land Markets in Africa', *Africa*, 80(1), pp. 1–13, DOI: 10.3366/E0001972009001235.

Cotula, L. and P. Mathieu (eds.) (2008) *Legal Empowerment in Practice. Using Legal Tools to Secure Land Rights in Africa* (London and Rome: IIED–FAO).

Cotula, L., S. Vermeulen, R. Leonard and J. Keeley (2009) *Land Grab or Development Opportunity? Agricultural Investment and International Land Deals in Africa* (London and Rome: IIED–FAO–IFAD).

Cousins, B., T. Cousins, D. Hornby, R. Kingwill, L. Royston and W. Smit (2005) *Will Formalizing Property Rights Reduce Poverty in South Africa's "Second Economy"? Questioning the Mythologies of Hernando de Soto*, Programme for Land and Agrarian Studies Policy Brief Debating Land Reform, Natural Resources and Poverty, No. 18, October (Cape Town: PLAAS), http://capri.cgiar.org/pdf/brief_land-10.pdf (accessed on 14 April 2015).

de Brauw, A., J. Huang, L. Zhang and S. Rozelle (2012) *The Feminization of Agriculture with Chinese Characteristics*, International Food Policy Research Institute Discussion Paper 01189 (Washington, D.C.: IFPRI), http://www.ifpri.org/sites/default/files/publications/ifpridp01189.pdf (accessed on 14 April 2015).

Deininger, K. (2003) *Land Policies for Growth and Poverty Reduction: A World Bank Policy Research Report*, Report No. 26384 (Washington, D.C., and Oxford: World Bank–Oxford University Press).

Deininger, K. and H. Binswanger (1999) 'The Evolution of the World Bank's Land Policy: Principles, Experience and Future Challenges', *The World Bank Research Observer*, 14(2), pp. 247–76, http://wbro.oxfordjournals.org/content/14/2/247.short?rss=1&ssource=mfr (accessed on 14 April 2015).

Deininger, K. and D. Byerlee (2010) *Rising Global Interest in Farmland: Can It Yield Sustainable and Equitable Benefits?* (Washington, D.C.: World Bank–International Bank for Reconstruction and Development), http://siteresources.worldbank.org/DEC/Resources/Rising-Global-Interest-in-Farmland.pdf (accessed on 14 April 2015).

De Schutter, O. (2011) 'How not to Think About Land-Grabbing: Three Critiques of Large-Scale Investments in Farmland', *Journal of Peasant Studies*, 38(2), pp. 249–279, DOI: 10.1080/03066150.2011.559008.

De Schutter, O., J. Swinnen and J. Wouters (2012). 'Introduction: Foreign Direct Investment and Human Development', in De Schutter, O., J. Swinnen and J. Wouters (eds.) *Foreign Direct Investment and Human Development. The Law and Economics of International Investment Agreements* (London and New York: Routledge) pp. 1–24.

de Soto, H. (2000) *The Mystery of Capital: Why Capitalism Triumphs in the West and Fails Everywhere Else* (New York: Basic Books).

Dwyer, M. (2015) 'Redirecting Regulation? Land Titling and Cambodia's Post-Neoliberal Conjuncture', in Pistor, K. and O. De Schutter (eds.) *Governance Access to Essential Resources* (New York: Columbia University Press).

——— (2013) *The Formalization Fix? Land Titling, State Land Concessions, and the Politics of Geographical Transparency in Contemporary Cambodia*, Land Deal Politics

Initiative (LDPI) Working Paper 37 (The Hague: LDPI), http://www.plaas.org.za/plaas-publication/ldpi-37 (accessed on 14 April 2015).

El-Ghonemy, M.R. (2003) 'Land Reform Development Challenges of 1963–2003 Continue into the Twenty-First Century', *Land Reform, Land Settlement and Cooperatives*, No. 2, pp. 32–43, ftp://ftp.fao.org/docrep/fao/006/j0415T/j0415T00.pdf (accessed on 14 April 2015).

Feder, G. and D. Feeny (1991) 'Land Tenure and Property Rights: Theory and Implications for Development Policy', *The World Bank Economic Review*, 5(1), pp. 135–153, http://www.jstor.org/stable/3989973.

Feder, G. and R. Noronha (1987) 'Land Rights Systems and Agricultural Development in Sub-Saharan Africa', *World Bank Research Observer*, 2(2), pp. 143–169, DOI: 10.1093/wbro/2.2.143.

Feder, G., T. Onchan, Y. Chalamwong and C. Hongladarom (1988) *Land Policies and Farm Productivity in Thailand* (Baltimore, MD: Johns Hopkins University Press).

Firmin-Sellers, K. and P. Sellers (1999). 'Expected Failures and Unexcepted Successes of Land Titling in Africa', *World Development*, 27(7), pp. 1115–1128, DOI: 10.1016/S0305-750X(99)00058-3.

Haralambous, S., H. Liversage and M. Romano (2009) *The Growing Demand for Land: Risks and Opportunities for Smallholder Farmers*, International Fund for Agricultural Development Discussion Paper for Round Table 2, Thirty-second session of IFAD's Governing Council (Rome: IFAD), http://www.ifad.org/events/gc/32/roundtables/2.pdf (accessed on 14 April 2015).

ICARRD (International Conference on Agrarian Reform and Rural Development) (2006) *Final Declaration*, 2006/3 (Porto Alegre: Food and Agriculture Organization), http://www.nyeleni.org/IMG/pdf/2006_03_FinalDeclaration_FAO_Conference_En-1-3.pdf (accessed on 14 April 2015).

Kugelman, M. and S.L. Levenstein (eds.) (2009) *Land Grab? The Race for the World's Farmland* (Washington, D.C.: Woodrow Wilson International Center for Scholars), http://www.wilsoncenter.org/sites/default/files/ASIA_090629_Land%20Grab_rpt.pdf (accessed on 14 April 2015).

Lipton, M. (2009) *Land Reform in Developing Countries: Property Rights and Property Wrongs* (Routledge: London).

Mann, H. and C. Smaller (2010) *Foreign Land Purchases for Agriculture: What Impact on Sustainable Development?*, Sustainable Development Innovation Brief No. 8, January (New York: United Nations Department of Economic and Social Affairs), https://sustainabledevelopment.un.org/content/documents/no8.pdf (accessed on 14 April 2015).

Mayo, S.K. and S. Angel (1993) *Housing: Enabling Markets to Work*, World Bank Policy Paper No. 11820, (Washington, D.C.: World Bank), http://documents.worldbank.org/curated/en/1993/04/1561159/housing-enabling-markets-work (accessed on 14 April 2015).

Mitchell, T. (2006) *The Properties of Markets: Informal Housing and Capitalism's Mystery*, Working Paper No. 2, Cultural, Political Economy Working Paper Series (Lancaster: Institute for Advanced Studies in Social and Management Sciences, Lancaster University).

Müller, F-V. (2012) *Commune-Based Land Allocation for Poverty Reduction in Cambodia: Achievements and Lessons Learned from the Project: Land Allocation for Social and Economic Development (LASED)*, paper prepared for presentation at the Annual World Bank Conference on Land and Poverty, Washington D.C., April 23–26.

OECD (Organisation for Economic Co-operation and Development) (2010) 'World Overview', in *Atlas of Gender and Development: How Social Norms Affect Gender Equality in non-OECD Countries* (Paris: OECD).

Palmer, D., S. Fricska and B. Wehrmann (2009) (in collaboration with C. Augustinus, P. Munro-Faure, M-P. Törhönen and A. Arial) *Towards Improved Land Governance*, Land Tenure Working Paper No. 11, September (Rome: Food and Agriculture Organization), http://www.fao.org/3/a-ak999e.pdf (accessed on 14 April 2015).

Payne, G. (1997) *Urban Land Tenure and Property Rights in Developing Countries: A Review* (London: Intermediate Technology Publications–Overseas Development Administration).

Payne, G., A. Durand-Lasserve and C. Rakodi (2007) *Social and Economic Impacts of Land Titling Programmes in Urban and Peri-Urban Areas: A Review of the Literature*, paper presented at the World Bank Urban Research Symposium, Washington, D.C., 14–16 May.

Penciakova, V. (2010) *Market-Led Agrarian Reform: A Beneficiary Perspective of Cédula da Terra*, London School of Economics Working Paper Series No. 10–100, March (London: LSE), http://www.lse.ac.uk/internationalDevelopment/pdf/WP/WP100 .pdf (accessed on 14 April 2015).

Place, F. (2009) 'Land Tenure and Agricultural Productivity in Africa: A Comparative Analysis of the Economics Literature and Recent Policy Strategies and Reforms', *World Development*, 37(8), pp. 1326–1336, DOI: 10.1016/j.worlddev.2008.08.020.

Platteau, J-Ph. (2000) 'Does Africa Need Land Reform?', in Toulmin, C. and J. Quan (eds.) *Evolving Land Rights, Policy and Tenure in Africa* (London: DFID–IIED–NRI) pp. 51–74.

Quan, J. (2006) *Land Access in the 21st Century: Issues, Trends, Linkages and Policy Options*, Livelihood Support Programme Working Paper No. 24 (Rome: Food and Agriculture Organisation), ftp://ftp.fao.org/docrep/fao/009/ah245e/ah245e00.pdf (accessed on 14 April 2015).

Ramachandran, N. (2006) *Women and Food Security in South Asia: Current Issues and Emerging Concerns*, United Nations University–World Institute for Development Economics Research Paper No. 2006/131 (Helsinki: UNU-WIDER), http://www.wider .unu.edu/publications/working-papers/research-papers/2006/en_GB/rp2006-131/ (accessed on 14 April 2015).

Santiago, A.M. (1998) 'Law and Urban Change: Illegal Settlements in the Philippines', in Fernandes, E. and A. Varley (eds.) *Illegal Cities Law and Urban Change in Developing Countries* (London: Zed Books) pp. 104–122.

Shipton, P. and M. Goheen (1992) 'Understanding African Land-Holding: Power, Wealth, and Meaning', *Africa*, 62(3), pp. 307–25, DOI: 10.2307/1159746.

Smith, R.E. (2003) 'Land Tenure Reform in Africa: A Shift to the Defensive', *Progress in Development Studies*, 3(3), pp. 210–222, DOI: 10.1191/1464993403ps0620a.

Special Rapporteur on Adequate Housing (2007) *Basic Principles and Guidelines on Development-based Evictions and Displacement*, Annex I of the Report of the Special Rapporteur on adequate housing as a component of the right to an adequate standard of living, Miloon Kothari, UN doc. A/HRC/4/18, 5 February.

———— (2006) *Report of the Special Rapporteur on adequate housing as a component of the right to an adequate standard of living*, Addedum: Mission to Cambodia, UN doc. E/CN.4/2006/41/Add.3, 21 March.

Toulmin, C. and J. Quan (eds.) (2000) *Evolving Land Rights, Policy and Tenure in Africa* (London: DFID–IIED–NRI).

UN-Habitat (United Nations Human Settlements Program) (2003) *Handbook on Best Practices, Security of Tenure and Access to Land. Implementation of the Habitat Agenda* (Nairobi: UN-Habitat), http://ww2.unhabitat.org/publication/hs5889ge/ hs5889ge.pdf (accessed on 14 April 2015).

Unruh, J. (2002) 'Poverty and Property Rights in the Developing World: Not as Simple as We Would Like', *Land Use Policy*, 19(4), pp. 275–276, http://ilc.landportal.info/ sites/default/files/poverty_prop_rights_lup.pdf (accessed on 14 April 2015).

von Benda-Beckmann, F. (2003) 'Mysteries of Capital or Mystification of Legal Property?', *European Journal of Anthropology*, 41, pp. 187–191.

Whitehead, A. and D. Tsikata (2003) 'Policy Discourses on Women's Land Rights in Sub-Saharan Africa: The Implications of the Re-Turn to the Customary', *Journal of Agrarian Change*, 3(1–2), pp. 67–112, DOI: 10.1111/1471-0366.00051.

World Bank (2007) *World Development Report 2008: Agriculture for Development* (Washington, D.C.: International Bank for Reconstruction and Development–World Bank), http://hdl.handle.net/10986/5990 (accessed on 14 April 2015).

———— (2004a) *Doing Business 2005: Removing Obstacles to Growth* (Washington, D.C.: International Bank for Reconstruction and Development–World Bank), http:// www.doingbusiness.org/~/media/FPDKM/Doing%20Business/Documents/ Annual-Reports/English/DB05-FullReport.pdf (accessed on 14 April 2015).

———— (2004b) *World Development Report 2005: A Better Investment Climate for Everyone* (Washington, D.C.: International Bank for Reconstruction and Development–World Bank) http://hdl.handle.net/10986/5987 (accessed on 14 April 2015).

Yngstrom, I. (2002) 'Women, Wives and Land Rights in Africa: Situating Gender Beyond the Household in the Debate over Land Policy and Changing Tenure Systems', *Oxford Development Studies*, 30(1), pp. 21–40, DOI: 10.1080/136008101200114886.

Zongmin, L. and J. Bruce (2005) 'Gender, Landlessness and Equity in Rural China', in Ho, P. (ed.) *Development Dilemmas: Land Reform and Institutional Change in China* (London: Routledge) pp. 270–295.

PART 2

Land Dynamics and Livelihoods in South-East Asia

∵

The Impact of Larger-Scale Agricultural Investments on Communities in South-East Asia: A First Assessment

James Zhan, Hafiz Mirza, and William Speller

Abstract

Since the mid-2000s, corporate sector investments in agriculture in developing countries have increased sharply, driven by rising commodity prices, the strategic concerns of food-importing countries, and commercial opportunities. Using the findings of fieldwork conducted by UNCTAD and the World Bank in countries across Africa and Asia, this chapter focuses on the impact of such investments on communities in South-East Asia. Relying on interviews with representative of the companies concerned and with members of local communities, as well as other stakeholders, carried out using a dyadic approach, the chapter provides detailed findings on the impact of investments in areas such as employment, incomes, land rights and the environment. It shows that both beneficial and negative consequences of agricultural investments can be traced to specific factors, such as decisions taken by investors (and governments) at the early stages of investment processes, the business models utilised, and investor-community relationships, as well as the degree to which responsible approaches are built into operations. The findings on Asia, as well as from the wider study on which this chapter is based, offer valuable information for governments, investors and civil society groups with regard to designing policies and practices, and to establishing relationships between these actors and monitoring areas relevant to the impact and performance of investments.

1 Introduction

The challenges facing global agriculture in the coming decades are monumental, both as a provider of food and, more broadly, as an engine of growth in developing countries. The sector will have to feed a projected population of 9 billion people by 2050. The Food and Agriculture Organization (FAO) estimates that an average annual investment of USD 209 billion is needed to meet the projected demand for food in 2050—and even more is required to eliminate hunger, and target poverty and malnourishment (FAO, 2012a). Moreover, faced with a number of common economic, social, and environmental challenges, developing countries require long-term sustainable, increased investment, including investment in agriculture; and in this context an *additional* average annual investment of some USD 250 billion per year until 2030 is required (UNCTAD, 2014). However measured, the agricultural investment gap is enormous and in many developing countries will most likely require larger scale corporate investment, over and above existing sources.

The central role of smallholder farmers' investment in any strategy for promoting agricultural development is widely recognised (IFAD and UNEP, 2013; HLPE, 2013). But since the mid-2000s, corporate sector interest in agriculture in developing countries has increased sharply, driven by rising commodity prices, the strategic concerns of food-importing countries, and various commercial opportunities in the sector. Corporate investment, both foreign and domestic, in agriculture has jumped accordingly, coming not only from traditional investors such as agribusiness enterprises, but also from state-owned enterprises and sovereign wealth funds, as well as private equity and other investment funds, although there is a high degree of uncertainty regarding scale, source of investment, and geographic scope (Schoneveld, 2014; FAO, 2012a; Anseeuw et al., 2012; UNCTAD, 2009).

Much of the research on investment in agriculture to date has focused on Africa, but Asia—especially South-East Asia—has also been a major target for investors. For instance, according to data available to UNCTAD, the stock of foreign direct investment (FDI) in 2012 in Cambodia, Malaysia, and Vietnam stood at USD 1.1 billion, USD 3.8 billion, and USD 3.8 billion, respectively (all of which figures are probably underestimates). Moreover, for some very poor countries such as Cambodia and the Lao People's Democratic Republic, investment in agriculture constitutes a very large share of total FDI (Figure 4.1), which reflects the larger number of investments from Cambodia in the sample. The following figure is based on recent flow data, but stock data are not too different, albeit highlighting the significance of FDI in agriculture in South-East Asian countries such as Malaysia and Indonesia, historical beneficiaries of investment in agriculture.

After decades of struggling to attract a significant level of corporate investment, including FDI, to their agricultural sectors, developing countries are now faced with a challenge: in what ways should they accept the type, size and number of such investments in order to maximise development benefits and minimise socio-economic and environmental risks (Deninger and Byerlee, 2011; Human Rights Council, 2011; Vermuelen and Cotula, 2010; Mann and Smaller, 2009)? In their initial naïveté as investment in agriculture began to

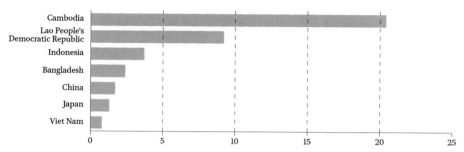

FIGURE 4.1 *FDI inflows to agriculture sector as a share of total FDI inflows, 2010–2012 (per cent).*
SOURCE: UNCTAD, FDI-TNC-GVC INFORMATION SYSTEM, FDI/TNC DATABASE
(www.unctad.org/fdistatistics).

surge from the mid-2000s many governments encouraged investment without carefully considering the consequences for the economy, rural areas, farmers or communities. As research has multiplied, and more importantly experience has been enriched, in Africa, South-East Asia and elsewhere, it is increasingly being recognised that overall net positive outcomes depend very much on the business models in place, the types of investor-community linkages, partnerships and relations established, etc.

The tenor of the arguments is that of more inclusive business models, achieved for instance by outsourcing as many activities as possible, be this 'outgrower' schemes with nucleus estates/operations outsourcing the farming, or franchised retail dealerships for local-market orientated operations.[1] Building on such business models, inclusive investor-community relationships can further involve many facets, including issues of ownership and control of assets (for instance, with respect to land and its associated use, communities can interface with investors through sale, lease, equity joint ventures and a large array of other types and combinations of arrangements); the risks and rewards of any arrangements; and the specificities of consultative, partnership, or other routes to communicating and addressing issues (Cotula and Leonard, 2010; Chaimberlain-Ven der Werf and Anseeuw, 2015; Rösler et al., 2013; Gaertner et al., 2014; Eaton, 2001).

However, while inclusive investor-community relationships might be a good idea in principle, in practice a number of major considerations must

---

1 In contrast, depending on local circumstances including the size of the investment relative to the local economy/community and so on, the investor might, in extreme cases, intertwine with the community through the provisions of education and health services (though in principle this would be taken on by the state as soon as feasible).

be taken into account when pursuing such goals. First, while the aims might be laudable, the reality could be different and not necessarily because of any intentional malice on the part of any party. For instance, outgrower schemes can widen participation in economic processes and widen the sharing of value added and benefits, but can also lock farmers into the imperatives of the principal investing company, a tension well summed up in the subtitle of De Los Reyes et al.'s (2015) paper on agribusiness and smallholder farmers in the Philippines: *A Free Hand, Increased Bargaining Power or Contract Regulation?* Secondly, neither investors nor communities are homogenous entities. The benefits and costs of an investment to a community, for example, even if 'net-positive', may fall differentially on the many individuals and groups of which it is composed. Outgrower farmers can be powerful and overbearing; agricultural workers will have different interests to those not engaged in the industry; how can women, minorities and other excluded groups have or attain voice? Thus perceptions of the value of an investment will vary within a community, in addition to the variation of perceptions between communities, investors, governments and other stakeholders. Finally, how an investment interacts with a community depends on a vast range of issues, including the crop involved, the value chain segment of the operation, the scale of the business activities, local conditions and circumstances and so on.

Thus, even if desirable, it is not possible to propose a simple model of investor-community dynamics and even less so one that can be deemed 'inclusive'. However, the literature is beginning to provide contingent good practices and tools that can be drawn on when striving for inclusive investor-community relationships and arrangements, be it in the context of an entirely new investment, or of an attempt to set an existing one on a different course (e.g. Lahiff et al., 2012; FAO, 2013; Deng, 2012). This chapter is based on an ongoing multi-stage study in this vein, whose ultimate aim is to draw detailed, practical knowledge, lessons and good practices from experiences on the ground to inform governments, investors, communities, civil society groups and international organisations engaged in tackling the opportunities, the challenges and the risks of agricultural investments of this type.

The chapter draws on a field-based, intensive survey of the conduct of agricultural operations at 39 larger-scale, mature agribusiness investments in sub-Saharan Africa and South-East Asia, focusing in particular on their approaches to social, economic and environmental responsibility.[2] Both the investors and

---

2   Elements of this chapter appeared in an earlier report (UNCTAD and World Bank, 2014); additional analysis carried out to discern specific issues concerning South-East Asia was conducted for this chapter.

the communities affected were interviewed. One of the intentions of this stage of the research was *not* to discern *the* most important impacts on local communities and the economy, but rather the *range of* the *perceived* important impacts of the investments, especially as seen by those locally impacted and other non-business stakeholders. At the same time, perceptions are grounded in realities, such as investors' performance in creating benefits (e.g. net job creation) or imposing costs (e.g. on the environment), albeit the perceived impacts will vary depending on a number of factors, including—for instance—the characteristics of the investment or the type of relationship between it and respondents. Hence the chapter includes discussion of, for example, investments with outgrower schemes, the performance of the investment, and the investor's approach to responsibility and sustainability. A critical incidents instrument was used to discern the range of impacts from the community and local stakeholder perspective.

This chapter examines the impacts of investments in the South-East Asian countries visited (Cambodia, Laos, Vietnam, Indonesia, and Malaysia), including impacts on land rights and access to land, drawing primarily on the answers received from local communities and stakeholders; at the same time it assesses how these impacts are influenced by the type of operations or decisions made by investors.[3] About a quarter of the investments surveyed were in South-East Asia, so—where relevant or useful—cross reference is made to the fuller sample of responses.

2   Methodology

A quota-based sample selection procedure was used to identify investors, drawing from a larger population of investors. The quota selection was based on a number of salient variables, including the size of the relative investment, coverage of different business models and value chains, inclusion of different types of companies and funds, coverage of key home and host countries (including investors from developed and developing economies), different crops and so on. The objective was to obtain a diverse sample of investors.

The sample includes both domestic investors and foreign investors from a range of countries, developed and developing. Of the ten investors, four were

---

3 Throughout this chapter the terms 'investment' and 'investor' are used interchangeably to describe the agribusinesses examined in this survey. Investment in agriculture involves a much wider set of actors apart from large-scale agribusinesses, and includes—most notably—small farmers investing in their own farms.

pure estate business models, four were processing operations and two were nucleus estate with outgrower models. The products included palm oil, rice, rubber, spices, vegetables, animal feed, and coffee. The size of land allocation ranged from less than 100 hectares to over 50,000 hectares. As such, the sample reflects a broad spectrum of agricultural investments. In South-East Asia, the sample comprises five investments in Cambodia, two in Vietnam and one each in Indonesia, Malaysia, and Lao People's Democratic Republic. Three investors were domestic, two were Thai, and one each were from India, China, Singapore, the UK, and the USA, respectively. The main products were palm oil (three investments) and rice (two), while there was one investment each in rubber, spices, vegetables, animal feed, and coffee. Five investments were operating on less than 100 hectares, three on between 100 and 10,000, one on between 10,000 and 50,000, and one investment had a land allocation greater than 50,0000 hectares.

Interviews were conducted on a confidential basis. This was an important condition for investors to be able to share information in a frank and open fashion. Nevertheless, the sample was constrained in that it could only include those investments that were willing to participate and, indeed, many investors contacted declined to participate or did not respond to our requests. In that regard, there is some bias in the sample towards relatively 'good' investors—that is to say, those with social and environmental programmes and those performing better operationally and financially. One would expect that these investors would be more likely to agree to allow researchers on-site. That caveat must be acknowledged but it should not be overplayed. In fact, the sample contained several investors that have been portrayed in a negative light in the media or by civil society groups.

Researchers spent around two to three days on-site with each agribusiness, conducting interviews with senior management to complete a semi-structured questionnaire, covering financial, human resources and operational information on the investment, as well details of the investor's approach to a wide range of socio-economic and environmental issues.[4]

---

4   The range of operational questions/variables included an orientation of the farm/business and its operations; copies of any useful background documents—farm map, concession agreement, model employment contract, environmental impact assessment, organogram, etc.; details of ownership structure and entities; details of farm size and enterprises; history of the operation and the surrounding area; personnel details—numbers, structure, employment conditions, training, etc.; outgrowers' details—contractual arrangements, prices, quality requirements, etc.; markets for product(s) and sources of inputs; perspectives on the success of the investment and the constraints experienced; and tax and incentives. A study of the investor's approach to social and environmental issues enabled an assessment of the extent to which a responsible agricultural approach to investments was being taken. These

A *further* two to three days were spent interviewing a wide range of stake-holders in local communities. These interviews were conducted on a confidential and anonymous basis and in an open-ended fashion, allowing stakeholders to raise the issues that are important to them. This approach was taken because (a) the intention was to elicit the issues and obtain some sort of 'qualitative weighting', without assuming that the results were definitive (the findings will be used to partly establish the parameters and framework for future work); and (b) when being asked for details of actual situations, interviewees can respond concretely not formulaically, and the interviewer is able to tease out issues during the discussion. The researchers sought to capture the views of a broad cross section of the community and other local stakeholders. Figure 4.2 provides the salient characteristics of the sample of stakeholders. One-third of the community interviewees were women. In total, 93 separate interviews were conducted. Some interviews included more than one person such that the total number of persons interviewed was 154.

In addition to the first-hand data obtained, media, civil society and other reports on each investor were consulted (including internal reports and documentation). A number of interviews were conducted with NGOs working on relevant issues, such as land rights or the environment, in the countries visited. These materials helped inform the thinking of the researchers, improved understanding of local contexts, and provided another lens through which to view information obtained through the fieldwork.

The write-ups of the company questionnaires and stakeholder interviews were imported into Nvivo, a software package designed for the analysis of large amounts of qualitative and quantitative data. The programme allows the researcher to classify (or 'code') the data according to particular themes (e.g. employment, resettlement, prices for outgrowers). Nvivo was also used to facilitate the quantification of qualitative socio-economic and environmental impacts obtained during the stakeholder interviews. This is in addition to the pure qualitative assessment of the extensive information received during the fieldwork, which was sorted, compared and analysed on a purely qualitative basis.

The remainder of this chapter is accordingly structured as follows: Section 3 provides a high-level assessment of the socio-economic impact of the investments studied, based on quantitative summary measures of information

---

questions/variables include land rights and natural resource rights; food security; consultation procedures; transparency; community development and social sustainability; impact assessments and monitoring; environmental impact and sustainability; grievance and redress mechanisms; human rights and best practice policies; and women and vulnerable communities.

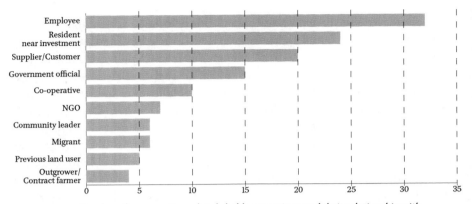

FIGURE 4.2 *Number of community and stakeholder interviews and their relationship with*
investing companies[a]
(a) Refers to the number of interviews conducted, some of which may have
included multiple interviewees. More than one category can apply to each interview:
for example an employee who was also a previous land user.
SOURCE: UNCTAD, FDI-TNC-GVC INFORMATION SYSTEM, FDI/TNC DATABASE
(WWW.UNCTAD.ORG/FDISTATISTICS).

obtained in stakeholder interviews. It then provides more detail on the key
issues identified using a quantitative and qualitative analysis of the material
obtained in both stakeholder interviews and interviews with investors. Section
4 translates those findings into potential policies and practices that can be
applied by investors, governments and civil society groups to maximise benefits and minimise risks, by applying observations of what has worked and what
has not worked at the investments studied. Finally, Section 5 concludes with a
discussion of complementary work and future research.

3　Findings: The Socio-Economic Impact on Communities in South-East Asia

3.1　*Overall Assessment*

The investments studied generated both positive and negative socio-economic
impacts on surrounding communities and host countries. Figures 4.3 and 4.4
show the most common positive and negative impacts of the investments
surveyed—as mentioned during the community and stakeholder interviews
detailed in Figure 4.2—providing an overview of how these investments were
perceived by those affected by them.

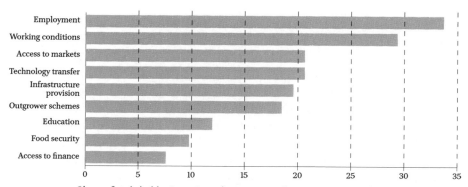

FIGURE 4.3 *Share of stakeholder interviews that mentioned a positive impact, by issue: investments in Asia.*

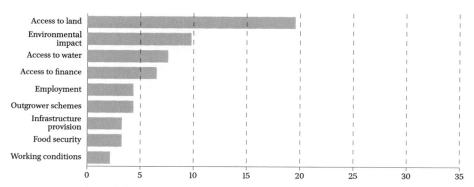

FIGURE 4.4 *Share of stakeholder interviews that mentioned a negative impact, by issue: investments in Asia.*

Notes: Figures 4.3 and 4.4 were created by classifying information from stakeholder interviews into whether the investment was perceived to have had a positive or negative impact, with the information further categorised by issue within each of these two top-level classifications. For example, an interviewee who stated he was happy to have a job with the investor would be classified as having described a positive impact with respect to employment. Some issues appear as both a positive and a negative impact because there can be both positive and negative dimensions to an investment's impact with respect to each issue. For example, an investor may have improved local water access by installing hand pumps, but may also have had a negative impact by polluting water sources used by local communities due to environmentally unsound agricultural practices. In total, 93 separate interviews were conducted. Some interviews included more than one person such that the total number of persons interviewed was 154.

SOURCE: UNCTAD-WORLD BANK SURVEY OF RESPONSIBLE AGRICULTURAL INVESTMENT DATABASE.

Overall, the indications are that local communities and other stakeholders interviewed felt that the benefits of the investments outweighed the negative impacts (Figure 4.5). Nevertheless, there is a wide range of outcomes arising from these investments in terms of their socio-economic and environmental impacts, their broader impact on the host country, and the operational and financial success of the investment itself. There are some operations that have generated mostly positive perceived outcomes, while others have produced mostly negative ones (Figure 4.6). Most exhibit a mixture of positive and negative impacts, performing well with respect to some aspects, but with significant room for improvement with regards to others. Investments in Asia were distributed throughout the sample, indicating that they had not systematically performed better or worse than investments in Africa.

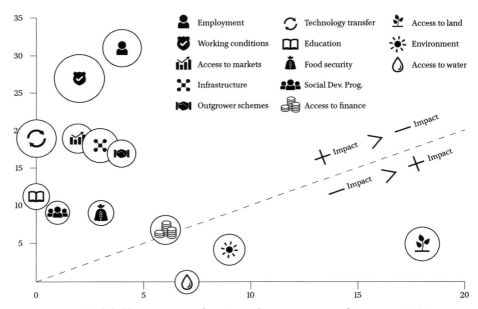

FIGURE 4.5 *Stakeholder perceptions of positive and negative impacts of investments in Asia, classified by issue[a].*
(a) The vertical axis shows the number of stakeholders who mentioned the investment as having had a positive impact on them with regard to that issue. The horizontal axis shows the number of stakeholders who mentioned the investment as having had a negative impact. The size of the bubbles represents the relative frequency with which each issue arose in stakeholder interviews, whether in a positive, negative, or neutral context.
SOURCE: UNCTAD-WORLD BANK SURVEY OF RESPONSIBLE AGRICULTURAL INVESTMENT DATABASE.

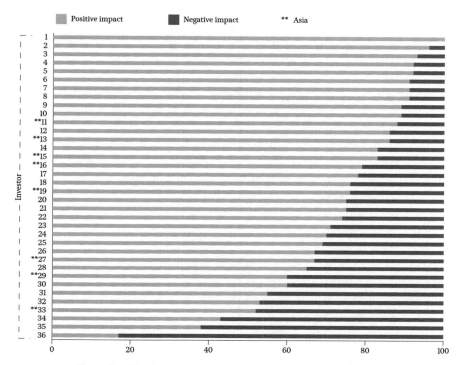

FIGURE 4.6 *Share of positive / negative socio-economic impacts mentioned in stakeholder interviews, entire sample (a).*

(a) All impacts of the investment mentioned in stakeholder interviews are classified as 'positive' or 'negative'. Chart shows the balance of positive and negative mentions for each investor.

SOURCE: UNCTAD-WORLD BANK SURVEY OF RESPONSIBLE AGRICULTURAL INVESTMENT DATABASE.

While figures 4.3–4.6 present an overview of the quantification of socio-economic and environmental impacts obtained during the stakeholder interviews, the detailed analysis in the following section relies on a qualitative assessment of the extensive information gathered during the fieldwork, information that has been examined and assessed on a primarily qualitative basis.

3.2   *Detailed Findings*
3.2.1   Employment
Job creation was the most frequently cited *benefit* arising from the investments. The investments studied in Asia employed around 7,000 people (Table 4.1) in total. This refers to direct employment by the investor, the number of indirect jobs created being difficult to assess. As an indication of the

possible scale of further job creation, two rice producers in Cambodia employed 12,500 and 30,000 contract farmers, respectively (though these farmers may not work exclusively for these investors). Similarly one coffee processor contracts to 1,500 distributors in Vietnam, and another works with 2,800 farmers, also in Vietnam. Beyond this, there are various multiplier and other indirect effects leading to further jobs being created—or destroyed. To get a full idea of the impact on job creation/destruction, further work is required.

Direct job creation was relatively more land-efficient in Asia—that is to say approximately 14 hectares per job in Asia (Table 4.1)—compared with investments in Africa. This is partly because the sample of Asian investors included more processing operations, underscoring the point that the benefits of investment in agriculture can arise even in the absence of large-scale land allocations. Large land allocations do not necessarily create the most jobs per hectare.

The share of permanent jobs as a proportion of total employment was higher in Asia than in the full sample, at around 70 per cent, compared with 50 per cent for the full sample. This is reflected in the more positive perception of working conditions that emerged from stakeholder interviews in Asia. Most investments visited paid higher wages than those available locally and those wages were sufficient for employees to maintain a decent standard of living. Several interviewees compared wages at agricultural investments favourably with those available in other industries in which foreign investors were present (for example, the garment industry in Cambodia).

TABLE 4.1   *Direct employment created, descriptive statistics: Asian investments*

	Sum of Asian Invest.	Mean	Median	Max.	Min.	Female share(a)	Expat share(a)	Hectare/ job
Total formal employment	6,825	683	252	2,647	120	32%	1%	14
Permanent	4,655	466	145	2,647	40	26%	2%	20
Temporary/Casual/ Seasonal	2,170	217	20	1,200	0	38%	0%	44

(a) Not all investors provided female and expat share figures. These percentages are based on the subset of investors that did (i.e. eight out of ten).

SOURCE: UNCTAD-WORLD BANK SURVEY OF RESPONSIBLE AGRICULTURAL INVESTMENT DATABASE.

Employment of expatriates was low in the sample, but not all jobs went to the population directly surrounding the investment. And expatriates were over-represented in management positions. In almost all cases, semi-skilled, unskilled, and casual or seasonal employment was sourced from the host countries. But employees were not necessarily from surrounding communities and sometimes came from other parts of the country, including the capital city. This in some instances led to tensions between the local community and the domestic migrant community.

There was a considerable gender imbalance at most investments, both in terms of numbers and the types of jobs on offer. Only around one-third of employees were women, and they were more likely to hold casual, temporary, or seasonal jobs. As such, women were overrepresented in the worst paid and most insecure jobs.

3.2.2   Impact on Outgrowers

Investors also contributed to employment opportunities by providing a stable market for outgrowers' produce: for example, the 11 investors with outgrower schemes helped to support—at least in part—the livelihoods of 30,000 contract farmers in total. According to stakeholders interviewed, the concomitant rise in rural incomes contributed positively to food security, directly and indirectly. As such, outgrower schemes interact significantly with several of the key benefits shown in Figure 4.3, notably technology transfer, access to markets, and food security. Impacts therefore had a wider dispersal vis-à-vis stakeholders than in cases where the investments were estates only, and perceptions of positive impact from the investment were generally higher, although arguably some of the perceived negative impacts were more diffused (i.e. blame, where it existed, assigned to outgrower farmers and not just to the principal investor). At the same time, the perceptions of the outgrowers also need to be taken into consideration.

Outgrower schemes can be effective in supporting livelihoods while allowing people to retain their most valuable asset—their land. Governments should consider which investors and business models are likely to maximise direct and indirect employment as these are key benefits of agricultural investment. Governments should consider the whole value chain and promote value-addition downstream of the raw materials produced from the land made available (a number of investors were processors, for instance), thereby maximising employment and other benefits. However, marginalised groups, including women and minorities, *were less likely to participate* in outgrower schemes. Consideration should be given to how to improve access for these groups.

The main advantage for outgrowers selling to major agricultural investors was higher prices and reliable, timely payments—a perception reiterated by senior management and outgrowers alike. But even major investors faced cash flow problems and some outgrowers—particularly those who have been assured a guaranteed minimum price for all their produce—have sometimes not been paid according to the agreed terms. More commonly, outgrowers lost money owed when investors faced capacity constraints. For crops that must be processed soon after they are harvested—including rubber, sugar, and palm oil—this occurred when investors did not facilitate timely pickups to transport outgrowers' produce to the processing site, or lacked sufficient factory space to process the raw materials once there.

Outgrowers tended to feel excluded from price-setting mechanisms— prices were usually set by the government, major industry players, the investors themselves, or a combination of these actors, always based in part on international market prices for the commodity. Despite company efforts to inform their outgrowers of current prices and mechanisms, pricing was often contentious, with many outgrowers voicing concerns about how their produce was quantified and assessed for quality, as well as about the final sum they received. Thus there is a need for good communication between farmers and company management about how prices are set, and for improved safeguards to ensure these prices are appropriately remunerative.

For instance, in Indonesia the price paid in each region for fresh fruit bunches of oil palm was set monthly through a multi-stakeholder process, involving members of the provincial plantation agriculture department, company management, and representatives of cooperatives. Those involved used a predetermined formula to fix the price; and one variable, the oil extraction rate, was the subject of much negotiation each month. Once a price was agreed, a formal notification was signed by the government, company, and outgrower representatives, obliging the investor to pay the set price.

3.2.3   Land Rights and Access to Land

The most prominent negative impacts arising in the investments examined were disputes over access to land. People's lives in rural communities are intimately tied up with their access to land and other natural resources and the arrival of an investor can have significant implications. Interviewees had, on balance, negative perceptions of the impact of investments across a range of land-related issues, including previous use of the land; the terms of, and process for, land acquisition; resettlement procedures; access to, and use of, the land by communities; the degree of land use practiced by the investor; and the rights of pastoral farmers and other customary land users.

Local communities often did not understand what rights to land they have under the laws of the country and frequently did not have formal titling deeds, even if they had been working the land for many years or generations. The situation was more complex in post-conflict countries where formal cadastral records had been lost during the conflict and a national land titling process was in progress.

Another common grievance was the failure to use the land in accordance with expectations. The under-use of allocated land was, however, a more prominent negative issue in Africa as compared with our Asian sample. Nevertheless, one investor in Cambodia appeared to be using its large land allocation for timber extraction only and not respecting its commitment to subsequently develop a rubber plantation on the land cleared. In this and other cases in the country, the failure to develop land resulted from inadequate financial capacity. Some investors have sufficient financial backing to acquire the land but not to develop it.

This risk can be minimised through full and early assessment and consultation of existing formal and informal rights to, and usage of, the land. Such consultations should be first and foremost the responsibility of the investor, with appropriate monitoring from state and non-state actors. It proved perilous to leave consultations to the host government; or for the investor to assume that the land acquired was being provided by the government without any existing land disputes. Similarly, it was unsatisfactory to outsource the consultation process to third parties such as land agents. Governments or land agents sometimes claimed to have 'prepared the land'—that is, left it issue-free for the investor to take over. Their claims that all land conflicts had been dealt with often proved spurious.

A lack of transparency with regard to the terms and process of land acquisition had important consequences. Uncertainty about investor actions and intentions created a sense of fear and resentment within communities nearby, with adverse consequences for the investment. For example, some members of one local community asked the researchers whether the investor nearby planned to take their land. This situation could in part have been avoided by greater transparency about the investor's operation.

Beyond such general aspects, a set of more financially-inclusive business models have begun to emerge and have been successful in forging partnerships with local communities, including over issues related to land. In explicit revenue-sharing arrangements, for example, an investor operates on community or native land and, rather than renting the land, enters into a revenue-sharing arrangement based on a certain percentage of the monthly turnover. These schemes are beneficial because they provide a continuous revenue stream across generations and genuine community-private partnerships in which communities take an interest in the success of the operation.

Since 2011, a palm oil company in Sarawak (Malaysia) has adopted a new business model whereby the company rents land from owners of Native Customary Rights (NCR) land to develop it for the cultivation of oil palm for a period of 30 years, after which the land and the palms will be returned to the land's owners. The company will bear the costs of development and after the third year—when the palms start to bear fruit—the company will pay each owner a fixed rental per tree until the expiry of the 30-year lease. The company has chosen this model as it is viewed as a more equitable and fairer proposition than the approach used by other companies in Sarawak whereby about 60 per cent of the ownership of the land would eventually be transferred to the company and the owners of NCR land would have only 30 per cent ownership.

3.2.4 Building In Responsibility and Sustainability: Initial Phases of the Investment

A key finding is that investor and host country actions at the pre-investment stage and during the initial phases of the investment are critical. This includes the investors' approach to consultations and engagement with local communities, impact assessments and transparency, and the host country government's pre-screening and monitoring of investors. While it is important that socially and environmentally responsible practices are embedded within the operation and monitoring of an investment on an ongoing basis, it is the processes followed, decisions taken, and requirements enforced in these early stages that dictate much of the future path of the investment.

In the investments studied, consultations were a key step in developing a strong relationship between the investors and the local communities. This generated more positive socio-economic outcomes and was in the interests of the investors because it contributed to financial and operational success, in particular by minimising the risk of land disputes. While initial consultations could be time-consuming and expensive, particularly for new investments, attempts to rush the process—due to the commercial expediency of getting the land acquisition settled quickly—led to negative long-term ramifications, both for the businesses and for the local communities, over a protracted period.

As mentioned above, stakeholder consultation was most effective when it was the responsibility of the investor. Host governments should establish regulations or guidelines for the conduct of such consultations and stringently monitor adherence, but not conduct these activities for investors. Ensuring community interests are represented requires the involvement of state and non-state actors. Some countries have enacted legislation requiring government oversight of community consultations. This has helped to ensure that investment projects have supported national and local development goals.

Formally established procedures through which stakeholders can raise grievances and seek redress also contributed to better relations with local communities. The best examples of grievance and redress mechanisms were those that were more formalised, typically involving a Community Liaison Committee on which the investor and the local community were represented.

In many cases, pre-screening of foreign investors can be improved to increase the prevalence of investors likely to make a positive contribution to the host country. Pre-screening should include, as a minimum, assessment of investors' financial strength and technical capabilities, their proposed approach with respect to consultations and impact assessments, and their commitments in terms of the benefits that the investor will bring to the host country.

Pre-screening, however, should not extend to producing business plans on behalf of investors, plans that are then in effect sold as part of the concession agreement. Business plans provided by host governments were often based on unrealistic assumptions and sub-standard assessments of crop suitability and other environmental factors. A rubber plantation in Cambodia was being operated on soil that interviews with surrounding communities quickly identified as being inappropriate for rubber production.

Social and environmental impact assessments (SEIAS) are another important tool for building responsibility and sustainability into the initial phases of an investment. There was a noticeable trend of investors taking their environmental responsibilities more seriously, undertaking social and environmental impact assessments, employing internal environmental management plans (EMPs), and making public their environmental policies. Investors cited increasing pressure from host country governments and the demands of certification processes as key drivers for this trend.

Yet SEIAS were too often 'box ticking' exercises, carried out merely to secure a license to operate rather than used as a tool to be actively incorporated into the conduct of the business. Many impact assessments were one-off assessments, not accompanied by a system of ongoing monitoring and adherence to recommendations for changes to operations. Some EMPs only existed on paper and were not authentic tools used to manage the environmental impact of the investment.

As with consultations, the government's role in impact assessments was most effective when limited to monitoring and ensuring proper conduct and implementation. This included providing detailed legal requirements covering what is expected of investors and the stipulation of requirements for third-party, independent auditing of such assessments.

SEIAS should also be transparent. In Malaysia, for example, assessments are published on the Department of Environment website. In other countries, much less information is available publicly. This lack of transparency applies to other areas too. In general, there was an insufficient amount of publicly available information to ensure the fully transparent and accountable conduct of agricultural investment.

Once these initial phases have been completed, commitments made as part of the consultation, screening, and impact assessment projects need to be monitored by the host government. Ongoing monitoring of agricultural investments by host governments was often limited and productivity-focused. All investors were subject to some form of monitoring, typically by departments of agriculture, land, labour, or the environment. But when government officials came to assess agricultural concessions, they often focused on ensuring the investor was meeting productivity targets, with little monitoring of the socio-economic and environmental impacts of an investment. The results or details of government monitoring were rarely made publicly available, making it difficult for other interested parties—be they local residents or civil society representatives—to hold investors to account.

Some governments had allowed foreign investment in agriculture to proceed at a pace beyond their ability to realistically assess and monitor the investors. Wherever necessary, governments should consider how to improve their monitoring capacity and, if necessary, consider slowing down the approval of new agricultural investments.

3.2.5   The Financial and Operational Performance of Investors
A somewhat surprising finding from the overall study, at least at first glance, is that many investors were in operational and financial difficulties. Around 45 per cent of investors were materially behind schedule or operating below capacity. About the same share were unprofitable at the time of the survey. The Asian investments tended to be performing better, with around 80 per cent profitable at the time of the survey and around one-third behind schedule.

A key distinction between the better or worse performers is linked to whether they have acquired substantial amounts of land or not. The Asian experience reflects findings in the wider sample that processing operations or those that do not involve large land allocations tended to be more successful—that is to say, processors/outgrowers as opposed to estates/estates plus outgrowers (Figure 4.7). Many of the latter investments were spending significant time and resources dealing with land disputes that could and should have

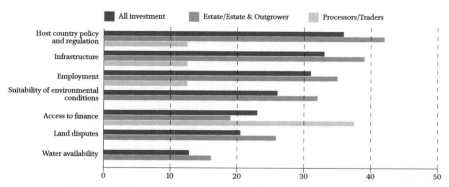

FIGURE 4.7 *Percentage of investors mentioning particular constraints on operations.*
SOURCE: UNCTAD-WORLD BANK SURVEY OF RESPONSIBLE AGRICULTURAL
INVESTMENT DATABASE.

been identified and appropriately handled via pre-investment consultation
and impact assessment procedures.

Investors highlighted a number of constraints that hindered their prospects
of success (Figure 4.7). They noted the importance of host country governments in creating an enabling environment that allows investors to survive,
thrive and contribute to the local community and the broader economy.
International investors in several countries experienced a lack of a clear, transparent and consistent approach towards foreign investment in agriculture,
including policies and procedures for the purchase or lease of land. Access to
finance, inadequate infrastructure and difficulties in sourcing local, qualified
staff were other key constraints on profitability.

Financial and operational success is an essential precondition for agricultural investments to make a positive contribution to development, whereas
failure can create lose-lose-lose situations for investors, host countries and local
communities alike. In this regard, investors noted the importance of striking
the right balance between, on the one hand, imposing necessary requirements
and regulations that promote responsible investment, and, on the other, ensuring that requirements were not so burdensome as to preclude much needed
investment by agribusinesses.

A key finding of this research is that a potentially win-win situation
vis-à-vis investment performance and investments' wider positive economic,
social, and environmental impact *is* achievable. In the survey, investors that
were financially and operationally successful tended also to be those that
had the most positive impact on their host economies and surrounding
communities—the result of more sophisticated approaches to social and

environmental responsibility. Similarly, those investments that were well-integrated within the host country and surrounding community were most likely to be financially successful. Investors that acquired land but did not conduct thorough impact assessments and consultations with communities, or left it to host governments to conduct them on their behalf, often found themselves subsequently dealing with costly and time-consuming land disputes.

3.2.6   Environmental Impact

Almost all investors had cultivation and operational models the environmental impacts of which are likely to be negative, and the assessment and management of which was often deficient. Most of the cultivation operations visited were undertaking intensive production operations of one or two crops, often involving extensive use of pesticides. Such intensive use of land and water contributes to degradation and depletion of these resources and a loss of biodiversity. Most investors have undertaken some measures to mitigate the negative environmental impact of their operations. Although these are initiatives that should be welcomed, it is important to note that they do not generate a positive or even a neutral environmental impact, but merely reduce to some extent the overall negative environmental impact of the investments studied in this research.

One exception was in Cambodia where one investor is promoting organic farming in a model farm that would comply both with guidelines under the International Foundation for Organic Agriculture (IFOAM) and with Indian Organic Certification Agency (INDOCERT) requirements for production of certified organic products. Agrochemicals and chemical fertilisers are not used. The farm maintains 30 cows to produce its own compost and organic fertilisers from cow dung and urine. Weeding is done manually.

Minimal tillage is practiced and the ground is protected by vegetation (mainly weeds) to prevent soil erosion. Crop rotation is practiced. The company is considering the feasibility of installing windmills to provide electricity to the farm and to the neighbouring village. The model farm is rain-fed for about 7–8 months in the year. In order to ensure that there is an adequate water supply during the dry months, the company has dug a network of 30 water-harvesting and retention ponds at low points around the farm. Rain harvesting is also carried out from the roof of the workers' quarters and other buildings.

More broadly, the environmental impact of the investments studies was difficult to discern, and so will be the subject of further research. Although environmental issues were not raised often in the stakeholder interviews, this cannot be taken as an indicator of limited environmental impact. Interviewees would tend to raise only those obvious issues that they directly experience (such as those mentioned above). But most environmental consequences materialise gradually and may not be immediately obvious to surrounding communities. Although some government environmental officials were interviewed, the results tended to reinforce the above conclusions about the inadequacy of environmental monitoring.

4   Lessons Learnt and Policy Implications

A number of key findings from the research described in this chapter have implications for investors, governments, and civil society. In particular, the research finds that issues such as due diligence, consultations with communities, financially inclusive business models, environmental impact assessments and transparency issues are crucial for investors to get right. In a similar vein, host governments need to pay special attention to aspects such as the pre-screening and selection of investors, ongoing monitoring of investments, conduct of consultations, impact assessments and business plans, phasing of investment approvals, and land rights. Finally, activities such as engagement with investors, monitoring of investors, and helping investors forge partnerships with marginalised groups are areas in which the active participation of local communities and NGOs can make a difference. Building on this, including the broader study of the sample of cases in Africa, it is possible to suggest policies and practices for governments, investors and civil society groups (in Asia and beyond) that, if implemented with due regard to local contingencies, can improve the chances of beneficial outcomes and minimise the risks of negative impacts associated with investments in agriculture.[5]

As discussed in the introduction to this chapter, and reinforced by the empirical findings of this study (and other research), the business models deployed and the investor-community relationships developed are central to both investment performance and impact on communities and economies. The differential outcomes of business models is most readily evinced, for example—in Section 3 of this chapter—in terms of employment generated and the performance of companies; while the investor-community relationship's importance can be discerned most readily in the analysis of land rights/

---

5   An UNCTAD and World Bank 2014 report provides numerous case study examples of best and worst practices, and a fuller discussion of lessons for investors, governments, and others.

access to land and investor actions vis-à-vis stakeholders in the early phases of an investment. Some of the key implications of these findings for the policies and practices of *investors* are:

- Early engagement and consultation with surrounding communities, including previous and existing users of the land.
- Transparency about the operation and ongoing dialogue with stakeholders, including the establishment of a formal grievance procedure.
- Social development programmes that reflect local communities' development visions.
- A financially inclusive business model.
- Proper conduct of social and environmental impact assessments (SEIAS) and their integration within business models.
- Setting of, and adherence to, realistic expectations about the pace of development of operations; use of land in accordance with commitments.
- Phasing of the investment, for example applying for and successfully developing a parcel of land before seeking a larger allocation.
- Fair and adequate remuneration, contractual conditions, and training for employees and outgrowers.
- Resolution of the business model prior to introducing outgrowers.

As knowledge of how to better the impact of investment in agriculture improves, there are policy implications for governments, often as counterparts to those for investors. Thus notable policy considerations for *governments* include:

- Rigorous pre-screening of potential investors' experience, financial capacity and technical capabilities.
- Obtaining from foreign investors commitments to social development programmes, employment, and other benefits to the host country, as well as a detailed schedule for the development of operations.
- Ongoing monitoring of investors' agreements and commitments.
- Monitoring consultations and SEIAS, but not conducting them on an investor's behalf.
- A clear, transparent regulatory framework for land acquisition (purchase or lease), consultations, resettlement, and compensation.
- Formalised local community tenure rights under a proper land registry system.
- Approval of foreign investment applications in line with the capacity to screen and monitor investors.

- Encourage phasing of investments, rather than mega-land deals; for example, providing an initial allocation of land, with further allocations contingent upon its successful development.
- Monitoring and enforcement of adherence to environmental and water regulations.
- Encouragement of innovation (new crops, technology, etc.), but not initially on a large scale.
- Reducing red tape and creating an enabling environment for foreign investment and the development of domestic industry.

Finally, civil society groups also have a vital role to play, not least in supporting local communities, for instance in the initial setting up of investment operations and longer-term monitoring. For instance, *civil society* groups could:

- Engage with investors to help them forge partnerships with marginalised groups and ensure that relevant stakeholders are included in decision-making processes.
- Help local communities to be well-organised, and to understand their rights and how to exercise them.
- Monitor conflicts between investors and stakeholders and constructively draw attention to important issues.

5   Conclusions and Further Work

The diversity of experiences, performance, and impacts of investments analysed in this chapter suggests that a wide range of factors influence the outcomes of an agricultural investment, and its impact on the local community and economy. Some factors are context specific. As such, one cannot be categorical about the types of investment that are most or least desirable, but business models adopted by investors, and specific approaches, policies, and practices adopted were shown to have a bearing on the outcome of investments. The nature of investor-community relationships, and the distribution of benefits (and costs) between the investor and the community, and within the community (the local economy) itself, also affect the overall impact. As discussed in the previous section, this can lead to actionable policies and practices for investors, governments, and communities.

The study on which this chapter is based has sought to contribute to the growing body of knowledge of what the responsible and sustainable conduct of agricultural investment consists of in practical, operational terms for communities, governments, and investors. In addition to the policy lessons outlined above, analysis of the range and type of impacts, and factors influencing the beneficial or negative outcomes of such impacts, can be used in concrete ways. For example, UNCTAD, the International Institute for Sustainable Development (IISD), and the World Bank are putting together a foundation for model contracts/contract clauses for investment in agriculture, using concrete examples of how to maximise the gains and minimise the risks of private sector participation in the agricultural sectors of developing countries, with information taken from this study and other works.

However, effective action by policymakers in specific areas of concern relating to investment in agriculture requires additional thoroughgoing work. Thus, in late 2014 UNCTAD and the World Bank embarked on a further, more concentrated (fewer cases), in-depth (focusing on specific issues gleaned from the first study, with a larger number of community/stakeholder participants) study on a selected sub-group of the original operations/communities visited. Among other aims, this research seeks to investigate the internal differences within local communities in terms of the impact of investments. That is, picking up on the variations in perceptions of impact within the communities mentioned in the introduction to this chapter, the study asks which particular groups or persons win or lose from investments and, more importantly, under what circumstances.

Finally, many of the decisions and actions that determine the ultimate outcome of investments are taken prior to the investment or during its initial phases. For this reason, UNCTAD and the World Bank, along with FAO and the International Fund for Agricultural Development (IFAD), also launched—in 2015—a new field programme working with investors, communities, governments, and other stakeholders from the *outset of new operations*. The primary objective of this next stage of the work is to infuse responsible and inclusive practices (taken from extant research, as discussed earlier) into agribusiness operations—*including vis-à-vis investor-community relationships*—from the outset, and to ensure that the outcomes of these operations work to the benefit of local communities, the environment and the economy as a whole. Along the way, the research aims to create context-aware procedures, processes, approaches and documentation—a toolkit, as it were—for building inclusive and development-friendly investment-community relationships and outcomes.

References

Anseeuw, W., L. Alden Wily, L. Cotula and M. Taylor (2012) *Land Rights and the Rush for Land: Findings of the Global Commercial Pressures on Land Research Project* (Rome: International Land Coalition), http://www.landcoalition.org/sites/default/files/publication/1205/ILCGSR report_ ENG.pdf (accessed on 7 May 2015).

Chamberlain-Van Den Werf, W. and W. Anseeuw (2015) *Making Land and Agricultural Investment Work for Development and Shared Prosperity—Assessment of Inclusive Business Models*, paper presented at the 2015 World Bank Conference on Land and Poverty, March 23–27, Washington, D.C., https://www.conftool.com/landand poverty2015/index.php/Chamberlain_-_Van_der_Werf-440-440_paper.pdf?page= downloadPaper&filename=Chamberlain_-_Van_der_Werf-440-440_paper.pdf& form_id=440 (accessed on 7 May 2015).

Cotula, L. and R. Leonard (eds.) (2010) *Alternatives to Land Acquisitions: Agricultural Investment and Collaborative Business Models* (London, Bern, Rome and Maputo: IIED–SDC–IFAD–CTV), http://www.ifad.org/pub/land/alternatives.pdf (accessed on 7 May 2015).

Deininger, K. and D. Byerlee (2011) *Rising Global Interest in Farmland: Can It Yield Sustainable and Equitable Benefits?* (Washington, D.C.: World Bank–International Bank for Reconstruction and Development), http://siteresources.worldbank.org/DEC/Resources/Rising-Global-Interest-in-Farmland.pdf (accessed on 7 May 2015).

De Los Reyes, V.R., J.L. Capacio, A. Garcia and J.V. La Chica (2015) *Agribusiness and Smallholder Farmers in the Philippines: A Free Hand, Increased Bargaining Power, or Contract Regulation?*, paper presented at the 2015 World Bank Conference on Land and Poverty, March 23–27, Washington, D.C., https://www.conftool.com/landand poverty2015/index.php/delos_Reyes-642-642.doc?page=downloadPaper&file name=delos_Reyes-642-642.doc&form_id=642 (accessed on 7 May 2015).

Deng, D. (2012) *Handbook on Community Engagement: A 'Good Practice' Guide to Negotiating Lease Agreements with Landowning Communities in South Sudan* (Juba: South Sudan Law Society), http://namati.org/resources/handbook-on-community-engagement-a-good-practice-guide-to-negotiating-lease-agreements-with-land-owning-communities-in-south-sudan/ (accessed on 7 May 2015).

Eaton, H. and A. Shepherd (2001) *Contract Farming: Partnerships for Growth*, FAO Agricultural Services Bulletin 145 (Rome: Food and Agriculture Organization), http://www.fao.org/docrep/014/y0937e/y0937e00.pdf (accessed on 7 May 2015).

FAO (Food and Agriculture Organization) (2013) *Trends and Impacts of Foreign Investment in Developing Country Agriculture: Evidence from Case Studies* (Rome: FAO), http://www.fao.org/docrep/017/i3112e/i3112e.pdf (accessed on 7 May 2015).

———— (2012a) *The State of Food and Agriculture: Investing in Agriculture for a Better Future* (Rome: FAO), http://www.fao.org/docrep/017/i3028e/i3028e.pdf (accessed on 7 May 2015).

———— (2012b) *Voluntary Guidelines on the Responsible Governance of Tenure of Land, Fisheries and Forests in the Context of National Food Security* (Rome: FAO), http://www.fao.org/docrep/016/i2801e/i2801e.pdf (accessed on 7 May 2015).

Gaertner, K.M., F. Ishikawa, T. Masuoka and B. Jenkins (2014) *Shared Prosperity Through Inclusive Business: How Successful Companies Reach the Base of the Pyramid* (Washington, D.C.: International Finance Corporation), http://www.ifc.org/wps/wcm/connect/bf203d80463da1548c90bd9916182e35/SharedProsperitythruiBiz_FINAL.pdf?MOD=AJPERES (accessed on 7 May 2015).

HLPE (High Level Panel of Experts) (2013) *Investing in Smallholder Agriculture for Food Security, A Report by the High Level Panel of Experts on Food Security and Nutrition* (Rome: Committee on World Food Security), http://www.fao.org/3/a-i2953e.pdf (accessed on 7 May 2015).

IFAD (International Fund for Agricultural Development) and TechnoServe (2011) *Outgrower Schemes—Enhancing Profitability*, Technical Brief, September (Rome and Washington, D.C.: IFAD and TechnoServe), http://www.technoserve.org/files/downloads/outgrower-brief-september.pdf (accessed on 7 May).

IFAD and UNEP (United Nations Environment Programme) (2013) *Smallholders, Food Security and the Environment* (Rome: IFAD), http://www.ifad.org/climate/resources/smallholders_report.pdf (accessed on 7 May 2015).

Lahiff, E., N. Davis and T. Manenzhe (2012) *Joint Ventures in Agriculture: Lessons from Land Reform Projects in South Africa* (London, Rome and Capetown: IIED–IFAD–FAO–PLAAS), http://pubs.iied.org/pdfs/12569IIED.pdf (accessed on 7 May 2015).

Mann, H. and C. Smaller (2009) *A Thirst for Distant Lands: Foreign Investment in Agricultural Land and Water* (Winnepeg: International Institute for Sustainable Development), http://www.iisd.org/pdf/2009/thirst_for_distant_lands.pdf (accessed on 7 May 2015).

Rösler, U., D. Hollman, J. Naguib, A. Oppermann and C. Rosendahl (2013) *Inclusive Business Models: Options for Support through PSD Programmes* (Bonn: Deutsche Gesellschaft für Internationale Zusammenarbeit), http://www.giz.de/fachexpertise/downloads/giz2014-ib-models-rz.pdf (accessed on 7 May 2015).

Schonevel, G.C. (2014) 'The Geographic and Sectoral Patterns of Large-Scale Farmland Investments in Sub-Saharan Africa', *Food Policy*, 48, pp. 34–50, DOI: 10.1016/j.foodpol.2014.03.007.

Special Representative on Human Rights (2011) *Guiding Principles on Business and Human Rights: Implementing the United Nations "Protect, Respect and Remedy" Framework, Report of the Special Representative of the Secretary General on the Issue of Human Rights and Transnational Corporations and Other Business Enterprises, John Ruggie*, UN doc. A/HRC/17/31, 21 March.

Tyler, G. and G. Dixie (2012) *Investing in Agribusiness: A Retrospective View of a Development Bank's Investments in Agribusiness in Africa and Southeast Asia and the Pacific*, Agriculture and Environmental Services Discussion Paper No. 1 (Washington, D.C.: World Bank), http://www-wds.worldbank.org/external/default/WDSContentServer/WDSP/IB/2013/09/23/000356161_20130923144055/Rendered/PDF/810830REVISEDootingoinoAgribusiness.pdf (accessed on 7 May 2015).

UNCTAD (United Nations Conference on Trade and Development) (2014) *World Investment Report 2014. Investing in the SDGs: An Action Plan* (New York and Geneva: United Nations), http://unctad.org/en/PublicationsLibrary/wir2014_en .pdf (accessed on 7 May 2015).

——— (2009) *World Investment Report 2009. Transnational Corporations, Agricultural Production and Development* (New York and Geneva: United Nations), http://unctad .org/en/pages/PublicationArchive.aspx?publicationid=743 (accessed on 7 May 2015).

UNCTAD and World Bank (2014) *The Practice of Responsible Investment Principles in Larger Scale Agricultural Investments: Implications for Corporate Performance and Impact on Local Communities*, Agriculture and Environmental Services Discussion Paper No. 8 and UNCTAD Investment for Development Issues Series (Washington, D.C., New York and Geneva: World Bank–UNCTAD), http://unctad.org/en/ PublicationsLibrary/wb_unctad_2014_en.pdf (accessed on 7 May 2015).

UNCTAD, FAO, IFAD, and World Bank (2010) *Principles for Responsible Agricultural Investment that Respects Rights, Livelihoods and Resources, A Discussion Note Prepared by FAO, IFAD, the UNCTAD Secretariat and the World Bank Group to Contribute to an Ongoing Global Dialogue*, UN doc. TD/B/C.II/CRP.3, 16 April.

Vermeulen, S. and L. Cotula (2010) *Making the Most of Agricultural Investment: A Survey of Business Models that Provide Opportunities for Smallholders* (Rome, London and Bern: FAO–IFAD–IIED–SDC), http://www.ifad.org/pub/land/agri_investment.pdf (accessed on 7 May 2015).

CHAPTER 5

Sweet and Bitter: Trajectories of Sugar Cane Investments in Northern Luzon, the Philippines, and Aceh, Indonesia, 2006–13

Mohamad Shohibuddin, Maria Lisa Alano, and Gerben Nooteboom

Abstract

This chapter aims to understand the complex process of investment and land deal making through the in-depth study of three cases of sugar cane investment in the Philippines and Indonesia. It focuses on three different trajectories of sugar cane schemes—one in northern Luzon, the Philippines, and two in Aceh, Indonesia. By means of a processual approach, the chapter identifies critical junctures—defined as crucial moments of dealmaking and interactions in which relations among actors are renegotiated—at which the investments took decisive turns. These are the collaboration of investors and bureaucratic cooperation between different levels of government; control of the development agenda; land deal making and control over land; control of labour; and curbing resistance. The chapter thus shows that investments in sugar cane and bioethanol—which often involve land deals—usually turn out differently than originally envisaged. Implementation problems arise due to the competing strategies and interests of investors, government departments, workers, landowners, and brokers, and due to specific historical and institutional constellations. Therefore, it can be argued that the implementation of investment schemes cannot simply be understood as the implementation of a contract or an already-planned programme; it should rather be understood as a constant process of negotiation and adaptation. In such a context, the identification of critical junctures is crucial for the conduct of monitoring activities and the adoption of adaptive policies during land deal processes.

This paper is based on the PhD fieldwork of Maria Lisa Alano (in northern Luzon) and Mohamad Shohibuddin (in Aceh), carried out in 2012–13. The authors are members of a research project on (trans)national land investments in Indonesia and the Philippines, funded by the Netherlands Organisation for Scientific Research (NWO) WOTRO Science for Global Development programme.

> ... *land grabbing may be as much the result of host state action and domestic power dynamics as of foreign pressure (Fairbairn, 2013, 352)*

1 Introduction

An integral part of the current boom in agricultural commodity production is investments in sugar cane and bioethanol—investments that often involve large land deals. So far, much attention has been paid to foreign investments and transnational actors who acquire or lease land and invest in commodity production as a response to the increase of prices at the world market. Evidence suggests that in many areas of Asia, the squeeze on natural resources and farmers' landholdings is caused by a less visible, longer-term process of land acquisition by local and national elites, often—but not necessarily—in conjunction with foreign investors (McCarthy et al., 2012). Relatively little consideration is given to the complexities and trajectories of deal making and implementation processes (Borras Jr. and Franco, 2010). Many deals turn out differently than originally envisaged by the investors, state agencies, stakeholders and NGOs. Once an investment scheme has been announced or a contract has been signed, implementation problems arise due to the competing strategies and interests of investors, government departments, workers, landowners, and brokers, and due to specific historical and institutional settings (Bakker et al., 2010, 168; Fairbairn, 2013, 137; Hall et al., 2011, 4).

In this chapter we argue that land deals are to be understood as processes of constant negotiation and adaptation. McCarthy et al. (2012, 556) emphasise the need to move beyond 'more structural accounts that privilege transnational forces that have a tendency to overlook local agency and difference'. In understanding these processes, we therefore build upon approaches that see the dynamics of changing regime interests, state policies, agribusiness agendas, traders, and farmers as being mutually constitutive, 'cumulatively shaping local production networks' (McCarthy et al., 2012, 556). The way these elements work together in a particular location affects the pathway of investments (McCarthy et al., 2012, 556). We are further inspired by writers such as Tsing (2005) who wrote that 'global forces are themselves congeries of local/global interaction' producing friction but also new coalitions and alternative forms of interaction.

This chapter aims to understand the complex processes of investment and land deal making through the in-depth study of three different implementation trajectories of sugar cane investment schemes—one in northern Luzon, the Philippines, and two in Aceh, Indonesia. Although investment and development policy play a central role in promoting and shaping large land deals in their initial stages, the relevance of policymaking and adaptation *during* the dealmaking process is often neglected. We argue that a processual approach to the analysis of land deals is needed to produce insights and tools that make monitoring and policy adaptation possible. Key questions concern which trajectories are unfolding, which actors are important, and how local conditions play a role. What can we learn from the different outcomes of these sugar cane investment schemes and how significant are the different investment trajectories for policy? To examine these questions, we reconstruct the social history of dealmaking in three schemes of government-supported sugar cane investment and the implementation processes relating to such deals. We begin this article with the current outcomes of the three investment schemes, after which their investment trajectories will be analysed and described in detail. We identify the collaboration of investors and bureaucrats; control of the development agenda; land deal making and control over land; control of labour; and curbing resistance as key junctures at which the land deal process took a decisive direction which affected or influenced the specific land deals presented in the paper.

2   Research Locations and Investment Trajectories

The research locations are Isabela in northern Luzon, the Philippines, and Aceh in Indonesia. In the former, one area was studied (Isabela); in the latter, two (Central Aceh and Bener Meriah). In all three locations the respective national governments tried to attract foreign companies to invest in sugar and biofuel production. The interest in sugar cane emerged as a result of the global boom in agricultural commodity production, the rising prices of sugar and biofuels, and the gradual abolishment of domestic subsidies due to global and regional free trade agreements. In 2006,[1] in Isabela, a biofuel production unit was established as a joint venture of foreign and domestic investors. In Aceh, sugar cane was a well-established crop in Central Aceh and was newly introduced to Bener Meriah in 2009.

The original plan of the Taiwanese, Japanese, and Philippine investors was to establish a biofuel company, Green Future Innovations Inc. A domestic company—Ecofuel Land Development Inc.—would supply the feedstock by developing 11,000 hectares of sugar cane plantation in the municipality of San Mariano using contract farming. However, the investment scheme was not executed as intended due to resistance from NGOs, the disinterest of farmers,

---

1   The activities began in 2006 although the companies were registered in 2009.

and complex property rights. In order for the plantation company to concretise its plans, it shifted to short-term lease contracts and brought in cheap and experienced sugar cane workers from elsewhere. The bioethanol plant to which Ecofuel supplies feedstock began operating in 2012, albeit with lower production levels than originally envisaged because Ecofuel could not yet comply with the required volume of delivery.

The two cases in the Gayo highlands of Aceh show very different investment processes, which result in opposite outcomes. Various local varieties of sugar cane have been grown by local smallholders in Central Aceh since the mid-1960s. Since then, sugar cane has been processed into red sugar for the local and regional market in simple, locally built and owned processing units. As part of a governmental programme to boost biofuel production, in 2009 the Indonesian government financed the establishment of a biofuel plant in Central Aceh. But this bioethanol plant could not compete with the local sugar factories, due to weak management, bureaucratic inefficiency, price distortions of the domestic biofuel market, and a lack of feedstock supply. As a result, the biofuel plant never became operational. Two years later, another attempt to establish an industrial processing plant took place when the Singapore-based company Indo-China Food Industries PTE Ltd began planning to develop a sugar factory. In 2011, Singaporean investors signed a contract with the Central Aceh district government to invest in a sugar processing plant. In 2012, a joint venture, PT Kamadhenu Ventures Indonesia, was established and by mid-2013, the construction of a sugar factory had begun and land was made available by the local government. The new investors managed to flexibly adapt to the local situation by starting with processing locally produced sugar cane so as not to compete with local production units.

The case of Bener Meriah provides a different story. The sugar investment area in Bener Meriah is situated on the old front line that separated the Free Aceh Movement (Gerakan Aceh Merdeka, GAM) and the Indonesian Army. The area was depopulated as a result of strategic evictions and war atrocities during the peak of the civil war from 2000 to 2003. The old front line separated ethnic Acehnese in the eastern coastal districts, who mainly supported GAM ideology, from native ethnic Gayonese and Javanese migrants in the highlands, who were neutral or in favour of the Indonesian government. Following the war, this depopulated area became a target of post-conflict development schemes aimed at reintegration and rehabilitation. The central Indonesian government, while trying to attract investors, spent a significant amount of money to introduce high-yield sugar cane varieties and boost smallholder sugar cane expansion. The district and central governments attempted to provide a labour force for the expected investors through resettlement and transmigration programmes oriented towards Gayo and Javanese migrants who had been evicted and lost land during the war. The district government also tried to provide large tracts of land for the investors by proposing a reduction in state production forest. However, despite policies and programmes from the national and provincial governments to attract foreign and domestic investors, overseas investors pulled out due to the many difficulties they experienced acquiring land in the post-war landscape, and therefore no processing plant was ever constructed.

The programmes to introduce sugar cane, implemented by the district government of Bener Meriah and financed from national and district budgets, were successful in the sense that settlers—some returnees and some newly resettled inhabitants—started to grow sugar cane. The programmes enabled local investors to invest in land and simple processing units of the same type as in Central Aceh. Ethnic Gayo elites and bureaucrats profited significantly from these programmes, while former landowners and Acehnese war victims were excluded. Large difficulties were encountered in the introduction of the crops and with regard to access to land and the distribution of benefits. Meanwhile, traders and small and medium-sized entrepreneurs, army personnel, and government officials from nearby towns and even from North Sumatra and Java did acquire land and started to grow and produce sugar cane for the local and regional market. Unrefined, red sugar is now produced, by smallholders, for the local and regional market in nearby district capitals (Takengon, Simpang Tiga Redelong, and Bireuen) and for soy sauce factories in Medan, in North Sumatra province.

In all three cases, interventions clearly had different results than expected and governance of the investments was a rather complex and ineffective process. The impact for local people was mixed. In the Philippines, the interventions resulted in land leases from smallholders and contract farming arrangements that benefitted mid- and large-scale farmers. The establishment of a partly foreign-owned bioethanol plant was facilitated, but not managed, by the government. In Central Aceh, initial government investments failed, but foreign, private investment materialised and investors manoeuvred through local mechanisms and by making use of an existing sugar cane market—a process which occurred without much government involvement. In Bener Meriah, many rural development schemes and government interventions were implemented and the national and district governments tried to convince companies to invest in the area, but following initial agreements and field surveys, foreign and domestic investments did not—in the end—materialise. The government then turned to rural development programmes aimed at growing sugar cane. These interventions can be understood as attempts to restore state control over the old front line area and to exercise security measures for sake of the Indonesian government vis-à-vis the GAM, which has dominated provincial politics since the 2006 elections. As a result, government officials and local and regional pro-Indonesian entrepreneurs did profit, while most of the war victims, especially the Acehnese, were left out.

A more detailed explanation and analysis will be provided in section 6 regarding the interventions and local outcomes.

3 Analytical Framework

In this chapter, we focus on sugar cane, since this agricultural commodity has attracted renewed interest not only from the government and investors but also from scholars researching the global land-grab phenomenon. Rather than focusing on international actors, here we will emphasise shifting power dynamics and competing actors at the sub-national level in the course of land investments. In doing so, we adopt a 'processual' approach to understanding the evolvement of investments in sugar cane crops and land over time in the Philippines and Indonesia. A processual approach involves the study of processes rather than of discrete events and separated actions. In our understanding, investments should be studied as trajectories of dealmaking, and understood as extended processes of negotiation and adaptation stretched over time. In the following, we will outline some basic elements of this processual approach to clarify the social reality of policy and business investments. We will also explain why this processual approach is relevant for policy.

A study of land deals as processes draws upon several bodies of literature. The first concerns an interactional perspective, understanding land deals as arenas of struggle and contestation in which different stakeholders compete over resources and profits (Bakker et al., 2010; Bierschenk, 1988; Long, 2001; Olivier de Sardan, 2005). In this competition, the issue of access to resources and the benefits of the intervention is pivotal. 'Access always involves insecurities due to contested forms of legitimisation, the opportunity of employing multiple sources of legitimisation (including state law, international human rights and claims of ancestry), the absence of a single regulating authority (such as the state) and the relative nature of access (relative to other contenders). Intervention is, therefore, subject to continuous contestation, renegotiation, bargaining and accommodation through which all the parties involved may land up with some access and control' (Bakker et al., 2010, 168). Local actors cannot predict the outcome of such interactive processes; neither can academics, who are also constrained when endeavouring to make absolute statements on rights of access.

We can also learn from the francophone research on development interventions, of which Bierschenk (1988; 2008) and Olivier de Sardan (2005) are major proponents. It is revealing to apply their earlier research—into the implementation of development projects—to investment schemes in agriculture, in order to understand the transformation of original goals into new outcomes and social realities. 'Project implementation does not mean carrying out an already-planned programme but is a constant process of negotiation. One must begin with an analysis of the project's participants and other interest groups, the goals and reasons for their negotiations, resources they have at hand—in short, of their own respective projects' (Bierschenk, 1988, 146).

In post-conflict areas, securitisation is the key force in this process, as competing parties articulate concerns on 'security matters' to legitimise their different political and economic stakes during the critical period of transition to peace. However, rather than reflecting on an objective threat, this kind of politicisation constitutes a 'securitising move' by powerful actors (especially, in this case, by former rebel and pro-Indonesia leaders), through which certain issues are elevated to the status of 'security matters' in order to be handled with the politics of emergency, thereby bypassing normal democratic procedures and necessary technical requirements (Buzan et al., 1998). In the context of post-war Aceh, such securitisation is not merely an appropriation of the language of peace building 'to justify [...] various predatory economic behaviours' (Aspinall, 2009, 17); rather, it is also a means for the national government to control certain areas and target loyal subjects through agribusiness and development schemes.

If we want to understand these processes in more detail and bring low-level actors and groups into focus with global developments, the market, and local and national structures of unequal power relations and state dominance, we need an understanding of 'the service of go-betweens or mediators who occupy a clearly strategic position' in this process (Olivier de Sardan, 2005, 173). Again, here we draw on the rich literature on development interventions and improvement schemes, particularly that of researchers who carried out pioneering work on understanding brokers and brokerage (Bierschenk et al., 2002; Lewis and Mosse, 2006; Olivier de Sardan, 2005). It is revealing to apply this literature on development interventions and improvement schemes to understanding investments and development schemes as interventions. '[Central] is the premise that [such an approach] can provide policymakers and aid managers with valuable reflective insights into the operations and effectiveness of international development as a complex set of local, national, and cross-cultural social interactions; and it is no longer possible to isolate interactions in the realm of development from those related to state apparatus, civil society, or wider national or international political, economic, and administrative practices' (Lewis and Mosse, 2006, 1).

The actions of investors, entrepreneurs, government officials, NGOs, go-betweens and middlemen are entangled in wider structures of power, dependency, inequality, culture and agro-ecological conditions. They are shaped by institutional legacies and historical repertoires that differ at different times and in different places. We thus cannot overlook the mediating role played by national-level institutions and domestic class inequality in determining the actually existing outcomes of agricultural commodity investment. We focus on the processes of brokerage between state development schemes, market opportunities, investor interests and local smallholders and labourers.

Such a focus on the role of domestic elite mediation is important, in part, because it belies the 'win–win' narratives on large deals currently being promoted by the World Bank and the FAO, among others. Fairbairn's (2013) study on foreign land investments in Mozambique finds that indirect land dispossession is the result of the mediating role played by domestic elites. She identified five sources of power that privileged domestic actors in their relation to foreign investors: traditional authority, bureaucratic influence, historical accumulation, locally based business knowledge and networks, and control over the development agenda. These largely correspond with the critical junctures we identified in Isabela and Aceh, as we shall see in the following sections.

4   Approach and Methodology

Investments are shaped and mediated by the institutional, political, and economic context in which they are made. A historical 'institutionalist' approach adds to the understanding of why certain investments materialise and others do not and what particular shapes investments take. 'When political institutions are weakened during transition periods, allocations of power and resources become open for competition' (Bertrand, 2004, 10). These periods of institutional change constitute 'critical junctures', during which the institutionalisation of social and economic relations is modified along with a reaffirmation, contestation, or renegotiation of the principles upon which these relations are based (Bertrand, 2004, 10). For this chapter, we identified the 'critical junctures' in the investment process—the crucial moments of dealmaking and interactions in which the relations between investors, the state, institutions, and local actors changed or were renegotiated, reconfirmed, and reconfigured.

During data collection, the extended case method (Lund, 2014; Van Velsen, 1967) was used to follow the dynamic interaction and the different processes in land deal making and investment concretisation. Fieldwork was spread over a 10-month period in Isabela and the Gayo highlands, and consisted of interviews, participant observation, and data gathering at the village, municipal, and provincial levels. A survey was also carried out at the village level where the biggest concentration of sugar cane interventions took place. In the research, respondents included women and men, farmers and farm workers, labour contractors, company field staff and officials, traders, local government officials, and representatives of government agencies. In Aceh, former GAM combatants and anti-GAM militia members were also interviewed.

5   National Policies around Sugar Cane Expansion

Agricultural commodities such as sugar cane have attracted renewed attention during the current agricultural boom following the convergence of multiple global crises involving finance, food, energy, and climate. The Philippine and Indonesian governments' decisions to exercise new policies for the expansion of sugar cane production can be understood as attempts to create economic opportunities from these crises through commodities characterised as 'flex crops'[2] (Borras Jr. et al., 2014). At the same time, the special treatment that sugar as a commodity demands, as a 'special/sensitive product' within free trade regime, provides some flexibility for both governments to establish a set of policies for allocating land, attracting private investments, and enhancing control over sugar cane downstream products (either biofuel or sugar).

5.1   Policies on Biofuels in the Philippines
Historically, the sugar cane sector had a special position in the Philippines, cane being its most important export commodity between the late eighteenth century and the mid-1970s. Large sugar estates, *haciendas*, were the basis of wealth for an important part of the Filipino elite—a landed elite that still has strong political influence as well as stakes in many agro-commodity firms. In 2007, the Philippines was the 10th largest sugar cane producer in the world and second to Thailand among South-East Asian countries (Fischer, et al., 2008, 31). The island of Negros can be considered as the sugar base of the country, with almost half of the country's total sugar cane being produced by its thirteen sugar mills. While a small proportion is still exported, production is now

---

2   Borras Jr. et al. (2014, 2) define flex crops as crops and commodities that have multiple uses (food, feed, fuel, industrial material) that can be, or are thought to be, flexibly interchangeable.

primarily for the domestic market, given the fast-growing population and rising domestic demand.

Investors are seeing sugar cane cultivation in a new light with respect to the growing popularity of green energy. The Philippines has joined the biofuel production hype with the aim of generating revenue while embarking on clean energy promotion, having become a signatory to the Kyoto Protocol. The country thus sees a future for biofuel use in the country and is now a marginal biofuel producer. Policies have been put in place to further this objective, most importantly the Republic Act 9367—better known as the Biofuel Act—of 2006. It requires the phasing out of harmful gasoline additives and the use of a minimum of 10 per cent bioethanol blend in all gasoline fuel sold and distributed in the country. Joint Administrative Order No. 1, Series of 2008 identifies proposed biofuel production sites as priority development areas for land conversion. Such areas are 'underutilized and marginal'; 'irrigated and irrigable lands, especially those used for rice production' cannot be used for biofuel crop production. At least two million hectares of the country's lands are targeted for agribusiness production, including crops for biofuel and agroforestry (NEDA, 2010). Sugar cane is expected to play an important role in this. In addition, sugar cane planters supported the Biofuel Act in view of the possible reduction of import tariffs on sugar because of the Association of Southeast Asian Nations (ASEAN) economic integration scheduled for 2015.

5.2   Overlapping Policies on Sugar Cane in Indonesia

In Indonesia, many paradoxes can be found in national sugar cane policies. One set of policies aims to increase national sugar production as part of national food security policies. Being heavily dependent on imported sugar, the government issued an ambitious policy in 2009 to achieve sugar self-sufficiency by 2014. To meet this target, as much as 350,000 hectares of new sugar cane area were to be developed, including Bener Meriah in Aceh (El Hida, 2011). Another set of policies targets sugar cane as a priority crop in an attempt to boost biofuel production by complementing the existing production of palm oil as biofuel. These policies are framed as a key part of the 'national energy mix' policy[3] stipulated by Presidential Regulation No. 5/2006, which envisions biofuel consumption constituting 5 per cent of total energy consumption in Indonesia by 2025.

---

3   The Indonesian 'national energy mix' policy envisages that fossil oil consumption would constitute less than 20 per cent of total energy consumption by 2025 as total energy demands would be met from various energy sources including fossil oil, biofuel, natural gas, liquefied coal, and other renewal energies.

With this kind of overlap in policies and agenda setting, the Indonesian case provides a sharp contrast to the Philippine case, where strong, clear-cut policies on biofuel production were put in place. In the Philippine policy context, downstream oil industry deregulation allows private companies to invest in the biofuel industry. Its clean air policy demands emission reduction and the promotion of biofuels as a cleaner fuel alternative. The government of the Philippines has clearly made an effort to promote biofuel production—also because the country has no oil itself. The Indonesian policies, on the other hand, got caught in contradictions and never manifested as intended. Reasons for this include conflicting policies for sugar self-sufficiency, a national energy mix, and post-conflict development assistance to facilitate the return of refugees and to involve them in sugar cane production.

6   Sugar Cane Interventions and Local Realities

As we indicated in the previous section, the differences between investments in biofuel and the need to enhance food production both in the Philippines and Indonesia have created conditions with regard to policy and institutional frameworks under which investments in sugar cane could thrive. However, as we will argue in this section, the specific outcomes of sugar cane interventions have a lot to do with sub-national power dynamics mediated by local elites with strong political and economic interests. The contrasting interests of local actors make straightforward implementation of national policies impossible.

6.1   Sugar Cane Investments in Isabela, the Philippines
In retrospect, the specific trajectory of sugar cane expansion and change in land and labour contracts in Isabela can be understood by taking a closer look at several critical junctures where a decisive direction was taken. In the following section, we follow the processual approach and identify the following junctures: protest and adaptations; bureaucratic support; the change from (intended) land acquisitions to land leases and contract farming; the establishment of beneficial labour contracts for local residents and the introduction of cheap and efficient labour from elsewhere; control of the development agenda; and the close cooperation between investors and local elites.

The investment plans evolved successfully due to a number of factors. In the beginning, the investment received a lukewarm reception in the villages because sugar cane cultivation was new to the locality. Some local farmers' groups associated with bigger groups campaigning against large-scale land investments in the Philippines also vigorously campaigned against it. To these groups, the establishment of the sugar cane investment violates the land and labour rights of local farmers, not to mention the threats to the environment and local food security (Aonishi et al., 2011) that such investment entails. Nevertheless, the investment scheme was established and has been operating now for eight years—albeit with deviations along the way. Local government played a crucial role in facilitating the entry of investors and the selection of the municipality of San Mariano as the main location of the investment. Once the area was identified by the central government, the investors had to deal with local government units. Ecofuel negotiated with provincial- and municipal-level officials in order to gain entry to the villages and identify plantation sites. The investment scheme received the endorsement of local government units and was hailed as one of the top investments in the province and the biggest active bioethanol project in the country. Provincial promotion brochures prominently feature Ecofuel's production areas and Green Future Innovation Inc.'s (GFII) bioethanol plant.

The decision-making process lacked transparency and it excluded small-holders. Village officials agreed to organise assemblies to promote the investment scheme at the village level, but the nature of the project and its possible implications for the community were not explained to the villagers, and nor was their input requested with regards to the introduction of sugar cane into their areas. The village officials could have played an active role in this. The village assemblies could have been utilised as platforms for dialogue on the acceptability of the investment scheme.

Ecofuel Land Development Corporation was registered as a corporation in 2009, but as early as 2006 had signed contracts with farmers and begun developing the sugar cane nurseries. Currently, two main types of arrangement are enforced by Ecofuel: lease and contract farming. Lease contract is the dominant scheme implemented by the company. The lease agreement usually covers three years and is renewable for another three years. The rent ranges from PHP 5,000–10,000 (roughly EUR 88–176 in 2014) per hectare per year depending on the distance of the farm from the processing plant. The company takes over the land for the duration of the contract, organising production and recruiting labourers.

The contract farming scheme requires that the landowners work or at least supervise the farm work themselves. The company advances the production costs, optionally including labour costs, then deducts these from the grower's earnings in the harvest period, computed at PHP 1,200 (approximately EUR 21 in 2014) per ton of sugar cane. Contract farming is the company's preferred option, as it makes controlling the quality and productivity of the land possible and saves on the cost of organising labour. Moreover, all production risks are born by the farmer, not by the company.

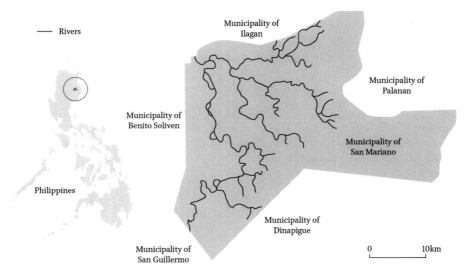

FIGURE 5.1 *Map of San Mariano, Isabela (the Philippines).*
SOURCE: MUNICIPAL PLANNING AND DEVELOPMENT OFFICE, SAN MARIANO,
ISABELA, 2012.

Another intervention, this time by the investor, was to capitalise on existing
social relations in the villages in order to acquire land and labour. The company hired locals as technicians and labour contractors. Company technicians
conducted house-to-house visits but only to convince farmers to lease their
lands and with very little explanation regarding the terms of the contract. The
farmers needed convincing, so technicians emphasised the possible earnings, the advance rental payment, and advances for production costs to be
provided by the company. Using its local personnel to promise incentives to
farmers already facing economic constraints was an effective approach for the
company.

Traditional big landowners turned out to be useful entry points for the company to gain access to land through lease or contract farming. They were the
first to be contacted during plantation development and their lands were used
for establishing nurseries. Despite the five-hectare ceiling on land ownership
imposed under the agrarian reform programme, there are still landowners
who possess at least 20 hectares, with one prominent landowner reportedly
owning about a hundred hectares in one village. During village assemblies, the
company officials used the experience of the big landowners in their dealings
with Ecofuel to entice small farmers to lease out their lands to the company as
well. The contract farming and lease arrangements with big landowners served

as a guarantee that the investor could be trusted. At present, the majority of the lessors and contract growers are small-scale farmers owning less than five hectares. Their areas converted to sugar cane were previously either not utilised, or used as pasture or cultivated for rice, corn, or vegetables.

The outcome of all these negotiations was that the planned contract farming arrangement preferred by Ecofuel did not materialise for the majority of its production areas. In the first years following the establishment of the scheme, almost all lands were leased for three years and workers were recruited to work on the leased lands. Labour contractors, on the other hand, were already experienced in pooling farmworkers to work in small groups on rice and corn farms. They could also easily mobilise labourers to work for Ecofuel. Nevertheless, a number of labour contractors recruited labour from traditional sugar-producing provinces in the Philippines beginning in 2006. Working for nine months in a year, the farmworkers are hired as migrant labour to perform the harder tasks avoided by the local farmworkers—for example the harvesting of canes and their transport to the processing plant.

Another setback for Ecofuel was that it could not develop its targeted 11,000-hectare plantation site in San Mariano because not all farmers wanted to give up farming. It changed its strategy and looked into adjacent municipalities and provinces for possible production areas. Lease and contract farming remained the two schemes offered by the company. In addition, Ecofuel encroached upon existing sugar cane-producing municipalities in neighbouring provinces and started buying sugar cane that was destined for the existing sugar mill in the region. The competition resulting from the entry of Ecofuel into these markets has been an unpleasant surprise for the existing sugar mill, but the resulting better prices for harvested cane have been welcomed by sugar cane farmers.

Existing socio-economic inequalities and political power differences provided leverage to the elite in dealing with Ecofuel. Members of the elite are able to bend company rules—such as not signing formal contracts or changing the nature of agreements, for instance from contract farming to self-financing. By comparison, smallholders were not given a choice as to which production arrangements were available to them, nor did they receive advice from local officials about the possible problems they could encounter if they contracted out their lands.

Smallholders also complain about the lack of government assistance with regard to the establishment of the sugar cane investment schemes. For them, the investments did not bring much benefit. But, true to its market-orientation, the Philippine government limited its role to identifying potential areas of production for large-scale land investments, leaving it up to companies and landowners to negotiate the terms of their engagement, as is the case with Ecofuel.

Due to all these difficulties, adaptations, and time-consuming negotiations, investing in Isabela was quite complex for Ecofuel. Moreover, they faced opposition from organised farmers' groups from early on. These groups had their own intervention strategies with which to resist the investment. The company suffered losses due to its equipment being burned by militant groups. Some mobilisations in 2011 and 2012 involved the uprooting of newly planted canes and the setting up of blockades to stop operations in areas where land ownership was contested. The workers also organised strikes in one of Ecofuel's farming areas and in the processing plant of GFII in 2012, which also paralysed operations at one point. Complaints of violation of environmental regulations were lodged against GFII but the company was only issued with a warning by the environmental management agency.

The company had its own strategies with which to respond to actions protesting against the investment scheme. Ecofuel pulled out from some of its production areas to counter such opposition. Halting operations affected the employment conditions of the local farmworkers. The lands of contract farmers were, in some areas, not maintained, which meant lower cane quality and thus a lower market price. Ecofuel alleged that local officials had not protected them from the militants' actions. Meanwhile, those campaigning against the investment criticised the inaction of local and national government agencies regarding environmental, labour, and land grabbing complaints lodged against Ecofuel.

We can observe a number of critical junctures in the investment and implementation processes. At these junctures, the interests and agendas of community elites, state actors, and investors came together. This collaboration (Tsing 2005) allowed the company to jump-start its operation in the municipality. Resistance to the investment was effective in the short term, but the investor was able to adapt and change its strategies, which restrained the opposition's initial gains. The investor also managed to control land and labour through its flexible adaptation of production schemes and the labour regime. The investment offered income and employment opportunities to small farming households, but the landed elite profited more through the better deals that they negotiated with the investor.

6.2   *Sugar Cane Interventions and Investments in Aceh, Indonesia*
In comparison with Isabela, the specific trajectory of sugar cane expansion and the establishment of a bioethanol plant in Central Aceh, and the failure of foreign investments in Bener Mariah, should be understood in the historical

context of post-conflict interventions and peace agreements. These sugar cane investments took place in a post-war environment. In this context, complicated land tenure as an outcome of war atrocities, and new provincial and district power reconfigurations following the peace agreement and the 2006 local elections, became the two main factors influencing the process of investment in sugar cane and land over time.

After the conflict, local elections were held throughout Aceh province in December 2006. In these elections, former GAM strategist Irwandi Yusuf was elected as Aceh's governor, (henceforth referred to as 'Governor Irwandi'), while in the Gayo highlands former anti-GAM leader Tagore Abubakar was elected as district head (*Bupati*) of Bener Meriah district (henceforth referred to as Bupati Tagore). Both these leaders, and other key players in the intervention, had access to development funds provided as a 'peace dividend' and soon engaged in intense contestations regarding post-conflict development agendas—including the agribusiness sector—contestations that replicated and even sustained conflict-era antagonism.

The specific trajectory of this intervention can again be understood by taking a closer look at the junctures at which critical decisions were made. In the following section, we look at critical junctures such as governmental and bureaucratic cooperation; control over and contestation regarding the development agenda; available production repertoires and agricultural histories; the control of land and labour; and the role of labourers, migrants, and local business elites.

Three mid-slope areas in the Gayo highlands were targeted by the national government for various sugar cane schemes following the conflict (see Figure 5.2). The first location, the Pantan Tau plateau in Central Aceh,[4] has been a sugar cane producing area since the mid-1960s. Pantan Perempusen (location 2) and Rime Mulie (location 3), both in Bener Meriah, are situated in the former frontier areas. Tens of hectares of sugar cane existed there just before the war, but all disappeared due to the conflict: war atrocities were rampant in the area. While only a few people were displaced in Pantan Tau and sugar cane production continued without major interruptions during the war, many villages in Pantan Perempusen and Rime Mulie sub-districts were depopulated, while most of the sub-districts' agricultural areas became grassland or shrub land. This not only created a drastic change in the rural landscape but also led to land tenure insecurity after the war.

---

4   Pantan Tau and other names used for sub-districts and villages in this paper are all pseudonyms.

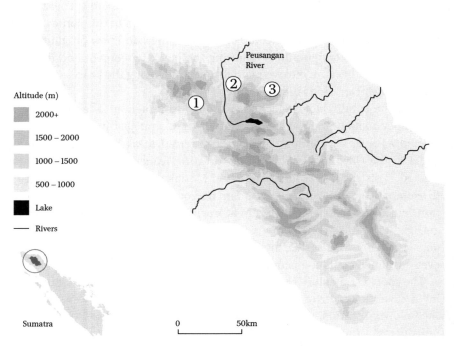

FIGURE 5.2 *Map of the Gayo highlands and areas targeted by sugar cane interventions*
            (Indonesia).
            Note: Location 1 is Pantan Tau plateau; location 2 is Pantan Perempusen sub-district,
            and location 3 is Rime Mulie sub-district.
            SOURCE: BOWEN (1991).

6.2.1   Sugar Cane Investments in Central Aceh
In contrast to the two areas in Bener Meriah, foreign investors found more
land in Pantan Tau, Central Aceh with which to pursue their investment plan.
Firstly, no 'post-war land' existed there since the area had been classified
as a 'white zone'.[5] Secondly, in the aftermath of the conflict, territorial and population control measures in this region had never become a matter of contestation or the subject of securitisation, such as they had in Bener Meriah. Last

---

5   During the war, the Indonesian military classified Aceh territory as 'black', 'gray', or 'white'
    zones according to the degree of their control over that territory and to the GAM's presence
    there (see Aspinall, 2008).

but not least, Pantan Tau is a well-established sugar cane area covering around 8,000 hectares of low productive sugar cane, which could provide the initial supply to feed the sugar cane processing plant.

The first attempt to invest there was made by the central government. In 2009, the Ministry of Industry built a plant to produce bioethanol—from sugar cane molasses—with a production capacity of around 3,000 litres per day. The plant cost IDR 16.172 billion (approximately EUR 1 million), and its construction was financed by the central government national biofuel programme. Its operation would depend on the supply of local sugar cane through free market mechanisms. The plant, however, never became operational since the plan did not work. Without adequate initial capital and due to the distortion of a highly subsidised fossil oil price, the plant's competition for feedstock with the local red sugar processing units made biofuel production uncompetitive. Thus, farmers continued to process their sugar cane for red sugar rather than selling it to the bioethanol plant, which offers much lower prices.

Soon afterwards, Pantan Tau was targeted for foreign investment by Singapore's Indo China Food Industries PTE Ltd. The investors were interested in investing in a sugar cane processing plant and in sugar cane estates. On 24 October 2011, a Memorandum of Understanding (MoU) was signed in Takengon, the capital of Central Aceh, by the managing director of the company and the *Bupati* of Central Aceh district. The MoU stated that the company would invest in the sugar cane processing complex, which would produce sugar, electricity, and ethanol.

For the first stage, a total of USD 7.5 million was to be invested in a processing plant capable of managing 3,500 tonnes of cane per day (TCD). This could be expanded to about 10,000 TCD depending upon the economic viability of such an expansion and the development of sugar cane estates around the factory. While the plant in its initial phase would depend on supplies from local farmers, in order to be able to increase its production capacity in the next operational step the company demanded that the Central Aceh district government allocate at least 10,000 hectares for a sugar cane plantation. If the plant's production capacity did expand to 10,000 TCD, a further 30,000 hectares was to be provided by the district government.

In response to this demand, the Central Aceh district government allocated 10,000 hectares of state land and of ex-plantation concession (*Hak Guna Usaha*, HGU) in Uning Gading, around 35 km from the north western side of Pantan Tau. An additional location was still to be found, which would most likely imply the reduction of production forest areas. Although the company had not yet started the land acquisition process in Uning Gading, rumours regarding the search for land for plasma estate[6] development had spread widely throughout the highlands since late 2011, triggering land speculation and a rush on land.

By mid-2012 the company had established a joint venture company, PT Kamadhenu Ventures Indonesia, and by early 2013 this joint venture had started to purchase 75 hectares of land in the centre of Pantan Tau to establish a factory complex. This process was accomplished in June 2013, and the following month the first stage of construction officially began. Although the construction process was interrupted by a big earthquake, which hit the area in July 2013, it resumed some months later. Factory construction was still in progress at the end of our fieldwork period.

Critical junctures in the investment process were: the co-optation of national and local units of government; converging development agendas; the ability of the foreign company to adopt a flexible and phased business plan; the shift to market based approaches, which curbed the opposition of farmers already producing sugar cane; the provision of land by the district government; and the availability of cheap labour and an experienced work force.

6.2.2   Sugar Cane Intervention in Bener Meriah
In the third case study area, Pantan Perempusen and Rime Mulie, in Bener Meriah—largely depopulated due to the massive outflow of refugees—any attempt to bring in agribusiness investments had to address the problem of a labour shortage and a general lack of agricultural inputs. The central and district governments, in their attempts to attract investors, therefore made great efforts and spent a significant amount of money to mobilise labourers and investments in crops and to allocate large tracts of land. In this regard, three interventions have been carried out by the government since 2007: the first was labour mobilisation, the second was the introduction of sugar cane, and the third relates to land allocation for sugar cane investments. These interventions were extremely complicated due to the problematic nature of securing the cooperation of local elites; conflicts over development agendas; GAM protests; and securitisation struggles, all of which constitute the key critical junctures in this case.

In relation to labour, in mid-2007 Bupati Tagore facilitated the arrival of 136 families of conflict refugees and resettled them in Blang Bintang village, Pantan Perempusen. Interestingly, these families were mostly former Javanese

---

6   The term plasma estate refers to a specific arrangement of contract farming between a company and smallholders in Indonesia in which smallholders are provided with agricultural supports (and sometimes with access to land) to produce a specific commodity as required by the company.

(trans)migrants who had fled from various parts of Aceh during the war, but none originated from Pantan Perempusen. Thus, rather than prioritising former inhabitants, this programme targeted a group of refugees completely foreign to the area, but loyal to the Indonesian state. In early 2009, after living in tents for more than a year, the families were provided with modest housing built by the Ministry of Social Affairs. The housing complex was located entirely on Bupati Tagore's own land.

Further, Bupati Tagore proposed a transmigration programme through which he expected not only to provide the 136 families in Blang Bintang with houses and pieces of land as promised, but also to mobilise more labours from other provinces in anticipation of the expected rise in labour demand due to the presence of the agro-industry investments. For this purpose, he allocated 9,320 hectares in Pantan Perempusen and 4,200 hectares in Rime Mulie. In addition, a plan to develop an integrated agro-industry in the transmigration area was prepared by the *Bupati*, all with significant support from the central government (notably from the Ministry of Manpower and Transmigration).

Strong criticism of these agribusiness and transmigration plans was, however, voiced by the GAM. Since mid-2006, GAM spokesperson Bakhtiar Abdullah had reportedly denounced the Indonesian government for discriminating against conflict refugees: 'Many (ethnic Acehnese) migrants who fled from Bener Meriah and Central Aceh are ignored, while transmigrant refugees previously [originating] from Java [have had their moves] fully facilitated and [are] taken care [of]' (Warsidi, 2006). Such criticism—typical of the GAM— was also echoed by Central Aceh's Governor Irwandi, and when a letter of recommendation from the governor was requested as part of the administrative requirements for proposing a transmigration programme, Irwandi refused to sign. A compromise was pursued, and the governor finally agreed to recommend the proposal on the condition that it should be a local rather than a national transmigration programme; that is, the participants could only be Aceh residents—not newcomers from other provinces.

Concerning the second category of interventions (i.e. those related to the introduction of sugar cane), a lot of investment was needed to re-establish the fertility of long-abandoned land in Blang Bintang. Most of the area had been covered by weeds (*imperata cylindrica*) and frequent grass fires had increased the acidity of the land. The newcomers were paid to clear the land. Yet it was a chaotic and frustrating period for them since certain people claiming to be the rightful owners of the land came to reclaim their parcels after that these had been cleared. Most such attempts failed, with the exception of a handful of pre-conflict landowners with political and economic power, such as government and police officials and army members living in the city, who succeeded to secure their land and even accumulated more of it after the end of the conflict. However, most people failed to get their land back.

The first attempts to introduce sugar cane to Blang Bintang took place in 2009. With his good political networks and links—since the war years—to national elites, Bupati Tagore succeeded in convincing the central government to designate Bener Meriah as an area targeted by the sugar self-sufficiency programme. Thus, during 2009–10 significant funds could be drawn from the national budget in order to provide farmers in Blang Bintang with cash assistance for preparing land, purchasing local varieties of sugar cane seedlings and establishing sugar cane plots. At the same time, to securitise the area and place it under his control, Bupati Tagore deployed military battalion 114/SM, purportedly to combat wild boar, the most damaging pest in Pantan Perempusen.

This introduction of sugar cane was a success. In late 2011 a further IDR 1.9 billion (around EUR 119,000) were provided by the Ministry of Agriculture to develop 50 hectares of nursery plots in Bener Meriah for the purpose of growing a high-yield variety—PSJT 941—in new sugar cane areas in the highlands. Bupati Tagore personally benefitted from these projects since he controlled the programme and located all nursery plots on his own land.

Since 2012, the third sugar cane intervention, again using the PSJT 941 variety produced by three farmers' groups on Tagore's land, has been pursued by the government in order to further expand smallholding sugar cane areas. This programme, to be implemented in several years, involves 120 new hectares of sugar cane production areas in three adjacent villages. The following year, the programme was executed again by the government targeting more land for sugar cane production. To support this programme, the district government of Bener Meriah allocated additional funds from its own budget. This sugar cane expansion attracted a rush of wealthy investors and entrepreneurs who wanted to acquire land and thus buy in to the sector.

In 2010, with the sugar cane introduction programme ongoing, the government started to offer areas of Bener Meriah to foreign investors. On 11 March 2010, the Director General of the Directorate General of Plantation, within the Ministry of Agriculture, chaired a meeting between Bupati Tagore and South Korean Park Energy PTE Ltd. In this meeting, Bupati Tagore offered the investors as much as 17,000 hectares in Pantan Perempusen and 20,000 hectares in Rime Mulie for sugar industry development. Since large parts of the areas designated for sugar cane were classified as state forest, the Director General promised to bring this issue to the attention of the National Team of Sugar Self-Sufficiency Programme, of which the Minister of Forestry became a member.

Following this meeting, on 29 March, the chairman of Park Energy PTE Ltd Shung Curk Park visited Bener Meriah to start an initial survey. A feasibility study was conducted some months later and delivered a promising result. The investors then stated their interest in investing around IDR 1.8 trillion in Bener Meriah in a sugar cane processing plant capable of handling 10,000 TCD. To feed this plant, the investors demanded that at least 20,000 hectares of land for sugar cane plantation be provided by the government.

Another attempt to attract investors was made by the Minister of Manpower and Transmigration. During his visit to Guangzhou on 28 May 2011, a public–private partnership (PPP) to develop sugar cane agro-industrial complexes in the transmigration area was agreed with Chinese state-owned Guandong Agribusiness Ltd. In this PPP scheme, a MoU was signed between the company and Indonesia's PT Pulau Sumbawa Agro (a subsidiary of PT Kapal Api Group). In accordance with this MoU, the CEO of PT Kapal Api Group and the Director General of Transmigration Area Preparation visited Bener Meriah from 12 to 15 July 2011 to survey potential areas for investment. During this visit, the allocation of at least 15,000 hectares of arable land was discussed with Bupati Tagore—the amount of land necessary to concretise the company's plan to invest in a sugar plant capable of handling 6,000 TCD.

In response to the demand for large tracts of land, the last type of intervention relates to attempts by the Bener Meriah district government to designate certain areas for agro-industry complexes and to allocate land for corporate sugar cane plantation. On 22 December 2010, Tagore issued a decree on the establishment of an integrated agro-industry development area named Garuda in Pantan Perempusen (the Garuda is the Indonesian national symbol and its use by Bupati Tagore reflects his ideological inclination vis-à-vis the GAM ethnonationalist movement). The area covers around 17,000 hectares of 'private land with and without land titling, all kinds of idle land, and state land'. In addition, on 21 February 2011, Bupati Tagore proposed a reduction of production forest to the Minister of Forestry, involving as much as 3,445.32 hectares in Pantan Perempusen and 12,119.25 in Rime Mulie.

Governor Irwandi, however, strongly opposed Tagore's proposal to reduce forest area in Bener Meriah, as he envisioned another agenda for managing Aceh's natural forest and protected areas—his 'Green Aceh' development plan. His refusal to issue a letter of recommendation for reducing forest area prevented the allocation of the large tract of land necessary for sugar cane investment, and with the land to be derived from forest areas no longer available, the investors found it impossible to continue their investment plan in Bener Meriah.

7   Discussion: Contrasting Outcomes and Critical Junctures

Despite the efforts of various schemes for foreign investment in sugar cane
plantation in the Philippines and in Aceh, Indonesia, involving investors
and the respective governments, of the three cases discussed, only two foreign investment programmes were realised. This outcome of the intervention
process can be understood by looking at the differences in the trajectories
of the investments and at the decisions taken, negotiations carried out, and
adaptations made during the process of implementation. The key decisive
moments—the critical junctures—reveal these differences and help to better
analyse and understand them.

    If we compare the different trajectories, we can identify five key junctures:
the collaboration of investors and bureaucratic cooperation between different
levels of government; control of the development agenda; land deal making
and control over land; control of labour; and curbing resistance.

    In Isabela, investments proceeded thanks to co-optation and agreement at
most junctures. However, ambitions and control over land and labour changed
during the trajectory partly due to refusal of landowners to engage in contract
farming and fierce opposition from civil society groups. Governmental policies
are clear and coherent and the government is cooperative on all levels. Local
landed elites have room to modify deals according to their interests and large
landowners profit more than small landowners. The decision to bring in sugar
workers from elsewhere and to pull out from conflict-ridden areas led to a further deterioration in the position of the rural poor. At present, short-term lease
agreements dominate the production arrangements of Ecofuel. The company
uses labour from both migrant and local farmworkers.

    In Central Aceh, eventually, the commercially viable investment made in a
Singaporean owned sugar plant thrived under free-market conditions. Critical
junctures were again the co-optation of national and local governments and
the existence of converging development agendas; a shift to market-based
approaches, which curbed the opposition of farmers already producing sugar
cane in combination with the ability of the foreign company to adopt a flexible
and phased business plan; the provision of land by the district government;
and the availability of cheap labour and an experienced workforce. Where
government investments failed due to mismanagement and as a result of contradictory food and energy policies in Central Aceh, once again the flexible
adaptation of the foreign investors turned out to be crucial for penetrating the
sugar area. The company did not intervene in the existing situation of local
land control. Instead, it adopted a phased business plan that allowed it to rely
on local supply for its initial production and only demanded large tracts of

land in the next phases of its business expansion plan. In the end, the state was largely absent; its attempt at involvement having failed due to mismanagement, conflicting national policies and poor adherence to market laws.

In Bener Meriah, Aceh, Indonesia, implementation of the investment scheme turned out to be much more of a struggle, filled with unexpected turns and moves in which local and regional governmental figures used agricultural investments to enhance political control and to cater to private gains. At most of the junctures conflicts could not be solved and antagonism prevailed. The power play of local authorities and the political, legal, and ethnic complexities present made foreign investors move out quickly. Government investment served other political goals than inclusive development and reconstruction agendas and the interventions were not market driven. However, when the agricultural investments did unfold, new opportunities were created and other parties came in, eager to profit from cheap available land, the introduction of improved cane varieties, and favourable post-conflict business circumstances. For indigenous Gayonese, small and medium-sized investors, and ethnic Gayo elites and bureaucrats, the outcomes of the agricultural development initiatives were rather sweet, and investments ended up being quite profitable, although these benefits were unevenly distributed among them.

For former landowners and pre-war inhabitants from various ethnic backgrounds, however, sugar cane investments provide a bitter outcome since most of them were excluded from these new opportunities. Meanwhile, for newly resettled Javanese settlers, the outcomes were rather ambiguous since only a few have been able to build up savings—from their participation in sugar cane programmes—with which to purchase land, thus becoming independent farmers. The state is significantly involved throughout the process, but juggles security interests, local power plays, and private interests. As a result, contestation and conflict were paramount at almost all the critical junctures and continued over longer periods of time, frustrating foreign investments but favouring ad hoc coalitions of local elites, small farmers, and local authorities.

8 Conclusion

Investments are usually understood to involve contracts, and contracts to involve two parties. As the cases described in this chapter show, in agricultural commodity investments in Asia, the reality is much more complex and investments are processes. Many more actors are involved and results locally differ from the original intentions of the government parties and investors who signed the contracts. Investors often operate as joint ventures, conjoined with local companies, brokers, and elites. It is typically national or provincial governments that facilitate deals and make land available to investors; but after that, other government bodies are involved, with different roles and interests. In the process of negotiations and adaptations to local agro-ecological circumstances and political realities, an increasing number of actors play a role. As a result, the investment process becomes unclear and outcomes are often unexpected and not always sweet.

Hence, while the investments and agricultural development projects represented a common arena of negotiation for all groups involved in the Isabela and Central Aceh cases, and while respective national biofuel and food security policies provided a common ground for legitimation, the different actors used very different frames of reference to guide their social interaction and the rationalisation of their actions. Where in the Philippines free-market narratives and strong anti-liberalist opposition dominated the debate, in Bener Meriah, Aceh, government investments proved essentially to be a fight over territory and people—a continuation of the war by other means. The specific outcomes of the sugar cane interventions thus have a great deal to do with subnational power dynamics mediated by local elites with strong political and economic interests and, in the case of the Philippines, by farmers' resistance.

The three case studies discussed in this chapter show how local tensions and circumstances, as well as conflicts, enable the specific outcomes of investments. In each case, the outcomes did not evolve exactly as planned. Moreover, local forces and power constellations also significantly influence the outcomes of investment schemes. Key junctures are control of the development agenda; collaboration between investors and the government; land deal making and control over land; control of labour; elite and bureaucratic cooperation; and curbing resistance. Our analysis makes clear that this is not a case of companies versus local people, but is rather a much more complex web of interests and struggles in which government parties can play different roles. Our analysis also shows the differential outcomes of investments in terms of control over land, territory, and labour, and of resources divided and distributed among multiple stakeholders; a series of battles over land, labour, and capital, culminating in a sequence of critical junctures. If agreement is reached at one juncture, interests can still be divided at another, critically determining the direction of the intervention. Further research should therefore examine the identification and comparison of such critical junctures and the possibilities for policies to monitor the process by focusing on these junctures. Our conclusions emphasise the unpredictability of intervention processes, as the outcomes of investment deals are far from clear at the start. We believe that understanding the processual nature of land deals and the identification of critical junctures have important implications for investment policies and land deal governance. A clear focus on critical junctures in this process will make adaptive and processual policies possible. Which might, in turn, make possible transforming some of the bitter consequences of interventions into sweeter realities along the way.

References

Aonishi, Y., F. Cosico, R. Gueta, H. Hatae, S. Lovera, E. Maguigad, J. Richardson and T. Roberts-Davis (2011) *Not One Idle Hectare: Agrofuel Development Sparks Intensified Land Grabbing in Isabela, Philippines*, Report of the International Fact Finding Mission, May 29th–June 6th 2011 (San Mariano: International Fact Finding Mission), http://www.foejapan.org/aid/land/isabela/pdf/20110822.pdf (accessed on 1 June 2013).

Aspinall, E. (2009) 'Combatants to Contractors: The Political Economy of Peace in Aceh', *Indonesia*, 87, pp. 1–34, http://www.jstor.org/stable/40376474.

——— (2008) 'Place and Displacement in the Aceh Conflict', in Hedman E-L. E. (ed.) *Conflict, Violence and Displacement in Indonesia* (Ithaca and New York: Cornell University Press).

Bakker, L., G. Nooteboom and R. Rutten (2010) 'Localities of Value: Ambiguous Access to Land and Water in Southeast Asia (Introduction)', *Asian Journal of Social Science*, 38(2), pp. 161–171, DOI: 10.1163/156853110X490872.

Bertrand, J. (2004) *Nationalism and Ethnic Conflict in Indonesia* (Cambridge: Cambridge University Press).

Bierschenk, T. (2008) *Anthropology and Development: An Historicizing and Localizing Approach*, Working Paper No. 87 (Mainz: Institut für Ethnologie und Afrikastudien, Johannes Gutenberg Universität), http://www.ifeas.uni-mainz.de/workingpapers/AP87.pdf (accessed on 4 May 2015).

——— (1988) 'Development Projects as Arenas of Negotiation for Strategic Groups: A Case Study from Bénin', *Sociologia Ruralis*, 28(2–3), pp. 146–160, DOI: 10.1111/j.1467-9523.1988.tb01035.x.

Bierschenk, T., J-P. Chauveau and J-P. Olivier de Sardan (2002) *Local Development Brokers in Africa: The Rise of a New Social Category*, Working Paper No. 13 (Mainz: Institut für Ethnologie und Afrikastudien, Johannes Guetenberg Universität), http://www.ifeas.uni-mainz.de/Dateien/Local.pdf (accessed on 26 May 2015).

Borras Jr., S.M. and J.C. Franco (2010) 'From Threat to Opportunity? Problems with the Idea of a "Code of Conduct" for Land-Grabbing', *Yale Human Rights and Development Law Journal*, 13, pp. 507–23.

Borras Jr., S.M., J.C. Franco, R. Isakson, L. Levidow and P. Vervest (2014) *Towards Understanding the Politics of Flex Crops and Commodities: Implications for Research and Policy Advocacy*, Think Piece Series on Flex Crops & Commodities No. 1 (Amsterdam: Transnational Institute), http://www.tni.org/sites/www.tni.org/files/download/flexcrops01.pdf (accessed on 4 May 2015).

Bowen, J.R. (1991) *Indonesia Sumatran Politics and Poetics: Gayo History, 1900–1989* (New Haven and London: Yale University Press).

Buzan, B., O. Wæver and J. de Wilde (1998) *Security: A New Framework for Analysis* (Boulder: Lynne Rienner Publishers Inc.).

El Hida, R. (2011) 'Butuh 25 Pabrik Gula Baru untuk Swasembada', *Detik Finance*, 18 July, http://finance.detik.com/read/2011/07/18/132717/1683408/1036/2/butuh-25-pabrik-gula-baru-untuk-swasembada (accessed on 23 January 2013).

Fairbairn, M. (2013) 'Indirect Dispossession: Domestic Power Imbalances and Foreign Access to Land in Mozambique', *Development and Change*, 44(2), pp. 335–356, DOI: 10.1111/dech.12013.

Fischer, G., E. Teixeira, E. Tothne Hizsnyik and H. van Velthuizen (2008) 'Land Use Dynamics and Sugarcane Production', in Zuurbier, P. and J. van de Vooren (eds.) *Sugarcane Ethanol: Contributions to Climate Change Mitigation and the Environment* (Wageningen: Wageningen Academic Publishers) pp. 29–62.

Hall, D., P. Hirsch and T.M. Li (2011) *Powers of Exclusion: Land Dilemmas in Southeast Asia* (Honolulu: University of Hawaii Press).

Lewis, D. and D. Mosse (2006) *Development Brokers and Translators: The Ethnography of Aid and Agencies* (Bloomfield: Kumarian Press).

Long, N. (2001) *Development Sociology: Actor Perspectives* (London: Routledge).

Lund, C. (2014) 'Of What is This a Case? Analytical Movements in Qualitative Social Science Research', *Human Organization*, 73(3), pp. 224–234, DOI: 10.17730/humo.73.3.e35q482014x033l4.

McCarthy, J., P. Gillespie and Z. Zen (2012) 'Swimming Upstream: Local Indonesian Production Networks in "Globalized" Palm Oil Production', *World Development*, 40(3) pp. 555–569, DOI: 10.1016/j.worlddev.2011.07.012.

Mitchell, J.C. (2006[1982]) 'Case and Situational Analysis', in Evens, T.M.S. and Don Handelman (eds.) *The Manchester School: Practice and Ethnographic Praxis in Anthropology* (New York: Berghahn Books) pp. 23–44.

NEDA (National Economic Development Authority) (2010) *Updated Medium Term Philippine Development Plan 2004–2010* (Manila: NEDA).

Olivier de Sardan, J-P. (2005) *Anthropology and Development: Understanding Contemporary Social Change* (London and New York: Zed Books).

Tsing, A. (2005) *Friction. An Ethnography of Global Connections* (Princeton: Princeton University Press).

Van Velsen, J. (1967) 'The Extended-Case Method and Situational Analysis', in Epstein, A.L. (ed.) *The Craft of Social Anthropology* (London: Tavistock) pp. 129–149.

Warsidi, A. (2006) 'GAM Tolak Transmigran Baru Asal Jawa', *Tempo Interaktif*, 15 March, www.tempo.co/read/news/2006/03/15/05875146/GAM-Tolak-Transmigran-Baru-Asal-Jawa (accessed on 12 August 2013).

CHAPTER 6

Marginal Land or Marginal People? Analysing Patterns and Processes of Large-Scale Land Acquisitions in South-East Asia

Peter Messerli, Amaury Peeters, Oliver Schoenweger, Vong Nanhthavong, and Andreas Heinimann

Abstract

This chapter aims to overcome the gap existing between case study research, which typically provides qualitative and process-based insights, and national or global inventories that typically offer spatially explicit and quantitative analysis of broader patterns, and thus to present adequate evidence for policymaking regarding large-scale land acquisitions. Therefore, the chapter links spatial patterns of land acquisitions to underlying implementation processes of land allocation. Methodologically linking the described patterns and processes proved difficult, but we have identified indicators that could be added to inventories and monitoring systems to make linkage possible. Combining complementary approaches in this way may help to determine where policy space exists for more sustainable governance of land acquisitions, both geographically and with regard to processes of agrarian transitions. Our spatial analysis revealed two general patterns: (i) relatively large forestry-related acquisitions that target forested landscapes and often interfere with semi-subsistence farming systems; and (ii) smaller agriculture-related acquisitions that often target existing cropland and also interfere with semi-subsistence systems. Furthermore, our meta-analysis of land acquisition implementation processes shows that authoritarian, top-down processes dominate. Initially, the demands of powerful regional and domestic investors tend to override socio-ecological variables, local actors' interests, and land governance mechanisms. As available land grows scarce, however, and local actors gain experience dealing with land acquisitions, it appears that land investments begin to fail or give way to more inclusive, bottom-up investment models.

1 Introduction

A growing body of scientific evidence on large-scale land acquisitions (LSLAS) is helping to inform the heated debate regarding this rapidly unfolding phenomenon. Some researchers—particularly those using qualitative, in-depth case studies—have examined land-acquisition processes within the dynamics of agrarian change and larger political-economic shifts. Other researchers have striven to establish quantitative inventories of LSLAs to improve our understanding of the scale and dimensions of land acquisitions at the national (Görgen et al., 2009; Schönweger et al., 2012; Üllenberg, 2009), regional (Friis and Reenberg, 2010), or global level (Anseeuw et al., 2012; Cotula, 2012; Deininger and Byerlee, 2011). Based on such inventories, the World Bank has deemed 445 million hectares (ha) of land worldwide to be 'marginal land' that could benefit from agricultural investments because it is not forested or under protection and has population densities below 25 people per km^2 (Deininger and Byerlee, 2011).

Both qualitative case-based approaches and quantitative inventory-based approaches have persistently met with difficulties and criticism when it comes to guiding policy on land investments. While case studies focussing on specific local contexts are good at capturing processes and interactions, they have limited geographical validity and are typically ill-suited to generalising and informing policy at higher spatial levels (Anseeuw et al., 2012; Messerli et al., 2013). By contrast, regional and global inventories based on quantitative approaches are useful for making large comparisons, but frequently lack insight into processes and fail to account for variety and differentiation; they have also been criticised for relying on faulty or incomplete data sources and for lacking verification on the ground (Edelman, 2013; Oya, 2013). Similarly, hasty assessments about unused or underused 'marginal' land have been consistently refuted by intensive case study research (Borras Jr. et al., 2011; Dwyer, 2013; Nalepa and Bauer, 2012). This research has shown that land targeted by international land deals is often not idle at all, but rather is subject to claims and is used by people who are increasingly being marginalised by processes of globalization.

From a policy perspective, it remains a point of dispute whether or to what extent LSLAs target marginal land and/or create marginalised populations. Overall, the policy-related evidence provided by researchers appears ambiguous and often contradictory. Because of this, recent proposals have recommended bringing together country-level and case-based research approaches, taking advantage of conceptual and methodological complementarities (Messerli et al., 2013; Scoones et al., 2013). Such a research agenda would aim at linking patterns of quantitative, place-based (spatially referenced) assessments of LSLAs to insights from processes-based, frequently qualitative case studies.

Supplying useful scientific evidence for decision-making and policymaking has also proven difficult in South-East Asia. Here, LSLAs have emerged mainly as a regional phenomenon, contrasting somewhat with the 'land rush' in Africa and Latin America where global drivers are seen as especially important (Anseeuw et al., 2012). Such acquisitions reflect a broader picture of agricultural and societal transformation, characterised by a rapid shift away from rural subsistence-oriented agriculture in favour of more urbanised societies and industrialised, market-based forms of land use. Often termed 'agrarian transition' (De Koninck, 2004; Rigg, 2006), this transformation comprises many simultaneously occurring processes such as agricultural intensification and territorial expansion, market-based economic integration, rural-urban migration, new forms of regulations governing agricultural production, and urbanisation. None of these processes necessarily follow a linear path and their pace differs from place to place. Rural transformation processes vary considerably across the region and across different scales, making it difficult to properly conceptualise and understand changes in the Asian countryside as they occur (Rigg, 2005). LSLAs have led to highly dissimilar outcomes from one place to another. Thus, using single case studies or locally obtained empirical results to formulate regional or national policy is highly problematic.

This paper focuses on land investments in Laos and Cambodia. The land resources in both countries are under significant pressure from LSLAs, especially as a result of foreign direct investment by neighbouring riparian countries. Our overall goal is to identify distinct spatio-temporal patterns of LSLAs across the two countries and to attempt to link them to recurrent or archetypal processes of implementation of land deals from concession granting to the final allocation of land. This encompasses two primary objectives: (1) methodologically, we aim to explore and illustrate how quantitative, place-based (spatial) analysis of land investments can be linked to process-based, qualitative studies; (2) as regards content, we aim to improve—based on better methodology—the generalisation of evidence on LSLAs for policymaking and decision-making.

The paper is structured as follows. In section 2, we describe our methodology and the results of analysing spatial patterns of LSLAs based on country-level inventories. Here, we focus on the origin of the investors, on crop types, and on geographical target contexts (including social and ecological characteristics). In section 3, we describe how we used a meta-analysis of case studies to identify key factors of LSLA implementation processes and recurrent linkages between these key factors. Based on these recurrent linkages, we propose four so-called archetypes of land acquisitions as the basis for a working typology of implementation processes. Finally, in section 4 we discuss whether and to what extent spatial patterns of land deals can be related to archetypes of implementation processes in order to improve the validity and generalisation of research results for policymaking purposes.

2 Analysing Spatial Patterns of LSLAs in Laos and Cambodia

2.1 *Materials and Methods*

In both Laos and Cambodia, national databases of LSLAs have been gradually built using different information sources furnished by different agencies and initiatives. In Laos, the bulk of data was collected through an inventory of land concessions and leases (from the local level to the national level) conducted between 2007 and 2010, with additional updates and data cleaning occurring in 2012 (Schönweger et al., 2012). Only 50 per cent of the granted deals collected in this inventory were spatially referenced. For the purpose of our analysis, only the spatially referenced deals were used, encompassing 597,600 ha of land (out of 1.1 million ha, in total, of granted land concessions and leases).

The Cambodian database was drawn together from a variety of information sources. It includes official data gathered by Open Development Cambodia (ODC, 2013); data from LICADHO (2013); data from NGO Forum (2012); and data from the Ministry of Agriculture, Forestry and Fisheries of Cambodia (2012); as well as our own field data. The resulting database combines data on land concessions (with spatial-reference data) comprising 490 deals that cover 4.5 million ha; the most recent updates and data cleaning took place in September 2013.

Using these unique data sets, we conducted a descriptive analysis looking at investors' country of origin, the intended purpose of the deal (by sub-sector), and the date of approval for each land deal. To gain some initial insights into the national-level characteristics of land acquisitions in Laos and Cambodia, we compared the geo-referenced land-deal data with other important spatially referenced country-level data sets, in particular those on poverty incidence, accessibility to provincial capitals, and land cover. Because the national land cover data sets for Laos and Cambodia were not comparable (due to differing methods and classifications), globally available data were used from the GlobCover 2009 land classification (Arino, 2010). We calculated the accessibility of provincial capitals (i.e. travel time in minutes) with cost–distance algorithms in ArcGis 10, using national road data sets, digital elevation models, land cover data, and main rivers as inputs (Messerli et al., 2008). For Laos, we used village-level poverty data—from Epprecht et al. (2008)—that were calculated using small-area estimation based on figures from the 2005 Lao Population and Housing Census and the 2003 Lao Expenditure and

Consumption Survey (LECS) III. For Cambodia, poverty measures were derived
from the Identification of Poor Households Programme data set (Kingdom of
Cambodia, 2012) and the Commune Database (NCCD, 2012) for 2008–2010.

2.2 Spatial Patterns of LSLAS in Laos and Cambodia

2.2.1 Dimensions and Scale of LSLAS

An openness to private investment in the form of land concessions has been
present in the economic development policies of both countries for many
years. In Cambodia, a new legal framework was adopted for land investment in
2001; the same occurred in Laos in 2003. In both countries, a series of additional
laws and decrees have reinforced and concretised the trend towards private
land investment (NAoL, 2004; GoL 2008; RGC, 2005). Investors' responses have
not been slow in coming, giving rise to a veritable 'land rush' in both countries.
The countries' respective governments have also made private investments in
land an explicit part of their official development strategies and policies. But
the growing scale and pace of land concessions have proven highly challenging to govern properly, sparking criticism both locally and internationally. The
total number of concessions granted in Laos increased fiftyfold between 2000
and 2009, rising steeply after 2005 (Figure 6.1). In Cambodia, there was also a

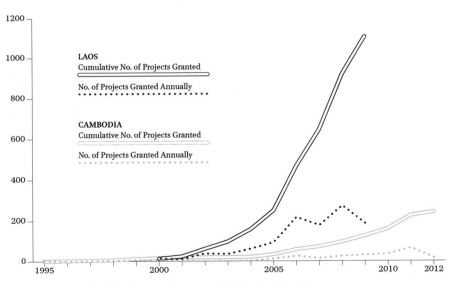

FIGURE 6.1   *Trends of land concessions granted in Cambodia and Laos.*
*Note: Figures for Cambodia do not include mining concessions, as no information
about the granting date of mining concessions was available.*
SOURCE: AUTHORS.

sharp increase in land deals after 2005. The most impressive observation, however, remains that—starting in 2000—it took only eight years to double the area granted to investors, from 0.5 million ha in 2000 to over 1 million ha in 2008, and only another four years to double it again, reaching over 2 million hectares in 2012.

Despite the announcement of moratoriums on new land concessions in Laos (2007, 2009, and 2012) and Cambodia (2012), these deals play a major role in the economies of each country and will continue to do so based on the sheer size of existing deals. Today, Laos has already granted approximately 2,640 land concessions for 1.1 million ha (Schönweger et al., 2012), while Cambodia has granted about 490 concessions for 4.5 million ha, including mining concessions. Notably, land granted as concessions or leases constitutes around 5 per cent of the territory of Laos and around 25 per cent of the territory of Cambodia.

2.2.2 Spatial Distribution of LSLAS

While land investments are spread throughout the two countries, there are regions where they are more clustered and more highly concentrated in terms of land area used (Figure 6.2): in the north of Laos, in the north and the north-east of Cambodia, and also in the south-western region of Cambodia. With regard to the origin of investors, domestic investments play an important role in terms of the absolute number of deals in both countries. These domestic investments are distributed in a similar manner to foreign investments across each country.

2.2.3 Investors and Main Sub-Sectors Behind LSLAS

While in Cambodia domestic deals account for almost 50 per cent of the entire land area granted, in Laos they account for less than 15 per cent (Table 6.1). Consequently, domestic investors in Laos have much smaller deals (by area) on average. Non-domestic investments are dominated in both contexts by the following neighbouring countries: China, Vietnam, and Thailand. The proximity of areas to country of origin of the investors who invest in those areas partly explains the distribution of these regional investments (Figure 6.2). Investments from foreign countries outside the region, aggregated here under the category 'international', only represent small shares (by area and number) of the remaining concessions (Table 6.1).

In terms of the intended purpose of deals, the forestry sub-sector—including all forms of tree crops (mainly rubber, eucalyptus, and teak)—outweighs the agricultural sub-sector in both countries based on land area used: the figures are 15,157 km² (forestry) versus 2,813 km² (agriculture) in Cambodia; and 2,878 km² (forestry) versus 834 km² (agriculture) in Laos. Again, regional investors from neighbouring countries are the main source of forestry-related

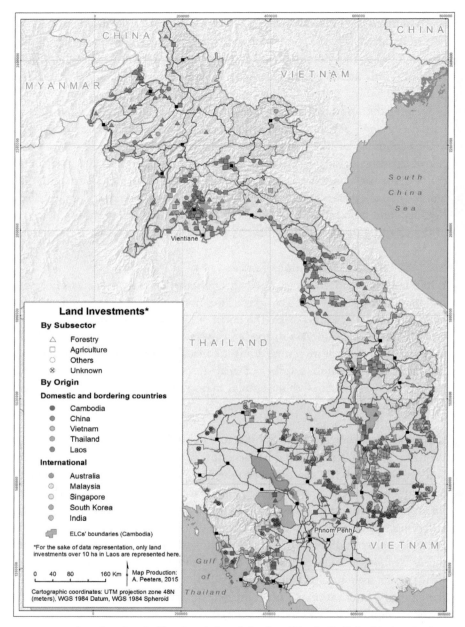

FIGURE 6.2 *Investment project locations in Laos (above) and Cambodia (below) by investors'*
           countries of origin and by subsectors.
           SOURCE: COMPILED BASED ON SCHÖNWEGER ET AL. (2012), ODC (2013),
           LICADHO (2013), NGO FORUM (2012), AND OUR OWN DATA COLLECTION.

TABLE 6.1 *Origin of investors, former land-cover status, and accessibility of land investments in Cambodia and Laos*

	Main sub-sectors	Deals No. #	Deals Area Km²	Domestic #	Domestic Km²	Regional* #	Regional* Km²	Internat. #	Internat. Km²	Unknown #	Unknown Km²	Forest %	Mosaic %	Cropland %	Other %	Total %	Access** Min.
Cambodia	Forestry	142	15,157	62	8,575	65	5,361	14	1,209	1	12	44.0%	37.1%	18.8%	0.1%	100%	199
	Agriculture	43	2,813	21	1,245	12	966	8	509	2	93	37.7%	41.1%	21.1%	0.1%	100%	143
	Other	11	723	4	213	3	461	0	0	4	49	38.2%	55.1%	4.4%	2.3%	100%	232
	Unknown	84	4,322	36	1,300	13	801	12	1,340	23	880	42.2%	40.1%	17.6%	0.1%	100%	171
	Total	280	23,014	123	11,333	93	7,588	34	3,058	30	1,034	42.8%	38.6%	18.5%	0.2%	100%	–
Laos	Forestry	262	2,878	80	257	150	1,818	32	803	0	0	39.3%	42.8%	17.8%	0.1%	100%	123
	Agriculture	149	834	53	87	64	664	32	83	0	0	22.7%	29.7%	47.0%	0.6%	100%	96
	Other	935	2,264	673	486	220	1,633	42	146	0	0	40.0%	42.0%	16.8%	1.2%	100%	257
	Total	1,346	5,976	806	829	434	4,115	106	1,032	0	0	37.2%	40.7%	21.5%	0.6%	100%	–
Cambodia & Laos	Forestry	404	18,035	142	8,832	215	7,179	46	2,013	1	12	43.3%	37.9%	18.6%	0.1%	100%	161
	Agriculture	192	3,646	74	1,332	76	1,630	40	592	2	93	34.5%	38.7%	26.6%	0.2%	100%	120
	Other	946	2,987	677	699	223	2,094	42	146	4	49	39.6%	45.1%	13.8%	1.5%	100%	244
	Unknown	84	4,322	36	1,300	13	801	12	1,340	23	880	42.2%	40.1%	17.6%	0.1%	100%	171
	Total	1,626	28,990	929	12,162	527	11,703	140	4,090	30	1,034	41.7%	39.0%	19.0%	0.2%	100%	–

* Regional refers to countries neighbouring Cambodia and Laos—namely, Vietnam, Thailand, and China.
** Accessibility refers to the time needed to travel to the nearest provincial capital (in minutes).
Source: Authors.

land deals in both countries taken together (53 per cent of deals), with domestic investors also being very important in Cambodia (44 per cent of deals). International investors hold only 11 per cent of all forestry concessions in both countries combined. Agriculture-related land deals are generally smaller than forestry-related land deals. Agriculture-related investments are dominated by regional (40 per cent of deals) and domestic stakeholders (39 per cent of deals) in Laos and Cambodia combined; international investors account for another 21 per cent of agriculture-related deals. It is also important to note the significance of the mining sector in Laos, as it accounts for the biggest share of land (92 per cent) among the sub-sectors classified under 'Other' for that country (Table 6.1).

2.2.4 Geographic Contexts of Land Acquisitions at the National Level

Overlaying our map of land deals with earlier land cover data revealed some interesting spatial patterns. Overall, land concessions are mainly granted in forested landscapes (42 per cent) and in landscape mosaics of forest, shrubland, and grassland (39 per cent); in Laos, such landscape mosaics have historically been the site of small-scale (mainly shifting) cultivation. Other general patterns emerging in both countries are that forestry-related concessions (e.g. tree plantations) tend to be granted in forested landscapes, while deals with an agricultural focus tend to be granted in landscapes of existing cropland. In Laos, agriculture-related concessions are twice as likely to be granted in cropland landscapes than in other types of landscapes.

Moreover, our spatial analysis reveals that the vast majority of investments are located in relatively easily accessible areas. Concessions in agriculture are the closest to provincial capitals in both countries, with an average travel time of two hours. Forestry concessions come next with an average travel time of two hours and 41 minutes to provincial capitals. Finally, concessions in other sub-sectors average over four hours of travel time—this especially reflects the importance of mining concessions in Laos, which must be situated where mineral deposits are located, of course, regardless of how remote that situation is. In Laos, land concessions tend to be more accessible than in Cambodia. Nevertheless, the main investors (domestic, Chinese, and Vietnamese) also run projects in very remote areas of both countries.

2.2.5 Summarising Patterns of Forestry- and Agriculture-Related LSLAS

Laos and Cambodia have both experienced a sharp increase in LSLAS over the past decade, corresponding to a fiftyfold increase in the number of land deals in Laos and a fourfold increase in the area granted in Cambodia. The land acquisitions in Laos are smaller in size but greater in number, and in Cambodia fewer but larger. Our analysis of the geography of LSLAS in both countries revealed some key commonalities and differences. Aware of the risks of over-simplification, we nevertheless identified and defined the following general patterns and socio-ecological contexts of LSLAs.

First, forestry is the most important concession-related sub-sector in Cambodia and Laos based on the amount of land involved. Investors from neighbouring countries—especially Vietnam and China—play a bigger role in these forestry-related concessions than do international investors from outside the region. In Cambodia, domestic investors also play a key role in this sub-sector. Forestry-related concessions are typically granted for large, contiguous plots of land, often relatively close to borders of riparian countries. In most cases, these plots are located in landscapes previously classified as 'forest'; this suggests that investors may also see opportunities to extract value from tim-ber obtained when clearing and preparing investment plots for their 'intended purpose'. In Laos, the areas where forestry concessions are located exhibit the highest poverty rates of all areas affected by LSLAs, while in Cambodia, forestry deals are in average below the national mean but concern less poor areas compared to agricultural deals. The agrarian systems affected are partly subsistence farming systems but more often semi-subsistence systems because their relatively good accessibility enables farmers to diversify their activities to include growing commercial crops or earning off-farm income.

Second, agriculture is the next most important concession-related sub-sector. Domestic and regional investors both play an important role in this sub-sector. Agricultural concessions are typically smaller in size than forestry concessions but are somewhat more accessible. In Laos, they tend to occur in areas displaying lower poverty incidence. Though some agricultural con-cessions target areas classified as forests, they more frequently target existing croplands and thus affect populations practicing lifestyles of semi-subsistence, commercial agriculture, and/or off-farm activities.

3   Analysing Patterns of LSLA Implementation Processes

After identifying these general patterns and socio-ecological contexts of land acquisitions, we sought to distinguish the different types of implementation processes that steer such acquisitions. We defined implementation processes as encompassing all phases, from the initial negotiation of a land concession to the final allocation of land in specific socio-ecological contexts. Our process-based analyses comprised three steps: (i) conducting case studies on different types of LSLAs in order to understand the actors, activities, and institutions that guide the implementation of land deals; (ii) conducting a meta-analysis of these case studies in which we identified common key factors and analysed their role in the implementation process; (iii) pinpointing and examining recurrent linkages between the key factors in an effort to distinguish archetypes of LSLA implementation processes as part of a broader typology. The following section describes each of these steps. While it provides a detailed account of the specific set of methods used and the results obtained, the case studies are initially described only briefly (number and type), as we wish to focus more attention on how they were used in our meta-analysis.

3.1   *Case Studies on Implementation Processes of LSLAS*

Our meta-analysis draws on 15 case studies primarily conducted as Master's thesis projects between 2011 and 2013 in Laos and Cambodia, as part of a broader research project (Michel, 2013; Sommer, 2013; Zurflueh, 2013). Each case study focused on a separate company that sought to acquire land in order to invest in a specific crop. The case studies were designed to improve our understanding of land-deal implementation processes over time (from negotiations to allocation of land) and across different scales, whether spatial or administrative. Each was conceptually based on a human actor model that differentiates the activities and agency of actors from the dynamic conditions of action and the intuitions in which actions are embedded (Wiesmann et al., 2011). The case studies were selected based on national inventories of land investments in Cambodia (LICADHO, 2013; ODC, 2013) and Laos (Schönweger et al., 2012) using factors such as crop type, investor origin, and size of concession area as sample criteria. A total of 22 case studies in seven Lao provinces and 8 case studies in two Cambodian provinces were conducted; of these, 15 were included in our meta-analysis (see Table 6.2).

3.2   *Meta-Analysis of Case Studies on LSLA Implementation Processes*
3.2.1   Identification of Key Factors

In general terms, our meta-analysis corresponds to an a posteriori comparison of already published case studies (Lambin and Geist, 2006). However, our approach differs from many meta-analyses in land science that investigate land use decision-making based on comparison of predefined direct or indirect drivers. Because each of our case studies followed a conceptual design based on a human actor model (Wiesmann et al., 2011), they revealed numerous interrelations between actors, actions, conditions of actions, and institutions. In order to maintain this broad range of important variables and also to focus our analysis on the most relevant, recurrent interactions, we performed a sensitivity analysis for each case study as a basis for our meta-analysis. The sensitivity model for the analysis of dynamic systems was initially developed by Vester and Hesler (1987), and then further adapted for the analysis of

TABLE 6.2   *Case studies used for the meta-analysis of LSLA implementation processes*

Crop	Investors' origin	Company	Location (Province)	Area granted (ha)
Rubber	China	Ruifeng	Luangnamtha	10,000
		Lilieng	Vientiane Prov.	2,500
		Rongxieng	Savannakhet	2,407
		Guangda	Savannakhet	1,800
	Vietnam	Daklak	Attapeu, Champasack	10,000
		Hoang Anh Ya Lay	Attapeu	10,000
		Ho Chi Minh Youth	Attapeu, Champasack	6,000
		Viet Lao Rubber Joint Stock	Champasack	10,000
	Thailand	Lao Thai Hua	Vientiane Prov.	30,000
Eucalyptus & Acacia	China	Sunpaper	Savannakhet	39,000
	India	Birla Lao	Khammuane, Savannakhet	50,000
	Japan	Oji Lao	Khammuane	50,000
Coffee	Singapore	Outspan	Champasack	2,900
	Thailand	Paksong Highland	Champasack	3,100
Sugar cane	Thailand	Mitr Lao	Savannakhet	10,000

SOURCE: AUTHORS.

socio-ecological systems by Messerli (2000). It initially requires researchers to define a set of key factors that: (i) are representative of the social, political, economic, and environmental dimensions of the system; and (ii) capture key interactions between these factors occurring in the system.

This narrowing down of key factors was discussed and carried out together with the researchers who conducted the original case studies. We defined three general domains considered to be important mutual conditions of action in the LSLA implementation process: the domain of *land investment*, the domain of *land governance*, and the domain of the *socio-ecological context*. For each of these domains, we then chose eight key factors covering relevant components of the human actor model and corresponding to the criteria mentioned above in (i) and (ii). Table 6.3 lists all 24 key factors identified across the three general domains, specifying their quality and rationale.

TABLE 6.3   *Key factors in LSLA implementation processes*

	#	Key factor	Quality and rationale
Domain of land investment	1.	Origin of investors	Country of origin
	2.	Type of crop	Intention of investment
	3.	Time of investment	Year when land was allocated
	4.	Access to political power	Investors' access to political power including historical ties and political backing in host country and country of origin
	5.	Access to cheap labour force	Perceived and actual availability and price of labour force
	6.	Size of company	Overall power of company including access to capital and stock exchange
	7.	CSR commitment	Investors' commitments to corporate social and environmental sustainability and a good reputation
	8.	Size of concession	Total size of land requested and granted for investment
Domain of land governance	9.	Economic growth strategies	Government endeavours to push economic growth through regional integration and foreign direct investment (FDI) in land
	10.	Policies related to land	Includes policies related to shifting cultivation, land use planning, infrastructure development, relocation, etc.
	11.	Top-down granting of concessions	Central level officials granting concessions and delegating implementation to lower administrative levels
	12.	Power of district/ provincial officials	Power of provincial and district officials actively involved in granting rights and support to investors
	13.	Experience with LSLAS	Decision makers' prior experience of LSLAS
	14.	Patronage and corruption	Patronage and corruption among different stakeholders and also across sectors and levels
	15.	Land tenure insecurity	Legal pluralism and relative power differentials of institutions governing land access and land use rights
	16.	Land surveys	Companies and/or government collecting information on land, involved stakeholders, and possible impacts

	#	Key factor	Quality and rationale
	17.	Available and suitable land	Land availability as perceived by local people or as constructed by powerful actors and policies
	18.	Land cover and land use	Pre-existing land use and land cover in areas targeted for land investments
	19.	Logging	Logging prior to investment is often seen as an important incentive for investors or/and authorities involved
Domain of socio-ecological context	20.	Biophysical factors and topography	Opportunities to acquire large and connected plots of land; biophysical factors influencing suitability such as soil, climate, altitude
	21.	Historical ties	Confidence of rural population and local authorities in investors from neighbouring regions and countries based on a shared history
	22.	Capability and assets of villagers	Includes factors of well-being/poverty and ethnicity, as well as social relations, networks, etc. of villagers and their representatives
	23.	Accessibility	Accessibility in travel time to nearby city centres, processing factories, and border crossings. Defined by topography, infrastructure, and land use
	24.	Land allocation	Final identification and allocation of land to the investor as a new land user

SOURCE: AUTHORS.

3.2.2   Meta-Analysis of Case Studies and Role of Key Factors

Having defined domains and representative sets of key factors, we were then able to focus in a comparative manner on our main object of interest: the diverse *interactions* between these key factors. For each case study, we assessed any possible interactions between the 24 key factors in either direction (i.e. influencing or being influenced). Referring back to the original research results of every case study, we assessed any possible interaction between any two factors. Based on their knowledge of the case-study settings, the researchers involved rated each possible interaction between key factors on a scale from absent (0), through weak (0.5) and moderate (1.0), to strong (2.0). This rating system enabled us to calculate the average strength of an interaction between any two key factors across all 15 case studies.

The matrix in Figure 6.3 summarises the most important interactions observed in each of the 15 case studies (shaded in dark gray). For example, reading across row 1 we see that the key factor (KF) Origin of Investor (KF 1) has a direct and strong influence on Access to Political Power (KF 4) and on the Size of Concession (KF 8). Similarly, reading down column 17 we see that Available Land (KF 17) is influenced by various key factors from different domains, including: Type of Crop (KF 2), Time of Investment (KF 3), and Size of Concession (KF 8) from the *land investment* domain; Policies Related to Land (KF 10), Land Tenure Insecurity (KF 15), and Land Surveys (KF 16) from the *governance* domain; and Capability and Assets of Villagers (KF 22), Accessibility (KF 23), etc. from the domain of *socio-ecological context*. Among other things, this powerfully demonstrates that, in practice, 'available land' (KF 17) cannot be observed strictly by means of remote sensing or according to environmental indicators; rather, it is something that is constructed based on power relations between actors and according to relevant policies.

Beyond looking at influences from a first factor on a second factor, we can use the matrix to examine how a second factor influences a third factor, and so on. This makes it possible to describe whole chains of interactions. For example, the Time of Investment (KF 3) is seen to strongly influence the Power of District/Provincial Officials (KF 12); indeed, during the early years of concession granting, alliances between provincial officials and investors flourished, and land deals did not require national-level approval. Provincial officials (KF 12), in turn, strongly influence the way Land Surveys are conducted (KF 16). As a consequence, provincial officials are able to define Available Land (KF 17) according to their own interests and those of investors. Finally, this definition of Available Land (KF 17) determines Land Allocation (KF 24) and the granting of contiguous plots and large Sizes of Concessions (KF 8).

Perhaps of even greater interest from a policy perspective is to identify which key factors play the biggest role in particular outcomes of the LSLA implementation process. Our meta-analysis provides information on the general role played by each factor, in particular how strongly each factor interacts with others in the system and whether it exerts or is subject to more influence overall. To this end, we calculated: (i) the sum of the influences that each factor *exerts* (referred to as the active sum, or AS, for each row), and (ii) the sum of the influences that each factor *is subject to* (referred to as the passive sum, or PS, for each column). By comparing the active sum of any given factor with its passive sum, we can calculate its activity ratio (AR=AS/PS)—that is, whether and to what extent it exerts a greater influence than it is subject to. In addition, it is

Key factors	1	2	3	4	5	6	7	8	9	10	11	12	13	14	15	16	17	18	19	20	21	22	23	24	AS	IR
		Land investment							Land governance								Socio-ecological context								AS	IR
Domain of land investment									A. Investments → Governance								B. Investments → Context									
1 Origin of investor		0.67	0.77	1.03	0.33	0.69	0.84	1.08	0.27	0.20	0.44	0.44	0.30	0.77	0.00	0.70	0.31	0.13	0.30	0.16	0.53	0.14	0.25	0.38	11	30
2 Type of crop	0.02		0.59	0.53	0.70	0.50	0.39	1.09	0.34	0.34	0.39	0.34	0.28	0.30	0.13	0.78	1.06	0.56	0.47	0.22	0.09	0.23	0.84	0.67	11	84
3 Time of investment	0.00	0.25		2.00	0.25	0.30	0.23	0.59	0.27	0.70	0.50	2.00	0.73	0.33	0.13	0.97	1.67	2.00	0.23	0.44	0.22	0.78	0.09	0.80	15	196
4 Access to political power	0.03	0.02	0.72		0.08	0.31	0.34	0.84	0.08	0.22	1.00	0.30	0.13	0.55	0.20	0.69	0.44	0.00	0.16	0.36	0.09	0.34	0.09	0.38	7	76
-5 Access to cheap labor force	0.02	0.41	0.34	0.09		0.08	0.17	0.88	0.14	0.13	0.00	0.00	0.00	0.05	0.06	0.06	0.28	0.08	0.03	0.00	0.06	0.00	0.38	0.20	3	17
6 Size of company	0.05	0.50	0.55	1.13	0.19		0.67	1.50	0.31	0.20	0.56	0.41	0.13	0.72	0.17	0.64	0.28	0.06	0.19	0.09	0.06	0.50	0.38	0.58	10	26
7 CSR commitment	0.06	0.09	0.28	0.42	0.16	0.08		0.09	0.02	0.19	0.11	0.13	0.08	0.69	0.22	0.72	0.47	0.22	0.36	0.09	0.06	0.78	0.00	0.34	6	38
8 Size of concession	0.09	0.13	0.64	0.97		0.11	0.20		0.25	0.41	0.81	0.80	0.22	0.66	0.61	0.84	1.34	0.48	0.19	0.47	0.16	0.84	0.53	1.05	12	213
Domain of land governance		C. Governance → Investments															D. Governance → Context									
9 Economic growth strategies	0.38	0.73	0.69	1.00	0.19	0.13	0.22	1.06		1.30	1.02	0.91	0.00	0.25	0.41	0.33	0.36	0.42	0.16	0.03	0.48	0.27	0.41	0.45	11	61
10 Policies related to land	0.30	0.97	0.67	0.27	0.23	0.00	0.70	0.72	0.28		0.45	0.78	0.00	0.28	1.08	0.83	1.27	2.00	0.33	0.03	0.06	0.73	0.20	0.61	13	114
11 Top-down granting of concessions	0.14	0.06	0.78	0.47	0.00	0.00	0.08	0.64	0.17	0.31		0.72	0.00	0.53	0.66	0.31	0.11	0.20	0.00	0.00	0.05	0.53	0.02	0.42	6	45
12 Power of district/province officials	0.27	0.44	0.97	0.55	0.00	0.00	0.27	1.25	0.52	0.31	0.31		0.02	0.95	1.17	1.47	1.31	0.78	0.28	0.16	0.39	0.75	0.19	1.11	14	205
13 Experience with LSLAs	0.02	0.19	0.20	0.06	0.42	0.02	0.08	0.41	0.00	0.13	0.00	0.17		0.02	0.33	0.34	0.11	0.16	0.25	0.13	0.16	0.89	0.00	0.22	4	10
14 Paronage and corruption	0.11	0.00	0.58	0.80	0.00	0.00	0.41	0.63	0.16	0.48	0.16	0.56	0.00		0.67	0.45	0.67	0.16	0.13	0.11	0.17	0.67	0.25	0.52	8	77
15 Land tenure insecurity	0.09	0.16	0.08	0.19	0.44	0.00	0.25	0.56	0.20	0.14	0.25	0.56	0.70	0.00		0.19	1.08	0.48	0.42	0.02	0.00	1.33	0.05	0.72	8	91
16 Land surveys	0.03	0.09	0.78	0.00	0.00	0.00	0.16	0.66	0.19	0.19	0.25	1.13	0.47	0.00	0.47		1.66	0.27	0.19	0.19	0.06	0.75	0.27	1.11	9	127
Domain of socio-ecological context		E. Context → Investments								F. Context → Governance																
17 Available and suitable land	0.45	0.75	0.94	0.23	0.17	0.13	0.13	1.53	0.86	0.72	0.23	1.38	0.11	0.45	0.91	1.13		0.64	0.31	0.73	0.00	0.94	0.48	1.91	16	306
18 Land cover and land use	0.11	0.28	0.50	0.00	0.47	0.00	0.09	0.63	0.36	0.84	0.13	0.95	0.00	0.22	0.94	0.64	1.50		0.36	0.75	0.00	0.48	0.67	1.22	11	133
19 Logging	0.06	0.41	0.33	0.13	0.00	0.06	0.00	0.30	0.27	0.30	0.00	0.42	0.00	0.45	0.38	0.20	0.56	0.23		0.22	0.00	0.14	0.27	0.38	5	33
20 Biophysical factors and topography	0.05	0.45	0.33	0.00	0.00	0.00	0.00	0.80	0.25	0.44	0.06	0.06	0.06	0.16	0.16	0.28	1.34	0.58	0.34		0.00	0.11	1.03	0.59	7	32
21 Historical ties	0.09	0.08	0.31	0.41	0.33	0.03	0.03	0.19	0.20	0.03	0.13	0.41	0.00	0.53	0.03	0.13	0.09	0.23	0.09	0.03		0.14	0.03	0.16	4	10
22 Capability and assets of villagers	0.00	0.00	0.17	0.00	0.23	0.03	0.53	0.56	0.00	0.27	0.31	0.88	0.06	0.70	1.08	0.55	1.34	0.42	0.00	0.02	0.03		0.08	1.23	8	112
23 Accessibility	0.42	1.06	0.52	0.03	0.05	0.08	0.08	1.08	0.28	0.33	0.03	0.66	0.23	0.23	0.36	0.73	1.42	0.84	0.63	0.16	0.11	1.08		0.98	11	78
24 Land location	0.00	0.02	1.02	0.06	0.47	0.17	0.28	0.41	0.03	0.03	0.34	0.34	0.14	0.19	0.78	0.41	0.94	0.97	1.13	0.22	0.00	0.83	0.63		9	145
Passive Sum (PS)	2.8	7.8	13	10	5.5	2.7	6.7	17	5.4	8.9	7.2	14	2.3	10	12	13	20	12	6.4	4.6	2.7	13	6.8	16		
Activity Ratio (AS/PS)	3.8	1.4	1.2	0.7	0.6	3.7	0.8	0.7	2.0	1.4	0.9	1.0	1.9	0.8	0.7	0.7	0.8	0.9	0.8	1.5	1.4	0.6	1.7	0.6		

FIGURE 6.3 *Meta-analysis of case studies using the sensitivity model.*

Note: *The matrix shows the average ratings of interactions between any of the 24 key factors in our 15 case studies. The ratings ranged from strong (2.0), through moderate (1.0) and weak (0.5), to absent (0.0). The active sum (AS) and passive sum (PS) of each factor were calculated in order to assess the factor's activity ratio (AS/PS) and its total strengths of interaction (IR).*

SOURCE: AUTHORS.

very useful to calculate how strongly each factor interacts with other factors. This can be done by multiplying the active sum by the passive sum to arrive at the total strength of interaction (IR =AS*PS).

Next, we identified all the factors that display activity ratios where the active sum outweighs the passive sum (AS/PS >1). These factors may be seen as having the biggest influence on the outcomes of the implementation process. In the *land investment* domain, these factors comprise Origin of Investor (KF 1), Type of Crop (KF 2), Time of Investment (KF 3), and Size of Company (KF 6). Indeed, the case studies we analysed showed that large companies— mainly from Vietnam and China—that arrived early and invested in forestry concessions (e.g. rubber, eucalyptus) were generally able to obtain large plots of land, where they wanted them, with little to no resistance or administrative obstacles. By contrast, relatively small companies and latecomers experienced significantly more problems and were required to cooperate with district officials, to conduct land surveys, and to negotiate the allocation of smaller plots of land with villagers. In the *land governance* domain, the most influential key factors comprise national-level Economic Growth Strategies (KF 9) and Policies Related to Land (KF 10), as well as different actors' Experience with LSLAS (KF 13). In the *socio-ecological context* domain, only Accessibility (KF 23) of urban centres appears to play an influential role; Biophysical Factors (KF 20) and Historical Ties (KF 21) exhibit positive activity ratios but appear only weakly interrelated.

Finally, we identified all the factors that display activity ratios where the passive sum outweighs the active sum (AS/PS<1) but which are highly interrelated. These factors may not have the power to influence the outcomes of the implementation process; however, because they are strongly influenced by many other factors, they serve as useful indicators of the type of implementation process in question. The most important of these indicative factors are the quantity and quality of Available Land (KF 17) and Land Allocation (KF 24), which vary substantially depending on whether the corresponding implementation process occurs in a more authoritarian/top-down or participatory/bottom-up manner. Further, Size of Concession (KF 8) serves as an excellent indicator of the type of implementation process, since careful negotiations and planning processes usually result in more fragmented, modestly sized plots than originally anticipated or desired by investors. Lastly, the following factors serve as useful indicators of the monitoring of the implementation process—that is to say, in terms of the role they play: the type and quality of Land Surveys conducted (KF 16), the role attributed to pre-existing Land

Use (KF 18), and the Capability and Assets of Villagers (KF 22). The fact that villagers' capabilities only serve as an indicator and not as an influential factor suggests that villagers' empowerment is subject to very real constraints. Indeed, from a systemic perspective, other factors have a much bigger role in the outcome of LSLA implementation processes.

3.3 *Archetypes of LSLA Implementation Processes and Resulting Typology*

As shown above, our meta-analysis enabled generalisation, based on 15 case studies, of the importance of different key factors in the LSLA implementation process. As we have also seen, however, the interactions between these factors display different qualities and levels of strength, involve feedback mechanisms and chain-like effects, and ultimately lead to different outcomes. In an effort to account for such differentiations in our meta-analysis, we looked for recurrent linkages between the key factors, links that may point to archetypal patterns. So defined, the resulting archetypes could provide the basis for a working typology of LSLA implementation processes.

For this purpose, we analysed how the three main domains of the implementation processes—namely, *land investment, land governance,* and *socio-ecological context*—influenced each other. For example, do the combined factors from the *land governance* domain exert a greater influence on the combined factors from the *land investment* domain or vice versa? To find out, we analysed the matrix of influences for every case study (Figure 6.3) and calculated the balance of influences between any two domains of the implementation process. Our analysis of all 15 case studies revealed four distinct archetypes in terms of the way the main domains influence each other (Figure 6.4). They are detailed below.

3.3.1 Archetype 1: Marginal People

Our analysis of the interrelations between the selected key factors revealed the following pattern among eight of the 15 case studies: a net influence exerted by the domains of *land governance* and *land investment*, respectively, on the domain of the *socio-ecological context*; and, at the same time, a net influence exerted by *land investment* on the *land governance* domain (observe the directions of the arrows in the outer ring of Figure 6.5). Based on this shared pattern, we posit an implementation-process archetype we refer to as 'Marginal People': land acquisitions in this category are essentially steered by the claims of powerful external actors, irrespective of local realities, thus exploiting and exacerbating the weak position of marginalised populations.

	Mutual influences between domains of Governance (G) and Investment (I)			Mutual influences between domains of Investment (I) and Socio-ecol. Context (C)			Mutual influences between domains of Socio-ecol. Context (C) and Governance (G)		
	z (G <= I)	z (I <= G)	Balance	z (I <= C)	z (C <= I)	Balance	z (C <= G)	z (G <= C)	Balance
Birla Lao (Pulp)	16.5	23.0	-6.5	9.5	7.0	2.5	12.0	16.5	-4.5
Daklak (Rubber)	17.0	27.5	-10.5	21.5	15.0	6.5	13.0	26.5	-13.5
Outspan (Coffee)	27.0	54.5	-27.5	35.0	19.0	16.0	29.5	38.0	-8.5
Hoang Anh Ya Lay (Rubber)	17.0	27.5	-10.5	21.5	15.0	6.5	13.0	26.5	-13.5
Sumpaper (Pulp)	15.5	18.0	-2.5	23.0	21.0	2.0	8.0	15.0	-7.0
Mitr Lao (Sugarcane)	12.5	15.0	-2.5	12.0	11.5	0.5	10.0	24.5	-14.5
Viet Lao Joint Stock (Rubber)	17.0	27.5	-10.5	21.5	15.0	6.5	13.0	26.5	-13.5
Paksong Highland (Coffee)	26.0	42.0	-16.0	37.0	28.5	8.5	26.0	34.0	-8.0
Archetype 1 (averages):	*18.6*	*29.4*	*-10.8*	*22.6*	*16.5*	*6.1*	*15.6*	*25.9*	*-10.4*
Guangda (Rubber)	24.0	29.0	-5.0	24.0	18.0	6.0	29.0	25.0	4.0
Lao Thai Hua (Rubber)	21.0	29.0	-8.0	40.0	28.0	12.0	34.5	33.0	1.5
Rongxieng (Rubber)	28.0	29.0	-1.0	26.0	18.5	7.5	31.0	27.5	3.5
Ruifeng (Rubber)	32.0	33.5	-1.5	53.0	18.0	35.0	49.0	43.5	5.5
Archetype 2 (averages):	*24.7*	*30.0*	*-3.9*	*33.1*	*19.8*	*15.1*	*31.8*	*31.0*	*3.6*
Oji Lao (Pulp)	21.0	18.5	2.5	11.5	17.5	-6.0	17.0	26.0	-9.0
Archetype 3 (averages):	*21.0*	*18.5*	*2.5*	*11.5*	*17.5*	*-6.0*	*17.0*	*26.0*	*-9.0*
Ho Chi Minh Youth (Rubber)	17.0	13.0	4.0	20.5	11.0	9.5	20.5	15.5	5.0
Lilieng (Rubber)	25.0	22.0	3.0	23.5	23.0	0.5	28.5	26.0	2.5
Archetype 4 (averages):	*23.5*	*22.6*	*3.5*	*25.5*	*17.8*	*5.0*	*27.3*	*28.0*	*3.8*

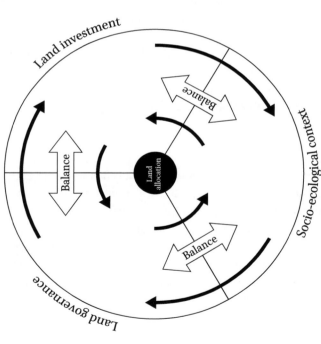

FIGURE 6.4 *Archetypes of ISLA implementation processes.*
Note: Archetypes were identified based on patterns in the way factors from one domain cumulatively influenced or were influenced by the factors in another domain: land governance, land investment, and socio-ecological context (see diagram). For every case study, the balance of influence (net cumulative effect of factors) was calculated between domain pairs. This resulted in four distinct types of archetypes (see table to the right of the figure).
SOURCE: AUTHORS.

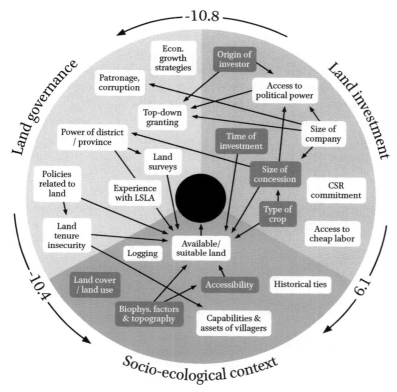

FIGURE 6.5 *Archetype 'Marginal People'.*
Note: Recurrent interactions among key factors in LSLA *implementation*
processes (displaying an average rating ≥ 1.25). The outer arrows indicate
the net balance of mutual influence between domains.
SOURCE: AUTHORS.

For the majority of the case studies in this category, analysis of the recurrent interactions between key factors (Figure 6.5) reveals strong ties in the *land investment* domain. Origin of Investor (KF 1)—typically neighbouring countries such as Vietnam, China, or Thailand—is positively correlated with the Size of Company (KF 6) and has a favourable influence on investors' Access to Political Power (KF 4). In many cases, strong alliances were established between investors and provincial authorities on either side of nearby national borders. These factors, corresponding to strong political and economic backing, in turn influence the intended Size of Concession (KF 8)—relatively large in these case studies (44,500 ha for pulp concessions and 10,000 ha for rubber concessions, on average). The strengths of the *land investment* domain led to recurrent influences on both the domain of *socio-ecological context* and on the domain of *land governance*. Notably, the definition of Available and Suitable Land (KF 17) appears to be defined by the Type of Crop (KF 2) and on the Size of Concession (KF 8) requested. Further, the efficient Top-Down Granting of Concessions (KF 11) corresponds to investors who arrived early on. Due to their lack of Experience with LSLAS (KF 13), local authorities and villagers could be easily swayed by empty promises. While key factors of the local *socio-ecological context* may influence the definition of Available and Suitable Land (KF 17) to a certain degree, they have limited influence on the Time of Investment (KF 3), Type of Crop (KF 2), or Size of Concession (KF 8). At the same time, key factors from the *land investment* domain influence processes in the domain of *land governance*. Investors' Access to Political Power (KF 4) and economic power corresponds to Top-Down Granting of Land Concessions (KF 11), which limits the Power of District/Provincial Officials (KF 12). Such access to power also strongly influences the conduct of Land Surveys (KF 16), contributing to greater Land Tenure Insecurity (KF 15). These factors together influence what is defined as Available and Suitable Land (KF 17) and to what degree the Capability and Assets of Villagers come into play (KF 22).

3.3.2   Archetype 2: Marginal Governance

Four cases of rubber investments from Chinese and Thai companies revealed a different pattern of recurrent interactions among key factors. While the net influence emerging from the *land investment* domain still dominates the influence of the *socio-ecological context* and the *land governance* domains, respectively, key factors in the *socio-ecological context* now clearly affect *land governance*. We refer to this archetype as 'Marginal Governance', since land governance here is shaped by specificities of the socio-ecological context, but still remains largely under the control of the *land investment* domain.

The recurrent interrelations of key factors in these four case studies (Figure 6.6) once again point to strong investors, namely two relatively small and two large companies (Ruifeng from China, and Lao Thai Hua from Thailand), which were initially granted concession areas of 10,000 ha and 30,000 ha, respectively. These large investments exerted powerful influences on the Power of Provincial/District Officials (KF 12) and the implementation of Land Surveys (KF 16). In addition, the Size of Concession (KF 8), Time of Investment (KF 3), and Type of Crop (KF 2) dictated what land was deemed available and needed to be allocated.

Also notable in these cases, key factors of the *socio-ecological context* were not simply overruled by outside forces. We observe in Figure 6.6 that Available

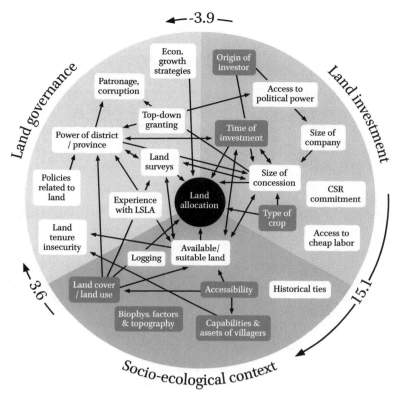

FIGURE 6.6 *Archetype 'Marginal Governance'.*
         Note: Recurrent interactions among key factors in LSLA implementation
         processes (displaying an average rating ≥ 1.25). The outer arrows indicate
         the net balance of mutual influence between domains.
         SOURCE: AUTHORS.

Land and Suitable Land (KF 17), Land Cover and Land Use (KF 18), Capability and Assets of Villagers (KF 22), and Accessibility (KF 23) exerted an influence on the Size of Concession (KF 8) and the Power of District/Provincial Officials (KF 12), and shaped the outcomes of the Land Survey (KF 16). In other words, the definition of available land and the final allocation of land were also influenced by people, by pre-existing land use, topography, and accessibility. This new pattern can be explained as follows: firstly, large companies with higher CSR standards (and a sensitivity to reputational risks), such as the Lao Thai Hua company, explicitly followed a bottom-up approach, paying careful attention to the context of the investment. Others, such as the Rongxieng Company, also adopted a more bottom-up approach, but only following initial bad experiences using an authoritarian approach (involving use of armed soldiers). The key characteristics of this archetype of implementation processes are strong investors who maintain control but pay careful attention to the socio-ecological context and allow it to shape land governance. Such investors are willing to accept a slower LSLA implementation process, smaller concessions than originally planned, or the subdivision of concessions into multiple plots. In one case, such perceived downsides were compensated for by means of high-value timber-extraction activities during land clearing.

3.3.3   Archetype 3: Marginal Investments

One case study involving a Japanese pulp production company exhibited a unique pattern of LSLA implementation, which did not fit with the other archetypes. In this case, the *land investment* domain was clearly dominated by factors in the *land governance* and *socio-ecological context* domains, ultimately threatening the whole project. While it is only a single case, we wish to highlight it as it may point to a unique archetype that we will refer to as 'Marginal Investments'.

In this type of LSLA implementation process (Figure 6.7) the company experienced a very smooth start because it was able to take over a pre-existing concession and benefited from Access to Political Power (KF 4) through high-level diplomatic ties. Despite its promising start, however, years have passed and the company continues to struggle to actually have the land allocated. They lack support from District/Provincial Officials (KF 12) and there is no longer enough Available and Suitable Land (KF 17) due to the earlier 'land rush' (Time of Investment—KF 3). Villagers and authorities from districts/provinces have also learned from past Experience with LSLAs (KF 13) and are now able to negotiate better conditions for land deals. In such cases, the Capability and Assets of Villagers (KF 22) and local authorities—that is, their ability to resist coercion or financial temptations and to negotiate effectively with companies and district officials—considerably influence contractual modalities (e.g. contract farming or concession type) and the overall terms of investment (e.g. land area, compensation). This has led the company in question to pursue a more bottom-up approach, fulfilling CSR commitments. However, this approach has allowed local socio-ecological factors—pre-existing Land Cover and Land Use (KF 18) and lack of Available Land and Suitable Land (KF 17)—to act as constraints, increasing the risk of investment failure. In response, the company recently diversified the crops it intends to produce from eucalyptus to a variety of agricultural products, and is conducting market and suitability studies.

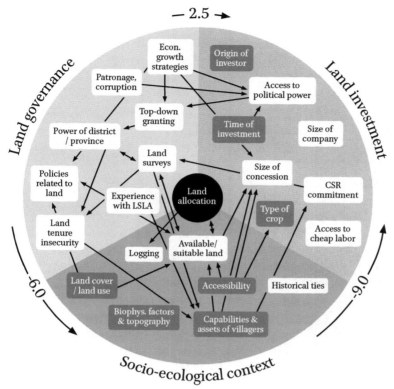

FIGURE 6.7   *Archetype 'Marginal Investment'.*
Note: Recurrent interactions among key factors in LSLA implementation
processes (displaying an average rating ≥ 1.25). The outer arrows indicate
the net balance of mutual influence between domains.
SOURCE: AUTHORS.

3.3.4   Archetype 4: Marginal Land

Finally, two case studies—involving a Vietnamese and a Chinese rubber investment, respectively—revealed yet another pattern of LSLA implementation. We believe these companies provide a good example of effectively targeting agricultural investments towards underused land, and we refer to the corresponding archetype as 'Marginal land'. In these cases: the *socio-ecological context* mainly influences *land governance; land governance* controls the *land investment* domain; and *land investment*, in turn, shapes the *socio-ecological context* (Figure 6.8).

First of all, the recurrent interactions observed between key factors indicate limited economic and political power on the part of the companies

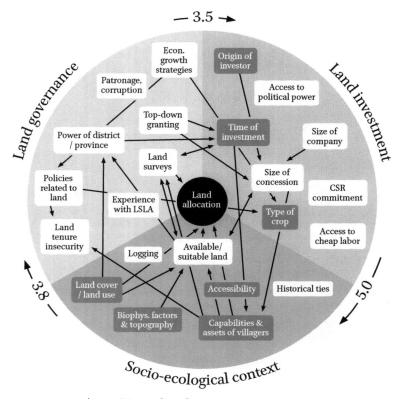

FIGURE 6.8 *Archetype 'Marginal Land'.*
Note: Recurrent interactions among key factors in implementation
processes of large-scale land acquisition (manifesting an average rating
≥ 1.25). Outer arrows refer to the net balance of mutual influences between
domains.
SOURCE: AUTHORS.

involved. While the *land investment* domain had some influence on the way
Land Surveys (KF 16) were carried out, it did not significantly influence Policies
Related to Land (KF 10) or Top-Down Granting of Concessions (KF 11). This
prevented the investors from manipulating aspects of land governance to their
advantage. The search for Available and Suitable Land (KF 17) proved to be a
very difficult endeavour for the investors. As they arrived later than other companies in the respective regions, their own interests—for example, obtaining a
large Size of Concession (KF 8) or producing a specific Type of Crop (KF 2)—
played a limited role in defining what was deemed available. They were obliged
to negotiate locally regarding available land and, as a result, key factors of the

socio-ecological context—such as Land Cover and Land Use (KF 18), Biophysical Factors and Topography (KF 20), Accessibility (KF 23), and Capability and Assets of Villagers (KF 22)—played a significant role. Though it was a lengthy and frequently complicated process, the resulting Land Allocation (KF 24) was the most inclusive of all those observed, with both villagers and investors agreeing to it. These actors then sought support in terms of land governance from provincial and district authorities, eventually requesting Land Surveys (KF 16) and formal recognition of the agreements. Ultimately, these processes positively influenced the implementation of Policies Related to Land (KF 10) and Land Tenure Insecurity (KF 15) (the latter in the sense that such insecurity was reduced).

4   Synthesis and Discussion

In previous sections, we have presented the results of applying two complementary approaches to the analysis of LSLAs, in an effort to provide better evidence for policymaking. On the one hand, we conducted a spatially referenced analysis of land acquisitions in Laos and Cambodia, revealing patterns of investor type, investment purpose (sub-sector), and socio-ecological contexts. On the other, we conducted a process-based analysis of LSLA implementation, reaching from initial negotiations to the final allocation of land. This was done by means of a meta-analysis of case studies in which we identified recurrent interactions between selected key factors of LSLA implementation. This enabled us to identify possible archetypes that could serve as a basis for a working typology of LSLA implementation processes.

Both approaches are capable of generating policy-relevant information, but each has clear limitations on its own (discussed below). That fact brings us back to our guiding question: can distinct spatial patterns be tied to specific types of LSLA implementation processes by means of common indicators? This would enable observers to either interpret spatial patterns in terms of underlying implementation processes, or to validate and generalise case-study findings regarding implementation processes to inform policies at higher spatial levels.

Our spatial analysis of LSLA inventories revealed two general patterns. (1) Numerous regional investors and some domestic investors have engaged in forestry sub-sectors, mainly focussing on rubber and eucalyptus or acacia plantations. The corresponding concessions are generally large, contiguous plots of land found in somewhat inaccessible landscapes once classified as forest or shrub land. The populations affected by these concessions are generally poorer than the respective national poverty line of each country and often practice small-scale agriculture (mainly, in Laos, shifting cultivation). (2) A mix of regional, domestic, and some international investors have engaged in agricultural sub-sectors. Their concessions are generally smaller and often compete with pre-existing cropping mosaics cultivated by smallholders. The affected areas are usually relatively accessible and populated by less-poor people in Laos and by poorer people in Cambodia.

These insights are consistent with a growing body of evidence showing that LSLAS are a strong driver of agrarian transition in South-East Asia (Anseeuw et al., 2012). LSLAS have increased exponentially, making rural areas the site of fierce competition over resources in settings where powerful investors from riparian countries play a key role (Schönweger et al., 2012). Our analysis shows that optimistic assumptions about investment mainly flowing to 'marginal land'—that is, land that is unused yet suitable for agriculture—are fundamentally flawed (Borras Jr. et al., 2011; Cotula et al., 2009; Messerli et al., 2014). Instead, land concessions are increasing resource competition, affecting two vulnerable groups in particular: smallholders in densely populated cropping mosaics; and poorer ethnic minorities in forest mosaics where shifting cultivation is common. Overall, spatial, quantitative analysis of land concessions clearly demonstrates that LSLAS are and will remain a driving force of agrarian transition in the region. Given the advanced stage of expansion into agricultural and forested landscapes and existing conflicts with affected land users, policymaking questions should no longer be limited to whether to permit, prevent, or regulate the arrival of LSLAS in the area. Rather, the focus must increasingly shift to policies relevant to conflict resolution, labour issues, and outmigration as new drivers of poverty.

In view of such questions, our analysis of spatial patterns remains very coarse and provides insufficient differentiation. While some general correlations can be posited between the origins of investors, the type of operations they conduct, and the socio-ecological contexts targeted, we neither understand the causalities of LSLA implementation processes nor can we identify the precise spatio-temporal contexts with the most vulnerable environments and populations.

However, our meta-analysis of case studies reveals a more differentiated picture of the processes behind the implementation of LSLAS. The majority of our case studies pointed to an archetype of LSLA implementation processes that we have termed 'Marginal People'. In this sort of authoritarian, top-down LSLA implementation process, 'available land' is defined less according to local socio-ecological factors than it is according to factors from the domains of investment and land governance. Contrary to the analysis of spatial patterns, we found that this type of implementation process can be observed both in the forestry sector and in the agricultural sector, encompassing crops as varied as rubber, eucalyptus, coffee, and sugar cane. Also, it involved investors from different countries of origin, both regional and international. Closely related to this type of LSLA implementation is the archetype we refer to as 'Marginal Governance'. It too is characterised by a strong investment domain but is somewhat shaped by the socio-ecological context, providing an empowerment to the socio-ecological context vis-à-vis policy pressures. Nevertheless, the economic and political power wielded by investors means that land governance is ultimately constrained in its effectiveness.

The remaining case studies were attributed to two more recent types of LSLA implementation processes. One type we refer to as 'Marginal Investments', in which investors struggle to obtain land. Accepting that available land—as defined by local land users—is very scarce, and lacking government support, investors in this category face the very real prospect of total failure. Investors also face possible failure in the final archetype we identified, 'Marginal Land'. This category comprises rubber companies that arrived late to the region and were forced to follow a more bottom-up approach in their search to find suitable land—by now exceedingly scarce. Their negotiations with local land users resulted in the most inclusive form of LSLA implementation we observed. After reaching an agreement about available land, villagers and investors jointly sought the support of district and provincial land governance institutions, which in turn lent their support to the investment domain.

Our analysis of LSLA implementation processes reveals various policy-relevant insights. First, we found that authoritarian forms of implementation dominate, as was suggested by the spatial patterns identified earlier. However, in contrast to our initial spatial observations, we found that investors from other countries besides Vietnam and China were also involved in top-down modes of implementation. In general, authoritarian implementation processes appear to be associated with powerful companies who arrived on the scene early, just after foreign direct investment had received policy approval, and had access to political elites within the government. These sorts of implementation processes occur very quickly, leaving little space for policy intervention. In these cases, openings for local people to voice their interests only appear to occur when they are granted by the investors themselves, whether for strategic reasons or because of commitments to corporate social responsibility.

Second, we found that new, more inclusive models of implementation emerge as land concessions begin to proliferate. Notably, these emerging models of implementation may provide spaces for policy intervention, whether at the national, provincial, or local level. Yet, it should be noted that they have not emerged due to regulatory measures, but rather due to the increasing scarcity of available land, competition between investors, and the learning processes of actors at different policy levels. One archetype emerging in this advanced stage of land acquisitions is that of failing land investments. This trend also appears to be reflected globally, as evidenced by the high rates of abandoned deals found in the Land Matrix (Land Matrix Partnership, 2014). Notably, failed deals could also provide space for a policy reboot in favour of more inclusive forms of land investment and agricultural development. Finally, the last archetype we identified—'Marginal Land'—points to alternative modes of agricultural investment that are actually beginning to occur. They appear to materialise once socio-ecological constraints—for example, demographic and environmental realities—begin to outweigh economic and political power. This newly emerging archetype has not received a lot of attention so far, but may come to play an increasingly important role worldwide.

We believe that such archetypes of implementation processes could contribute to a better, more differentiated and policy relevant understanding of LSLAS as driving forces of agrarian transitions. But this requires us to validate and generalise such archetypes to inform policies at higher spatial levels. Ideally, this could be done by linking our process-based archetypes with observable place-based (spatially referenced) patterns of LSLAS. In other words, we wish to identify whether these archetypes display spatial signatures that can be extrapolated using spatio-temporal data sets spanning larger geographic areas. Table 6.4 lists the key factors of our process-based archetypes and highlights the key factors for which spatio-temporal data sets are readily available.

As seen in Table 6.4, the key factors for which data from inventories and spatial layers are available (shaded rows in Table 6.4) only marginally overlap with the most important indicators of the different archetypes of LSLA implementation processes. With the exception of the Size of Concessions, it seems that no other key factor differentiating the four archetypes can be quantified with currently available spatio-temporal data sets. Conversely, many of the indicators that are decisive to LSLA implementation processes are difficult or impossible to capture fully using spatially explicit, country-level data; the most prominent example being Available and Suitable Land (KF 17). No statistics or map can adequately capture the characteristics of this factor. Correspondingly, spatial signatures differentiating these four archetypes can scarcely be extrapolated in time and space. However, a closer look at the indicators shows that expanding the information collected by existing inventories could make a big difference. If factors such as Time of Investment (KF 3) and characteristics of

TABLE 6.4 *Synthesising implementation processes and spatial patterns of land acquisitions*

Key factors		Marginal people	Marginal governance	Marginal investment	Marginal land
Domain of land investment					
Origin of investor	1				
Type of crop	2				
Time of investment	3	Early arrivals	Early arrivals		Late arrivals
Access to political power	4	High level ties, diplomatic			
Access to cheap labor force	5				
Size of company	6	Large size	Large size	Large as well as small	Large as well as small
CSR commitment	7		Generally high		
Size of concession	8	Large, connected plots	Large, connected plots		Small, flexible
Domain of land governance					
Economic growth strategies	9				
Policies related to land	10				
Top-down granting of concessions	11				
Power of district/province officials	12	High, influencing land surveys	Weak, infuenced by investment	High	Strong, drawing on soc.-ecol. context
Experience with LSLAS	13				
Patronage and corruption	14				
Land tenure insecurity	15				
Land surveys	16	Not or partly implemented	Implemented	Carefully implemented	Carefully implemented
Domain of socio-ecological context					
Available and suitable land	17	Defined by investment and governance	Defined by investment and soc.-ecol. context	Defined by soc.-ecol. context	Defined by investment and soc.-ecol. context
Land cover and land use	18		Reflected in lad survey		Reflected in land survey
Logging	19				
Biophysical factors and topography	20				Reflected in land survey
Historical ties	21				

TABLE 6.4   *Synthesising implementation processes and spatial patterns* (cont.)

Key factors		Marginal people	Marginal governance	Marginal investment	Marginal land
Capability and assets of villagers	22		Indications of needs expressed	Strong negotiation power	Strong negotiation power
Accessibility	23				
Land allocation	24	Fast, majority of concession allocated	Parts of concession, slow, change of location	Slow, fragmented, small share of	Slow, fragmented

Note: The table lists the key factors of our four archetypes and existing spatio-temporal data sets that capture these key factors. Shaded rows indicate key factors for which statistical and spatial data are readily available.
SOURCE: AUTHORS.

Land Allocation (KF 24) were made publicly accessible and were more exhaustive, they could serve as excellent proxies for the type of implementation process. Furthermore, existing LSLA monitoring systems could additionally incorporate indicators such as the role of provincial or district authorities in the implementation process, the way Land Surveys (KF 16) were implemented, and the Capabilities and Assets of Villagers (KF 22). Finally, refining methods to understand who and what define the availability of land would represent a breakthrough for understanding the processes of land allocation.

5   Conclusions

The research we have described is intended to help overcome certain persistent difficulties of providing adequate, robust evidence on LSLAs for the purpose of decision-making and policymaking, specifically in Laos and Cambodia. Much of this difficulty stems from the existing gap between case study research—which typically provides qualitative and process-based insights—and national or global inventories that typically provide place-based (spatially referenced) and quantitative analyses of broader patterns. Using a meta-analysis of case studies that focuses on recurrent interactions between selected key factors, we defined four archetypes of implementation processes. We argue that this type of generalisation not only provides insights for land-related policies, but also represents a precondition for linking process-based insights with spatial patterns emerging from place-based studies.

Methodologically, we conclude that both approaches generate valuable yet incomplete evidence for policymaking. Spatial patterns mask important differentiations and do not enable causal understanding. At the same time, a working typology of LSLA implementation processes such as ours is difficult to assess in terms of its validity for higher levels of policymaking and scaling up to different contexts. Finding ways of linking these two perspectives remains a crucial task. At present, there is a dearth of available indicators serving both perspectives, making it difficult to properly link them. Yet, the solution is clearly within reach: inventories of land acquisitions could make these kinds of indicators available with little extra effort. They would need to document how the size and contiguity of a land deal changes over time from the granting of concessions to the final allocation of land. Additionally, information on the use and form of land surveys as well as the time and type of involvement of different actors represents an important proxy for implementation processes.

We believe that this type of combined approach is capable of generating important evidence to inform policy. It enables a better understanding of the overall dimensions and relevance of LSLAs in agrarian transitions. Our own quantitative results point to a highly advanced stage of LSLA proliferation in South-East Asia, necessitating new policies capable of addressing conflicts, impacts on pre-existing land use and natural resources, threatened livelihoods, and outmigration, which could all drive new waves of poverty. At the same time, our analysis of implementation processes clearly shows that there is little space for participatory forms of agricultural investment when large and powerful companies initially arrive on the scene in a new region and are essentially given a pass by senior government authorities. For a long time, the prevailing processes of land allocation in Laos and Cambodia were top-down and authoritarian, further marginalising vulnerable populations. Only now, as land has become scarcer and competition between investors has increased, are new, more inclusive implementation processes emerging. These implementation processes enable various stakeholders to agree on what land is truly underused or 'marginal', and thus ripe for investment. In terms of future land policies, this suggests a role for spatially differentiated moratoria on land concessions. In other words, policymakers could ban concessions in certain areas and allow them in others, encouraging competition between investors and negotiation with local land areas in certain places, while keeping other places free of land concessions to protect vulnerable smallholders.

References

Anseeuw, W., M. Boche, T. Breu, M. Giger, J. Lay, P. Messerli and K. Nolte (2012) *Transnational Land Deals for Agriculture in the Global South: Analytical Report Based on the Land Matrix Database* (Bern, Montpellier and Hamburg: CDE–CIRAD–GIGA), http://publications.cirad.fr/une_notice.php?dk=564980 (accessed on 16 March 2015).

Arino, O. (2010) *GlobCover 2009*, http://epic.awi.de/31046/1/Arino_et_al_GlobCover 2009-a.pdf (accessed on 16 March 2015).

Borras Jr., S.M., D. Fig and S.M. Suárez (2011) 'The Politics of Agrofuels and Mega-Land and Water Deals: Insights from the ProCana Case, Mozambique', *Review of African Political Economy*, 38(128), pp. 215–234, DOI: 10.1080/03056244.2011.582758.

Cotula, L. (2012) 'The International Political Economy of the Global Land Rush: A Critical Appraisal of Trends, Scale, Geography and Drivers', *Journal of Peasant Studies*, 39(3–4), pp. 649–680, DOI: 10.1080/03066150.2012.674940.

Cotula, L., S. Vermeulen, R. Leonard and J. Keeley (2009) *Land Grab Or Development Opportunity? Agricultural Investment and International Land Deals in Africa* (London and Rome: IIED–FAO–IFAD).

De Koninck, R. (2004) 'The Challenges of the Agrarian Transition in Southeast Asia', *Labour Capital and Society*, 37(1–2), pp. 285–288, http://lcs-tcs.com/ PDFs/37_12/15-de%20Koninck.pdf (accessed on 26 May 2015).

Deininger, K. and D. Byerlee (2011) *Rising Global Interest in Farmland: Can It Yield Sustainable and Equitable Benefits?* (Washington, D.C.: World Bank–International Bank for Reconstruction and Development), http://siteresources.worldbank.org/ DEC/Resources/Rising-Global-Interest-in-Farmland.pdf (accessed on 14 April 2015).

Dwyer, M.B. (2013) 'Building the Politics Machine: Tools for "Resolving" the Global Land Grab', *Development and Change*, 44(2), pp. 309–333, DOI: 10.1111/dech.12014.

Edelman, M. (2013) 'Messy Hectares: Questions about the Epistemology of Land Grabbing Data', *Journal of Peasant Studies*, 40(3), pp. 485–501, DOI: 10.1080/ 03066150.2013.801340.

Epprecht, M., N. Minot, R. Dewina, P. Messerli and A. Heinimann (2008) *The Geography of Poverty and Inequality in the Lao PDR* (Bern: Geographica Bernensia).

Friis, C. and A. Reenberg (2010) *Land Grab in Africa. Emerging Land System Drivers in a Teleconnected World* (Copenhagen: Global Land Project International Project Office), http://www.ihdp.unu.edu/docs/Publications/GLP/GLP_report_01.pdf (accessed on 26 May 2015).

GoL (Government of Lao People's Democratic Republic) (2008) Decree On the Implementation of the Land Law, No. 88/PM, 3 June, Ventiane, http://www .prflaos.org/sites/default/files/policy/40.%20PM%20Decree%20on%20the%20 Implementation%20of%20the%20Land%20Law.pdf (accessed on 16 March 2015).

Görgen, M., B. Rudloff, J. Simons, A. Üllenberg, S. Väth and L. Wimmer (2009) *Foreign Direct Investment (FDI) in Land in Developing Countries* (Eschborn: Deutsche Gesellschaft für Technische Zusammenarbeit, GTZ), http://www.giz.de/expertise/downloads/Fachexpertise/giz2010-en-foreign-direct-investment-dc.pdf (accessed on 26 May 2015).

Kingdom of Cambodia (2012) *Identification of Poor Households Programme*, http://www.idpoor.gov.kh/en/home (accessed on 16 March 2015).

Lambin, E.F. and H.J. Geist (eds.) (2006) *Land-Use and Land-Cover Change. Local Processes and Global Impacts* (Berlin: Springer).

Land Matrix Partnership (2014) *Land Matrix Newsletter*, January 2014, http://www.landmatrix.org/media/filer_public/b2/48/b24869d1-ff17-4cb2-8bc3-5c55ef6a3e0c/lm_newsletter_3-4.pdf (accessed on 20 April 2015).

LICADHO (Cambodian League for the Defense of Human Rights) (2013) *The Great Cambodian Giveaway: Vizualizing Land Concessions over Time*, http://www.licadho-cambodia.org/concession_timelapse/ (accessed on 16 March 2015).

Messerli, P. (2000) 'Use of Sensitivity Analysis to Evaluate Key Factors for Improving Slash-and-Burn Cultivation Systems on the Eastern Escarpment of Madagascar', *Mountain Research and Development*, 20(1), pp. 32–41, DOI: 10.1659/0276–4741(2000)020[0032:UOSATE]2.0.CO;2.

Messerli, P., M. Giger, M.B. Dwyer, T. Breu and S. Eckert (2014) 'The Geography of Large-Scale Land Acquisitions: Analysing Socio-Ecological Patterns of Target Contexts in the Global South', *Applied Geography*, 53, pp. 449–459, DOI: 10.1016/j.apgeog.2014.07.005.

Messerli, P., A. Heinimann, M. Epprecht, S. Phonesaly, C. Thiraka and N. Minot (eds.) (2008) *Socio-Economic Atlas of the Lao PDR—An Analysis Based on the 2005 Population and Housing Census* (Bern: Geographica Bernensia).

Messerli, P., A. Heinimann, M. Giger, T. Breu and O. Schönweger (2013) 'From "Land Grabbing" to Sustainable Investments in Land: Potential Contributions by Land Change Science', *Current Opinion in Environmental Sustainability*, 5, pp. 528–534, DOI: 10.1016/j.cosust.2013.03.004.

Michel, L. (2013) *Key Factors Influencing Decision-Making on Large-Scale Land Acquisitions in Cambodia*, unpublished MSc Thesis (Bern: University of Bern), http://www.cde.unibe.ch/v1/CDE/pdf/MSc%20Thesis%20Lukas%20Michel.pdf (accessed on 16 March 2015).

Ministry of Agriculture, Forestry and Fisheries of Cambodia (2012) http://www.maff.gov.kh/ (accessed on 16 March 2015).

Nalepa, R.A. and D.M. Bauer (2012) 'Marginal Lands: the Role of Remote Sensing in Constructing Landscapes for Agrofuel Development', *Journal of Peasant Studies*, 39(2), pp. 403–422, DOI: 10.1080/03066150.2012.665890.

NAoL (National Assembly of Lao People's Democratic Republic) (2004) Law on the Promotion of Foreign Investment, No. 11/NA, 22 October, Vientiane, http://www.ilo.org/dyn/natlex/natlex_browse.details?p_lang=en&p_country=LAO&p_classification=01&p_origin=SUBJECT (accessed on 16 March 2015).

NCCD (National Committee for Sub-National Democratic Development) (2012) *Commune Council Database*, http://db.ncdd.gov.kh/ccd/home/index.castle (accessed on 16 March 2015).

NGO Forum (2012) http://www.ngoforum.org.kh/ (accessed on 16 March 2015).

ODC (Open Development Cambodia) (2013) http://www.opendevelopmentcambodia.net/ (accessed on 16 March 2015).

Oya, C. (2013) 'Methodological Reflections on "Land Grab" Databases and the "Land Grab" Literature "Rush"', *Journal of Peasant Studies*, 40(3), pp. 503–520, DOI: 10.1080/03066150.2013.799465.

RGC (Royal Government of Cambodia) (2005) Sub-Decree on Economic Land Concession, Sub-Decree No. 146, 27 December, Phnom Penh, http://www.cambodiainvestment.gov.kh/sub-decree-146-on-economic-land-concessions_051227.html (accessed on 16 March 2015).

Rigg, J. (2006) 'Land, Farming, Livelihoods, and Poverty: Rethinking the Links in the Rural South', *World Development*, 34(1), pp. 180–202, DOI: 10.1016/j.worlddev.2005.07.015.

———— (2005) *Living in Transition in Laos: Market Integration in Southeast Asia* (London: Routledge).

Schönweger, O., A. Heinimann, M. Epprecht, J. Lu and P. Thalongsengchanh (2012) *Concessions and Leases in the Lao PDR: Taking Stock of Land Investments* (Bern: Geographica Bernensia).

Scoones, I., R. Hall, S.M. Borras Jr., B. White and W. Wolford (2013) 'The Politics of Evidence: Methodologies for Understanding the Global Land Rush', *Journal of Peasant Studies*, 40(3), pp. 469–483, DOI: 10.1080/03066150.2013.801341.

Sommer, L. (2013) *Deciding on Large-Scale Land Acquisitions in the Lao PDR: Case Studies on Land Concessions in the Agroforestry Subsectors from Central Laos*, unpublished MSc Thesis (Bern: University of Bern), http://www.cde.unibe.ch/v1/CDE/pdf/MSc%20Thesis%20Laura%20Sommer_15%2001%202014.pdf (accessed on 16 March 2015).

Üllenberg, A. (2009) *Foreign Direct Investment (FDI) in Land in Madagascar* (Eschborn: GTZ).

Vester, F. and A.V. Hesler (1987) *Sensitivitätsmodell* (Frankfurt: Umlandverband).

Wiesmann, U., C. Ott, C. Ifejika Speranza, U. Müller-Boeker, P. Messerli and J. Zinstag (2011) *An Actor's Model as Conceptual Orientation in Research for Sustainable Development* (Bern: Geographica Bernensia), http://www.north-south.ch/publications/Infosystem/On-line%20Dokumente/Upload/11_Wiesmann%281%29.pdf (accessed on 20 April 2015).

Zurflueh, J. (2013) *Vietnamese Rubber Investments in the South of the Lao* PDR: *Key Factors Influencing Decision Making in Large-scale Land Acquisitions by Vietnamese Investors in the Agro-forestry Sector of the Lao* PDR, unpublished MSc Thesis (Bern: University of Bern), http://www.cde.unibe.ch/Pages/Publication/2499/Default .aspx (accessed on 16 March 2015).

CHAPTER 7

From Lagging Behind to Losing Ground: Cambodian and Laotian Household Economy and Large-Scale Land Acquisitions

Christophe Gironde and Gilda Senties Portilla

Abstract

Large-scale land deals in the agriculture and forestry sectors have significantly affected livelihoods in South-East Asia. This chapter analyses the implementation of land deals for rubber plantations since the mid-2000s and their consequences for rural livelihoods in north-eastern Cambodia and southern Laos. The analysis provides empirical material on how these deals were facilitated by previous policies and how they were implemented on the ground. It further highlights different levels of dispossession in in a series of villages studied and examines the uneven transformations in people's livelihoods. The conclusions complement scholarly assessments of land deals' immediate impact with a medium-term analysis of the consequent transformation of livelihoods. The chapter indicates that land acquisitions and related crop booms have set in motion dynamic, market-based developments including changes in social attitudes and lifestyles. Yet, the majority of the population has been caught in an insecure environment, where it is vulnerable to the opportunistic behaviours of more powerful actors. Family farming-based livelihoods are no longer 'lagging behind', as they were once considered; they are now losing ground, as opportunities to diversify their means of subsistence remain inadequate. Finally, the chapter provides policy-relevant recommendations on how to alleviate some of the worst short-term consequences for the local rural populations.

1   Introduction

Cambodia and Laos have both placed export-oriented, cash crop agriculture at the core of their development strategies. To do so, the two countries have leased vast areas of land to foreign and domestic companies in order that they invest in large-scale agricultural production. Addressing cases of rubber investment in Ratanakiri province in north-eastern Cambodia and Champasak

© Graduate Institute of International and Development Studies, 2016 | DOI 10.1163/9789004304758_008

province in southern Laos, this chapter analyses the implementation of these land deals and their medium-term consequences for rural livelihoods.

The chapter contributes to bridging the existing gaps in the 'land grab' literature by addressing three main scholarly challenges. The first challenge is to complement standard assessments of immediate impact—mostly measured in terms of land loss—with a medium-term analysis[1] including how households respond to new constraints and opportunities, and to what extent they have, or have not, managed to adapt their productive activities to create sustainable livelihoods. The second challenge is to go beyond the winners–losers picture (Borras Jr. and Franco, 2012), which opposes outside investors and local communities, by analysing the outcomes of the social differentiation induced by large-scale land acquisitions. The third is to include various types of investors and land deals of all sizes (Edelman et al., 2013) in order to highlight to what extent different types of rubber sector land acquisitions have different consequences.

This chapter has three sections. The first presents the debate on the region's agricultural model for export-oriented cash crops and provides the analytical framework and methodology. The second section is dedicated to case studies, describing and analysing local contexts, the process of land acquisitions, and changes in livelihoods over a period of 5–7 years. In the third section we synthesise and discuss our case studies. In the conclusion we reflect on the current stage of agrarian transition in the spaces studied and draw some policy recommendations based on people's own reflections on their realities.

2 Research Background and Methodology

Our research relates to the debate on whether the outcomes of agrarian transitions are 'disruptive' or 'more developmentally positive' (Rigg et al., 2012, 1469–70). We discuss to what extent local livelihoods are 'disrupted' (Cotula, 2013) by large-scale land acquisitions and what new opportunities or alternative economic occupations are available in relation to such acquisitions. We also address the issue of the social differentiation that occurs in relation to the dynamics of land acquisitions and the changing farming system. More specifically, the chapter contributes to the discussion on the capacity of smallholders to engage with crop booms (Hall, 2011), in a context in which their land tenure

---

1 By 'medium-term', we refer to the period of 5 to 7 years that followed the acceleration of large-scale land acquisitions for rubber plantation, which occurred in 2006–08.

and access to resources are increasingly being challenged by radical changes in property regimes and actors (Peluso and Lund, 2011; Bakker et al., 2010; Guérin et al., 2003). Our analysis is particularly inspired by the attention drawn to 'new actors' by Peluso and Lund (2011, 668), and the call from Tania Li (2011) for more attention to be paid to labour regimes, as non-farm job creation and access to salaried work are of increasing importance in agrarian transitions (Rigg, 2006).

Numerous South-East Asian experiences show that smallholders can grow rubber successfully (Delarue, 2011; Sikor, 2012; Sturgeon, 2012). In line with a broad consensus that public support to farmers is crucial to the diffusion of technology, the key lesson from those experiences is that farmers have been successful when they have benefited from secure land tenure (Sikor, 2012) and that their performance depends greatly on the support they receive, or do not receive, from the state (Gouyon, 1995; Fox and Castella, 2013). Another important factor in farmers' performance is the learning process, as illustrated by the cases of farmers in northern Thailand, who could learn tapping in plantations in the south before developing their own farms, and of northern Laotian farmers who benefited from 'sharecropping arrangements with relatives' from China who 'extended their rubber holdings across the border' (Sturgeon, 2012).

For Cambodia, it is argued that rubber is more profitable than other trees, such as acacias, eucalyptus, cashew nut or oil palm (Hansen and Top, 2006). The study by Fox et al. (2009) similarly shows that rubber is the best alternative to current natural forest uses and argues that it provides a 'better economic position' to local populations. And rubber is deemed attractive 'due to its fewer (agricultural) inputs, long economic life and high market demand' (CDRI, 2009, 13). Other studies draw attention to the fact that rubber plantations 'require huge investment in both financial and technical resources' (Yem et al., 2011), and that small producers might not be paid adequately for their rubber because of the commercialisation system (Gironde and Fortunel, 2014). Predictions made over the last decade are not optimistic about the sustainability of local populations' livelihoods, particularly when considering the rate of forest loss (Fox et al., 2008), the unavoidable abandonment of traditional farming practices (Ruohomäki, 2004), and 'neo-patrimonialism' practices and abusive power relations (Un and So, 2011; Ironside, 2009). As most populations are left out of complex registries of land-use rights (Simbolon, 2002; Luco, 2008) the risk of marginalisation and forced displacement is deemed high, in particular for ethnic minorities (Bourdier, 2009).

For northern Laos, economic gains for smallholders have been observed under certain market conditions and incentives from contract farming and governmental policies (Manivong and Cramb, 2008). However, studies have found that these investments are often accompanied by unfair and uncertain terms for farmers (Diana, 2008; Gerbert, 2010; Lin, 2010) and by losses in terms of food security due to soil degradation and deforestation (Luangmany and Kaneko, 2013). In southern Laos, where contract farming is unusual for rubber,[2] farmers' land has been enclosed in rubber estates that are managed by public/private (mainly foreign) companies (Schönweger et al., 2012). Engagement with rubber is limited to a few local elites who have the necessary capital and know-how. A growing body of literature has mostly documented the negative outcomes—for local communities and the environment—induced by these deals (Barney, 2007; Baird, 2011; Kenney-Lazar, 2012; McAllister, 2012). Farmers at large, however, are not necessarily averse to certain changes brought about by the rubber boom, but are limited in terms of their capital, secure land rights, and access to markets. They often become easy prey to 'price dictation, oligopsony and unscrupulous practices' (Fullbrook, 2011, 15), a risk that is more pronounced for ethnic minorities.

The case studies in this chapter are based on the authors' personal field research carried out in villages of Ratanakiri (Cambodia) and Champasak (Laos) provinces, respectively. Data were mostly collected through semi-structured interviews with households, local authorities, and company representatives. Villages were selected based on the presence of large-scale rubber land concessions for at least five years, accessibility during rainy and dry seasons, and different processes of land acquisitions reported by district authorities. Fieldwork in Cambodia was spread over four 10-day missions in 2012–13, covering three villages: Pra Lai and Trang in Loum Choar Commune (O'Yadav district) and Malik in Malik Commune (Andounge Maes district). Data collection in Cambodia included a questionnaire-based survey of 240 households— that is to say, 24 per cent of the population of the villages. In Laos, fieldwork took four months spread across 2012 to 2014 in four villages: Thongpao, Huaytong, and Lak Sip Kao in Bachiang district, and Lak Sao Paet in Paksong district. Interviews in Laos were complemented with participant observation[3] and focus group discussions with the elderly and the youth of the village.

Due to the sensitivity of the topic, interviewees remain anonymous and comments made by public officials are not openly credited to any particular

---

2 The government in Champasak has recently unveiled a 'land as equity' model, including rubber, in which farmers will allegedly receive more benefits as they will hold shares in the concession contracts and retain land ownership rights if a venture fails (Vientiane Times Reporters, 2015).

3 This included household activities, such as farming chores in the dry and rainy seasons, cooking and meal times, collection of non-timber forest products (NTFPS), fishing, and village festivals or social gatherings. Situations, symbols, or objects indicative of the transformation of livelihoods were also observed, such as cash-related actual work and consumer goods.

individual. Direct quotes of respondents are not literal citations, but are trans-lations of the original statements made in Khmer, Lao, or in the local indig-enous language.

A further note on terminology is pertinent. While the term 'land acquisi-tions' is used to refer to any type of land deal regardless of origin and type of investment, (economic) 'land concessions' specifically refers to state grants of land, in either concession or lease form, to foreign and national investors in areas that are categorised as pertaining to the state (Schönweger et al., 2012).

3   Case Studies

3.1   *Ratanakiri*

3.1.1   Local Context and Background

In the area studied, local livelihoods—until the mid-1990s—were based on customary land tenure consisting of oral recognition of farming use-rights (Springer, 2013). Families had to inform or ask the village chief or more simply agree with neighbours on the demarcation of plots to be farmed. Testimonies gathered from people native to Loum Choar and Malik, indicating that access to land was not an issue because there was plenty of land, corroborate those gathered by Fox and Vogler (2009, 316), who report on a neighbouring commune (15 km away) in which each person had access to approximately 11 hectares (ha) in the late 1980s. Social differentiation was low with respect to farming land and access to forest areas, which provided the core of necessary resources. All families had equal access to land and equal use rights as well as access to forest resources. Families could be distinguished by their possession of cattle and buffaloes and prestigious handicraft goods (White, 1996). Food crops—mostly rice and vegetables—were dominant in a rotational cropping system including 10–15 years fallow after 2–3 years use of the same plot. Rain-fed crops were, if necessary, completed by paddy rice in lowlands. Fruit trees, husbandry, fishing, hunting, and the collection of non-timber forest products (NTFPs) in the areas surrounding the villages completed resources from cultivation. Non-farming activities were minimal. Cash crops, mostly soya and cashew nut, were progressively developed during the 1990s.

Prior to the mid-2000s land rush, local livelihoods were impacted by public policies implemented in the 1990s. Once the state of warfare and instability ended, the government developed its administrative capacity in remote and border areas such as Ratanakiri. New villages were established closer to roads, public services, and communal administrations. Displaced inhabitants were assigned areas of land to which neither the traditional inheritance system nor communal management provided them with legitimate access and use-rights.

At the same time, the 'Khmerisation' policy, which aimed to settle people of ethnic Khmer origin in ethnic minority areas, brought newcomers to these remote territories. Pioneer in-migrants would later open the door to their relatives and networks, which led in turn to additional cohorts of newcomers acquiring land during the 1990s, in some cases to the point where indigenous populations decided to move away from in-migrant clusters (Tang, 2014, 30–31).

Rubber plantation in Cambodia was revived from the mid-1990s on, when former state plantations were privatised (Fortunel, 2014). Then, powerful members of the state apparatus and 'entrepreneurial groups sympathetic to the Cambodian People's Party' (Hugues, 2003) acquired large tracts of land, mostly for logging. In the early 2000s, a series of government initiatives and development projects—model farms, planting schemes, training courses, etc.—were set up to promote rubber. Until that time, populations had preferred to invest in cashew nut; rubber being not well known and seedlings difficult to find. However, the conditions necessary for a rapid spread of rubber plantation were met. The rubber boom started with the sharp increase in rubber prices in 2005, triggering an unprecedented change in land cover and land use (Fox et al., 2008) driven by Khmer entrepreneurs (accounting for up to several hundreds ha holdings), medium-rank officials and their relatives (up to a few dozens of ha), and in-migrants (a few ha). In parallel, the first economic land concession (ELC) contracts were signed; their numbers increased from 2009 onwards. In 2012, there were 16 ELCs for a total of approximately 114,000 ha for the entire province.

3.1.2 Land Acquisitions

In Pra Lai, Trang, and Malik, rubber expansion started about eight to ten years ago. This is corroborated by the dominance of rubber plantations that are not yet productive, large areas of cleared land not yet planted, and the influx of in-migrants who nowadays represent 31.5 per cent (one family in three) of the total population of the two Communes in which these villages lie.

In Pra Lai village, two main investments affect the population's access to land: a 5,000 ha ELC to a Khmer-Vietnamese joint-venture named Chea Chenrith (contract signed in 2002; revised in 2012) and a Khmer company named Mekong Express, which bought 480 ha of land between 2007 and 2010.[4] The closest point of the Chea Chenrith joint-venture land's perimeter is located approximately four kilometres from the village; no demarcation marks—fences, pillars, or marked trees—could be seen. The land encompasses an area that has not yet been prepared for rubber trees, and Pra Lai

---

4 The 480 ha now the property of Mekong Express are spread across the two villages of Pra Lai and Trang; it is not possible to quantify how much land is on each village's territory.

inhabitants have, so far, continued farming in this area. Surprisingly, we even found rubber trees planted by villagers on land that, they say, is part of Chea Chenrith's territory. These trees—two dozen ha—belong to five well-off families, including the chief of the village and his close relatives. The rest of the Pra Lai villagers have also continued to cultivate annual crops on this unused portion of the ELC landholding. In 2012, villagers applied for the measurement of the land plots they farmed, in accordance with Prime Minister Directive 01 (D01) (issued in May 2012), which stipulated that citizens could claim back the land plots that had been granted as part of ELCs and that they cultivated at the time when the ELC was set up. During August 2012, government officials measured a total of 173 ha of land plots; fallow land plots were not measured and are considered as being the property of the company. In Pra Lai, 72 families (56 per cent) reported that their land was measured and received land titles that, so far, guarantee that they can 'keep' these plots. The situation is significantly different with Mekong Express, which in one to two years prepared the land and planted rubber trees. No attempt by villagers to continue farming on the Mekong Express landholding was reported. Apart from the rapid plantation of rubber trees, villagers explained this situation by stating that this acquisition cannot be contested since part of the land was sold by villagers themselves, and another part was sold by representatives of the communal authorities. Villagers also reported being afraid of contesting the acquisition as the land's owner is Khmer. Furthermore, D01 applies only to ELC-companies, not to ordinary private ones such as Mekong Express.

The situation differs in Trang where the population was impacted by Mekong Express and Khmer in-migrants. The purchases there by Mekong Express took place in two phases: in 2007–08, the company bought its first land plots directly from villagers; in a second phase, the company dealt with the local authorities and bought communal land. At the same time, the village experienced many acquisitions by Khmer in-migrants, who settled first along the main road, in Oun village, where they opened shops, restaurants, etc. They then progressively bought land plots further from the road, in Trang. The villagers explained that between 2007 and 2009, they had sold part of their fallow plots assuming that there was enough land left to be cleared for the next rotation; they simply could not have known that—at that moment—large tracts of land were in the process of being sold to Mekong Express. As a result, since 2010, Trang families have been left with stripes or dots of land between the landholdings of the migrants and the hundreds of hectares now the property of Mekong Express. The process has not stopped: about a third of Trang families (31 per cent) report that they have sold land since 2010 and 40 per cent of Trang families report having less land than in 2010.

The third village, Malik, is surrounded by two Vietnamese ELCs—Heng Brother and Chieng Ly Investment—since they were granted, respectively, 2,361 ha in 2009 and 5,080 ha in 2011. In addition, numerous Khmers have acquired land plots on the outskirts of the village. The ELCs deprived Malik villagers not only of land they could farm but also of fishing and hunting in an area that, they explain, was particularly rich for such activities. Monetary compensation for cultivated plots—USD 150–200 per ha, based on the cost of labour for clearing—were derisory when compared to the income that could be made from certain crops on those plots. But the most important distinctive feature in Malik village is the population's response. First, Malik villagers opposed Heng Brother when the company started to expand beyond its granted area. The opposition benefited from the support of local organisations, which helped to forward villagers' formal claims to provincial government representatives. Although it is not possible in the field to measure the area that may have been saved, the Malik population certainly stopped the further expansion of the company. In parallel, those Malik villagers who had the resources—that is to say, a work force or/and cash to hire workers, rushed to clear land plots at the edge of Heng Brother's landholding to fix these areas as their land. They opened new plots, continuously grew annual crops and built wooden houses. The other ELC beneficiary, Chieng Ly, a Khmer-Chinese company, encountered organisational challenges and delays, such as securing adequate budget and machinery for land clearing or for developing rubber nurseries. These contingencies gave Malik villagers time to react and limit dispossession; like with Heng Brother, they could continue farming as the company was slow in expanding the planted area. In some places, the villagers were able to continue farming until 2012, and their efforts were rewarded: of the three villages studied, Malik is the one with the highest proportion of families (90 per cent) who had land measured in 2012. The measurement operation is not negligible, as the average area families had measured—and for which they later received a land certificate—was 4.63 ha. The Chieng Ly development was also challenged by Khmers, as explained by one of its managers, who complained about powerful 'Khmer land-grabbers' that the company is not able to chase out.

We thus have three sites, each with various dispossession dynamics of uneven magnitude: Pra Lai, where, despite the ELC-related, large land loss on paper, villagers are—overall—left with enough land to meet their basic needs; Trang, where the entire village lacks land to satisfy its basic needs; and an in-between situation in Malik. At all three sites, land acquisitions generated differentiation among families depending on their respective capacities to compensate for land loss by clearing other plots. The families who had a large enough workforce could rapidly compensate for the land they had lost; others could not or could only to a lesser extent. Differentiation increased further, as those who could clear land were also able to sell the wood thus gathered. This gave them the financial capital needed to pay workers for further clearing. Moreover, in a context in which state control over forest clearing and 'illegal' logging was intensifying, the families who had political and social capital could clear land and sell wood, whereas ordinary families were forbidden to do so and were at risk of having the wood they had gathered confiscated. The arrival of new landholders, companies, and in-migrants opened new avenues for access to productive capital. Representatives of communal authorities, who had eased the settlement of these newcomers, were the first to get access to the start-up package for rubber—that is, good quality rubber seedlings, fertilisers, and technical advice for planting. Meanwhile, the majority of the indigenous population could—at best—only find jobs clearing the lands of the new landholders.

3.1.3   Livelihood Change

For communities who did not know any limitation to access to land and forests other than the availability of the workforce needed to clear them, the foremost difference in current livelihood systems is the comparably limited natural areas they use. According to the survey conducted in 2013 in the three villages studied, for all villages almost two-thirds of the families (64 per cent) had less than 5 ha of land to farm, which is deemed the minimum area for meeting basic needs (with the current, ordinary cropping system including mostly rice, vegetables, cassava, and soya). The median land area per family is 3.9 ha and the mean is 5 ha. This is roughly about half the area that average families used to farm, including fallow areas, before the acceleration of land acquisitions a decade ago. The limitation in land available for farming is uneven across the three villages and within each village, as shown in Table 7.1. Land loss is more acute in Trang village, where half of the families have less than 2 ha each, whereas in Pra Lai and Malik villages this figure is 9.4 and 4.8 per cent, respectively. One-fifth (18.7 per cent) of Trang families reported being landless, compared to 6.2 and 2.4 per cent, respectively, in the two other villages. From our qualitative interviews, we did not find any indication that land areas were less abundant in Trang than in Pra Lai or Malik prior to the land acquisitions analysed above. The difference is explained mostly then by the purchases of land by Khmer migrants, who—so far—have not reached Pra Lai.

The reduction in the land indigenous populations can have access to has led first to an intensification of land use, typically farming the same plot more times and reducing fallow duration, until rice yield significantly declines.

TABLE 7.1 *Distribution of households by size (in ha) of land parcel owned (percentage of all surveyed households)*

	<0.1 ha	0.1–1.9 ha	2–3.9 ha	4–5.9 ha	6–7.9 ha	8–9.9 ha	≥10 ha
Pra Lai							
Percentage of households	6.2%	3.1%	18.7%	25%	6.2%	12.5%	28.1%
Cumulative percentage		9.4%	28.1%	53.1%	59.4%	71.9%	100%
Trang							
Percentage of households	18.7%	31.2%	31.2%	0.0%	0.0%	6.2%	12.5%
Cumulative percentage		50%	81.2%	81.2%	81.2%	87.5%	100%
Malik							
Percentage of households	2.4%	2.4%	17.1%	36.6%	19.5%	7.3%	14.6%
Cumulative percentage		4.8%	21.9%	58.5%	78.5%	85.4%	100%

SOURCE: SNIS PROJECT QUESTIONNAIRE-BASED SURVEY, AUGUST 2013.

Traditional 10–15 year-long fallow periods no longer exist; fallow land is at risk. A total of 63 per cent of respondents reported that they did not have any fallow area at the time they were interviewed; the proportion reaches 70 per cent among households who hold less than 6 ha, and 81 per cent for those who hold less than 4 ha. The intensification of land use is also related to the fact that families tend to be made up of an increasing number of people to feed, as there is no land left for the youth to open new fields. Furthermore, farming what is left of land is not always profitable: in Trang, we found cases where near-landless families explained they had not farmed the entire area they have access to because of soil exhaustion. They also explained that they had abandoned farming their land because the output was less than what they can expect from off-farm activities, although the availability of job opportunities is rather random.

A second transformation in cropping systems is a reinvestment in paddy rice for those who have access to low, wet land which had been relatively neglected

TABLE 7.2   *Distribution of households by size (in ha) of rubber land area (percentage of all surveyed households)*

	<0.1ha	0.1–1.9 ha	2–3.9 ha	4–5.9 ha	6–7.9 ha	8–9.9 ha	≥10 ha	Total
Number of households	204	12	14	8	1	0	2	241
Percentage of households	84.6%	5.0%	5.8%	3.3%	0.4%	0.0%	0.8%	100%
Cumulative percentage		89.6%	95.4%	98.7%	99.1%	99.1%	100%	

SOURCE: SNIS PROJECT QUESTIONNAIRE-BASED SURVEY, AUGUST 2013.

as farmers invested in cash crops. Of the total number of households, 56 per cent grow paddy in low, wet land. A third transformation is the increasing share of farmed land dedicated to cassava, and to a lesser extent to soya beans, rather than to rice and associated vegetables. Cassava is grown by 82 per cent of the households, on a mean area of 1.98 ha per household, whereas soya is grown by 37 per cent of the households. Cassava has become the cornerstone of farming systems as it provides farmers' main income in the context of an increasing need for cash; cassava is also the main source of savings for capital expenditure (housing and transportation) and eventual investment into rubber. A fourth transformation is the plantation of rubber trees, rather than cashew nut trees, although there were only 15 per cent of the families who reported owning rubber trees.

Another major change explained by our interviewees consists in the reduction of the cattle that they own due to several reasons: families sell animals to raise much-needed cash; there is increasingly less space for grazing and people cannot spend the required time to walk their cattle; finally, owing to the limited space available, they fear the possible damages that the animals might make to rubber trees, and the fines or retaliations (especially in terms of animals killed) on the part of the companies. At the time of interview, seven households out of ten did not own one single buffalo and eight out of ten did not have a single cow.

Household members are increasingly searching for salaried employment in the various types of rubber plantations. New landholdings at first created jobs, to clear and prepare the areas to be planted and to take care of the plantations during their early years; then, the plantations needed fewer workers—mechanisation developed and companies hired workers with skills that indigenous people do not have. Also, job creation benefits migrants more than native populations: Khmer owners have made it very clear that they hire Khmer workers because native populations lack not only skills but also commitment—that is to say, they do not commit durably to their employers' companies as they must also pursue their own farming activities, whereas Khmer in-migrants work full-time and remain with their employers longer. Only 8.7 per cent of people reported having a regular salaried occupation. The overall process of rural development has certainly created petty opportunities in food processing (typically pealing cassava tubers), local trade, transportation services, etc., but most of these are taken up by in-migrants. Similar to the low proportion of households the members of which have regular salaried jobs, only 11 per cent of households reported members having non-farming occupations of their own, and they were almost exclusively non-native households. Out-migration is not an option for the inhabitants of Trang, Pra Lai, or Malik: only 3.7 per cent of families reported they have one member living outside the commune and 4.1 per cent reported that they receive remittances. While respondents lack acquaintances outside the area and do not know anyone living in cities, the need and the motivation—of the area's youth in particular— for leaving the village is strong, as illustrated by the number of interviewees who said that they would be ready to move, even when considering the risks they have heard of associated with migration.

Differentiation among families is increasing, in particular with respect to land area. When comparing change in land area between 2010 and 2013 with land area in 2013, we found that among the families who reported having less land in 2013 than in 2010, seven out of ten belong to the group with less than 6 ha of land, whereas three out of ten belong to the group holding more than 6 ha. The difference in land assets is even more acute between the native population and the newcomers, as shown in Table 7.3. Forty per cent of the native population report having less land, whereas the proportion is only 10.7 per cent

TABLE 7.3   *Change in households' land assets between 2010 and 2013 (percentage of relevant population category)*

	Less land	Same land	More land	Total
Entire population	32.6%	56.1%	11.3%	100%
Native	40.0%	54.5%	5.5%	100%
Non-native	10.7%	60.7%	28.6%	100%

SOURCE: SNIS PROJECT QUESTIONNAIRE-BASED SURVEY, AUGUST 2013.

for the non-native population. Similarly, 28 per cent of the non-native population have increased their land area over the period, whereas this figure is only 5 per cent in this case of the native population.

3.2   *Champasak*

3.2.1   Local Context and Background

After the failure of the first rubber plantation in Laos, established by the French in the southern province of Champasak in 1930, a few other public and private attempts at developing the crop were made during the 1990s (Manivong and Cramb, 2008; Baird, 2010). Yet, only recently has rubber become a widespread distinctive feature of the rural landscape. Through large land concessions granted by the central or provincial government, Vietnamese investors have revitalised rubber in Champasak, mainly in Bachiang and, to a lesser degree, Paksong districts[5] (Schönweger et al., 2012). Both districts are located on the Bolaven Plateau—Bachiang in its western hillsides; Paksong in more altitudinal areas—a region predominantly inhabited by autochthonous Mon-Khmer ethno-linguistic groups (Goudineau, 2008; Baird, 2010) and also by non-native Lao-Tadai groups (Fortunel, 2007). These groups rely on semi-subsistence farming, most of which is carried out manually.

The villages studied—Thongpao, Huaytong, Lak Sip Kao (all in Bachiang), and Lak Sao Paet (in Paksong)—were founded shortly before or amid the US heavy bombardments that followed the escalation of the Laotian Civil War.[6] Despite movements of people related to the war, collective memory stresses a time of plentiful land resources, with livelihoods tied to the cultivation of rice, coffee, vegetables, fruit, peanuts, and cardamom, and to the raising of livestock. After a brief and only feebly enforced period of collectivisation,[7] farming continued as usual: '[in principle] families could clear as much as they wanted'[8] under customary arrangements mediated by village chiefs or between families. Due to labour limitations, families usually cleared and farmed up to 5 ha. Social differentiation at the time was minimal; the founders of the village and party-appointed leaders, including war veterans, enjoyed more social prestige, but not necessarily larger productive assets. Households in possession of cattle and irrigated rice paddies were regarded as wealthier. Subsistence farming

---

5   In Paksong, land concessions for coffee outweigh those for rubber.

6   This war (1955–1975) was fought between the royalist government forces (backed by the US) and the communist Pathet Lao (supported by North Vietnam).

7   Except for Lak Sip Kao's collectivisation (1976–89), other villages participated only loosely for 2–3 years.

8   Interview with village authorities, 26 February 2014.

was practiced in rotational mixed-cropping systems with long fallow periods of a minimum of five years. In lower areas, paddies complemented rain-fed rice. Rivers and forests also provided a major source of nutrition (fish, wild game, NTFPS), especially in between the dry and wet periods (February–April), coinciding with the end of the coffee harvest and the start of a new rice farming cycle.

The Land and Forest Allocation Programme (LFA), implemented in the 1990s, brought about a crucial change in people's modus vivendi. Aimed at distinguishing forest from other lands, the LFA was a nationwide programme that covered processes from mapping and zoning village land to issuing temporary use certificates for farmland and degraded forest (Fujita and Phanvilay, 2008). It was coupled with a ban on rotational cultivation and with other poverty-reduction plans, often entailing the relocation of villages to focal areas—close to roads, markets, schools, and clinics (Evrard and Goudineau, 2004). Although the cases studied here did not involve relocation, the imposition of different land zones both created confusion and limited people's access to resources. Government and development aid agencies encouraged intensive cash-crop agriculture over 'unproductive' fallow land. Paksong, with a small coffee industry fruitfully initiated by the French in the 1920s (but interrupted by wars), saw a boom in coffee production (Sallée and Tulet, 2010). Coffee (mostly of the robusta variety) has since become the main source of income in Lak Sao Paet. Without proper, elevated soils for coffee and without sufficient attempts at developing higher-value cash crops, the usual rainy-season crops for sale in Bachiang remain corn, peanuts, and fruit, in reduced rotational systems. Cassava is a recent addition, sold in the dry season. Households in Lak Sao Paet and Lak Sip Kao have recently diversified incomes by turning to, or increasing a long-established small trade in, artisanal baskets and brooms, and machetes, respectively.

On the ground, since the LFA was barely enforced at all by the relevant authorities, rotational farming and NTFP collection had somehow persisted prior to the granting of concessions. Weaknesses in the LFA's implementation also meant that the step of handling land use certificates went largely missing in the studied sites, especially for fallow land, which would later facilitate the granting of concessions.

3.2.2   Land Concessions

Between 2004 and 2006, up to 30 per cent of Bachiang district land (of a total of 78,676 ha) featured in announced concession plans for three Vietnamese rubber companies: Viet-Lao Joint Stock Rubber, Yao Tieng Rubber Partnership, and Dak Lak Rubber (Srikham, 2010). Although the companies started clearing land at the time, the total concession area after approval, as registered by the National Land Management Authority (NLMA, 2009–2011), represents a lower, yet still significant, share of the district land (18.4 per cent). Yao Tieng was granted a total area of 1,489 ha in Bachiang, and 333 ha in Paksong; Viet-Lao was granted a concession for 10,316 ha, and Dak Lak for 2,677 ha, both in Bachiang (NLMA, 2009–2011). Concession areas coincided with the locations of the studied villages (and many others) for reasons of soil suitability, land availability, and relatively easy access.[9] Lak Sip Kao is the closest to the provincial capital of Pakse (19 km away); Thongpao is the farthest (circa 70 km away). Given its location in a less elevated area, adequate for the rubber crop, Lak Sao Paet (28 km from Pakse) is currently the only village in Paksong with a rubber plantation, operated by Yao Tieng since 2008 (Department of Agriculture and Forestry, 2013). Table 7.4 shows the hectares cleared on each site per company, relative to the village size beforehand. Concession areas span from 34 to 95 per cent of total village area cleared—with 89 per cent as the average for Bachiang villages. As rubber was rapidly planted, companies had reached the tapping phase by 2013.

TABLE 7.4   *Magnitude of land concessions in four selected villages*

Village	Company	Village size prior to concession (ha)	Area cleared by concession (ha)	Percentage of village area cleared
Thongpao[10]	Yao Tieng	400	273	68%
Huaytong,	Viet-Lao	144	68	47%
Lak Sip Kao[11]	Dak-Lak / Yao Tieng	563	536	95%
Lak Sao Paet	Yao Tieng	717	245	34%

SOURCE: FIELD RESEARCH BY SENTIES PORTILLA, 2012–13.

9   Interview with district authorities, 15 July 2013.

10   According to an anonymous source, Dak Lak's concession also contained Thongpao, but village records of 2006 only register Yao Tieng. Discussions with two village chiefs led the researchers to conclude that the land in question was part of Thongpao, but had been lost to a neighbouring village following a border dispute in 2005—and then granted to Dak Lak.

11   The area cleared is for two companies (Dak Lak and Yao Tieng); areas for each were not specified.

The way land concessions unfolded on the ground is described in similar terms across all the villages. The central or provincial government had planned and approved land allocations for the companies without previous consultations with village authorities and local populations. Villagers were told that the companies would adequately compensate them. The base average payment for one hectare was 1 million Laotian kip (LAK),[12] which was not enough to cover the purchase of the rice required for two months by the average (eight-member) family interviewed. With rare exceptions, families believed they could not (or should not) oppose the concessions, especially because higher authorities had taken those decisions. Most villagers felt pressured by the fact that district officials organised village meetings to announce the approval of grants by provincial or central level authorities (showing papers not necessarily signed yet), and did so in the presence of company representatives and, in some cases, the district police. Village chiefs did not have any say in the investment plans and decision-making process, but most served as facilitators of the concessions. When some families were reluctant to agree, village chiefs warned them that the company would take their land anyway without providing any compensation.

The outcomes of such dispossession vary across and within the sites due to the magnitude of land loss, the new actors drawn into the land rush, and livelihood assets and trajectories up until the concessions were granted. Lak Sip Kao has suffered the most serious loss, as 95 per cent of its land has been absorbed by two different concessions. An estimated 80 per cent of the total 270 households in Lak Sip Kao had in between 2–5 ha of land. Most of the families interviewed in this group were left with none, despite their attempts to avoid their land being cleared by planting fruit trees on their 'idle' swidden land. At the other end of the spectrum lies Lak Sao Paet, where, since the cultivation of coffee entails more permanent uses of land, some coffee smallholders were able to demonstrate that land was 'in use'—as opposed to being kept fallow, in which case it was given away in the form of concessions with no compensation being received in return. Notwithstanding these differences, it was found that the majority of households in all villages experienced serious land loss, as illustrated by Table 7.5 below.

A comparison of the situations prior to and after companies planted rubber indicates that the average size of household farmland for all villages combined fell from 3.96 to 1.17 hectares. Households who had 3–5 ha prior to concessions being granted were left—post-concessions—with around 1–2 ha of farming

---

12   USD 125 at current conversion rate (May 2015). Conversion rate around the time when the concessions were granted was USD 1 = LAK 9,000.

TABLE 7.5   *Average household farmland size in four selected villages (2003 and 2013, in ha)*

Village	Average household land size in 2003 (ha)	Average household land size in 2013 (ha)
Thongpao	3.11	0.85
Huaytong	5.24	0.66
Lak Sip Kao	3	0.75
Lak Sao Paet	4.25	2.45
Total average	3.96	1.17

SOURCE: FIELD RESEARCH BY SENTIES PORTILLA, 2012–13.

land, usually paddy or coffee plots. This is true for approximately 70 per cent of households of all the studied villages combined. Consequently, swidden agriculture is—for the majority—no longer possible, in a context where most villagers were rotational farmers. None of the families interviewed had temporary land certificates for farmland, which the LFA had meant to provide. This supported the argument that villagers' 'idle' swidden land was to become the property of the state, a transfer for which no compensation would be provided. Some certificates had been given to villagers in Lak Sip Kao, Huaytong, and Lak Sao Paet. These, however, only covered land close to the main road, including houses, paddy fields, and fruit or coffee trees; but not larger, more distant plots of farming land.[13] District and village authorities claimed that no such certificates had (yet) been provided in Thongpao. In Lak Sao Paet, there were cases in which villagers approached the company themselves to sell some of their previously 'certified' plots; sales for which they had allegedly received a higher price—compared to the average base payment on other sites, the difference was not significant.

In addition to the Vietnamese plantations, a few cases were encountered in which provincial government officials hold concessions. In Huaytong, 2.2 ha of the first colonial plantation—presumably the same plantation that a state-owned company later revamped in the 1990s—was recently granted to a public official from Pakse. Employees have been brought in from outside the area,

---

13   These findings confirm a previous study in Lak Sip Kao (Hall et al., 2011). Respondents from our study remained unclear as to whether these certificates were land titles within the framework of a titling programme, the second phase of which (in rural areas) began in 2003.

allegedly because the local inhabitants are already occupied at the Viet-Lao plantation or with their own farming activities. In Lak Sip Kao, other civil servants have set up smallholdings (figures unspecified) growing rubber, which has required buying whatever land is left from the local inhabitants. These cases of land acquisition by Lao nationals seem, however, to be operating with more ease because locals think of these investors primarily as 'government people', against whom any open resistance is unthinkable.

Margin for manoeuvre or for avoiding major losses is limited to very few households. Farmers at large, including those with permanent land use rights, had greater chances of keeping some or all of their land if they had acquaintances in the government and/or some information about their land rights under statutory land laws. There were also exceptional cases, seemingly without the aforementioned advantages, in which households negotiated or opposed their dispossession. In Huaytong, a villager successfully pushed for a higher price per hectare, even though a Viet-Lao representative threatened to have provincial officials sent to 're-educate' him. In Lak Sao Paet, an elderly widow refused altogether to sell her land to Yao Tieng because their proposed payment was not enough to make up for her loss in crops. She threatened to cut down their rubber trees if the dispossession went ahead. In these cases of seemingly limited or no dispossession, other losses come into play.

The proximity of the rubber plantations to local farming land (a range of 0.5–3 km) has created a scenario in which households who have kept enough land prefer not to carry on with shifting cultivation due to fears that nearby rubber trees will catch fire when those households' own fields are burned. In addition to farming land loss and disruption of traditional cultivation, there has been a reduction in forest land and watercourses have been polluted. This means that the enclosure of plantations and their proximity to villagers' farm lands have also prevented villagers from continuing to pursue other livelihoods, such as cattle grazing, fishing, hunting, and collecting NTFPs. Some families have observed reductions in fish populations in nearby rivers and blamed this on the use of chemicals on the plantations, chemicals that have created health problems for workers.

3.2.3   Livelihood Change

Over the past seven years, households have substantially decreased family farming activities, which were their main occupation until the onset of the concessions, and have instead increased their salaried activities. Some now devote their time entirely to wage labour, a trend that is more pronounced in Bachiang. For households with more than 1 ha of land left, (now insufficient) farming output is complemented with paid work, typically at the rubber plantations. These households have continued with the cultivation of traditional cash crops (corn, peanuts, coffee), and they are increasingly planting cassava, especially in Bachiang. In the initial two years of rubber plantation, Bachiang families could continue planting peanuts and corn in between the young rubber trees, but as the trees have now grown, people have turned to their remaining plots, where rotation is very limited. In Lak Sao Paet, in Paksong, most households have continued with coffee cultivation, but reportedly more are now engaged in basket- and broom-making, or in selling the raw materials for these activities to intermediaries who then sell these for a higher price in Pakse or Chong-Mek, the border checkpoint with Thailand. While old cash crops, and newer ones such as cassava, have provided incomes to meet growing needs, land is at risk of exhaustion when it is cultivated without rotation. This intensification is also found in the case of upland rice, where fallow duration has been shortened to a maximum of three years.

For families with less than 1 ha, farming only takes place if family members cannot find anything (salaried) else to do. There are a few instances in Thongpao and Huaytong where those who were landless prior to the concessions were already salaried workers for other landed families, mainly outside their villages. Now they also work at the plantations.

The availability of work at the plantations has, however, fluctuated over time and cannot be taken for granted. In the early years, companies were reluctant to engage local inhabitants because they were perceived as 'unreliable *sompao* [ethnic] people', who are 'difficult to work with because they do not commit for long'.[14] Companies brought in labour from outside, including Vietnamese workers. In some cases, this reluctance was mutual, as villagers mentioned not wanting to work for the companies either out of expressed feelings of resentment, or because they believed they could not compete with the Vietnamese, who are said to be 'better and faster' at the tasks. In Huaytong, the village authorities reported that in 2006 Viet-Lao only hired ten people from the village (i.e. 4 per cent of the population). Eventually, the companies had to engage more local labour due to the amount of clearing required, but when those tasks were complete less labour was needed. Hiring experienced another resurgence when the rubber tapping started.

Jobs at the plantations are mostly for young people; 'old' people (>40 years old) are often considered ineligible. Working conditions and salaries were systematically reported to not match people's expectations and household needs. Whereas male rubber tappers earn, on average, LAK 1 million per month across all studied sites, female tappers reported an average wage of LAK

---

14   Informal conversation with a Vietnamese company representative, 26 July 2013.

TABLE 7.6   *Main livelihood activities in four selected villages (2003 and 2013)*

Village	2003	2013
Thongpao	– *Agriculture* a) Rain-fed rice, for consumption b) Peanuts and corn in swidden systems, as cash crops	– *Salaried work* a) Rubber plantations b) For other families in village or nearby – *Agriculture* a) Remaining farmland turned to cassava production
Huaytong	– *Agriculture* a) Irrigated and rain-fed rice, for consumption b) Fruit trees, cassava, and coffee in permanent land, for consumption	– *Salaried work* a) Rubber plantations b) Factory and domestic work outside village – *Agriculture* Fruit trees, coffee, and cassava
Lak Sip Kao	– *Agriculture* a) Irrigated and rain-fed rice, for consumption b) Fruit trees and coffee in permanent land, as cash crops – *Machete-making*	– *Salaried work* a) Rubber plantations b) Construction work c) For other families outside village – *Machete-making*
Lak Sao Paet	– *Agriculture* a) Coffee (mainly robusta) in permanent and swidden systems, as a cash crop – *Basket- and broom-making*	– *Agriculture* a) Coffee and fruit trees – *Salaried work* a) Rubber plantations b) Coffee plantations – *Basket- and broom-making*

SOURCE: FIELD RESEARCH BY SENTIES PORTILLA, 2012–13.

700,000. Other tasks, such as clearing, provide lower (daily) wages.[15] The most frequently cited reason for gender-based wage differences was 'you get paid depending on how much rubber you tap', followed by 'the boss in your team decides how much you get'.

In their search for jobs, some villagers have had to go further away from their place of residence. Such mobility, which is temporary in most cases, depends on networks outside the area, which are developed in all the studied villages, but to a lesser degree in Thongpao. For the few young people in Thongpao who have experienced temporary work outside their home village, having a rubber plantation located in the area has meant that they 'can now choose to stay', even though they are aware of the poor employment conditions and their limited future prospects as small landholders. Across villages there is a general perception among the young that having cash is relatively better than having land that produces only food for the household. Cash, and its perceived regular availability (on-site) with the coming of the plantations, can provide young villagers with their three main desires: 'you can buy a motorbike', 'you can have a better [concrete] house', and 'it gets you clothes and nice things [consumer goods]'. Although the majority of the young acknowledged that cash could also be obtained from family farming, they highlighted various constraints: a lack of labour input; a lack of necessary capital and/or skills in their households to have a good, copious harvest; and—above all—that land was becoming scarcer. Another constraint mentioned was a lack of the knowledge necessary to market their produce at a higher price. A few of them—chiefly those who had experienced more years of schooling outside their village, but had 'no money to continue'—mentioned they were 'not so interested in farming; we just do it, we have no choice'. For the middle-aged and older villagers, things are not worse or better: 'Before, we had land and we had food; now we have almost no land but we can find money to buy food.'

In Lak Sip Kao, where households have so far coped by combining salaried employment (at the plantations or elsewhere) with machete-making, the situation is now uncertain because possible village relocation plans for a stadium construction are underway. According to village authorities, at the time of latest interview (21 January 2014), the project's approval was being discussed in Vientiane.

Growing rubber, although appealing, remains impossible due to a lack of land and start-up capital and/or know-how. Only one interviewed family, in Huaytong, has invested in rubber. Since the household head is a war veteran and an influential figure in the village, particularly with regard to land

---

15   Interviews, 16 July 2013, and group discussion, 29 January 2014.

issues, he was able to retain some of his land. After family members acquired knowledge of rubber by working for Viet-Lao, they bought rubber trees from the company and planted them in two hectares. The family is confident and enthusiastic about the potential of their small rubber plantation, which will turn profitable in 2016: 'By then, others will see [the benefit] and perhaps start doing the same.'

4 Synthesis, Comparisons, and Discussion

Our case studies present several points of resemblance. In contrast to depictions of poverty and vulnerability as endemic and intrinsic to traditional cultivation systems, we found that local populations' vulnerability prior to the mid-2000s was mostly generated by public policies, which pertain mainly to the population's displacement for Ratanakiri, Cambodia, and to restrictions on access to and use of farmland in Champasak, Laos. In both countries, the agrarian transition was marked by the introduction of cash crops prior to the wave of land acquisitions, coupled with more radical changes driven by the arrival of large-scale rubber plantations, which are similar in size in our case studies—4,147 ha on average for Ratanakiri; in Champasak, an average of 4,938 ha.

In both areas, the acceleration of land deals and the development of new crops—rubber but also cassava—has greatly changed the economic environment in which indigenous populations lead their lives and experience their social systems. Rural interconnectedness has increased thanks to new and better-maintained roads and because most of the families nowadays own at least one motorcycle. Secondary towns, district-centres, rural marketplaces, and crossroads have grown rapidly. The supply of agricultural inputs, tools, construction materials, medicine, consumption goods, etc. has increased. Small retail shops have opened in villages—people who travel back and forth on motorcycles supplying them regularly—and the range of goods has diversified. In addition, travelling sellers make tours of the villages, where they sell meat, fish, vegetables, etc. However, urban and market development are not systematically synonymous with betterment for the bulk of the population. Some of the foods that these travelling sellers offer for sale in the villages are items that villagers used to produce or collect by themselves, and that they must now pay for, as these products are now produced less and because populations are increasingly busy with other off-farm tasks. Trade and markets have developed, but farmers sell their harvests mostly at home. Although sale prices are higher a few kilometres outside villages, producers do not know how to operate in those marketplaces.

The major difference between Champasak and Ratanakiri lies in the magnitude of land loss and the consequent importance of non-farming activities to new livelihoods. Land loss in Champasak has overall been more severe than in Ratanakiri. Yet, our research in Cambodia shows that 'the bigger, the more severe' is a premise that does not always stand. In Ratanakiri, the pace of development of the (large) ELCs left some time and space for former users to respond, whereas no such time was given to the population of Champasak. Several factors can explain this difference, including the proximity to/distance from, and overlap with, areas that were previously used. In Ratanakiri companies did not have sufficient physical capital to plant the large granted areas. A second major difference is the involvement of a wider range of new actors in Ratanakiri, including medium-sized Khmer companies operating outside the frame of ELCs and numerous in-migrants who settled in the villages, all of whom contributed significantly to the process of land acquisitions. Incoming migration in Champasak villages, in relation to salaried work at the rubber plantations, was found to be much lower and more temporary. Champasak families have found more, although intermittent, job opportunities in rubber plantations than their peers in Ratanakiri, who suffer from the tough competition of Khmer in-migrants.

We also observed differences in populations' attitudes towards the new holders of land. In Ratanakiri, populations dared to respond to and in some cases to contest central government-signed ELCs, whereas in Champasak villagers rarely contested upper-level decisions, and even less so challenged acquisitions by public officials. This may reflect the fact that the state in Laos has a tighter and more effective control over its populations than does the state in Cambodia—whether this is real or merely perceived as such by those who are governed. Another marked difference was found in Ratanakiri where local populations express a fear of Khmer landowners, who they say are high-ranking and well-connected people with unlimited power, which is not the case with foreign-held land concessions. Local populations responses are also telling regarding the subjective meanings underlying power relations, as illustrated by the Ratanakiri population, which expresses having lower capabilities compared to the Khmer, who they say they are 'more clever'. Similar expressions from villagers in Champasak (non-Lao ethnic and Lao alike) were also heard regarding the Vietnamese.

We can thus distinguish two levels of dispossession that we will hereafter label as 'partial' and 'severe'. As dispossession levels are uneven across households within a single village, we then draw on a typology of the transformation of household livelihoods across our cases.

Partial dispossession, as found to be predominant in Pra Lai and Malik (Cambodia) and Lak Sao Paet (Laos), comprises situations in which villages were left with enough land for the majority of families to—so far—satisfy their basic needs from farming. *Partial* also means that livelihoods remain centred around family-based activities, although families are increasingly in search for salaried jobs. The magnitude of partial dispossession is tied to the capacity of local populations to make up for their land loss by clearing other areas, to negotiate with companies the retention of some of their (the populations') land, to get incorporated into rubber companies, or to receive monetary or non-monetary compensation. Apart from the size of land loss relative to the total area previously farmed by the local population, some cases of partial dispossession are related to a slower pace of development achieved by companies, and the consequent opportunity for the local population to anticipate and respond to land acquisitions. Thus, the transformation of partial dispossession into severe dispossession might just be a matter of time; the time it will take for investors to plant the full holding they were granted.

Severe dispossession, as observed in Trang and the three villages in Bachiang, depicts situations in which access to land and other natural resources is not enough to satisfy basic needs. Dispossession is severe particularly for swidden land, as both national governments concerned have facilitated the granting of land areas left fallow, with the argument that those areas were 'not used' or were 'state land'. Using the same argument, swidden plots were frequently not eligible for any type of compensation. Severity relates to the size of and a faster pace of plantation development; to people's powerlessness or perceptions of powerlessness in reacting to dispossession, particularly vis-à-vis certain types of investors or authority levels granting the concessions; and to the derisory amount of compensation, if compensation is provided at all. In some cases, severe dispossession also relates to the combination of large-scale land deals with a wave of small-scale acquisitions by in-migrants or public officials.

The typology of livelihood transformations reflects (1) how households were affected by and could respond to the politics of dispossession, (2) the main transformation of their economic activities over the last five to seven years, and (3) how they have managed, or not, to engage in the rubber boom.

A first group, which mostly includes village elites and their close relatives, has managed to retain some land or avoid being dispossessed altogether by orienting investors far enough away from their land. This represents around 2 per cent of households in Champasak and 4 per cent in Ratanakiri. Thanks to their status and power in their respective villages, they could easily compensate for any loss by obtaining access to other land. As they themselves often facilitated the land acquisitions, their acquaintance with investors enabled them to obtain access to inputs (seedlings) and/or technical advice to develop rubber plantations of their own on areas ranging from 2 to 10 ha. Only one case of a member of a village elite who planted rubber was documented in Champasak. This group also includes some of the oldest and well-off in-migrants.

A second group has thrived on the wave of land acquisitions and rubber boom-induced local development. It includes shop owners, traders, and households providing services such as transport, restaurant, repair work, brokerage, worker recruitment, and money lending. In Champasak, this group does not exceed 10 per cent of households of all the studied sites combined. In Ratanakiri, this group represents 7 per cent of the sample; members of the group are mostly outsiders to the places in which they have settled and established their business, and some of them invested in rubber at a time when land was still cheap, and they today possess plantations similar in size to those of the first group.

For the third group, farming activities have remained at the core of their livelihoods; farming-based livelihoods include an increasing share of land dedicated to cash crops, cassava and fruit trees, and a little rubber (1–2 ha). In this group, which accounts for 12 per cent of the total population surveyed in Ratanakiri, households have engaged in rubber through their own investments; only one such case was encountered in southern Laos. The engagement process has been slow or came later than for the two previous groups, as these households did not possess the necessary start-up capital and were not acquainted with the rubber companies. We cannot predict if these households will manage to turn their investment into profitable cropping systems, as the trees are not productive yet. So far, they have not had to work for others, or only occasionally.

For the fourth group, livelihood transformation is marked by an increasing share of salaried work—or petty commodity production for a few—as a proportion of their total income. They have become part-time farmers who do not have the capacity to engage in rubber. Their best achievement lies in finding more regular salaried jobs and possibly semi-skilled better-paid ones. Their prospects at home are much constrained by in-migrant workers; and their future elsewhere depends much on the social networks needed to facilitate migration. This group represents around 49 and 75 per cent of the totals, respectively, in Ratanakiri and Champasak.

A last group consists of rural workers for whom farming is practiced only when there is nothing else to do. In Champasak, this situation is reflected in an estimated 13 per cent of households, all studied sites combined. In Ratanakiri,

28 per cent of households belong to this group. Salaried work has become the pillar of their livelihoods. Engagement in rubber was never an option. The existence of this group relates to severe cases of dispossession, where households sold too much of their land at an early stage, an occurrence in Ratanakiri, or to households that had large plots of swidden land falling in concession areas, as was the case in Champasak. In Ratanakiri, this group also includes in-migrants who have not yet acquired land and who came in search for work. Although regular jobs are rare, selling labour has become a more rational pursuit than farming. As job opportunities are not sufficient at home, out-migration of one or several household members tends to increase. Those who are not capable of migrating are left with limited choices, including 'desperate' sales of their remaining land assets.

5   Conclusion

In the seven villages that feature in this chapter, an agrarian transition from dominant subsistence-oriented swidden forms of agriculture had started prior to the acceleration of land acquisitions. However, as local government only loosely implemented public policies, and the development of cash crops for outside markets remained limited, the 'powers' of regulation and the market (Hall et al., 2011) were not strong enough to include these communities in the market economy. Yet, those public policies eroded the former agrarian system and thus paved the way for an 'insecure boom' (Hall, 2011, 3).

The power and pace of transition changed from the mid-2000s. The effectiveness of regulation increased because local governments were involved in its implementation process; furthermore, they contributed to its legitimation or rather its acceptance by local populations. At the same time, the power of the market increased: the booming demand for rubber, stronger than for any previous crop, made it more profitable for local government representatives to comply with central government strategy; it also convinced smallholders that rubber could be profitable. The transition strengthened further, as small landholders themselves became 'agents' of land transactions, with opportunistic village elites—in some cases—becoming agents of land grabbing within their own communities.

Despite substantial land acquisitions by outsiders, most local populations have until now managed to keep some land and to maintain farming activities for themselves. However, this state of affairs is bound to change at some point as large-scale companies are increasing their planted acreage and medium-scale companies are pursuing their search for surrounding areas to expand, and as the flow of in-migrants, in the case of Ratanakiri, is continuing. Furthermore, in response to the reduction in land available, families have intensified their cropping systems—of cassava in particular—in ways that might not be sustainable.

Beyond the reduction and depletion of those natural resources that are left to local populations, the majority are cornered by a socio-economic environment that increases their need for cash, while their former household farming-based livelihoods are not providing enough of a livelihood anymore, and rubber remains out of reach. In reference to the agrarian transition as described by Rigg et al. (2012), our cases show some major nuances. First, at the provincial level, the increasing share of non-farming activities is found in urbanising areas, market places, and along the main transportation networks; but for native populations the process is not advanced, despite their need and wish to get out of farming solely. Second, the process of 'delocalisation of life and living' is reflected in the shift of spaces created by land acquisitions, but the 'mobility' of native populations is confined to within the vicinity of their villages. Third, a dis-embedding of households and families is occurring, but not so much because of social and economic relations being 'stretched across space', but rather because of the development of individual interests, notably among the youth of the areas in question. Last, the dissociation of the village-community is strong, as illustrated by the uneven opportunities brought about by newcomers and the opportunistic behaviour of village elites.

Family farming is not lagging behind; it is losing ground, as illustrated by land sales that are no longer even a short-term cash opportunity, but fall more and more into the category of 'desperate' sales to cover existing deficits. As opportunities to diversify economic activity remain insufficient, people will have to turn to the diversification of localities; out-migration is likely to become one of the key features of this agrarian transition.

Needless to say, a political commitment from the two national governments concerned to seriously and substantially reassess their development strategies in light of these consequences is urgent, and not simply a matter of procedural design or wishful, responsible thinking on the part of investors. The usual recommendation of prior informed consultations about land deals has not only—in our cases—become outdated, its presumed effectiveness for future investments remains more than uncertain in the light of current development drives. Furthermore, we cannot expect much from the Voluntary Guidelines for responsible investments,[16] as investors on the ground have no incentive to abide by such guidelines, and nor will they feel under any pressure to harm their business with such instruments.

---

16   http://www.fao.org/3/a-au866e.pdf (accessed on 26 May 2015).

There are indeed other remarkable issues that people are facing on a daily basis for which a broad palette of interrelated human rights instruments could be called upon for action. These include the right to food, the right to water, and the right to a livelihood. Nevertheless, international governance mechanisms will remain ineffective if they have no links or outreach to civil society organisations on the ground. In both countries studied in the context of this chapter, such organisations are few and often only mildly familiar with the work of global governance structures, and their intervention capacity is rather limited when compared to the magnitude of continuing land acquisitions.

Beside a structural policy change that would be needed to halt an agrarian transition that is undermining the livelihoods of the majority, it is also important to take into account that the process of losing ground has also been accompanied by a process of dislocation/disruption of family-based livelihoods. In such a situation, younger generations, which have—or can expect to secure—some autonomy by obtaining salaried employment, are considering moving away as they are faced with limited options at home, notably a lack of land for the foreseeable future. Moreover, having a salaried job has—locally— become a perceived way of 'moving forward' or 'improving oneself'. Since such a direction 'forwards' is already leading some, and is very likely to lead many more, into exploitative situations, development practitioners should complement their advocacy of land rights, land tenure security, and access to information with assessments of capabilities and learning needs, in terms of vocational training, in a number of areas for which these populations express an interest; agriculture remaining one of them.

In Cambodia, salaried employment is developing with the rubber boom— tapping rubber for instance—but indigenous peoples cannot access it because they lack the necessary skills. Even the indigenous elites hire Khmer in-migrants to tap their trees. In Laos, there is growing interest in pursuing the benefits from farming products and other activities that, for some years, have been practiced in parallel to household farming (e.g. basket-making and machete-making), and in newer activities such as mechanised textile sewing and hairdressing, particularly among the country's youth. Therefore, training programmes to support the development of such activities and the marketing of agricultural and non-agricultural products and services should be encouraged. Further, for the growing number of people who are in search of work outside their villages, vocational training could also make a great difference. In addition, awareness raising and legal advice should be provided regarding the risks associated with migration.

Although we do not take the socio-economic transformation described in this chapter as given and irreversible—and therefore we do not intend, by any means, to accept it—we do recognise that, while waiting for solutions to its structural causes, whose search, we hope, will no longer be delayed, we need to address the negative consequences of this transformation currently affecting local populations.

References

Baird, I. (2011) 'Turning Land into Capital, Turning People into Labour: Primitive Accumulation and the Arrival of Large-Scale Economic Land Concessions in the Lao People's Democratic Republic', *New Proposals: Journal of Marxism and Interdisciplinary Inquiry*, 5(1), pp. 10–26, http://ojs.library.ubc.ca/index.php/newproposals/article/viewFile/2264/2265 (accessed on 23 April 2015).

———— (2010) 'Land, Rubber and People: Rapid Agrarian Change and Responses in Southern Laos', *Journal of Lao Studies*, 1(1), pp. 1–47, http://lad.nafri.org.la/fulltext/2042-0.pdf (accessed on 23 April 2015).

Bakker, L.G.H., G. Noteboom and A. Rutten (2010) 'Localities of Value. "Ambiguous Access to Land and Water in Southeast Asia"', *Asian Journal of Social Science*, 38(2), pp. 167–171, DOI: 10.1163/156853110X490872.

Barney, K. (2007) *Power, Progress and Impoverishment: Plantations, Hydropower, Ecological Change and Community Transformation in Hinboun District, Lao PDR* (Toronto and Washington, D.C.: YCAR Papers/Rights and Resources Initiative), http://www.cifor.org/publications/pdf_files/books/bbarney0701.pdf (accessed on 26 May 2015).

Borras Jr., S.M., and J.C. Franco (2012) 'Global Land Grabbing and Trajectories of Agrarian Change: A Preliminary Analysis', *Journal of Agrarian Change*, 12(1), pp. 34–59, DOI: 10.1111/j.1471–0366.2011.00339.x.

Bourdier, F. (2009) 'When the Margins Turn One's Step Toward an Object of Desir: Segregation and Exclusion of Indigenous Peoples in Northeast Cambodia', in Hammer, P.J. and M. Khmersiksa (eds.) *Living on the Margins: Minorities and Borderlines in Cambodia and Southeast Asia* (Phnom Penh: Center for Khmer Studies) pp. 177–185.

CDRI (Cambodia Development Research Institute) (2009) *Agricultural Trade in the Greater Mekong Sub-Region. Synthesis of the Case Studies on Cassava and Rubber Production and Trade in GMS Countries*, CDRI Working Paper Series No. 46 (Phnom Penh: CDRI), http://www.cdri.org.kh/webdata/download/wp/wp46e.pdf (accessed on 23 April 2015).

Cotula, L. (2013) *The Great African Land Grab?: Agricultural Investments and the Global Food System* (London and New York: Zed Books).

Delarue, J. (2011) *Thailand: The World's Leading Exporter of Natural Rubber Owing to its Smallholders*, Working Paper No. 96 (Paris: Agence Française de Développement), http://www.afd.fr/webdav/site/afd/shared/PUBLICATIONS/RECHERCHE/ Scientifiques/Documents-de-travail/096-document-travail-VA.pdf (accessed on 23 April 2015).

Department of Agriculture and Forestry (2013) *Information of Lease and Concession of Government Land to Private Entities, Foreign and Domestic Companies in 2012–2013 in Paksong District* (Paksong District Office).

Diana, A. (2008) *Navigating the Way through the Market: A First Assessment of Contract Farming in Luang Namtha* (Vientiane: Deutsche Gesellschaft für Technische Zusammenarbeit, GTZ) http://rightslinklao.org/wp-content/uploads/downloads/ 2014/05/Navigating-the-Way-through-the-Market-A-First-Assessment-of-Contract-Farming-in-Luang-Namtha.pdf (accessed on 23 April 2015).

Edelman, M., C. Oya and S.M. Borras Jr. (2013) 'Global Land Grabs: Historical Processes, Theoretical and Methodological Implications and Current Trajectories', *Third World Quarterly*, 34(9), pp. 1517–1531, DOI: 10.1080/01436597.2013.850190.

Evrard, O. and Y. Goudineau (2004) 'Planned Resettlement, Unexpected Migration and Cultural Trauma in Laos', *Development and Change*, 35(5), pp. 937–962, DOI: 10.1111/j.1467–7660.2004.00387.x.

Fortunel, F. (2014) 'Kampong Cham et Ratanakiri, regards croisés sur l'évolution des grandes plantations cambodgiennes', in Fortunel, F. and C. Gironde (eds.) *L'Or Blanc, Petits et grands planteurs face au "boom" de l'hévéaculture (Viêt-nam-Cambodge)* (Bangkok: Institut de Recherche sur l'Asie du Sud-Est Contemporaine) pp. 123–142, http://www.irasec.com/ouvrage113 (accessed on 23 April 2015).

——— (2007) 'Le plateau des Boloven et la culture du café, entre division interne et intégration régionale', *L'Espace géographique*, 36(3), pp. 215–228, www.cairn.info/ revue-espace-geographique-2007-3-page-215.htm (accessed on 23 April 2015).

Fox, J. and J.-C. Castella (2013) 'Expansion of Rubber (*Hevea brasiliensis*) in Mainland Southeast Asia: What are the Prospects for Smallholders?', *The Journal of Peasant Studies*, 40(1), pp. 155–170, DOI: 10.1080/03066150.2012.750605.

Fox, J. and J.B. Vogler (2009) 'Understanding Changes in Land and Forest Resource Management Systems: Ratanakiri, Cambodia', *Southeast Asian Studies*, 47(3), pp. 309–329, http://hdl.handle.net/2433/109765 (accessed on 23 April 2015).

Fox, J., D. McMahon, M. Poffenberger and J. Vogler (2008) *Land for my Grandchildren: Land Use and Tenure Change in Ratanakiri: 1998–2007* (Honolulu: Community Forestry International (CFI)–East West Center).

Fujita, Y. and K. Phanvilay (2008) 'Land and Forest Allocation in Lao People's Democratic Republic: Comparison of Case Studies from Community-Based Natural Resource Management Research', *Society and Natural Resources*, 21(2), pp. 120–133, DOI: 10.1080/08941920701681490.

Fullbrook, D. (2011) *Smallholder Production Agreements in the Lao PDR: Qualifying Success* (Vientiane: Laos Extension Agriculture Project, LEAP), http://www.fao.org/

uploads/media/2%20%20Smallholder%20Production%20Agreements%20in%20
Lao%20PDR-%20qualifying%20success.pdf (accessed on 23 April 2015).

Gebert, R. (2010) *Farmer Bargaining Power in the Lao PDR: Possibilities and Pitfalls*
(Vientiane and Berlin: LEAP–National Agriculture and Forestry Research Institute),
http://lad.nafri.org.la/fulltext/2237-0.pdf (accessed on 23 April 2015).

Gironde C. and F. Fortunel (2014) 'Le "boom" de l'hévéa au Cambodge: une conversion hasardeuse pour les petits producteurs autochtones de Ratanakiri?', Fortunel,
F. and C. Gironde (eds.) *L'Or Blanc, Petits et grands planteurs face au "boom" de
l'hévéaculture (Viêt-nam-Cambodge)* (Bangkok: Institut de Recherche sur l'Asie du
Sud-Est Contemporaine) pp. 143–171, http://www.irasec.com/ouvrage113 (accessed
on 23 April 2015).

Goudineau, Y. (2008) 'L'anthropologie du Sud-Laos et la question Kantou', in
Goudineau, Y. and M. Lorrillard (eds.) *Recherches nouvelles sur le Laos* (Vientiane
and Paris: EFEO) pp. 639–664.

Gouyon, A. (1995) *Paysannerie et hévéaculture dans les plaines orientales de Sumatra*,
unpublished PhD thesis (Paris: Institut National Agronomique Paris-Grignon).

Guérin, M., A. Hardy, S.T. Boon Hwee and N. Van Chin (2003) *Des montagnards aux
minorités ethniques: quelle intégration pour les habitants des hautes-terres du Viêt
Nam et du Cambodge?* (Bangkok: IRASEC).

Hall, D. (2011) 'Land Grabs, Land Control, and Southeast Asian Crop Booms', *The Journal
of Peasant Studies*, 38(4), pp. 837–857, DOI: 10.1080/03066150.2011.607706.

Hall, D., P. Hirsch and T.M. Li (2011) *Powers of Exclusion: Land Dilemmas in Southeast
Asia* (Honolulu: University of Hawai'i Press).

Hansen, K. and N. Top (2006) *Natural Forest Benefits and Analysis of Natural Forest
Conversion in Cambodia*, Working Paper No. 33 (Phnom Penh: CDRI).

Hughes, C. (2003) *The Political Economy of Cambodia's Transition 1991–2001* (London
and New York: Routledge).

Ironside, J. (2009) 'Poverty Reduction or Poverty Creation? A Study on Achieving the
Millennium Development Goals in Two Indigenous Communities in Ratanakiri
Province, Cambodia', in Bourdier, F. (ed.) *Development and Dominion: Indigenous
Peoples of Cambodia, Vietnam and Laos* (Bangkok: White Lotus Press) pp. 79–113.

Kenney-Lazar, M. (2012) 'Plantation Rubber, Land Grabbing and Social-Property
Transformation in Southern Laos', *Journal of Peasant Studies*, 39(3–4), pp. 1017–1037,
DOI: 10.1080/03066150.2012.674942.

Li, T.M. (2011) 'Centering Labor in the Land Grab Debate', *The Journal of Peasant Studies*,
38(2), pp. 281–298, DOI: 10.1080/03066150.2011.559009.

Lin, S. (2010) *FDI in Agriculture in Northern Lao PDR: A Case Study of Luang Namtha
Rural Development in Mountainous Areas of Lao PDR, Component 1: Sustainable
Resource Use and Local Economic Development* (Vientiane: GTZ), http://laocs-kis.

org/index.php?option=com_sobipro&task=download.file&fid=206.1171&sid=132& lang=en (accessed on 23 April 2015).

Luangmany, D. and S. Kaneko (2013) 'Expansion of Rubber Tree Plantation in Northern Laos: Economic and Environmental Consequences', *Journal of International Development and Cooperation*, 19(3), pp. 1–13, http://ir.lib.hiroshima-u.ac.jp/00035036 (accessed on 23 April 2015).

Luco, F. (2008) ' "Manger le Royaume"—Pratiques anciennes et actuelles d'accès à la terre au Cambodge', in Forest, A. (ed.) *Cambodge contemporain* (Bangkok and Paris: IRASEC–Les Indes savants) pp. 419–444.

Manivong, V. and R.A. Cramb (2008) 'Economics of Smallholder Rubber Expansion in Northern Laos',*Agroforestry System*, 74(2), pp. 113–125, DOI:10.1007/s10457-008-9136-3.

McAllister, K. (2012) *Rubber, Rights and Resistance: the Evolution of Local Struggles against a Chinese Rubber Concession in Northern Laos*, paper presented at the International Conference Global Land Grabbing II, October 17–19 (Ithaca: Cornell University), http://www.cornell-landproject.org/download/landgrab2012papers/mcallister.pdf (accessed on 23 April 2015).

NLMA (National Land Management Authority) (2009–2011) *Reports on the 'Findings of State Land Lease and Concession Inventory Project' for the Provinces of Attapeu, Bokeo, Champasak, Khammuan, Luangnamtha, Luangprabang, Saravan, Vientiane, Xayabouly and Xiengkhouang* (Vientiane: Land and Natural Resource Information and Research Centre).

Obein, F. (2007) *Assessment of the Environmental and Social Impacts Created by the VLRC Industrial Rubber Plantation and Proposed Environmental and Social Plans*, Final Report (Vientiane: Agence Française de Développement), http://dev.rightslink lao.org/wp-content/uploads/downloads/2014/06/04-afd-vlrc_rubber_plantation_in_bachiang_district.pdf (accessed on 26 May 2015).

Peluso, N.L. and C. Lund (2011) 'New Frontiers of Land Control: Introduction',*Journal of Peasant Studies*, 38(4), pp. 667–681, DOI: 10.1080/03066150.2011.607692.

Rigg, J. (2006) 'Land, Farming, Livelihoods, and Poverty: Rethinking the Links in the Rural South', *World Development*, 34(1), pp. 180–202, DOI: 10.1016/j.worlddev .2005.07.015.

Rigg, J., A. Salamanca and M. Parnwell (2012) 'Joining the Dots of Agrarian Change in Asia: A 25 Year View from Thailand', *World Development*, 40(7), pp. 1469–1481, 10.1016/j.worlddev.2012.03.001.

Ruohomäki, O. (2004) 'Encounters in Borderlands: Social and Economic Transformations in Ratanakiri, Northeastern Cambodia', *Moussons*, 7, pp. 71–94, http://moussons.revues.org/2482 (accessed on 23 April 2015).

Sallée, B. and J-C. Tulet (2010) 'Développement de la caféiculture paysanne et concessions de terres sur le plateau des Bolovens (Sud Laos): synergie ou antagonisme?', *Cahiers d'Outre-Mer*, 249, pp. 93–120, DOI: 10.4000/com.5886.

Schönweger, O., A. Heinimann, M. Epprecht, J. Lu and P. Thalongsengchanh (2012) *Concessions and Leases in the Lao PDR: Taking Stock of Land Investments* (Bern and Vientiane: Geographica Bernensia), http://www.cde.unibe.ch/v1/CDE/pdf/Concessions-Leases-LaoPDR_2012.pdf (accessed on 23 April 2015).

Sikor, T. (2012) 'Tree Plantations, Politics of Possession and the Absence of Land Grabs in Vietnam', *The Journal of Peasant Studies*, 39(3–4), pp. 1077–1101, DOI: 10.1080/03066150.2012.674943.

Simbolon, I. (2002) *Access to Land of Highland Indigenous Minorities: the Case of Plural Property Rights in Cambodia*, Working Paper No. 42 (Halle: Max Planck Institute for Social Anthropology).

Srikham, W. (2010) *The Effects of Commercial Agriculture and Swidden-Field Privatization in Southern Laos*, paper presented at the RCSD International Conference on Revisiting Agrarian Transformations in Southeast Asia: Empirical, Theoretical and Applied Perspectives, 13–15 May, Chiang Mai, Thailand.

Sturgeon, J. (2012) 'The Cultural Politics of Ethnic Identity in Xishuangbanna, China: Tea and Rubber as "Cash Crops" and "Commodities" ', *Journal of Current Chinese Affairs*, 41(4), pp. 109–131, http://journals.sub.uni-hamburg.de/giga/jcca/article/view/576/574 (accessed on 23 April 2015).

Tang, S.M. (2014) *The Immigrants' Settlement Strategies and Immigration Dynamics within the Framework of Large Scale Lands Acquisitions and their Impacts on Local Populations' Livelihoods in Selected Village of Ratanakiri Province, Cambodia*, unpublished Master thesis, Master en Etudes Asiatiques (Geneva: University of Geneva).

Un, K. and S. So (2011) 'Land Rights in Cambodia: How Neo-Patrimonial Politics Restricts Land Policy Reform', *Pacific Affairs*, 84(2), pp. 287–306, DOI: 10.5509/2011842289.

Vientiane Times Reporters (2015) 'Champasak Moves Towards "Land as Equity" Project Model', *Vientiane Times*, 14 January, Issue 11, p. 1.

White, J. (1996) 'The Highland People of Cambodia: The Indigenous Highlanders of the Northeast, an Uncertain Future', in *Interdisciplinary Research on Ethnic Groups in Cambodia: Final Draft Reports for Discussion at the National Symposium on Ethnic Groups in Cambodia Held in Phnom Penh* (Phnom Penh: Center for Advanced Study).

Yem, D., T. Neth and L. Vuthy (2011) *Rubber Plantation Development in Cambodia: At What Cost?* (Los Banos, Philippines: Economy and Environment Program for Southeast Asia), http://www.eepsea.org/o-k2/view-item/id-397/Itemid-385/ (accessed on 26 May 2015).

CHAPTER 8

'Better-Practice' Concessions? Lessons from Cambodia's Leopard-Skin Landscape

Michael B. Dwyer, Emily Polack, and Sokbunthoeun So

Abstract

In the context of the global land rush, policy debates are split on the question of state land concessions: are smallholder-centric 'inclusive' investment models the only real form of responsible agricultural investment, or are 'responsible' concessions possible when it comes to the protection of local land access? To help move this debate forwards, this paper examines two case studies in Cambodia—an oil palm plantation recently certified by the Roundtable on Sustainable Palm Oil (RSPO) and a teak plantation certified by the Forest Stewardship Council (FSC)—which we refer to as 'better-practice' concessions. These cases reflect efforts to operationalise the Cambodian government's 'Leopard-Skin' policy, which stipulates that concessions be developed around smallholders rather than directly on top of them. We argue that regularisation is not inherently objectionable, but carries risks when carried out on a concession-by-concession basis, because it distances vulnerable land users from the potentially protective effects of the law and defers to localised, and often unequal, relations of authority. The paper thus highlights the challenges that investors and communities are likely to face even when concession developers seek to respect existing local land claims, and suggests that models based on empowered communities with more secure forms of tenure are likely to work better for all parties involved.

1 Introduction

In many destination countries in the global land rush, the state lays legal claim to large swathes of land, including land occupied and used by smallholders and managed under a variety of customary governance systems. This disjuncture between formal and de facto property is exacerbated by many states not even knowing the extent of their landholdings (FAO et al., 2010), and has in recent years been used to put large amounts of land into play through the blurring of both legal and cartographic boundaries (Cotula et al., 2009; Deininger and Byerlee, 2011; HLPE, 2011; Borras Jr. and Franco, 2012). This imprecise legal geography has major implications for investors who have been lured into so-called 'frontier' markets by promises of cheap and abundant state land (Adler and So, 2012; Borras Jr. and Franco, 2012; de Leon et al., 2013). If state land is *actually* state-owned in the sense of being demarcated and uncontested, it can give investors attractive incentives: 'one-stop' acquisition, efficient regulation and, most important, low cost of access. But when land is state-'owned' in only the formal sense—that is, when it remains occupied, used, or even locally held under soft forms of title—investors are vulnerable to a range of delays, additional costs, and reputational risks (Munden Project, 2012; de Leon et al., 2013). Whether state ownership of land is actual, merely formal, or somewhere in between is thus a subject of great interest.

The role of the private sector in helping bridge the gap between formal and de facto property remains a key point of contention in debates about land grabbing, responsible agricultural investment, and the gulf in between (Cotula and Leonard, 2010; FAO et al., 2010; UNCFS, 2012). In many ways Cambodia is exemplary of the global land grab problem, in which local elites and foreign investors collaborate with each other and with state officials to acquire and develop large concessions of putatively state-owned (but previously un-demarcated) land. State land concessions in Cambodia, various estimates of which range between 1 and 3 million hectares (Titthara and Boyle 2012a; ADHOC, 2013; 2014), have reportedly flouted legal provisions on landhold-ings and community protection, and many have reportedly involved substan-tial violence and displacement yet delivered minimal or no benefit to locals (LICADHO, 2009; Chak, 2011; Müller, 2012; Kuch and Zsombor, 2013; Neef et al., 2013). But while this may be the standard story within the Cambodian land sector (see Gironde and Senties Portilla; Cismas and Paramita, both in this vol-ume), this pattern has nonetheless become a growing liability for the actors involved—not just companies and their investors, but also state officials at multiple levels, and even foreign donors. This article focuses on two cases where companies have sought to develop more socially benign—and, they believe, more profitable and sustainable—plantation concessions in a context that is still marred by extensive land conflict. The first is the Mong Reththy Investment Cambodia Oil Palm (MRICOP) Company (Preah Sihanouk prov-ince); the second is the Grandis Timber Company (Kampong Speu province). We examine each case empirically, investigating how two well-intentioned yet strategically oriented companies navigate the complex landscape of mul-tiple entitlements and competing claims that lurk beneath the surface of state ownership in Cambodia's rural hinterland. In doing so, we interrogate the pri-vate sector's role in helping address the state land problem, both in Cambodia and elsewhere.

The two cases sit within a national regulatory context that is increasingly linked to what government officials, private sector actors and the media call the government's Leopard-Skin (*Sbek Khla*) policy. The term, apparently coined by state officials around 2010 and circulated increasingly since (CDC, 2010; RGC, 2012a; 2012c), remains vague for some, and contested for others in its status as well as its intended operational meaning (Milne, 2013; Beban, 2014). For some, it is a clear policy, carrying significant government weight (if not quite the force of law), while for others it is more like a concept, approach, or formula that is still being tested, but that holds significant appeal because of its contrast with the status quo (ADHOC, 2014). The basic idea behind it boils down to concession development through *regularisation rather than eviction*: treating illegal smallholders—occupants whom official discourse often terms 'encroachers'—as legitimate parts of the economic landscape, and developing concessions *around* them rather than by evicting them first (CDC, 2010; RGC, 2012c; ADHOC, 2014). One foreign advisor to the Cambodian land sector described the policy as 'leaving the people where they are and just using the rest' (Müller, 2012, 10). Similarly, the *Phnom Penh Post* (Becker 2012) called the approach a 'workaround strategy' in the literal sense of leaving small-scale farmers in place and making companies work around them.

Regularisation is hardly a new idea in Cambodian policy circles. A preference for avoiding evictions has been stated in various policy documents and discussions for over a decade (see e.g. CLP, 2002, 27; RGC, 2007; MAFF, no date). Yet, as has often been noted, the concept has been minimally implemented (Müller, 2012). What is notable about the last few years is the political currency that regularisation has gained, as land conflicts, evictions, and land-related arrests mushroomed, especially in the run-up to Cambodia's national elections in July 2013 (ADHOC, 2013; Un, 2013). The case studies presented below are notable for providing a closer look at what regularisation efforts in Cambodia have actually looked like. The cases were chosen for their ability to show Leopard-Skin development in practice—both companies have publicly committed to avoiding eviction and made the business case for leaving local land users in place (Chakrya and Sherrel, 2011; Becker 2012)—and because each has been identified by outside experts, including third party certifiers (Intertek-Moody International, 2012; GFA Certification, 2013), as being a positive example in a concession landscape defined largely by its governance failures (for MRICOP, see UNCOHCHR, 2007, 20; Chakrya and Sherrel, 2011. For Grandis Timber, see IWA, 2011; Müller, 2012, 11; and Becker, 2012).

Looking at how private sector actors negotiate the landscape of existing property claims and entitlements that confront their efforts to develop concessions of so-called state land is useful because it provides a window into the social, political-economic and legal dynamics that exist in pluralist contexts where statutory, use-based, and patronage-based ownership norms all vie for supremacy—contexts where, in short, 'the law is not the law' (Adler and So, 2012). Studying private sector efforts to take advantage of state-legal land claims while also acknowledging local, use-based understandings of ownership—at least in part—provides insight into the political economy of concession development, framing regularisation as a strategic move for legitimising state land concessions at a moment of crisis, and showing how the private sector performs for the state the difficult task of making the legal abstraction of state land operational on the ground. In examining this reciprocity, we show how concession development risks blurring the lines between public authority and private interest, but also suggest that at least some in the private sector are thinking *more* pragmatically than the government about local land entitlements. Whether this pragmatism should be equated with good practice, however, is a difficult question; the cases thus show the need to look closely at how Leopard-Skin development deals with entrenched relations of power and marginality in rural landscapes. Finally, by gesturing to both the needs and challenges associated with getting accurate information about how land acquisition occurs, the cases provide opportunities to connect with wider debates on transnational regulation, including third-party certification and soft law (see Cismas and Paramita in this volume).

This paper is based on findings from desk research and a field study involving key informant interviews (including company directors, project staff, local officials, and residents of project-area communities) conducted in November and December 2011, as well as additional investigation during 2012 and early 2013, the periods during which both projects were being evaluated for third-party certification. The study is based on best available information. However, as is typical in the Cambodian agribusiness sector, most project documents such as impact assessments and land inventories remained unavailable to us. While rough project timelines could be constructed from fieldwork and online data, access to project documents would have increased our ability to analyse and explain the cases more substantially. Opacity is typical of the Cambodian agribusiness sector (and of investment in Cambodia more generally), but this lack of access to documents presented a limitation nonetheless. Second, our focus, both conceptually and methodologically, is on questions of land access; while these are inevitably connected to larger issues of livelihood, sustainable development, and so on, such wider issues as such are beyond the scope of this chapter. (For linkages to livelihood, human rights, and a governance analysis of agricultural investments in Cambodia, see Messerli et al., Gironde and Senties Portilla, and Cismas and Paramita, all in this volume).

2 Background: The Political Economy of 'Anarchic Encroachment'

While Cambodia has featured centrally in the 'global land grab' debate of recent years (GRAIN, 2008; Deininger and Byerlee, 2011; Neef et al., 2013; Baird, 2014), land grabbing and related problems of unmapped state land are hardly new. Dating back to the social and economic dislocations of Khmer Rouge rule (1975–1978) and its aftermath (during the 1980s and 1990s), the distribution of land and associated questions of access and ownership have long been at the heart of contemporary Cambodian politics (Chandler, 1993; Gottesman, 2003; Hughes, 2007; Un and So, 2009; Cock, 2010; Heder, 2011). One of the central motifs through which this history has unfolded is 'anarchic encroachment', a term that state officials often use to describe the activities of smallholders on lands that are claimed as state property. Anarchic encroachment is far more complicated than just smallholders, however, harkening back not just to the legal disarray that followed the Khmer Rouge's removal in 1979, but also—and, we argue, especially—to contemporary Cambodian state policy predicated on the allocation of state land for development purposes.

Despite having an official policy of collectivised production (as in Vietnam and Laos at the time), the Cambodian government that came to power in 1979 had little choice, given the memory of Khmer Rouge rule, but to allow the traditional model of smallholder farming to return on a wide scale (Chandler, 1993; Gottesman, 2003). This occurred during the 1980s, and in preparation for the Vietnamese military withdrawal from Cambodia at the end of the decade (and presaging the formal UN-mediated transition period of 1992–1993) the government offered farmers the chance to formalise these entitlements; by the end of 1991, roughly 4 million applications had been filed (So, 2009, 106). Only a fraction of these applications were eventually converted into actual certificates of ownership, however, in part because the Land Law of 1992 excluded agricultural land from eligibility for private ownership (Van Acker, 1999, 37; Cooper, 2002, 17). Instead, in a move that favoured elite patronage over smallholder populism, state officials focused on handing out concession rights to powerful individuals, most (in)famously for logging. Thus neoliberalism, in the form of 'public enterprise privatization' (RGC, 1994; MEF, 1995), articulated with the politics of patronage; timber concessions, for example, increased from roughly 2.2 million hectares in 1994 (World Bank et al., 1996, 4; also see Global Witness, 2002, 3) to as much as 8 million hectares by the end of the 1990s (Chan et al., 2001; also see Springer, 2011).[1] Writing in 1999, an Oxfam legal advisor lamented

---

1 Cambodia is hardly unique in this regard, although a wider comparison is beyond the scope of this chapter.

the growing landlessness that accompanied this first concession boom, noting that 'the current system is unable to cope with the pressure it has come under from the newly opened market economy and the growing population [...] [F]or the first time in its history, Cambodia is experiencing a shortage of arable land' (Williams, 1999, 2).

The discourse of 'anarchic encroachment' (RGC, 1999) came into widespread use during this period as government officials sought to describe the rural land situation without directly implicating economic elites, whose activities were a key part of the problem, but who were also key political allies. Encroachment on state (e.g. forested) land, then as now, frequently involves the supervision, resources, and political connection of elites who offer access to land and/or work to the poor and socially vulnerable. This system held steady for a time, especially during the 1990s when the Khmer Rouge were still a military threat from the forests of the Thai border region (Le Billon, 2000), and elite resource patronage could be widely tolerated 'as a necessary evil' because it provided much-needed economic stability and development (Hughes, 2007, 840). But as the Khmer Rouge threat receded, neo-patrimonialism's blatant unfairness—its 'discriminatory enforcement of laws and regulations, discretionary provision of monopoly franchises, concessions and contracts, and diversionary collection of public revenues and disbursement of state lands, funds and employment' (Cock, 2010, 263)—became increasingly disruptive. Seeking to place land development on a firmer legal basis, the government rewrote the Land Law in 2001.

The 2001 Land Law is notable for its strategic orientation: much like that which the Leopard-Skin policy is currently attempting to achieve (see below) The 2001 Land Law is also notable for including provisions that recognise smallholder entitlements at both the household and community scale, but that also develop a flexible and powerful doctrine of state land ownership, particularly when it comes to the allocation of concessions. In the spirit of continuing the process of 'reconstituting ownership over immovable property after the period of crisis from 1975 to 1979' (Article 29), the new law thus reversed the 1992 Land Law's exclusion of agricultural land from the legal definition of smallholder ownership, and outlined pathways for titling both individual smallholdings and indigenous communal lands (see also Grimsditch and Henderson, 2009; Adler and So, 2012). At the same time, however, it *ended* the establishment of new rights of possession, singling out 'the private property of the state and public legal entities' as a priority area where the practice of 'encroachment' via the establishment of possession rights needed to be stopped (Article 17).

The new law also created a powerful doctrine of state land, strengthening the legal foundation for ongoing 'public enterprise privatisation' and positioning concessions as a key piece of the state's development repertoire. 'State public' lands, which include areas of natural and cultural significance, as well as areas with infrastructure for general public use, were protected from alienation (Article 15), although they could be transferred out of state-public status 'when they lose their public interest use' (Article 16); Everything else—all state lands that were not state-*public* lands—were state-private lands by default, and eligible for allocation via concessions (Articles 48–62). Concessions could take two broad forms: economic land concessions (ELCs), aimed at cultivating large-scale investment, and social land concessions (SLCs), aimed at alleviating landlessness through the provision of surplus state land.

ELCs were already in existence, but needed legal grounding and protection after the free-for-all of the 1990s. Building on a 1989 Council of Ministers' Instruction (No. 3) and the 1994 Investment Law, the 2001 Land Law extended their maximum duration to 99 years, stipulated that ELC land be put to use within twelve months, and imposed a limit of 10,000 hectares per concessionaire. Existing ELCs over 10,000 hectares, of which there were roughly a dozen at the time (UNCOHCHR, 2007), were allowed to maintain their size if reduction 'would result in compromising the exploitation in progress' (Article 59). SLCs were a new invention, oriented explicitly towards replacing 'encroachment' with a more orderly and managed solution to landlessness and demographic expansion. After prohibiting further 'encroachment' on state land, Article 17 of the new law thus contained a provision for allowing 'vacant lands of the State private domain [to] be distributed to persons demonstrating need for land for social purposes in accordance with conditions set forth by [a future] sub-decree.' The new Land Law, anticipating a move that would be repeated in 2012–2013 (see below), thus sought to harness the allocation of state land to the aspirations of the landless and land-poor.

Unfortunately, the geography of ELCs and SLCs has never approached anything like parity. Although the enabling sub-decree for SLCs was issued more than a year and a half before the one for ELCs, the SLC-granting process has continued to lag far behind that of ELCs. A German advisor to the Cambodian land sector recently put the number of SLCs at a few thousand hectares, lamenting that 'as a gross summary, it has to be stated that 99 per cent of the distributed state land was handed over in long-term leases of up to 99 years to national and international investors, to the detriment of the rural poor, who got only a 1 per cent share' (Müller, 2012, 3–4). This asymmetry was mirrored in the accompanying bureaucracy: the slow allocation of SLCs is often explained by its adherence to rules, while ELC allocation has proceeded apace (Un and So, 2011; Müller, 2012: 3; ADHOC, 2013). The same advisor quoted above noted that despite the extensive regulatory requirements governing ELCs—

including social and environmental impact assessments, community consultations, legal efforts to avoid relocation, and formal land use planning, *all in
advance* of signing a contract—these prescriptions have been 'widely ignored'
(Müller, 2012, 6).

The current landscape of Cambodian concessions thus poses a problem. On
the one hand, the allocation of ELCs has been so extensive that many worry
that Cambodia's arable land is 'all but gone' (Titthara and Boyle, 2012a). On the
other hand, much of this land—land that is located inside formal concessions
but has yet to be actually alienated—is still being used by local communities.
Even as the intersection of post-2001 neo-patrimonialism and the global land
rush has created widespread (and putatively low-rent) corporate land access,
land conflicts and entitlement losses for Cambodia's rural poor and indigenous
communities have become a growing political liability. It is into this breach
that the Leopard-Skin policy has sought to step.

3   Blurred Boundaries: The Case of Mong Reththy Investment Cambodia Oil Palm Company (MRICOP)

In July 2011, one of Cambodia's most famous tycoons delivered an unexpected
lecture to his fellow members of the Cambodian senate. Publicised widely
in the days that followed, *Oknha* Mong Reththy's speech criticised the rash
of evictions and legal violations that have plagued Cambodia's land sector in
recent years. Referring to 'some investors' who 'claim that they need to evict
people to develop their concessions' Reththy said: 'I disagree with this tactic—
these people have been living on their land for generations. Where will they go
when they're kicked out?' According to Chakrya and Sherrel (2011), he 'urged
investors to employ local residents on their concessions rather than hiring
outsiders,' and 'called on the government to create a panel to verify that companies granted ELCs abided by their [legal] conditions.' At the time he made
this speech, Reththy was himself confronting land tenure-related business risk.
Just days later, a prospective USD 115 million joint venture with France's largest sugar company was reported to have fallen through (Hul, 2011); while the
precise timing and details remain unclear, Reththy's speech suggested that
Cambodia's business elite—many of whom rely on foreign capital for joint-
venture partnerships—were feeling the need to distance themselves publicly
from the scourge of land grabbing.

Reththy's comments were not just posturing, however. They were based on
his experience developing his flagship MRICOP concession, an oil palm plantation that was named in an influential United Nations human rights report

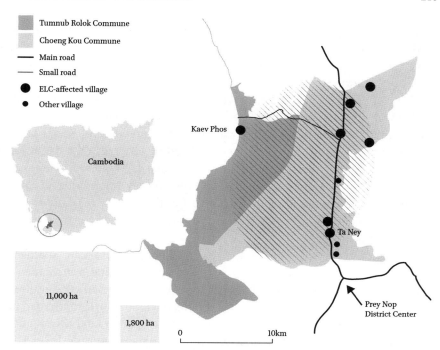

FIGURE 8.1 *Mong Reththy Project Area (hatch), Northern Preah Sihanouk Province (Cambodia).*
Note: The precise location of his ELC was not specified, and is approximated here;
granted ELC sizes are shown at lower left for reference.
SOURCE: AUTHORS.

as Cambodia's only 'successful' ELC (UNCOHCHR, 2007, 20). This project had its roots back in 1993, when Reththy purchased some land in northern Preah Sihanouk province with the help of a local intermediary (Pal, 2010, 233–234). Two years later, Reththy submitted a proposal to the Council for Development of Cambodia, requesting land on which to develop an oil palm plantation. By November 1995, he had been approved for an 11,000-hectare concession in Ta Ney village, in the southern part of Choeng Kou Commune (Figure 8.1); by January 1996 the contract was signed.[2] In March of 2000, Reththy signed a second contract, adding a second, smaller ELC of 1,800 hectares. Despite having

2 MAFF, ELC profile section, Mong Reththy Investment Cambodia Oil Palm Co., Ltd, 'Legal Papers and Right for Investment' (http://www.elc.maff.gov.kh/en/profile/23-shv/82-sihanuk-mongreththy.html) (accessed 2011; for contemporary access, see http://OpenDevelopmentCambodia.net).

areas, Reththy's ELCs were not given precise *locations*; other than commune and village names, no concession maps existed at the time. As this case illustrates, the ELC therefore functioned in practice more like a general license to develop the northern part of Preah Sihanouk province.

Soon after its initial contract was signed, MRICOP conducted a study with local officials to identify area residents who would be impacted by the plantation.[3] This study, while not an Environmental and Social Impact Assessment (ESIA) of the type later mandated by law, created a list of local occupants and provided a basis for the negotiations that followed.[4] Three compensation options were documented in different key informants' accounts: (i) monetary compensation in exchange for their land; (ii) land-for-land exchange outside the concession area; and (iii) exclusion of the person's land from the project.

MRICOP's ELC acquisition in the 1990s was characterised by a situation in which Reththy was viewed by many local residents (and even some officials) not only as an investor, but also as someone who carried state authority. Interviews with area residents who lived along the main north-south road (see Figure 8.1), and thus tended to experience the company's land access efforts early in MRICOP's history, tended to give rather critical accounts (also cf. Lang, 2000). While respondents took pains to avoid directly criticising Reththy himself, they nonetheless raised concerns about their unequal relationship with the company, a pattern typical of the Cambodian context more generally. In a few instances, residents explained that they felt pressure to accept cash compensation or land exchange simply by virtue of living near the plantation of a wealthy and powerful developer. They reported that people were told they could remain on and continue to cultivate their land as they normally would but were also warned about causing damage to the new plantation crops. In this context, rumours and innuendo were used to significant effect. One area resident reported deciding to sell after 'hearing people say that my land was under a development project and would be taken' anyway.

The presence of the company also created a speculative land market geared towards providing MRICOP with land. Some residents reported the presence of speculators who used the name of the company to undermine residents'

3   Interview with village and commune officials, December 2011. Unless otherwise indicated, interviews and informants referenced in this section refer to fieldwork in the Choeng Kou commune, December 2011.

4   According to local officials, this study was carried out by a MRICOP associate designated personally by Mong Reththy. We were unable to obtain a copy of the actual study, and thus base our account solely on interviews.

faith in their own land tenure, thus acquiring land that would have otherwise sold at higher prices (or possibly have been kept). One villager explained that land brokers bought from people at lower prices and sold to MRICOP at higher prices (for example buying at USD 200 per hectare and selling for USD 700–800). Residents reportedly sold to speculators out of fear they would lose the land anyway. This pressure to sell was reportedly sometimes the result of collusion between speculators and government officials, or in some cases between officials and people claiming to be Reththy's employees.

These accounts point to a heterogeneous mix of property claims encountered by the company; this hardly accords with the notion of a state-owned countryside. In this context, farmers who lacked documentary proof of ownership were able to have their entitlements recognised. But these entitlements were also precarious. Rumours of living 'under the *Oknha*'s development project' were mobilised by rival elites, land brokers, and even some who claimed to be Reththy's employees, and were used to convince reluctant smallholders to sell 'before it was too late.' While it is impossible to determine how often this took place, it is clear that various actors exploited the fears of poor land users, capitalising on the fact that the MRICOP concession area was geographically ill-defined. This is hardly a situation of prior state landownership. Rather, it is a case where locally existing landholdings were recognised to a point, but also rendered precarious through the granting of a concession to a powerful businessman over a general area.

At later stages, MRICOP's land acquisition efforts were more positively experienced, especially when they were paired with the work opportunities and expanded infrastructure that accompanied the conversion of Kaev Phos—a coastal village in the concession's western zone—into a port facility. During the building of 'Oknha Mong' Port in Kaev Phos in 2003–2004 (see Figure 8.1), residents described having their pictures taken in front of their old homes, and receiving land transfer documents certified by local authorities with these pictures attached. This process of land exchange was the same regardless of the gender of the residents and was described by respondents as being widely accepted. One resident explained that locals had not only received new land but gained access to a health centre, a school, and better roads thanks to the company. Another resident of 'Reththy 1', a village built to resettle Kaev Phos's former residents, described actually making money after he sold some of the land he received as part of the compensation process.[5]

This diversity of responses highlights the issue of timing: negative responses were related to MRICOP's land acquisition in the 1990s, whereas positive

5   This paragraph is based on interviews with residents of Reththy 1 Village, December 2011.

responses referred to events in the following decade, when MRICOP had more business relations with clients around the world, including European companies. Presumably to facilitate selling in European markets, MRICOP began the process of joining the Roundtable on Sustainable Palm Oil (RSPO) in the mid-to-late 2000s. While the company's membership was initially delayed due to the land conflict reported by Lang (2000), it was granted in late 2011 after certifiers determined that the dispute had been resolved in an acceptable manner (Intertek-Moody, 2012, 12).

4   Managing the Frontier: The Case of Grandis Timber

Grandis Timber is a teak plantation company that has been developing an ELC in western Kampong Speu province since 2009. Catering to a small but growing group of sustainability-oriented 'frontier' investors,[6] the company aims to turn its plantation into 'an asset class [that] hits [...] financial returns and is socially responsible and environmentally sustainable' (Daniel Mitchell, manager, quoted in Becker, 2012). Most of its plantation land is a former logging concession, and the company emphasises its mix of reforestation, conservation, and economic development activities. The company is a joint venture between the SRP International Group and Danish and Swedish pension funds, and was certified by the Forest Stewardship Council in July 2013 (FSC, 2013).

Like MRICOP, Grandis has attracted significant attention for its publicised belief that it is cheaper, as a feature about the company in the *Phnom Penh Post* (Becker, 2012) put it, 'to treat people well and have them stay in their homes and work their small farms, rather than pushing them off the land.' Grandis was featured as a field-trip destination by the International Woodfibre Association (IWA, 2011), and lauded by the *Phnom Penh Post* in the paper's above-mentioned feature as a company that was successfully implementing the Prime Minister's Leopard-Skin approach to development. Grandis's emphasis on local entitlements also caught the attention of German cooperation (Gesellschaft für Internationale Zusammenarbeit, GIZ) land sector advisors, who have been working with the Cambodian government's SLC program in recent years (Bickel and Löhr, 2011; Müller, 2012; Neef et al., 2013). This interest relates to the company's policy of working around existing land users even if they do not have legal rights to the land (Müller, 2012)—a preference for

---

6 See also Frontier Investment Development Partners (http://www.fidp-funds.com/) and Leopard Capital (http://www.leopardasia.com/) (both accessed on 16 March 2015).

regularisation over eviction that exemplifies the Leopard-Skin approach. As this case demonstrates, however, this is rarely a straightforward process.

Grandis's ELC is located in the foothills of western Cambodia's Cardamom Mountains (Figure 8.2), a part of Kampong Speu province where permanent settlement is comparatively recent. During the 1980s the area was insecure and therefore sparsely populated, especially following a Khmer Rouge offensive in 1989 that scattered many residents and left Reaksmey Samaki Commune (to the north) almost entirely empty (see Gottesman, 2003). Repopulation began in significant numbers in the late 1990s, and especially in the early years of the twenty-first century, right around the time the 2001 Land Law was passed. Some settlers were drawn by the low density of farmsteads, others by reports that government officials were distributing land. Local officials identified areas where new settlement could occur, and in many cases helped settlers file applications for legal possession rights. One commune chief described the rapid but erratic expansion of settlements and farmland as producing 'villages that stretched like rubber bands', with residences and agricultural plots frequently separated by wide distances, and with few ways for authorities to regulate the geography of settlement and production.[7]

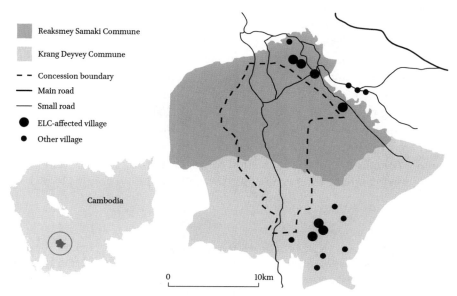

FIGURE 8.2 *Grandis Timber Project Area, Western Kampong Speu Province (Cambodia).*
SOURCE: AUTHORS.

---

7 Interview with commune official, Phnom Srouch District, December 2011.

In 2007 a local commune chief proposed a 1,200-hectare Social Land Concession to be established in Prey Torteng and Krang Deyvay villages, at the southern end of what eventually became the Grandis concession (Figure 8.2). The SLC was approved. But when, in early 2009, Grandis proposed using the same area for its own ELC, the SLC had not yet materialised.[8] Ultimately, it was decided to move the proposed SLC to a different location nearby, and to develop the Grandis ELC in the area where the SLC had been proposed.[9]

Setting its sights on full legality, social responsibility, and environmental sustainability, Grandis embarked on an effort to delimit its concession from locally used land, to carve out patches of good forest for conservation, and to begin the certification process with the FSC. A feasibility study conducted by company representatives and local authorities was finalised in late July 2009, and identified 682 hectares of landholdings, used by 310 families. These lands were mapped using GPS and demarcated with cement posts in order to show local residents that Grandis intended to respect their land boundaries, and, presumably, to help prevent encroachment on the company's land. The survey also identified large areas of intact forest to be set aside for a variety of environmental uses. Excluding these forest lands and the 682 hectares of local landholdings, Grandis's final proposal for its ELC came in at 9,820 hectares, just under Cambodia's legal limit. A month after the proposal, the company signed an 'Agreement in Principle' with Cambodia's Council of Ministers. On the last day of 2009, Grandis signed a concession contract with the government, giving the company the legal right to develop a teak plantation in the area identified by the survey.[10] Land clearing began in early 2010.

Many residents we spoke to described the company's activities, including its ongoing presence, in positive terms. One resident of Krang Deyvey village, for example, noted that many locals, including those living inside the concession area, were working for the company. Although this was day labour work on the Grandis ELC, the combination of wages (USD 2.5 per day) and transportation ('company trucks come into local villages every morning to pick up

---

8   Interview, same as previous.

9   Despite being moved, the SLC fared better than many (cf. Neef et al., 2013), and was final-
     ised in 2012; see http://lwd.org.kh/lwd/land-allocation-for-poor-families-in-kampong-
     speu-kicks-off/ (accessed on 16 March 2015).

10   http://www.elc.maff.gov.kh/en/profile/13-ksp/33-ksp-grandis.html (accessed 2011; for
     contemporary access, see http://OpenDevelopmentCambodia.net). In accordance with
     Cambodian law, an environmental and social impact assessment (ESIA) was apparently
     conducted sometime during this period as well; this was not made available to us, as is
     unfortunately standard practice in Cambodia.

workers and drop them off in the evening') suggested that it was a relatively good option compared to other local alternatives. A local official also praised Grandis for its provision of work opportunities, although noting the challenge of not enough skilled people locally to meet the company's needs. This meant some skilled workers were recruited from other provinces.[11]

The company has also allowed local residents to harvest tree stumps from its concession area. These are a valuable resource for charcoal production—an important source of cash, especially for land-poor and landless households. Taking wood for charcoal in other areas is classified as illegal and regulated by the forest administration with serious consequences for those found extracting wood. A local official we spoke to thus also praised Grandis's policy on providing access to tree stumps, albeit that it is also a means of clearing the land and therefore of benefit to the company.

Somewhat surprisingly, Grandis's decision to respect existing land *uses* rather than legal land *rights* eventually brought the company into conflict with state authorities. Following the 2009 survey and corner marker placement, company staff drew up GPS-referenced paper maps to hand out to residents. These 'farm map documents' were not intended to carry legal meaning, but rather to formalise the company's commitment not to encroach on villagers' land;[12] presumably they could also have been used as a form of prior agreement if cases of encroachment emerged in the future. However, cadastral officials worried that the documents could be (mis)interpreted as proof of legal tenure rather than simply as company-acknowledged limits on its own concession land. Faced with the charge of encroaching on the state's authority to define and demarcate property, Grandis backed off its initial plan and decided not to distribute the documents.

5   Discussion and Conclusion

In a context of widespread land conflict marked by a mix of unequal power relations, insufficient land administration capacity, and the popular perception that land rights are a reform-unfriendly area, this paper has examined the possibility of 'better practice' within the modality of state land concessions. As the economic and political liabilities of land conflict are increasingly felt, both in Cambodia and elsewhere in the global south, a key question that remains is the extent to which this room to manoeuvre hinges on local contextual

---

11   Interviews with residents and local officials, Krang Deyvay Commune, December 2011.
12   Interview with a Grandis employee, December 2011.

circumstances versus more general factors. The cases examined above provide a number of insights.

Notwithstanding their individual differences, one of the most striking features of both the MRICOP and Grandis Timber cases is their family resemblance to the Land Law revision that took place in 2001, albeit with a key difference. As noted in Section 2, the 2001 Land Law moved in two directions simultaneously: it offered significant potential benefits to smallholders and communities in the form of titles, but it also strengthened the legal doctrine of state land by drawing a 'line in the sand' when it came to establishing *new* rights of possession. Cutting off the establishment of new possession rights (after 2001) was a key feature of the new Land Law, and was part of the larger project of strengthening the state's legal claims to land as a way of replacing the allegedly 'anarchic' development of land with more governable and efficient means. The cases presented here show how the Leopard-Skin approach is pursuing a variant of this 'line in the sand' approach, but this time with respect to *actual possession* rather than *legal* possession *rights*. By acknowledging the de facto right to keep lands that are already under concession-area-households' possession, MRICOP and Grandis are pursuing a version—from their perspective a much more practical one—of the possession rights compromise enshrined in the 2001 Land Law. The difference is that, unlike the 2001 Land Law (where legal respect for possession rights was limited by the state's ability to formalise those rights in a timely manner), these companies are actively working on the ground. By developing the lands that come up to the borders of current smallholder plots, companies like MRICOP and Grandis can enforce the 'line in the sand' compromise in ways that the 2001 Land Law failed to.

This shift from recognising legal to actual possession has major implications. The intention to mitigate conflict and avoid needless and harmful evictions should be acknowledged and built upon. As global supply chains (not only in palm oil and teak, but in timber, sugar, rubber, maize and other commodities) become increasingly transparent, tenure-related risk is growing; as it does, the business case for these types of steps increases. However, the ad hoc approach examined above is forced to rely on local power relations to regulate land-related negotiations between local users, companies, and state officials. This is a tough sell to communities and their advocates; while third-party certification may be able to alter incentives by increasing transnational oversight, the degree to which it can tip the balance towards equality is doubtful. One advantage of law is that it can, in theory, give equal rights to parties who, in practice, do not have equal power. Moving the basis of land-related negotiation from law to case-by-case negotiation may work well in particular cases (and as the MRICOP case shows, within the same case at particular times), but it depends on the benevolence of the powerful, and it further attenuates the already weak capacity of law to protect the most vulnerable members of society.

The shift towards recognising (without *legally* recognising) local land possession seems, then, to be geared towards improving the legitimacy of the state land concession system at a time when it is facing increasing strain from both local communities and transnational investors (see e.g. Brinkley, 2013; de Leon et al., 2013). This essentially tactical dimension is important because it highlights the issue of timing in maintaining power asymmetry between local land users and would-be concessionaires. The German advisor quoted above in Section 2 described (in another part of the same paper) the rationale of the Cambodian Ministry of Land Management, Urban Planning and Construction (MLMUPC) when it came to Grandis's significance: the ministry, he said, 'was initially reluctant to implement Circular 02 [on regularisation], giving the reason of *not wanting to encourage further encroachments*. But MLMUPC [began] to pilot Circular 02 [in 2012] [...] in Kampong Speu province where an institutional investor from Denmark [i.e. Grandis Timber] [...] has already anticipated the 'leopard skin' feature of the Prime Minister' (Müller, 2012, 11; emphasis added). The cases examined above show how Leopard-Skin development is attempting to prevent 'further encroachments': namely, by allocating concessions first, and conducting regularisation only in areas where smallholders are already surrounded.

This approach is expanding. In May 2012, the Cambodian government expanded the 'Leopard-Skin formula' significantly with the issuing and implementation of a prime ministerial order (No. 01BB) on 'strengthening and increasing the effectiveness of the management of economic land concessions' (RGC, 2012a). Implementation has focused largely on demarcating rural landholdings, especially in concession-contested areas, and issuing titles or small-scale concession agreements to occupants (Titthara and Boyle, 2012b; ADHOC, 2014; Grimsditch and Schoenberger, forthcoming). While this process was initially praised for reorienting land titling *towards* rather than away from socially marginal communities, it has come under substantial criticism for its opacity, its uneven implementation, its inability to actually address the land conflicts it encounters, and its creation of social divisions in indigenous communities forced to choose between individual and communal titles (Titthara and Boyle, 2012b; Rabe, 2013; Milne, 2013; Beban, 2014; ADHOC, 2014). Notwithstanding these issues, the significance of the process is clear for the purposes of this paper. Order 01BB represents a model of Leopard-Skin development based on the allocation of state land to deserving recipients ('in order to favour the conditions of land development'—RGC, 2012b), rather than the provision of title based on existing legal rights. The Order-01BB campaign was thus widely criticised as an election-year ploy—and it may well have been that—but it is also significant in that, much like the cases examined here, it acknowledged occupation-based rights in exchange for the acknowledgment of the state's right to distribute land. In this move *away* from a rights-based model of property recognition, like the cases presented above, it exemplifies the reciprocity between public authority and property-making described by Sikor and Lund (2009). If the MRICOP and Grandis cases showed how private actors can blur the lines that surround this authority—substantially in the case of MRICOP, and merely in the form of a threat (exemplified by the farm map documents) in the Grandis Timber case—the Order-01 campaign illustrates the state's efforts to claim the mantle of Leopard-Skin development clearly for itself.

The cases of MRICOP and Grandis Timber raise the questions of where the line between 'better' and 'good' concession practice lies, and of the degree to which those concerned with reforming land governance in the interest of smallholders should pursue good concessions in addition to their efforts to promote alternatives. These are fraught questions, and we refrain from trying to answer them definitively here. Our research found evidence pointing in both directions, with significant improvements over time (in the MRICOP case) as well as significant proactive work carried out by both companies (especially by Grandis) to minimise community contestation up front. But the jury is still out; high-quality, responsible, and sustainable investments go beyond the short term (and beyond the issue of land access alone). What is needed most, both in the cases examined above and in other investments more broadly, are improved transparency to allow greater public scrutiny; free, prior, and informed consent of local land users; independent investigation; and effective grievance mechanisms—all of which are basic components of most guidelines and regulatory frameworks on land and investment governance. Third-party certification has provided some of this in our two case studies, and its impacts should not be minimised. But the limits of audit-based research are also significant: it is limited to occasional visits and forms of remedy (i.e. additional investigation, and ultimately denial or revocation of certification) that may not enable or inspire communities to voice concerns openly. Indeed, much like the community-based natural resource management (CBNRM) paradigm, without adequate transparency and local ownership, certification could end up legitimising enclosure and thus stifling expressions of discontent by affected communities (cf. Tubtim and Hirsch, 2004).

Time will thus tell whether private sector efforts to 'work around' local land uses will produce truly sustainable development. While we would prefer to see an investment model that allows communities to deal with investors directly as empowered landowners, we realise the gulf between these positions is nontrivial. Acknowledging communities' de facto rights not only in the present, but for future needs as well, entails a business model predicated on the community having a much greater role in representing the public interest. Current experiments at the 'better practice' end of the concession spectrum are likely to shape the contours of this debate for the coming years. In the meantime, their ability to sustain their investments and the communities in their midst remains to be seen.

References

Adler, D. and S. So (2012) 'Reflections on Legal Pluralism in Cambodia: Towards Equity in Development when the Law is not the Law,', in Sage, C., B. Tamanaha and M. Woolcock (eds.) *Legal Pluralism and Development Policy: Dialogues for Success* (Cambridge: Cambridge University Press).

ADHOC (Cambodian Human Rights and Development Association) (2014) *Land Situation in Cambodia in 2013* (Phnom Penh: ADHOC), http://www.adhoc-cambodia. org/?p=4580 (accessed on 16 March 2015).

——— (2013) *Turning Point? Land, Housing and Natural Resources Rights in Cambodia in 2012* (Phnom Penh: ADHOC), http://www.nachdenkseiten.de/upload/pdf/ ADHOC-A_Turning_Point_Land_Housing_NRM_2012.pdf (accessed on 16 March 2015).

Baird, I. (2014) 'The Global Land Grab Meta-Narrative, Asian Money Laundering and Elite Capture: Reconsidering the Cambodian Context', *Geopolitics*, 19(2), pp. 431–453, DOI: 10.1080/14650045.2013.811645.

Beban, A. (2014) 'How the Leopard got its Spots: Gender Dimensions of Land Reform in Cambodia', *Voices from the Sylff Community*, 10 October, http://www.tokyofoundation.org/sylff/14378 (accessed on 16 March 2015).

Becker, S.A. (2012) 'Largest Teak Nursery in Cambodia', *Phnom Penh Post*, 4 July, http://www.phnompenhpost.com/special-reports/largest-teak-nursery-cambodia (accessed on 16 March 2015).

Bickel, M. and D. Löhr (2011) 'Pro-poor Land Distribution in Cambodia' *Rural 21: International Platform*, March, http://www.rural21.com/fileadmin/_migrated/content_uploads/rural_2011_3_33-35_01.pdf (accessed on 26 May 2015).

Borras Jr., S.M. and J.C. Franco (2012) 'Global Land Grabbing and Trajectories of Agrarian Change: A Preliminary Analysis', *Journal of Agrarian Change*, 12(1), pp. 34–59, DOI: 10.1111/j.1471–0366.2011.00339.x.

Brinkley, J. (2013) 'Coca-Cola Steps up for Cambodian Land-Grab Victims', *Chicago Tribune*, 3 December., CDC (Council for the Development of Cambodia) (2010) *Keynote Address by Samdech Akka Moha Sena Padei Techo Hun Sen, Prime Minister of the Kingdom of Cambodia, for the Third Cambodia Development Cooperation Forum* (*CDCF*), Government House, 2 June, http://www.cdc-crdb.gov.kh/cdc/third_cdcf/opening/shs_third_cdcf_en.htm (accessed 16 April 2015).

Chak, S. (2011) '"Development" Does not Justify Land Grabs in Cambodia', *Future Challenges*, 17 December, http://futurechallenges.org/local/development-does-not-justify-land-grabs-in-cambodia/ (accessed on 16 March 2015).

Chakrya, K.S. and D. Sherrel (2011) 'Tycoon Lands Surprise', *Phnom Penh Post*, 28 July, http://www.phnompenhpost.com/national/tycoon-lands-surprise (accessed on 16 March 2015).

Chan, S., S. Tep and A. Sarthi (2001) *Land Tenure in Cambodia: A Data Update*, Cambodia Development Resource Institute Working Paper 19 (Phnom Penh: CDRI).

Chandler, D. (1993) *The Tragedy of Cambodian History: Politics, War, and Revolution since 1945* (New Haven: Yale University Press).

CLP (Council for Land Policy) (2002) *Strategy of Land Policy Framework: Interim Paper*, September 6 (Phnom Penh: Royal Government of Cambodia).

Cock, A. (2010) 'External Actors and the Relative Autonomy of the Ruling Elite in Post-UNTAC Cambodia', *Journal of Southeast Asian Studies*, 41(2), pp. 241–265, DOI: 10.1017/S0022463410000044.

Cooper, G. (2002) 'Land Policy and Conflict: The Cambodia Portion of an Eight-Country Study by the North-South Institute for the World Bank' (Ottawa: North-South Institute), http://info.worldbank.org/etools/docs/library/35466/LAND%20POLICY%20AND%20CONFLICT.pdf (accessed on 26 May 2015).

Cotula, L. and R. Leonard (eds.) (2010) *Alternatives to Land Acquisitions: Agricultural Investment and Collaborative Business Models* (London, Bern, Rome and Maputo: IIED–SDC–IFAD–CTV).

Cotula, L., S. Vermeulen, R. Leonard and J. Keeley (2009) *Land Grab Or Development Opportunity? Agricultural Investment and International Land Deals in Africa* (London and Rome: IIED–FAO–IFAD).

de Leon, R., T. Garcia, G. Kummel, L. Munden, S. Murday, and L. Pradela (2013) *Global Capital, Local Concessions: A Data-Driven Examination of Land Tenure Risk and Industrial Concessions in Emerging Market Economies*, paper prepared for the Rights and Resources Initiative (Manila, Paris, London and Chicago: The Munden Project), http://www.rightsandresources.org/documents/files/doc_6301.pdf (accessed on 16 March 2015).

Deininger, K. and D. Byerlee (2011) *Rising Global Interest in Farmland: Can it Yield Sustainable and Equitable Benefits?* (Washington DC: World Bank–International Bank for Reconstruction and Development).

FAO, IFAD, UNCTAD and the World Bank Group (2010) *Principles for Responsible Agricultural Investment that Respects Rights, Livelihoods and Resources* (*Extended Version*), discussion note, 25 January, http://siteresources.worldbank.org/

INTARD/214574-1111138388661/22453321/Principles_Extended.pdf (accessed on 16 March 2014).

FSC (Forest Stewardship Council) (2013) *Certificate Holder Listing, Grandis Timber*, http://info.fsc.org/Detailprint?id=a0240000008IdhFAAS (accessed on 15 July 2013).

GFA Certification (2013) *Public Summary, Main Audit Report, Grandis Timber Limited*, http://fsc.force.com/servlet/servlet.FileDownload?file=00P4000000FADzkEAH (accessed on 15 July 2013).

Global Witness (2002) *Deforestation without Limits: How the Cambodian Government Failed to Tackle the Untouchables*, July (London: Global Witness).

Gottesman, E. (2003) *Cambodia After the Khmer Rouge: Inside the Politics of Nation Building* (New Haven and London: Yale University Press).

GRAIN (2008) *Seized! The 2008 Land Grab for Food and Financial Security* (Barcelona: GRAIN), http://www.grain.org/briefings_files/landgrab-2008-en.pdf (accessed on March 16 2015).

Grimsditch, M. and N. Henderson (2009) *Untitled: Tenure Insecurity and Inequality in the Cambodian Land Sector* (Phnom Penh and Geneva: Bridges Across Borders Southeast Asia–Centre on Housing Rights and Evictions–Jesuit Refugee Service), http://www.babcambodia.org/untitled/untitled.pdf (accessed on 16 March 2015).

Grimsditch, M. and L. Schoenberger (forthcoming) '"New Actions and Existing Policies": The Implementation and Impacts of Order 01', *NGO Forum on Cambodia*.

Heder, S. (2011) 'Cambodia in 2010: Hun Sen's Further Consolidation', *Asian Survey*, 51(1), pp. 208–214, DOI: 10.1525/as.2011.51.1.208.

HLPE (High Level Panel of Experts on Food Security and Malnutrition) (2011) *Land Tenure and International Investments in Agriculture* (Rome: Committee on World Security), http://www.fao.org/fileadmin/user_upload/hlpe/hlpe_documents/HLPE-Land-tenure-and-international-investments-in-agriculture-2011.pdf (accessed on 16 March 2015).

Hughes, C. (2007) 'Transnational Networks, International Organizations and Political Participation in Cambodia: Human Rights, Labour Rights and Common Rights', *Democratization*, 14(5), pp. 834–852, DOI: 10.1080/13510340701635688.

Hul, R. (2011) 'Planned Multimillion-Dollar Sugar Plantation Suspended', *Cambodia Daily*, 29 July, https://www.cambodiadaily.com/archives/planned-multimillion-dollar-sugar-plantation-suspended-66247/ (accessed on 16 March 2015).

Intertek-Moody International (2012) *Mong Reththy Investment Cambodia Oil Palm Co. Ltd (MRICOP), Main Assessment on RSPO Certification*, public summary report No.: R9280/12–2 (MRICOP-PMU), http://www.intertek.com/WorkArea/DownloadAsset.aspx?id=39943 (accessed on 16 March 2015).

IWA (International Woodfibre Association) (2011) *International Woodfibre Association Conference Program*, http://www.woodfibreconference.com/2011/fieldtrip.html (accessed 2012).

Kuch, N. and P. Zsombor (2013) 'Arrests Over Land Disputes Doubled in 2012', *Cambodia Daily*, 15 February, https://www.cambodiadaily.com/archives/arrests-over-land-disputes-doubled-in-2012-10538/ (accessed on 16 March 2015).

Lang, C. (2000) 'Oil Palm Plantation in Cambodia', *World Rainforest Movement Bulletin*, No. 39, http://www.ecoearth.info/shared/reader/welcome.aspx?linkid=93201 (accessed on 16 March 2015).

Le Billon, P. (2000) 'The Political Ecology of Transition in Cambodia 1989–1999: War, Peace and Forest Exploitation', *Development and Change*, 31(4), pp. 785–805, DOI: 10.1111/1467–7660.00177.

LICADHO (Cambodian League for the Defense of Human Rights) (2009) *Land Grabbing and Poverty in Cambodia: The Myth of Development* (Phnom Penh: LICADHO), http://www.licadho-cambodia.org/reports/files/134LICADHOREportMythofDevel opment2009Eng.pdf (accessed on 16 March 2015).

MAFF (Ministry of Agriculture, Forestry and Fisheries) (no date) *Model Contract for Economic Land Concession*, formerly available at http://www.maff.gov.kh/pdf/ Agreement_en.pdf (accessed on 7 April 2012).

MEF (Ministry of Economy and Finance) (1995) *Prakas on Directives to Implement (Prakas Nainoam Anuvat) Public Enterprise Privatization*, PKN NO. 280 PrK. SHV. TR., 3 August.

Milne, S. (2013) 'Under the Leopard's Skin: Land Commodification and the Dilemmas of Indigenous Communal Title in Upland Cambodia', *Asia Pacific Viewpoint*, 54(3), pp. 323–339, DOI: 10.1111/apv.12027.

Müller, F-V. (2012) *Commune-based Land Allocation for Poverty Reduction in Cambodia: Achievements and Lessons Learned from the Project: Land Allocation for Social and Economic Development (LASED)*, paper prepared for presentation at the Annual World Bank Conference on Land and Poverty, Washington D.C., April 23–26.

Munden Project (2012) *The Financial Risks of Insecure Land Tenure: An Investment View*, paper prepared for the Rights and Resources Initiative (Manila, Paris, London and Chicago: The Munden Project), http://www.rightsandresources.org/documents/ files/doc_5715.pdf (accessed on 16 March 2015).

Neef, A., S. Touch and J. Chiengthong (2013) 'The Politics and Ethics of Land Concessions in Rural Cambodia', *Journal of Agricultural and Environmental Ethics*, 26(6), pp. 1085–1103, DOI: 10.1007/s10806–013–9446-y.

Pal, V. (2010) *Gold Paved Road: Biography of His Excellency Okhna Doctor Mong Reththy*, (Phnom Penh: Mong Reththy Group).

Rabe, A. (2013) *Directive 01BB in Ratanakiri Province, Cambodia: Issues and Impacts of Private Land Titling in Indigenous Communities*, report written in collaboration with the Ratanakiri Communal Land Titling Working Group (Chiang Mai: Asia Indigenous Peoples Pact).

RGC (Royal Government of Cambodia) (2012a) *Order 01BB on the Measures Strengthening and Increasing the Effectiveness of the Management of Economic Land Concessions (ELC)*, 7 May, http://www.mlmupc.gov.kh/mlm/imgs/20130213%20Manual%20for%20Implementing%20Govt%20Order%2001_ENG.pdf (accessed on 16 March 2015).

———— (2012b) *Council of Ministers' Letter 666 SCN from Deputy PM Minister in Charge of Council of Ministers to the Senior Minister of LMUPC*, 26 June, http://www.mlmupc.gov.kh/mlm/imgs/20130213%20Manual%20for%20Implementing%20Govt%20Order%2001_ENG.pdf (accessed on 16 March 2015).

———— (2007) *Circular No. 02.SR, Measures Against Illegal Holding of State Land*, 26 February.

———— (1999) *Declaration (Sechkdey Prakas) on the Measure of Eliminating Anarchical Land Encroachment*, No. 06 BRK, 27 September, http://www.skpcambodia.com/Laws%20&%20Regulations%20of%20the%20Kingdom%20of%20Cambodia/Property%20&%20Land%20Law/PKS-RGC-06-99-Land%20enroachment_Road%20Reservation-E.pdf (accessed on 16 March 2015).

———— (1994) *Declaration of the Royal Government on Privatization of Public Enterprise*, No. 01 SRBK, 20 December, http://www.skpcambodia.com/Laws%20&%20Regulations%20of%20the%20Kingdom%20of%20Cambodia/Property%20&%20Land%20Law/PK-RGC-01-94-Privatization-E.pdf (accessed on 16 March 2015).

Sikor, T. and C. Lund (2009) 'Access and Property: A Question of Power and Authority', *Development and Change*, 40(1), pp. 1–22, DOI: 10.1111/j.1467–7660.2009.01503.x.

So, S. (2009) *Political Economy of Land Registration in Cambodia*, unpublished PhD thesis (DeKalb, IL: Northern Illinois University).

Springer, S. (2011) 'Articulated Neoliberalism: the Specificity of Patronage, Kleptocracy, and Violence in Cambodia's Neoliberalization', *Environment and Planning–Part A*, 43(11), pp. 2554–2570, DOI: 10.1068/a43402.

Titthara, M. and Boyle, D. (2012a) 'Kingdom's Arable Land all but Gone', *Phnom Penh Post*, 1 March, http://www.phnompenhpost.com/national/kingdom's-arable-land-all-gone (accessed on 16 March 2012).

———— (2012b) 'PM's Land Titling Scheme Full of Ambiguity', *Phnom Penh Post*, 6 July, http://www.phnompenhpost.com/national/pms-land-titling-scheme-full-ambiguity (accessed on 12 July 2012).

Tubtim, N. and P. Hirsch (2004) 'Common Property as Enclosure: A Case Study of a Backswamp in Southern Laos', *Society and Natural Resources*, 18(1), pp. 41–60, DOI: 10.1080/08941920590881925.

Un, K. (2013) 'The Cambodian People Have Spoken', *The New York Times*, 9 August, http://www.nytimes.com/2013/08/10/opinion/global/the-cambodian-people-have-spoken.html?_r=0 (accessed on 16 March 2015).

Un, K. and S. So (2009) 'Politics of Natural Resource Use in Cambodia', *Asian Affairs*, 36(3), pp. 123–138, DOI: 10.1080/00927670903259921.

———— (2011) 'Land Rights in Cambodia: How Neopatrimonial Politics Restricts Land Policy Reform', *Pacific Affairs*, 84(2), pp. 289–308, DOI: 10.5509/2011842289.

UNCFS (United Nations Committee on World Food Security) (2012) *Report of the 39th Session of the Committee on World Food Security (CFS)* (Rome: FAO), http://www.fao.org/docrep/meeting/026/mf120e.pdf (accessed on 22 February 2013).

UNCOHCHR (United Nations Cambodia Office of the High Commissioner for Human Rights) (2007) *Economic Land Concessions in Cambodia: A Human Rights Perspective* (Phnom Penh: UNCOHCHR), http://cambodia.ohchr.org/WebDOCs/DocReports/2-Thematic-Reports/Thematic_CMB12062007E.pdf (accessed on 26 May 2015).

Van Acker, F. (1999) *Hitting a Stone with an Egg? Cambodia's Rural Economy and Land Tenure in Transition*, CAS discussion paper No. 23, April, (Antwerp: Centre for ASEAN Studies–Centre for International Management and Development Antwerp).

Williams, S. (1999) *Review of Current and Proposed Cambodian Land Legislation*, Cambodia Land Study Project (Oxford: Oxfam).

World Bank, UNDP and FAO (1996) *Forest policy assessment, Cambodia*, report No. 15777-KH, August 14 (Washington D.C., Geneva and Rome: World Bank–UNDP–FAO).

PART 3

Human Rights and Large-Scale Land Acquisitions

∵

CHAPTER 9

Identifying and Monitoring Human Rights Violations Associated with Large-Scale Land Acquisitions

A Focus on United Nations Mechanisms and South-East Asia

Christophe Golay

Abstract

This chapter aims to contribute to the debate on contemporary 'land grabbing' and its impact on human rights. It describes the role played by United Nations (UN) human rights mechanisms in monitoring violations associated with large-scale land acquisitions (LSLAs), with a focus on UN treaty bodies. A typology of human rights violations associated with LSLAs is presented, on the basis of the assessment that UN treaty bodies have made in examining the impact of LSLAs in Cambodia, Indonesia, Laos, and Vietnam. Three common threads can be extracted from this assessment. The first relates to the actual or potential human rights implications of the internal displacement and forced evictions caused by LSLAs, which often lead to drastic changes in livelihood opportunities. The second involves the impact of LSLAs on the procedural rights of indigenous peoples, in particular their right to free, prior, and informed consent to policies and activities that directly affect their land, territory and livelihoods. The third concerns the disproportionately negative effect that LSLAs have on individuals and groups who are vulnerable to discrimination and marginalisation, including women, children, indigenous peoples, rural communities, and small-scale farmers. The example of Laos, where we conducted research in 2012 and 2013, confirms the assessment made by UN treaty bodies. The overall conclusion is that human rights are well recognised in international law and that national laws seem to be adequate in many countries, including

The author was joint coordinator of the Swiss Network for International Studies (SNIS)-funded project "Large-Scale Land Acquisitions in Southeast Asia: Rural Transformations between Global Agendas and Peoples' Right to Food". He would like to thank Irene Biglino for her contribution to this chapter, and for her invaluable support in the research that led to the writing of this contribution. Ioana Cismas, Patricia Paramita and Samuel Segura Cobos should also be thanked for previous research done on the subject in the context of the SNIS-funded project (www.snis.ch).

in South-East Asia. Yet, human rights instruments and national laws are poorly implemented on the ground, or not implemented in favour of local communities.

1   Introduction

The aim of this article is to contribute to the debate on contemporary 'land-
grabbing' and its impact on human rights (Cotula, 2009; De Schutter, 2011a; De
Schutter, 2011b; Monsalve Suárez, 2013; Cotula, 2012; Narula, 2013; Künnemann
and Monsalve Suárez, 2013; Clays and Vanloqueren, 2013; Golay and Biglino,
2013) and, more specifically, to present a typology of human rights violations
associated with large-scale land acquisitions (LSLAs) and present the role
played by United Nations (UN) mechanisms in monitoring these violations.

The focus in this contribution will be on UN monitoring mechanisms, which
can be classified as political or quasi-judicial (Golay, 2009), and not on access
to justice, despite the fact that a key principle of human rights law is that
victims of human rights violations should have access to justice (Borghi and
Postigione Blommestein, 2006, IX). Access to justice has also been described
as a powerful tool for giving meaning to human rights 'in small places close
to home' (Robinson, 2003, 1). For the UN Committee on Economic, Social and
Cultural Rights (CESCR),[1] '[a]ny person or group who is a victim of a violation
of [a human right] should have access to effective judicial or other appropriate
remedies at both national and international levels. All victims of such violations are entitled to adequate reparation, which may take the form of restitu-
tion, compensation, satisfaction or guarantees of non repetition' (1999, 32).

As we will see with the example of Laos, access to justice for victims of
human rights violations is often very difficult in practice (Special Rapporteur
on Extreme Poverty, 2012). And in the great majority of cases, mechanisms that
monitor human rights violations associated with LSLAs are not judges, but
administrations at the local and national levels and UN human rights monitoring bodies and experts at the international level. This contribution will focus
on the second category, with an emphasis on their role in monitoring human
rights violations in South-East Asia.

The second part of this chapter presents the international legal basis that
can be used to monitor human rights violations associated with LSLAs. The
third part focuses on the role played by UN treaty bodies in monitoring human
rights violations in Cambodia, Laos, Indonesia, and Vietnam, and presents a

---

1   The Committee on Economic, Social and Cultural Rights (CESCR) oversees compliance with
     the International Covenant on Economic, Social and Cultural Rights (ICESCR).

typology of human rights violations associated with LSLAs. The fourth part takes the example of Laos as a case study.

2   International Legal Basis for Monitoring Human Rights Violations Associated with LSLAs

International human rights law includes a number of treaties and soft-law instruments. With regard to the first category, treaties relevant to monitoring the impact of LSLAs include the International Covenant on Civil and Political Rights (ICCPR), the International Covenant on Economic, Social and Cultural Rights (ICESCR), the International Convention on the Elimination of All Forms of Racial Discrimination (ICERD), the Convention on the Elimination of All Forms of Discrimination against Women (CEDAW), the Convention on the Rights of the Child (CRC) and the Convention on the Rights of Persons with Disabilities (CRPD).

Under these treaties, state parties have the obligation to respect, protect and fulfil human rights in the context of LSLAs, without any discrimination (Special Rapporteur on the Right to Food, 2009). They should also implement policies to support particularly vulnerable individuals and groups, such as women and indigenous peoples. Women's rights to land and property are specifically protected in the CEDAW Convention (Arts. 14(2) and 16), and the rights of indigenous peoples in the UN Declaration on the Rights of Indigenous Peoples and in the International Labour Organization (ILO) Convention No. 169 concerning Indigenous and Tribal Peoples. Indigenous peoples' rights of ownership, possession and control of their land, territories and resources, and states' obligations to guarantee their effective protection, as well as the requirement of indigenous peoples' prior, free, and informed consent—all recognised in international law—are particularly important in the context of LSLAs.

If we except ILO Convention No. 169, these international treaties have been accepted by all or a great majority of states, and therefore potentially offer a good basis for UN bodies to monitor human rights violations associated with LSLAs.

Turning to soft law, it must be highlighted that in recent years a number of instruments have been developed with a view to reaffirming the relevance of human rights in the context of LSLAs (UN Special Rapporteur on the Right to Food, 2009; Golay and Biglino, 2013). The most important step in this area was the adoption, by the UN Committee on World Food Security, of Voluntary Guidelines on the Responsible Governance of Tenure of Land, Fisheries and Forests in the Context of National Food Security (*Governance of Tenure Guidelines*) in May 2012. The main objective of the *Governance of Tenure Guidelines* is to promote secure tenure rights and equitable access to land, fisheries and forests in order to reduce poverty and realise the right to food. Two central elements of the guidelines are the need to identify, record and respect legitimate tenure rights, whether formally recorded or not, and to protect tenure rights holders against forced evictions (guidelines 3.1.1. and 3.1.2, respectively). Special protection should be accorded to smallholders and to indigenous peoples and other communities with customary tenure systems (guideline 7.3). The guidelines also recommend that states provide safeguards to protect legitimate tenure rights, human rights, livelihoods, food security and the environment from risks that could arise from LSLAs (guideline 12.6) and that responsible investments should do no harm, safeguard against dispossession of legitimate tenure right holders and environmental damage, and respect human rights (guideline 12.4). The guidelines further underline that redistributive reforms can facilitate broad and equitable access to land and inclusive rural development (guideline 15.1).

In March 2010, the UN Special Rapporteur on the right to food, Olivier De Schutter,[2] submitted a report to the Human Rights Council in which he described the phenomenon of LSLAs and its causes and presented a set of 11 human rights principles applicable to LSLAs (Special Rapporteur on the Right to Food, 2009).[3] The report's objective was to delineate the 'minimum human rights obligations' that states, but also investors and financial institutions, must comply with when negotiating and concluding LSLAs. For De Schutter, the principles 'are not optional; [but] follow from existing international human rights norms' (Special Rapporteur on the Right to Food, 2009, 5).

The 11 principles describe the obligation of states and investors to conduct negotiations leading to LSLAs in a fully transparent manner and with the participation of local communities; the requirement of free, prior, and informed consent of the local communities concerned; the general prohibition of forced evictions; the obligation to recognise and protect the land tenure rights of local communities; the importance of the sharing of revenues generated by LSLAs

---

2   Olivier De Schutter's mandate began in May 2008 and ended in May 2014. Jean Ziegler was the first mandate holder between September 2000 and April 2008. Hilal Elver replaced Olivier De Schutter in June 2014.

3   Among the many other UN Special Rapporteurs who could have played a role in response to LSLAs (Piccone, 2012; Subedi et al., 2011; Golay et al., 2011; Nifosi, 2005), the UN Special Rapporteur on human rights in Cambodia offered the most important response in monitoring the impact of LSLAs in this country in 2012. See Golay and Biglino, 2013, 1637–1638; and Cismas and Paramita in this volume.

with the local population; the necessity of choosing labour-intensive farming systems in countries facing high levels of rural poverty and few employment opportunities in other sectors; the need to protect the environment; the necessity of including clear and detailed obligations for investors in the agreements, with sanctions for non-compliance; the need to include a clause providing that a certain minimum percentage of the crops produced will be sold in local markets in food-importing countries, to contribute to local food security; the necessity to undertake prior impact assessments, including on food security, the environment and employment; the obligation to protect indigenous peoples' rights; and the obligation to respect the applicable ILO instruments (Special Rapporteur on the Right to Food, 2009, 5).

De Schutter's principles were not received unopposed and attracted some criticism from certain states and civil society organisations, which feared that they would 'legitimise' land grabbing, instead of contributing to halting the phenomenon (Clays and Vanloqueren, 2013). But De Schutter's principles have also been used to assess the implications of LSLAs in concrete cases.[4]

3   Identifying and Monitoring Human Rights Violations Associated with LSLAs in South-East Asia: the Role Played by United Nations Treaty Bodies

Several UN mechanisms have monitored human rights violations associated with LSLAs (Golay and Biglino, 2013). This section focuses on UN treaty bodies, with particular emphasis on the monitoring role they have played in relation to South-East Asian countries.[5]

The UN treaty bodies are committees made up of independent experts, established under the international human rights treaties, which monitor the implementation of the treaties through the periodic review of reports submitted by state parties (Vandehole, 2004; Bassiouni and Schabas, 2011; Keller and

---

4   For example, in 2010 the Government of Switzerland participated in a public symposium, alongside the Director of Addax Bioenergy, a Geneva-based company investing in Sierra Leone, and civil society organisations representing communities affected by the LSLA in Sierra Leone. During the event, the human rights impact of Addax's LSLA was discussed with reference to De Schutter's principles. The symposium *Business and human rights. Clearing the path to foster corporate accountability* took place on 18 October 2010 in Geneva. More information is available at http://www.reports-and-materials.org/Land-grabbing-symposium-Geneva-18-Oct-2010.pdf (accessed on 27 April 2015).

5   This second part is largely inspired by Golay and Biglino (2013, 1635–1642), but the focus here is on South-East Asia.

Ulfstein, 2012). Most of them also have the competence to receive individual or collective complaints—also called 'communications'—in cases of human rights violations (Golay, 2009, 32–33).

Many UN treaty bodies have monitored human rights violations associated with LSLAs in the context of the periodic review of reports submitted by state parties; these include the CESCR, the Committee on the Elimination of Racial Discrimination (CERD), the Committee on the Elimination of Discrimination against Women (CEDAW Committee), and the Committee on the Rights of the Child (CRC Committee). Based on a review of their examination of state parties' reports since 2006, at least three common threads can be extracted from their monitoring and recommendations.

The first overarching concern relates to the actual or potential human rights implications of internal displacement and forced evictions caused by LSLAs, which often lead to drastic changes in livelihood opportunities. A connected concern is that in many cases the displaced groups are not resettled and compensated for their livelihood losses. In its consideration of Cambodia, the CESCR examined issues relating to the human rights impact of LSLAs in quite some detail (see also Cismas and Paramita in this volume), and concluded that, 'authorities of the [state] party are actively involved in land-grabbing' (CESCR, 2009, 30). The CESCR expressed grave concerns over the vast concessions granted to private companies and noted the increase in forced evictions and threats of eviction linked to such concessions and expressed deep concern about the lack of effective consultation with persons affected by the forced evictions. It also called attention to the inadequate compensation or relocation provisions for families forcibly removed from their properties (CESCR, 2009, 30).

The second common thread involves the impact of LSLAs on the procedural rights of indigenous peoples, and in particular the fact that policies and activities that directly affect their land, territory and livelihoods require their free, prior, and informed consent. For example, the CESCR examined the impact of land concessions on indigenous peoples during its assessments of Cambodia. In its recommendations, the committee highlighted the need for carrying out environmental and social impact assessments and consultations with affected communities with regard to economic activities, including mining and oil explorations, 'with a view to ensuring that these activities do not deprive the indigenous peoples to the full enjoyment of their rights to their ancestral lands and natural resources' (2009, 16). In further pointing out that legislation providing for the titling of indigenous communities' lands had not been implemented in an effective manner, the CESCR urged Cambodia to provide for the implementation of the provisions without delay.

The CERD has also extensively monitored the impact of LSLAs on the rights of indigenous peoples. In 2007, for instance, it expressed concerns about the denial of indigenous peoples' rights in Indonesia in connection with LSLAs made for agro-industrial purposes, such as the expansion of oil palm plantations on indigenous territories (2007, 17). The committee called on Indonesia to secure indigenous peoples' ownership rights to their lands, territories and resources and to obtain their consent prior to further oil palm development. The CERD voiced similar concerns in 2012 in its review of Vietnam (2012b, 15).

In examining the situation in Cambodia, the CERD noted that such transactions were in many cases being conducted 'to the detriment of particularly vulnerable communities such as indigenous peoples' (2010, 16). Another concern related to reports that concessions affecting land traditionally occupied by indigenous peoples were being granted without full consideration, or the exhaustion of procedures provided for by national legislation. The committee strongly encouraged the development of a series of protective measures, such as procedures to delay the issuing of concessions on indigenous lands and only issue such concessions pursuant to free, prior, informed consent being given by the affected communities. The reach of the committee's recommendations extended even further, as it called on business entities negotiating concessions to take into consideration their corporate social responsibility as it relates to the rights and well-being of local populations (CERD, 2010, 16).

The third recurrent theme is the disproportionately negative effect that LSLAs have on other populations that are vulnerable to discrimination and marginalisation. In addition to indigenous peoples, concerns have been raised about negative impacts on women, children, rural communities, and small-scale farmers. CEDAW focused its attention on female heads of households in Cambodia who had lost their sources of livelihood because of the confiscation of land by private companies and were excluded from decision-making processes concerning land distribution (2006, 31). Similarly, in its concluding observations on Cambodia in June 2011, the CRC expressed a deep concern that thousands of children and families, especially the urban poor, small-scale farmers and indigenous communities, were continuing to be deprived of their land 'as a result of land grabbing and forced evictions carried out by people in positions of power' (2011, 61). The committee recommended the establishment of a 'national moratorium on evictions until the determination of the legality of land claims is made' (CRC, 2011, 61). As an overarching recommendation in its assessment of Cambodia, the CERD requested that a proper balance be struck between development objectives and the rights of citizens and that the former not be enacted 'at the expense of the rights of vulnerable persons and groups covered by the Convention [on the Elimination of All Forms of Racial

Discrimination]' (2010, 16). Following CEDAW's review of Laos, it was recommended by the committee that the state party ensure that development projects are implemented only after gender impact assessments involving rural women have been conducted (2009, 44–45).

Finally, a separate issue relates to land policy reforms financed and promoted through development cooperation and assistance, which in certain cases have been found to lead to human rights violations (Künnemann and Monsalve Suárez, 2013, 127). One of these cases came to the CESCR's attention: the involvement of the German Agency for International Cooperation in financing the land titling system in Cambodia. It has been suggested that the scheme—aimed at recognising individual and not collective rights—contributed to weakening the tenure status of vulnerable and marginalised communities, exposing them to the risk of eviction as a result of LSLAS (Künnemann and Monsalve Suárez, 2013). Following that reasoning in its review of Germany in 2011, the CESCR explicitly cited the land-titling scheme in Cambodia to illustrate the concern that 'the [state] party's development cooperation programme has supported projects that have reportedly resulted in the violation of economic, social and cultural rights' (2011, 11).

An overview of UN treaty bodies' monitoring function must also briefly consider communication procedures. A number of international human rights treaties are supplemented by Optional Protocols allowing for the consideration of individual or collective complaints usually referred to as 'communications'. Avenues that are potentially relevant for monitoring human rights violations associated with LSLAS are those established by the Optional Protocol to the ICCPR, by Article 14 of the ICERD, and by the Optional Protocol to the CEDAW that has been ratified by Cambodia, the Philippines, and Thailand (Golay, 2009, 32–33). Turning to practical cases, there are some examples from the Human Rights Committee, the body entrusted with monitoring the ICCPR, in which indigenous communities have sought protection of their way of life, their economic activities and their means of subsistence (Human Rights Committee, 2000 and 2009; Golay and Özden, 2009, 55). These cases, although not dealing necessarily with LSLAS and cases in South-East Asia, provide some useful lessons on how these UN mechanisms may be used in the future to monitor the actual or potential human rights violations associated with LSLAS in South-East Asian countries.

A communication procedure that has recently become available is the one established by the Optional Protocol to the ICESCR (Biglino and Golay, 2013). The optional protocol, which entered into force on 5 May 2013, provides for the right of individuals and groups to submit complaints regarding violations of the rights contained in the covenant. This makes this procedure ideally suited to victims of human rights violations associated with LSLAs who wish to submit communications to the CESCR, but no South-East Asian country has yet accepted it.

4 The Example of Laos

We undertook field research with colleagues in Laos in 2012 and 2013 in the context of a research project on the impact of LSLAs on the right to food in South-East Asia.[6] The presentation of Laos as a case study in this part of the chapter complements information and cases analysed in other chapters of this volume, in relation to Laos and Cambodia (see Messerli et al., Gironde and Senties Portilla, and Cismas and Paramita in this volume). This part begins with a presentation of the relevant legal framework in Laos, followed by an analysis of the examination of human rights violations associated with LSLAs in Laos by UN treaty bodies.

4.1 Legal Framework and Lack of Access to Justice and Effective Remedies at the National and Regional Levels

In Laos, like in Cambodia (see Cismas and Paramita in this volume) and several other countries, there is a solid legal framework that, in principle, offers numerous safeguards in human rights terms. However, there is an important gap between what constitutes 'law on paper' and how that law is actually implemented and applied 'on the ground'.

Laos has ratified the most important international human rights treaties, including the ICCPR, ICESCR, ICERD, CEDAW, CRC, and CRPD. But it has not ratified optional protocols allowing for individual or collective communications in cases of human rights violations.

The Constitution of Laos (adopted in 2003) recognises a list of fundamental rights, including the right to education (article 38), the right to health (article 39), the right to submit complaints and petitions (article 41), and the rights and freedoms of expression, assembly, and association (article 44). It also provides that the '[s]tate, society and families attend to implementing development policies and supporting the progress of women and to protecting legitimate rights and benefits of women and children' (article 29). It is worth mentioning however that many human rights are not enshrined in the

---

6　For a description of the two-year research project and to access the outputs that were produced by the researchers, visit http://www.snis.ch/project_large-scale-land-acquisitions-southeast-asia-rural-transformations-between-global-agendas.

Constitution, such as the right to life, the right to food, and the right to housing, and that the Constitution does not mention international human rights instruments ratified by Laos. It is also important to note that Laos's legal framework does not recognise indigenous peoples but ethnic groups (articles 8 and 22).

The most important national law in the context of LSLAs is the 2003 Land Law, which creates eight land categories: agricultural land, forestland, water area land, industrial land, communication land, cultural land, land for national defence and security, and construction land. When it was adopted, one of its main objectives was to support small-scale farmers in better using agricultural land, and to provide them with a secure legal environment. However, more than ten years after its adoption, the great majority of people living in Laos' rural areas remain untouched by or unaware of these potential benefits (Gironde et al., 2014, 40). Senties Portilla found that, in practice, the Land Law 'paved the way for foreign investment in land through [...] legally defining the circumstances under which land can be conceded to investors [, with] enormous implications [for] the typically rural and subsistence-oriented agrarian structures of the country, which [...] largely remain founded on customary practices' (2012, 61–62, 69). She also observed that the titling of communal lands that could be used to protect villagers against restrictions imposed by corporations, for example to accessing food and water, is poorly implemented (2012, 67–69).

What also emerges with great clarity in Laos is that access to justice and effective remedies in cases of human rights violations is extremely difficult, or non-existent. Individuals affected by LSLAs encounter many hurdles in their attempts to access justice (Gironde et al., 2014, 47). In a report presented to the UN General Assembly in 2012, the UN Special Rapporteur on extreme poverty and human rights Magdalena Sepulveda Carmona developed an analytical structure for the analysis of the obstacles, experienced when attempting to access justice, faced by people living in poverty. The special rapporteur's framework identifies a set of macro-categories whereby obstacles can be classified (Special Rapporteur on Extreme Poverty, 2012). A large number of issues identified in the framework reflect barriers that exist to accessing justice in Laos, including 'institutional and structural' as well as 'social and cultural' obstacles.

Access to other kind of remedies, including those of an administrative nature, is also extremely difficult in Laos for victims of human rights violations associated with LSLAs (Gironde et al., 2014, 47). The main avenue that exists is a hotline, created in 2012, to the national assembly. According to many, a great number of complaints submitted through this hotline were related to land disputes (Baird, 2011). In one case at least, it allegedly led to a member of the national assembly visiting the community and compensation being given to its members (Gironde et al., 2014, 47). But as the process is purely oral it is difficult to gather more information regarding the efficiency of this remedy.

This lack of access to justice and effective remedies in Laos is representative of a context in which human rights education is extremely poor, or non-existent, and speaking about and reporting human rights violations is extremely difficult. Illustrative of this context is the fact that two people who spoke out on human rights issues were either forced to leave the country or disappeared. On 9 December 2012, the country director of Helvetas, a Swiss non-governmental organisation (NGO) working in the field of development and with rural communities in Laos, Anne-Sophie Gindroz, was given 48 hours to leave the country because she criticised the government for creating a difficult environment for development actors and civil society organisations by restricting freedoms of expression and association (Radio Free Asia, 2012).[7] One week later, on 15 December 2012, Sombath Somphone, a well-known Lao activist, disappeared. More than two years later, the government of Laos still stands accused of not conducting a proper investigation into Somphone's disappearance, and his family has no information on where he could be (APHR, 2014).[8] It also seems that there is no hope of a rapid improvement of the human rights situation in Laos, with new laws being proposed to Parliament to further restrict the freedoms of association and expression of NGOs and their members (APHR, 2014).

Unlike Africa, the Americas, and Europe, Asia is a region in which there is no regional human rights treaty, human rights court, or commission covering the region in its entirety (Golay, 2009, 37–46). When victims of human rights violations face difficulties accessing justice and effective remedies at the national

---

7   In a letter addressed in November 2012 to participants at a round table on foreign aid strategy in Laos, A.-S. Gindroz wrote: 'We are working in a challenging environment: this is a country governed by a single-party regime, where there is little space for meaningful democratic debate, and when taking advantage of that limited space, repercussions follow.' (Radio Free Asia, 2012). Before being evicted from the country, Ms. Gindroz chaired a coalition of civil society organisations working on land issues in Laos—the land issues working group (http://www.laolandissues.org) (accessed on 28 April 2015).

8   After a visit to Laos in September 2014, C. Santiago, Malaysian parliamentarian and vice-president of the Association of Southeast Asian Nations (ASEAN) Parliamentarians for Human Rights (APHR) declared: 'The Lao authorities have erected a brick wall of silence on this investigation, so much so that the only intelligent conclusion is that there is in fact no investigation taking place at all and that the obstinacy is part of a cover up for state officials implicated in his abduction' (APHR, 2014).

level, it is therefore impossible for them to use regional monitoring bodies. Two positive developments in this sphere were the establishment of the Association of Southeast Asian Nations (ASEAN) Intergovernmental Commission on Human Rights and the ASEAN Commission for the Promotion and Protection of the Rights of Women and Children, in 2009 and 2010, respectively.[9] But the commissions' added value in the area of LSLAs and human rights remains unclear, as does their engagement with the topic (Gironde et al., 2014, 39).

4.2   The Role Played by UN Mechanisms in Monitoring Human Rights Violations Associated with LSLAs in Laos

In a context in which access to justice and effective remedies is extremely difficult at the national and regional levels, national (Gender and Development Group—Alliance for Democracy in Laos)[10] and international (INDIGENOUS[11] and UNPO)[12] NGOs have used international treaties ratified by Laos to denounce the negative impacts of LSLAs. They have done so through the submission of parallel reports—parallel to the government report—when UN treaty bodies examined Laos's human rights record (Alliance for Democracy in Laos, 2012; INDIGENOUS, 2012; UNPO, 2012; GDG, 2008). These NGOs have targeted the CERD and the CEDAW committees, which have responded by evaluating human rights violations associated with LSLAs in Laos and issuing recommendations to the government (CERD, 2012a; CEDAW, 2009).

The CERD has examined the need to better protect the livelihoods—and the right to an adequate standard of living—of ethnic groups. In its consideration of reports concerning Laos, the committee reiterated the right of communities to give, or withhold, their free, prior, and informed consent and called for the state to ensure that this decision is respected in the planning and implementation of large-scale projects affecting these communities' lands and resources

---

9   In 2009 and 2010, these two institutions (composed of states' representatives) were created by ASEAN to monitor existing international human rights obligations of ASEAN members, in agreement with Article 14 of ASEAN's charter, adopted on 20 November 2007 and in force since 15 December 2008.

10   The Alliance for Democracy in Laos presents itself as a worldwide network of Lao political opposition organisations and active advocates committed to a peaceful change towards genuine democracy in Laos. It is an NGO and is based in Germany. Its website can be found at www.laoalliance.org (accessed on 28 April 2015).

11   INDIGENOUS is the International Network for Diplomacy Indigenous Governance Engaging in Nonviolence Organizing for Understanding & Self-Determination.

12   UNPO is the Unrepresented Nations and Peoples Organization, and is based in The Hague and Brussels. Its website can be found at www.unpo.org (accessed on 28 April 2015).

(2012a, 16–17). Express references were made to the importance of 'the cultural aspect of land, as an integral part of the identity of some ethnic groups' (CERD 2012a, 16–17). Following its examination of the situation in Laos, the CEDAW committee recommended that the government ensure that development projects are implemented only after conducting gender-impact assessments involving rural women (2009, 44–45).

On the basis of the assessments made by UN treaty bodies, and field research conducted in 2012 and 2013 in the context of a project on the human rights impact of LSLAs in South-East Asia, it is possible to conclude that the typology of human rights violations associated with LSLAs that we presented in the second part of this chapter (see part 2, above) is relevant when discussing human rights violations in Laos (Gironde et al., 2014, 43–46). As is the case in many other countries, such violations include the human rights implications of internal displacement and forced evictions caused by LSLAs, which often lead to drastic changes in livelihood opportunities, and in the great majority of cases leave the displaced individuals and communities without adequate resettlement and compensation for their losses in livelihood (see the cases in the province of Champasak described in the contribution by Gironde and Senties Portilla in this volume). They also include violations of ethnic minorities' right to give, or to withhold, their free, prior, and informed consent to externally imposed policies and activities that directly affect their livelihoods, and the disproportionately negative effect that LSLAs have on other individuals and groups who are vulnerable to discrimination and marginalisation, including women, children, rural communities, and small-scale farmers (Gironde et al., 2014, 43–46). Inadequate participation and consultation, and information asymmetry, also appear to constitute a dominant trend in Savannakhet and Luang Prabang provinces in Laos (Gironde et al., 2014, 45–46).

These violations also include the disproportionately negative effect that LSLAs have on individuals and groups who are vulnerable to discrimination and marginalisation. To give a concrete example, a study of the impacts of a land concession—of 7,000 ha, granted to a Chinese rubber company (Sino Company) in 2006—on a local community in Nambak District, Luang Prabang Province in Laos, revealed that the implementation of the concession led to the large-scale enclosure of upland resources that these villages depended on (Friis, 2013). This also implied the imposition of a strict penalty scheme for damage to rubber trees caused by roaming animals, which led to a prohibition on villagers continuing to rear livestock, which had negative impacts on soil fertility and led to a decline in paddy rice yields. In a number of reported cases, individuals and their families were left with no option but to purchase food on the market although, due to their precarious economic conditions, they could not afford the rich, nutritious and diverse diet they had enjoyed when they had had agricultural land on which to grow food and access to forest areas that provided additional food sources (i.e. fish and wild animals) (Gironde et al., 2014, 45).

5   Conclusion

In the second and third parts of this contribution, we have presented the international legal basis that can be used to monitor human rights violations associated with LSLAs, and have provided examples of the role that UN treaty bodies can play in monitoring these violations, with a focus on South-East Asia. We have also presented a typology of human rights violations associated with LSLAs. In the fourth part, we presented Laos as a case study.

We conclude that three common threads can be extracted from this assessment. The first concern relates to the actual or potential human rights implications of the internal displacement and forced evictions caused by LSLAs, which often lead to drastic changes in livelihood opportunities. The second thread involves the impact of LSLAs on the procedural rights of indigenous peoples, in particular their right to give, or to withhold, their free, prior, and informed consent to policies and activities that directly affect their land, territory and livelihoods. The third recurrent theme is the disproportionately negative effect that LSLAs have on individuals and groups who are vulnerable to discrimination and marginalisation, including women, children, indigenous peoples, rural communities, and small-scale farmers.

Taking a step back, we can conclude that human rights are well recognised in international law and that national laws seem to be adequate in many countries, including in Cambodia and Laos. These rights and laws represent a good basis from which to evaluate the impacts of LSLAs. But these human rights instruments and national laws are poorly implemented in the ground, or not implemented in favour of local communities (see also Cismas and Paramita in this volume). And despite a constructive role played by UN monitoring mechanisms, which certainly offer one of the few avenues that exist for denouncing human rights violations associated with LSLAs, violations continue to be widespread in the countries affected by the phenomenon and evaluated by UN experts.

References

Alliance for Democracy in Laos (2012) *Report of the Alliance for Democracy in Laos about the Human-Rights Situation and the Race Discrimination in Laos,* presented to the UN CERD, Hagen (Germany), http://tbinternet.ohchr.org/Treaties/CERD/Shared%20Documents/LAO/INT_CERD_NGO_LAO_80_9467_E.pdf (accessed on 28 April 2015).

APHR (ASEAN Parliamentarians for Human Rights) (2014) *Lao Government's Deceptive Game on Sombath Investigation Must End,* press release, 23 September, http://www.aseanmp.org/?p=3101 (accessed on 27 November 2014).

Baird, I. (2011) 'Turning Land into Capital, Turning People into Labour: Primitive Accumulation and the Arrival of Large-Scale Economic Land Concessions in the Lao People's Democratic Republic', *New Proposals: Journal of Marxism and Interdisciplinary Inquiry,* 5(1), pp. 10–26, http://ojs.library.ubc.ca/index.php/newproposals/article/view/2264 (accessed on 28 April 2015).

Bassiouni, M.C. and W.A. Schabas (eds.) (2011) *New Challenges for the UN Human Rights Machinery. What Future for the UN Treaty Body System and the Human Rights Council Procedures?* (Cambridge, Antwerp and Portland: Intersentia).

Biglino, I. and C. Golay (2013) *The Optional Protocol to the International Covenant on Economic, Social and Cultural Rights,* Geneva Academy In-Brief No. 2 (Geneva: Geneva Academy of International Humanitarian Law and Human Rights), http://www.geneva-academy.ch/docs/publications/The%20optional%20protocol%20In%20brief%202.pdf (accessed on 28 April 2015).

Borghi, M. and L. Postigione Blommestein (eds.) (2006) *The Right to Adequate Food and Access to Justice* (Bruxelles and Genève: Bruylant–Schultess).

CEDAW (Committee on the Elimination of Discrimination against Women) (2009) *Concluding Observations of the Committee on the Elimination of Discrimination against Women: Lao People's Democratic Republic,* UN doc. CEDAW/C/LAO/CO/7, 14 August.

——— (2006) *Concluding Comments of the Committee on the Elimination of Discrimination against Women: Cambodia,* UN doc. CEDAW/C/KHM/CO/3, 25 January.

CERD (Committee on the Elimination of Racial Discrimination) (2012a) *Concluding Observations of the Committee on the Elimination of Racial Discrimination: Lao PDR,* UN doc. CERD/C/LAO/CO/16–18, 13 April.

——— (2012b) *Concluding Observations of the Committee on the Elimination of Racial Discrimination: Viet Nam,* UN doc. CERD/C/VNM/CO/10–14, 9 March.

——— (2010) *Concluding Observations of the Committee on the Elimination of Racial Discrimination: Cambodia,* UN doc. CERD/C/KHM/CO/8–13, 1 April.

———— (2007) *Concluding Observations of the Committee on the Elimination of Racial Discrimination: Indonesia*, UN doc. CERD/C/IDN/CO/3, 15 August.

CESCR (Committee on Economic, Social and Cultural Rights) (2011) *Concluding Observations of the Committee on the Economic, Social and Cultural Rights: Germany*, UN doc. E/C.12/DEU/CO/5, 12 July.

———— (2009) *Concluding Observations of the Committee on the Economic, Social and Cultural Rights: Cambodia*, UN doc. E/C.12/KHM/CO/1,12 June.

———— (1999) *General Comment 12: The Right to Adequate Food (art. 11)*, UN doc. E/C.12/1999/5, 12 May.

Clays, P. and G. Vanloqueren (2013) 'The Minimum Human Rights Principles Applicable to Large-Scale Land Acquisitions or Leases', *Globalizations*, 10(1), pp. 193–198, DOI: 10.1080/14747731.2013.760940.

Cotula, L. (2012) ' "Land Grabbing" in the Shadow of the Law: Legal Frameworks Regulating the Global Land Rush', in Rayfuse, R. and N. Weisfelt (eds.) *The Challenge of Food Security. International Policy and Regulatory Frameworks* (Cheltenham and Northampton: Edward Elgar) pp. 206–228.

———— (ed.) (2009) *The Right to Food and Access to Natural Resources. Using Human Rights Arguments and Mechanisms to Improve Resource Access for the Rural Poor* (Rome: Food and Agriculture Organization), http://pubs.iied.org/pdfs/G03065.pdf (accessed on 28 April 2015).

CRC (Committee on the Rights of the Child) (2011) *Concluding Observations: Cambodia*, UN doc. CRC/C/KHM/CO/2, 20 June.

De Schutter, O. (2011a) 'How not to Think of Land-Grabbing: Three Critiques of Large-Scale Investments in Farmland', *The Journal of Peasant Studies*, 38(2), pp. 249–279, DOI: 10.1080/03066150.2011.559008.

———— (2011b) 'The Green Rush: The Global Race for Farmland and the Rights of Land Users', *Harvard International Law Journal*, 52(2), pp. 504–559.

Friis, C. (2013) *Land, Livelihoods and Access to Resources in Laos PDR—Large-Scale Land Acquisitions in a Dynamic Context of Agrarian Transformation*, unpublished Master's thesis (Copenhagen: Faculty of Science, University of Copenhagen), http://www.snis.ch/system/files/master_thesis_cecilie_friis_complete_0.pdf (accessed on 28 April 2015).

GDG (Gender and Development Group) (2008) *Implementation of the CEDAW Convention. List of Key Issues to be Submitted to the CEDAW Committee*, CEDAW pre-session November 2008, http://www2.ohchr.org/english/bodies/cedaw/docs/ngos/GDG_Laos_44.pdf (accessed on 28 April 2015).

Gironde, C., C. Golay, P. Messerli, A. Peeters and O. Schönweger (2014) (with the contributions of I. Biglino, I. Cismas, C. Friis, P. Paramita, G. Senties Portilla and S. Seng) *Large-Scale Land Acquisitions in Southeast Asia: Rural Transformations between Global Agendas and Peoples' Right to Food'*, Working Paper (Geneva: Swiss

Network for International Studies), http://www.snis.ch/system/files/gironde_working_paper_lsla_southeast_asia_17.08.2014_0.pdf (accessed on 28 May 2015).

Golay, C. (2009) *The Right to Food and Access to Justice: Examples at the National, Regional and International Levels* (Rome: Food and Agriculture Organization).

Golay, C. and I. Biglino (2013) 'Human Rights Responses to Land Grabbing: A Right to Food Perspective', *Third World Quarterly*, 34(9), pp. 1630–1650, DOI: 10.1080/01436597.2013.843853.

Golay, C., C. Mahon and I. Cismas (2011) 'The Impact of the UN Special Procedures on the Development and Implementation of Economic, Social and Cultural Rights', *The International Journal of Human Rights*, 15(2), pp. 299–318, DOI: 10.1080/13642987.2011.537472.

Golay, C. and M. Özden (2009) *The Right of Peoples to Self-Determination* (Geneva: CETIM).

Human Rights Committee (2009) Ángela Poma Poma v. Peru, Comm. No. 1457/2006, Views of 27 March, UN doc. CCPR/C/95/D/1457/2006.

——— (2000) Apirana Mahuika et al. v. New Zealand, Comm. No. 547/1993, Views of 27 October, UN doc. CCPR/C/70/D/541/1993.

INDIGENOUS (International Network for Diplomacy Indigenous Governance Engaging in Nonviolence Organizing for Understanding & Self-Determination) (2012) *Shadow Report Regarding the Periodic Reports of Laos under the UN Convention on the Elimination on the Elimination of All Forms of Racial Discrimination*, for consideration at the 80th Session of the United Nations CERD, 28–29 February, http://tbinternet.ohchr.org/Treaties/CERD/Shared%20Documents/LAO/INT_CERD_NGO_LAO_80_9469_E.doc (accessed on 28 April 2015).

Keller, H. and G. Ulfstein (eds.) (2012) *UN Human Rights Treaty Bodies: Law and Legitimacy* (Cambridge: Cambridge University Press).

Künnemann, R. and S. Monsalve Suárez (2013) 'International Human Rights and Governing Land Grabbing: A View from Global Civil Society', *Globalizations*, 10(1), pp. 123–139, DOI: 10.1080/14747731.2013.760933.

Monsalve Suárez, S. (2013) 'The Human Rights Framework in Contemporary Agrarian Struggles', *Journal of Peasant Studies*, 40(1), pp. 239–290, DOI: 10.1080/03066150.2011.652950.

Narula, S. (2013) 'The Global Land Rush: Markets, Rights, and the Politics of Food', *Standford Journal of International Law*, 49(1), pp. 101–175, http://ssrn.com/abstract=2294521.

Nifosi, I. (2005) *The UN Special Procedures in the Field of Human Rights* (Antwerp and Oxford: Intersentia).

Piccone, T. (2012) *Catalysts for Change: How the UN's Independent Experts Promote Human Rights* (Washington: Brookings Institution Press).

Radio Free Asia (2012) *'NGO Director Expelled'*, press release, 7 December, http://www
.rfa.org/english/news/laos/expulsion-12072012153813.html (accessed on 27 November
2014).

Robinson, M. (2003) 'Making Human Rights Matter: Eleanor Roosevelt's Time Has
Come', *Harvard Human Rights Journal*, 16, pp. 1–11.

Senties Portilla, G. (2012) *Land Concessions in Lao PDR: Transforming Rural Livelihoods
and Aspirations*, unpublished preliminary thesis dissertation (Geneva: Graduate
Institute of International and Development Studies).

Special Rapporteur on Extreme Poverty (2012) *Report of the Special Rapporteur on
Extreme Poverty and Human Rights, Magdalena Sepulveda Carmona*, UN doc.
A/67/278, 9 August.

Special Rapporteur on the Right to Food (2011) *Mission to Madagascar*, Addendum to
the Report of the Special Rapporteur on the right to food, Olivier De Schutter, UN
doc. A/HRC/19/59/Add.4, 26 December.

———— (2009) *Large-Scale Land Acquisitions and Leases: A Set of Minimum Principles
and Measures to Address the Human Rights Challenge*, Annex to the Report of the
Special Rapporteur on the right to food, Olivier De Schutter, UN doc. A/HRC/13/33/
Add.2, 28 December.

Subedi, S., S. Wheatley, A. Mulherjee and S. Ngane (2011) 'The Role of the Special
Rapporteurs of the United Nations Human Rights Council in the Development
and Promotion of International Human Rights Norms', *The International Journal of
Human Rights*, 15(2), pp. 155–161, DOI: 10.1080/13642987.2011.537463.

UNPO (Unrepresented Nations and Peoples Organization) (2012) *Parallel Report
Presented by Unrepresented Nations and Peoples Organization*, Alternative Report
submitted to the UN Committee on the Elimination of Racial Discrimination at the
80th Session during the consideration of the 16th–18th Periodic Reports of Laos
(UNPO: The Hague).

Vandehole, W. (2004) *The Procedures Before the UN Human Rights Bodies: Divergence or
Convergence?* (Antwerp and Oxford: Intersentia).

CHAPTER 10

Large-Scale Land Acquisitions in Cambodia: Where Do (Human Rights) Law and Practice Meet?

Ioana Cismas and Patricia Paramita

Abstract

Being anchored in the broader policy debate on the effectiveness of international human rights standards on the ground, this chapter inquires whether human rights carry any relevance in the Cambodian landscape of contestation of large-scale land acquisitions (LSLAs) and long-term leases. The chapter first establishes that substantive and procedural obligations relevant to LSLAs result from Cambodia's ratification of human rights treaties. It then examines whether and to what extent this normative framework informs the acts and actions of the government in relation to land transactions, and the strategies employed by affected communities. The study relies on legal analysis to unearth tensions between processes set in motion by land laws and shortcomings in their implementation in terms of transparency and participation, accountability and redress, and identification of vulnerable groups. It also draws on desk and field research in a rural and an urban area of Cambodia to examine the mobilisation strategies employed by the two communities affected by LSLA-related forced evictions; the focus is on processes of appropriation and adaptation of human rights by affected local communities, known as 'vernacularization'. The chapter shows that the rural-urban spatiality, a constructed element, is of relevance in explaining the different configurations of social activism occurring in each setting and these configurations' use of human rights. It finds that, contrary to similarly LSLA-affected rural citizens, urban dwellers made extensive use of human rights language and human rights mechanisms to challenge their forced evictions and also achieved a certain success. Furthermore, the chapter shows that deficient governmental practice, in particular in the area of information and access to justice may play a role in entertaining this divided spatiality, especially by incapacitating the vernacularization of human rights in rural settings.

1 Introduction

Unlike past rushes for land, the wave of large-scale land acquisitions and long-term leases (LSLAs) of the last two decades in Africa, Asia, and parts of Eastern

Europe is embedded in a liberalised world economy and involves new actors, new labour processes, and new legal instruments (White et al., 2012; Peluso and Lund, 2011). This recent expansion of LSLAs has triggered debates on whether the phenomenon represents an opportunity for investment and development or corresponds to an exclusionary process that specifically marginalises vulnerable individuals and societal groups (Arezki et al., 2012; Borras Jr. et al., 2011; Cotula et al., 2009; Kachika, 2010; Moyo and Chambati, 2013). This antagonism is best reflected in the two terms most often used to describe the phenomenon: 'land investment' and 'land grab.' Beyond the symbolism that these terms encapsulate, it becomes clear that LSLAs are intertwined at the junction of development economics, land use and land governance, colonial memory, and post-colonial practice, against the background of states' obligations under international human rights law (Gironde et al., 2011; de Schutter, 2013).

These complex intersections are certainly present in the case of LSLAs in Cambodia. As one of the fastest growing economies in South-East Asia, Cambodia has experienced, over the past two decades, a rapid increase in foreign investment, often taking the form of economic land concessions (ELCs).[1] In parallel to the economic phenomenon, and as a consequence of land becoming scarcer, disputes over land have become more intense, frequent, and often violent, involving state authorities and company representatives, stakeholders from rural communities, urban dwellers, politicians, human rights activists, and journalists (ADHOC, 2013; Special Rapporteur on Cambodia, 2013). In this landscape of contestation, do human rights have any relevance? Put differently, our aim here is to examine whether and to what extent human rights standards inform the acts and actions of the government in relation to LSLAs, and the strategies employed by affected communities.

This chapter is premised on the understanding that '[h]uman rights are not just abstract', they acquire value through their application in practice (Marks and Clapham, 2005, 388). As such, the chapter is anchored in the broader policy debate on the effectiveness of international human rights standards on the ground. To explain and strengthen state compliance with international human rights norms, scholars have focused on the national and international mechanisms monitoring or adjudicating the obligations of states[2] and the internalisation/domestication of human rights (Golay, 2011), the reputational damage that would result from non-compliance (Chayes and Chayes, 1995),

---

1   Estimates of the number of, and area covered by, ELCs vary. In this volume, Messerli et al. estimate that Cambodia has 486 land deals comprising 4.5 million hectares.

2   An illustrative example for this strand of the literature is Christophe Golay's contribution in this volume.

on processes such as material inducement, persuasion, and acculturation (Goodman and Jinks, 2013), and the legitimacy of international instruments and modalities for enhancing ownership thereof in various (cultural) contexts (Franck, 1995; An-Na'im, 1990). While drawing on some of these descriptive and proscriptive approaches to verify where human rights law and practice meet in the case of LSLAs in Cambodia, our particular interest lies with the process of appropriation and adaptation of human rights by affected local communities, known as 'vernacularization' (Merry, 2006), and the impact of rural-urban spatiality thereon.

Structurally the chapter has three parts. The first part lays out the human rights framework relevant to LSLAS as it can be distilled from the UN treaty bodies' process of review of Cambodia's implementation of its international obligations. Second, relevant domestic legislation and governmental actions are contrasted with the previously identified human rights framework. The third part addresses the practices of affected communities in an urban and a rural area of Cambodia and inquires whether and how these actors utilise human rights law to prevent LSLAS or challenge the effects thereof. The conclusion appraises our findings.

Methodologically, the chapter relies on legal analysis, including Cambodia's history of ratification of human rights instruments and their transposition into domestic law, and on analysis of data obtained through desk research and fieldwork. It presents case studies from a rural area (the village of Sein Serrey in Kampong Thom province) and an urban one (the Boeung Kak lake, Phnom Penh). In selecting these cases we sought to ensure that processes of land commercialisation were pronounced, that different land transfer and livelihood scenarios could be identified, and that there was at least some evidence of awareness of human rights.[3] The information for the rural case was collected through semi-structured qualitative interviews with 30 evicted families and local authorities, conducted from January to April 2013. The urban case study is examined through the prism of the academic literature, NGO reports, videos of interviews, and interviews with non-residents involved in social activism. These cases allow us to illustrate the Cambodian version of the rural-urban 'dichotomy' and the connotations and meanings attached to it, and to

---

3 Phnom Penh, the capital city, was selected because it has witnessed both a significant change of land use and urban forced evictions, and it is 'home' to many non-governmental organisations (NGO) that have articulated LSLA-related demands in human rights terms. Sein Serrey, meanwhile, is a newly established village surrounded by forest and plantations, and is a place where residents who were forcibly evicted to make space for LSLAS had little contact with and received little support from NGOS.

ultimately deconstruct this dichotomy and examine how it informs debates on the dissemination of human rights and claim-making in Cambodia.

2   Mapping Cambodia's Human Rights Obligations Relevant to LSLAS' Contexts

In the legal positivist tradition a state's consent to be bound by international norms is central to determining the sources of its human rights obligations. Cambodia's obligations stem from international human rights instruments to which it has become party, notably the International Covenant on Civil and Political Rights; the International Covenant on Economic, Social and Cultural Rights (ICESCR); and sectoral treaties on the elimination of racial discrimination, on the elimination of discrimination against women, on the rights of the child, and the rights of people with disabilities.[4] Whilst these instruments are silent as to the permissibility of LSLAS as such, the concluding observations of bodies monitoring their implementation reveal that the treaties have created a human rights map, or framework, which entails substantive and procedural obligations of relevance to land transactions in Cambodia and beyond (Cismas, 2013; Golay and Biglino, 2013; Golay et al., 2014).[5]

As to the substantive features, Cambodia has a triadic obligation to respect (refrain from interfering with the exercise of an existing right), protect (ensure against abuse by third parties, including powerful individuals and companies), and fulfil human rights (take positive action to ensure enjoyment of rights). In addition, it has a general obligation not to discriminate against individuals or groups, inter alia, on grounds of ethnicity, gender, social origin, or their rural–urban residence. In their concluding observations on Cambodia, treaty bodies have emphasised the negative consequences of LSLAS and flagged possible non-compliance with the respect and protect obligations in relation to a number of rights. These include the prohibition of forced evictions, the right to livelihood, the rights to food and housing, and the rights of indigenous people to dispose of their lands and natural resources (CESCR, 2009; CEDAW, 2006). In the Cambodian context forced evictions and internal displacement without adequate resettlement and compensation have triggered a wider range of abuses perpetrated by or with the involvement of third parties, including violations of the rights to freedom of expression and assembly, violence against land

---

4 A comprehensive ratification history of Cambodia can be consulted at http://indicators .ohchr.org (accessed on 16 March 2015).

5 See also Golay's contribution in this volume.

rights defenders, and the criminalisation of the latter (Amnesty International, 2012; ADHOC, 2011).

Treaty bodies have consistently emphasised the disproportionately negative effect, in human rights terms, that land transactions in Cambodia have on populations that are vulnerable to discrimination, or are marginalised or disadvantaged, such as indigenous people, rural communities, the urban poor, women, and children (Golay et al., 2014). The situation is in profound contrast with the state's obligation to fulfil human rights specifically through the identification and implementation of measures for the benefit of vulnerable groups. Therefore, the government has been urged to pursue the demarcation of state public land and state private land,[6] the implementation of titling of the communal land of indigenous people (CESCR, 2009), and—importantly—the establishment of a 'national moratorium on all evictions until the proper legal framework is in place and the process of land titling is completed' (CESCR, 2009; CRC, 2011). It is clear that the fulfil dimension under the ICESCR entails a strong social justice component: 'the granting of economic concessions [should] take into account the need for sustainable development and for all Cambodians to share in the benefits of progress rather than for private gain alone' (CESCR, 2009).

The substantive rights stipulated by human rights conventions are underpinned by a number of procedural safeguards of paramount relevance in the context of LSLAs in Cambodia. These can be grouped for analytical purposes under two headings: transparency and participation, whereby an obligation to obtain prior free and informed consent is linked to the holding of effective consultations and to the participation of stakeholders, in particular vulnerable groups; accountability and redress, which includes holding perpetrators of human rights violations responsible and affordable access of victims to courts and other administrative mechanisms for seeking an effective remedy including adequate relocation and compensation. The Voluntary Guidelines on Responsible Governance of Tenure of Land, Fisheries and Forests in the Context of National Food Security, a recent addition to the flurry of soft-law instruments applicable to land transactions (see Annex), hold great potential

---

6   The 2001 Land Law divides state land into state public land and state private land—together these account for approximately 75–80% of Cambodia's total land area (USAID, 2012). State public land refers to land of a natural origin (such as rivers, lakes, or forests) which has general public use, and to archaeological and cultural heritage sites. State private land is state land that does not provide a public service and which does not come under any of the other categories of state public land. The 2001 Land Law and Sub-Decree No. 146 stipulate that ELCs can be granted only for state private land (RGC, 2001; RGC, 2005a).

for guiding Cambodia's actions in particular in relation to procedural safe-guards. The effective performance of these safeguards may not be sufficient for land transactions to be human rights friendly or even neutral. However, it is clear from Cambodia's process of review by human rights mechanisms that a failure to uphold these guarantees would, with great likelihood, result in violations of human rights and the country's non-compliance with its international obligations.

3   Governmental Performance with Regards to Human Rights
       Obligations

'Context matters' has long been one of the mantras of the social sciences. As an agriculture-based society, Cambodia has witnessed, through the centuries, massive changes to its land tenure system. It is important to recall that the genocidal evictions and the collectivisation campaign implemented by the Khmer Rouge in which over 1.7 million individuals lost their lives represented a process of 'population geography: a discipline of bodies through a control of space' (Tyner, 2009, 134). As such, not only was private property abolished but most of the land tenure and cadastral records were obliterated (Sar, 2010), which led to the current situation where an estimated two-thirds of Cambodians do not possess proper deeds to the land they inhabit (IRIN, 2013).

To take this context seriously means to recognise that land reform in Cambodia, including land titling, will be a strenuous and lengthy process. At the same time, it is the context of past violations and land-related conflict that recommends the integration of the human rights framework ensuing from Cambodia's ratification of international treaties as a necessary and particularly auspicious step in the country's efforts to undertake land reform and pursue economic development.[7] Along these lines, our analysis agrees that, at a formal level, land legislation in Cambodia is 'relatively well developed' (Special Rapporteur on Cambodia, 2012). Nonetheless, important human rights concerns derive from tensions between processes set in motion by the same and/or different bodies of legislation, and by major shortcomings in the implementation of domestic legislation.

---

7   Importantly, Cambodia's Constitution recognises, in Article 31, that international instruments supersede domestic legislation.

3.1   *Processual Tensions*

The 2001 Land Law recognises the possession of rights by those people who enjoyed land prior to 2001, in a manner that is 'unambiguous, non-violent, notorious [sic] to the public, continuous and in good faith', even if those people have not yet been formally recognised as owners of the land[8] (RGC, 2001, chapter 4; Special Rapporteur on Cambodia, 2012). The law also distinguishes between state public land and state private land, whereas the 2005 Sub-Decree on State Land Management provides the framework for the identification, registration and classification of state land, and the process of re-classifying state land from one category into another (Special Rapporteur on Cambodia, 2012; RGC, 2005b). But the 2001 Land Law also provides for the possibility of granting ELCs. The latter are 'a legal right established by a legal document issued under the discretion of the competent authority, given to any natural person or legal entity or group of persons to occupy a land and to exercise thereon the rights set forth by this law' (RGC, 2001). Article 4 of Sub-Decree 146 on ELCs (RGC, 2005a) lists among the criteria that need to be cumulatively respected for land to be eligible for concessions, the following:

> The land has been registered and classified as state private land in accordance with the Sub decree on State Land Management and the Sub decree on Procedures for Establishing Cadastral Maps and Land Register or the Sub decree on Sporadic Registration.

As can be gauged from the above, there is a processual tension that arises as a result of the provisions of the 2001 Land Law, the 2005 Sub-Decree on State Land Management, and Sub-Decree 146 on ELCs. The effective implementation of the latter sub-decree relies on the output of the processes established by the former acts. As such, as long as the titling programme and the identification, registration, and classification of state land are ongoing, the mere opportunity to request and grant ELCs (as provided by Sub-Decree 146) will invariably skew the latter processes and open the door to abuse in relation to what land receives title and what land is classified as state public land. Unsurprisingly, UN mechanisms and land activists have requested a moratorium on ELCs until such time as titling and other land programmes are finalised. On 7 May 2012, Prime Minister Hun Sen announced a moratorium on new ELCs. Direct causality of the compliance of the Cambodian government with the request made by

---

8   The Law stipulates that a title for this land can be requested, which then converts possession into full ownership rights.

human rights mechanisms cannot be established; however, it is interesting to note that the moratorium was announced during the UN Special Rapporteur's mission to Cambodia, which was undertaken with the aim of examining the country's human rights situation.

3.2   *Major Shortcomings in Implementation*

Beyond the above-mentioned tensions set in motion by legislative acts with regards to land, the implementation of such legislation raises major concerns. Evidence suggests a striking failure to adequately implement existing domestic legislation, and to respect international obligations, in three areas: transparency and participation, accountability and redress, and identification of vulnerable groups.

'The granting and management of economic and other land concessions in Cambodia suffer from a lack of transparency and adherence to existing laws'— this was the bleak assessment on transparency and participation provided by the UN Special Rapporteur on Cambodia (2012). NGO reports confirm that the majority of people living in concession areas have not had the opportunity to participate in decision-making processes, have not been consulted, and have not given their consent to ELCs. Amnesty International (2009) found that 'evictions are routinely carried out without any court order or verification of the claim of ownership' of the land. Other sources suggest that, at the most basic level, villagers have not been informed about the land transactions taking place, including the exact location of a concession, its dimensions, companies involved, intended use of the land, and other similar aspects (FIDH, 2012). Research points to relevant links between lack of access to information and lack of access to redress, and conversely suggests a positive correlation between information and compensation (Golay et al., 2014).

Turning to accountability and redress, it may be observed that in principle, there are several options for settlement of land disputes in Cambodia, largely depending on whether the disputed land is officially registered or not (BABC, 2010; LICADHO, 2009; Sithan, 2012). When the land is registered, disputes will be settled in national courts. When land is not registered, complaints over land issues are to be submitted to the Administrative Commission and the Cadastral Commission (CC). Despite these existing avenues, institutional, structural, and social factors often serve as barriers to accessing justice in LSLA-related disputes (Golay et al., 2014; Special Rapporteur on extreme poverty, 2012).

The CC, for instance, is portrayed as institutionally weak due to limited budgetary resources and monitoring capacities (BABC, 2010). Physical inaccessibility (affecting rural communities in Cambodia since these courts are clustered in urban areas) and economic inaccessibility (due to fees for lodg-ing a complaint, costs related to transportation, lost wages, and legal counsel) represent structural barriers that deprive individuals of their right to access a remedy (Golay et al., 2014).

The corruption-retaliation-mistrust triad presents another obstacle in the path of accountability and access to remedies. The bias of dispute mechanisms towards, those who could generally be termed, the rich, and against poorer communities and land rights activists is an aspect that plagues the implemen-tation of ELC legislation (ADHOC, 2011; LICADHO, 2012). A recent communica-tion addressed to the Cambodian government by the Special Rapporteur on Cambodia (OHCHR, 2014) notes that

> Too often, court cases submitted by families contesting ownership of land with wealthy business owners are denied their day in court, whereas those filed by the company against the villagers have been diligently pro-cessed and resulted in numerous convictions.

It has been reported that, because of corruption or due to fear of retaliation, judges side with companies, dismiss cases on jurisdictional grounds, or use legal tactics to delay proceedings indefinitely (Golay et al., 2014). That retalia-tion in LSLA contexts is a serious concern is evidenced by the high number of land rights activists and journalists who have been prosecuted (ADHOC, 2011), and the repercussions, including 'raw remarks descending to the personal level', which the Special Rapporteur on Cambodia (2013) was faced with in the aftermath of his reports. The consequence of such practice is that corruption and fear of retaliation has led to a generalised mistrust of the justice system among the population (Golay et al., 2014). It becomes evident that effective and accessible remedies and affordable and prompt enforcement—as stipu-lated by the Voluntary Guidelines on Land Tenure, for instance—remain ele-ments that exist solely on paper for a high number of Cambodians.

Lastly, it should be noted that the obligation to identify vulnerable groups and the promotion and implementation of policies targeting the realisation of their rights is echoed by Article 61 of the Constitution of Cambodia (Kingdom of Cambodia, 2010), which stipulates that

> The State shall promote economic development in all fields, especially in agriculture, handicraft, industry, to begin with the remotest areas, with concern for water policy, electricity, roads and means of transportation, modern techniques and credit system.

A report of the then Special Representative of the Secretary-General for human rights in Cambodia (2007) states that 'a large number of economic land concessions have been granted in favor of foreign business interests and prominent Cambodian political and business figures'. Importantly, the report underlined that the benefits for rural communities were not evident and that not even the purported positive effects on state revenue stemming from these concessions were apparent (Special Representative on Cambodia, 2007). In a similar vein, the current UN Special Rapporteur on Cambodia (2012) noted more recently: '[T]hroughout my analysis, I struggled to fully comprehend the benefits of many land concessions that the Government has granted. In general, it is not clear to what extent the people of Cambodia have actually benefited from land concessions'. Here again, the gap between law and practice remains glaringly wide.

4   LSLA-Affected Communities and Human Rights Vernacularization: Two Case Studies from Rural and Urban Cambodia

National and international NGOs including the Cambodian Human Rights and Development Association (ADHOC), the Cambodian Human Rights Portal, the Community Legal Education Center (CLEC), the Cambodian League for the Promotion and Defense of Human Rights (LICADHO), the Cambodian NGO Forum, Amnesty International, Bridges Across Borders Cambodia (BABC), and the Centre on Housing Rights and Evictions (COHRE) have put forward a human rights framework in their advocacy efforts and strategic litigation campaigns against 'land grabbing' in Cambodia. Against such a background, the authors' engagement with communities affected by LSLA-related forced evictions in one urban and one rural area in Cambodia was concerned with how these communities made sense of their experiences, which—according to international law—may be classified as human rights violations. Did 'human rights' become their language in enunciating their situation? In what ways did they rely on human rights ideas and law, if at all? How did particular cultural, historical, and social contexts and spatiality play out in the use of human rights ideas and law?

4.1   *The Relevance of the Cambodian Rural-Urban Divide in Human Rights Vernacularization*
Our analysis of social mobilisation in LSLA contexts in rural and urban settings draws on scholarship on cultural circulation and translation. Numerous authors have become preoccupied with the dissemination of human rights

ideas; among them Margaret Keck and Kathryn Sikkink (1998), and Sanjeev Khagram et al. (2002), who scrutinise the role of transnational advocacy networks and the process of institutionalisation. In their works, Sally Merry and Peggy Levitt introduce the term 'vernacularization' to describe the process of appropriation and local adaptation of human rights ideas (Merry, 2006; Merry et al., 2010; Merry and Levitt, 2011). They contribute to the classic rights-culture and universalism-relativism debates by looking at these as a continuum, instead of a binary opposition. In their account, universal ideas and cultures are negotiated and adapted by the 'brokers'[9] in a certain cultural setting.

Other scholars, while noting that social behaviour is context specific, have studied the mutual incubation processes between space and society (Leitner et al., 2008). Their argument is that an analysis of social processes needs to include an examination of multiple spatialities. John Allen suggests that space and spatiality are essential to our understanding of power (Allen, 2003). At the same time, places and spaces are deemed to be products of political contestations over access, control, and participation (Tonkiss, 2005). As such, actors including local communities and brokers are embedded in spaces; spaces are constructed by a power constellation that is socially and historically specific; and spaces constrain as well as enable certain types of social activism and behaviours, including the vernacularization of human rights ideas and claims based on such ideas.

Our working hypothesis is that, in the case of Cambodia, victims of LSLA-related human rights violations in rural areas articulate their grievances differently than those in urban areas, despite what might appear to be a shared cultural and historical background. We postulate that it is these different spaces that shape, in a distinct way, the rural and urban communities' narratives and strategies of response to LSLAs, including their vernacularization of human rights.

Before proceeding to the case studies, it is important to provide an insight into the construction of the rural-urban divide in Cambodia. In our interviews, we could grasp that the division between rural and urban is always present especially in the way our interviewees labelled themselves as either *neak chamkar* ('farmland people') or *neak krong* ('city people'). This sense of division has been engrained in Cambodian society at least since the beginning of French colonialism. During that period, cities located in the strategic areas around the Mekong River, and in particular Phnom Penh, were given priority

---

9 'Brokers' move between local, national, regional, and global contexts and meaning systems; they take, negotiate, translate, and adapt ideas that apply in a certain locality to be transplanted into another (Merry, 2006).

in terms of development and 'modernisation'; beyond geographic rationality, at stake was the stigmatisation of farmers from rural areas as 'poor', 'lazy', and 'easily contented' (Derks, 2008, 31). During the Vietnam War, the United States military expanded their air campaigns to the rural areas of Cambodia to target Vietnamese communist troops installed there, destroying multiple villages and creating further rural impoverishment (Osborne, 2008). During the Khmer Rouge regime, inhabitants of cities were forcibly displaced to rural areas in order to boost agricultural production—millions died in the collectivisation processes in rural areas (McIntyre, 1996). After this series of wars, the rural-urban dichotomy continued to exist and exert its effects, not least as a consequence of the massive socio-economic reconstruction of Phnom Penh. In addition to the income gap between city and farmland people, discrepancies can be found in relation to access to information and public facilities, including electricity, infrastructure, education, housing and health care. For instance, the main channel for accessing news in rural areas is battery-driven radio, for which broadcast content remains very much controlled by the government; main roads in rural areas are mostly gravel and can only be used during dry weather.

This socio-historical lens allows us to understand that a number of constructed factors are at stake, which may contribute to different types of social mobilisation in rural and urban areas. That the two worlds are a construction is further evidenced by the fact that many of those who had been forcibly moved during the Khmer Rouge period, subsequently moved once again in order to start a new life (Heuveline, 1998). At that time, rural-urban conceptions were hardly a matter for consideration. Today, larger cities like Phnom Penh are expanding with the birth of peri-urban areas, whereby national roads are built to connect cities to remote areas—development that ultimately provides more avenues for rural-urban interaction (Derks, 2008). Despite the porous boundary, and duly acknowledging that the divide between rural and urban Cambodia is constructed, one cannot neglect that there are indeed discrepancies between the two types of areas when it comes to resources and access to information, in particular.

4.2   Bonteay Rongeang, Sein Serrey Village

In 2008, Tan Bien, one of the main Vietnamese rubber companies, was granted an ELC comprising 8,100 ha in the area covering the Bonteay Rongeang settlements. Information provided to the affected community concerning the ELC was limited to the setting up of wooden noticeboards (although authorities would have been aware that the literacy rate is generally low in rural areas) and the reading, on several occasions by district officers of official letters (individuals who lived far from the village would have been unable to attend).

Our data clarify that there were no consultation campaigns, nor was any express consent for the relocation and the ELC itself sought. Based on the interviews undertaken with individuals from the affected community, we can conclude that the type of information and means of dissemination were inadequate; authorities did not provide the villagers with an accurate understanding of how their livelihoods would be impacted upon by the ELC, or inform them about available avenues to contest the project. In our view, the lack of adequate information partially explains why the community did not seek to organise in order to oppose the ELC.

Later that year, several villagers' houses were bulldozed and the land was turned over to the company. The villagers' first organised efforts came in response to the evictions and the destruction of their houses, and took the form of setting ablaze bulldozers and heavy equipment owned by the company. Seven villagers were subsequently arrested by the local authorities (Sarat,[10] personal communication, 2013).

ADHOC was reportedly the only NGO involved in the advocacy efforts related to this case. Its involvement changed the dynamic of the social activism to a certain extent: it provided the community with direct assistance and consultation, as well as with a channel for conveying the villagers' concerns by the initiation of a three-party negotiation process. As a result, the aforementioned nebulous actions conducted by dispersed villagers and some of their representatives were replaced by coordinated mediation between the villagers, Tan Bien, and local authorities. The subsequent negotiations resulted in the release of the arrested individuals and a commitment from the central government to grant compensation in the form of residential land (40×20m) and cultivatable land (1–2 ha) for all evicted households. Nevertheless, most of the villagers refused to relocate from Bonteay Rongeang as they had invested a comparatively large amount of capital in growing their crops.

In late 2009, the Government of Cambodia mobilised a military battalion to evict individuals—the military, reportedly, exhibited a very aggressive and threatening attitude towards the villagers. One interviewee recalled that 'No one dared to refuse [to leave], they were holding electric tasers. They would electrocute anyone who stood up [to their instructions]'. As a consequence, 673 families were forcibly relocated to a new village, Phum Thmay,[11] carrying with them whatever belongings they could gather and leaving most of their

---

10   ADHOC Coordinator for Kampong Thom.

11   The literal translation of this name is 'the new village'. Phum Thmay was considered too large to accommodate a population of more than 700 families and, in 2011, was divided into two villages, Serrey Monkul and Sein Serrey.

possessions behind. Whilst they were granted the 40x20m of residential land per household, contrary to the negotiated agreement, compensation in cultivatable land was never provided. Living conditions upon arrival in their new village further illustrate the inadequacy of the compensation package. Although roads around and inside the village had been built, no housing was available for the newly arrived villagers. Upon reaching their respective residential plots, they had to clear the area in order to build their houses. No assistance was provided by the authorities; during the first months of their relocation, the villagers were forced to live in tents.

When asked about their response to the breached compensation agreement, most interviewees said that they did not know who was responsible for overseeing the process. They also concluded that their lack of legal know-how and the absence of a recognised ombudsperson presented a serious constraint to their ability to formulate and make their grievances known, specifically in the case of filing legal complaints with the authorities. A former representative of the community, belonging to the opposition party, explained that he independently prepared a petition demanding that the cultivatable land promised be provided—more than six hundred villagers from Phum Thmay had signed it. At the time of the interview, he had not submitted the petition and expressed uncertainty as to the appropriate addressee. The interviewees expressed their view that without advocacy and legal assistance from NGOs (they specifically mentioned ADHOC) their petition would remain largely ineffective.

It appears that the villagers interviewed felt a strong sense of disappointment towards the injustice they were experiencing. Yet this was rarely articulated in terms of injustice per se, rather they used the language of failed economic development. For example, they emphasised that their landlessness that resulted from their eviction due to the ELC had further impoverished them instead of providing them with more economic opportunities. It must be noted that the terms 'human rights' and 'human rights violations' were not used to describe either their eviction, or the general situation they experienced as a result of the ELC.

Some preliminary conclusion can be drawn. First, the failure of the authorities to provide villagers with adequate information relating to the ELC (including what the concession entailed and how it could be contested) increased the vulnerability of the Bonteay Rongeang community; it prevented them from organising and considering alternatives. Once confronted with the evictions, forward-looking planning was not at the heart of their actions; rather, their activism took a spontaneous and reactionary form. In our view, the burning of the company's heavy machines was fuelled by shock, anger, and a desire to maintain their homes and possessions 'on the day'—the outburst was not part of a strategy intended to lead to a long-term resolution of the dispute through violence. Similarly, the petition that they started remains, so far, unused due the lack of a concrete plan about what to do with it. Although there is a sense among the community that an injustice has been done, this has not been articulated in human rights terms, nor has recourse to courts been envisaged as a possibility of securing domestic rights. Vernacularization of rights is limited in this case, yet not inexistent as is reflected by the collaboration with a human rights NGO (ADHOC) and the shared opinion that the latter's ongoing support would be essential for the resolution of the villagers' dispute. Second, the relevance of space should be noted. The movement was concentrated and isolated in the sense that the actors involved are local authorities and villagers, and their concerns were rarely heard outside the disputed area.

4.3   Boeung Kak Lake, Phnom Penh

In 2007, the Municipality of Phnom Penh announced that it had entered a 99-year lease agreement with a private developer, Shukaku Ltd[12] covering a 133 ha area including the Boeng Kak Lake. The lake, once well known as an affordable touristic destination, is one of the largest urban wetlands in Phnom Penh, and a source of the city's aquatic life (Cultivate Understanding Multimedia, 2012). The plan of the municipality envisages the transformation of the area into 'pleasant, trade, and service places for domestic and international tourist [sic]' (Phnom Penh Government, 2011). According to the UN Special Rapporteur on Cambodia (2012), the project has affected over 4,000 families, 'most of whom were forcibly evicted, relocated involuntarily, or who accepted sub-standard compensation under duress'.

In an effort to challenge the evictions and the ELC itself, the residents of Boeung Kak organised themselves and pursued multiple strategies. Shortly after the company started developing the project, the residents sought legal counsel and submitted complaints to Cambodian courts demanding the discontinuation of the development (Channyda, 2008). As their legal motions were rejected, in February 2011 they petitioned a number of relevant governmental authorities and presented an alternative proposal for in situ resettlement and onsite housing on 12 per cent of the leased area (BABC, 2010).

---

12   In 2010, Erdos Hong Jun Investment Co., Ltd, a Chinese firm, formed a joint venture company with Shukaku, and the Boeng Kak Lake lease agreement was re-registered under the name of the joint venture, Shukaku Erdos Hong Jun Property Development Co., Ltd (BABC, 2012).

With the support of a coalition of NGOs—The Housing Task Force—they requested the concessioner company to endorse their alternative proposal as part of the company's corporate social responsibility (CSR) policy. While these efforts were unsuccessful, it is notable that the community shifted its strategy from litigation to advocacy, including by attempting to capitalise on business practices such as CSR.

The Boeung Kak residents further diversified their advocacy through protests timed to coincide with the visits of UN and foreign dignitaries, by expressly articulating their grievances as human rights violations, by drawing on cooperation and support from local and international NGOs, and by petitioning international complaint mechanisms.

The urban dwellers' protests organised on the occasion of the UN Secretary General's visit to Cambodia in 2010 were met with violent attacks by police forces, and by arrests—a number of press releases from local and international NGOs served to further internationalise the grievances of the Boeung Kak community (House and Billo, 2011; BABC, 2010; LICADHO, 2009). In 2012, during the visit to Cambodia, for the East Asia Summit, of US President Barack Obama and Secretary of State Hillary Clinton, dwellers of Boeung Kak organised an 'Obama Save Our Souls (SOS)' march through the city of Phnom Penh, particularly taking in eviction sites. They demanded that the US dignitaries increase political pressure on the Government of Cambodia to respect human rights and stop forced evictions. It should be noted that women representatives of the Boeung Kak Lake community have been at the forefront of these and other demonstrations. Reportedly, there was an assumption that protests led by women were less likely to be targeted by police forces—however, violence against women and arbitrary arrests have multiplied (UN Special Rapporteur on Cambodia, 2012). In March 2012, women 'bared their breasts publicly, ostensibly to avoid apprehension by the police, demonstrating unprecedented desperation' (UN Special Rapporteur on Cambodia, 2012).

In comparative perspective, we recognise that it would be difficult for rural communities, such as Bonteay Rongeang village, to organise protests that target specific international actors during their visits to Cambodia. The city dwellers were undeniably 'advantaged' by physical proximity to different locations where international meetings and visits took place and to the offices of national and international NGOs, and by better access to information in general. The ease, due to such proximity, of collaborating with human rights advocates should also be emphasised.

The level of sophistication of the toolbox of strategies that the Boeung Kak community employed is attested by their petitioning of the World Bank

Inspection Panel.[13] Represented by the Geneva-based NGO the Centre on Housing Rights and Evictions (COHRE), the former residents of Beoung Kak Lake requested that the Inspection Panel review the land management and administration project (LMAP), alleging that the design and the implementation of the project 'denied urban poor and other vulnerable households protection against widespread tenure insecurity' and increased forced evictions in Cambodia (COHRE, 2009). The World Bank and other donors financed the LMAP with the aim of assisting Cambodia in the issuance and registration of land titles and the implementation of a land administration system (Inspection Panel, 2010). When the Boeung Kak Lake area was adjudicated in the LMAP scheme in January 2007, despite their legitimate claims under the 2001 Land Law residents were denied titles (COHRE, 2009). The Inspection Panel found evidence in favour of the petitioners' claim that the World Bank's failure to properly design and supervise the LMAP had ultimately led to their forced eviction and involuntary resettlement (Inspection Panel, 2010; Special Rapporteur on Cambodia, 2012). It ceased the related loans to Cambodia after December 2010.

Another recipient of petitions from the former residents of Boeung Kak is the Special Rapporteur on Cambodia. The Rapporteur submitted to the Cambodian government a number of communications concerning the case, visited the area while on mission to Cambodia, and reported regularly on the human rights violations that these individuals had experienced, thereby maintaining international pressure and demanding a resolution of the dispute (OHCHR, 2012; Special Rapporteur on Cambodia, 2012; 2013). The dispute found a partial resolution when, in August 2011, a sub-decree was issued to adjust the size of the Boeung Kak Lake Development, providing title to communities living on a 12.44 hectare stretch of land. In the words of the Special Rapporteur (2012) 'a positive development in this long-standing dispute. Nevertheless, this was not as inclusive as it should have been, and some families were subsequently evicted and continue to protest the eviction and relocation.'

Two aspects should be noted at this stage. First, the aim of the Boeung Kak Lake movement goes beyond maintaining the status quo (defending dwellers' houses at the time the eviction took place). The intention appears to be to effect long-term social change by generating social awareness and political pressure on the government. Second, spatiality played a central role in the case

---

13   The Inspection Panel is an independent complaints mechanism that is open to petitions from individuals and communities that have been adversely affected by a World Bank-funded project.

of the urban dwellers. Unlike the movement in Sein Serrey, the efforts of the urban dwellers are not limited by and localised in the commune or municipality. They are supported by national and transnational networks and target an international audience. A wide array of actors were supportive of the movement—local attorneys and NGOs that joined forces under the banner of The Housing Task Force, international NGOs, and other types of non-resident human rights activists—exposing the Boeung Kak Lake story (including via media outlets) to a worldwide audience. As they had access to factual and legal information relevant to their cause, the urban dwellers were able to use their advocacy efforts to strategically target foreign governments, financial institutions, and high-level UN officials. The language of human rights in which they chose to express most of their grievances and the appeals to courts and international human rights mechanisms may have 'come easier' to the Boeung Kak community (compared to the villagers) for reasons of space (proximity to and support from human rights groups, physical proximity to courts). Beyond the adoption of human rights ideas and the utilisation of specific mechanisms, a process of adaptation is at stake: a vernacularization, in so far as the successful appeal to the World Bank's Inspection Panel (a non-traditional human rights mechanism) is concerned.

5   Conclusion

This chapter has established that a human rights framework entailing substantive aspects (the requirement to respect, protect, and fulfil human rights), and procedural safeguards (transparency and participation, accountability and redress) carries legally binding force for Cambodia. Not least in situations regarding land transactions. Notably, much of the domestic legislation regarding land, and even the decree on ELCs, mirror these human rights standards. It is the implementation of these laws, the actual practice, that gives rise to what one close observer calls 'chronic disputes' in LSLA contexts (Special Rapporteur on Cambodia, 2012). Our findings suggest that this deficient governmental practice, in particular in the areas of information, consultation, and access to justice, to a certain extent incapacitated the vernacularization of human rights ideas in the studied rural setting; it did, in a sense, and without aiming at extrapolation, reinforce the (constructed) division between the rural and the urban space. Contrary to the affected community in Sein Serrey village, the urban dwellers of Boeung Kak Lake have made extensive use of human rights language and mechanisms to challenge their forced evictions and have achieved a certain success. In joining a small category of other communities from elsewhere in the world they have pursued non-traditional avenues for adjudication of human rights—as such their contribution may have a wider significance for human rights compliance and for mechanisms that are able to induce such compliance. Spatiality, it should be recognised, played a major role: the proximity to information and a network of 'brokers', including national and international NGOs, have enabled Boeung Kak Lake dwellers to advocate and claim their rights.

Appraising the findings of our research, we can conclude that in Cambodia, in the context of LSLAs, human rights law and practice meet halfway. On the one hand, we have solid domestic legislation, backed by a moratorium on ELCs. And while our two case studies do not permit generalisation, they do speak for a certain activism of affected communities and the solidarity of civil society organisations. One the other hand, however, we have major shortcomings in the implementation of the said legislation and the reality of a moratorium, which by definition is temporary and reversible.

References

ADHOC (Cambodian Human Rights and Development Association) (2013) *Turning Point? Land, Housing and Natural Resources Rights in Cambodia in 2012* (Phnom Penh: ADHOC), http://www.nachdenkseiten.de/upload/pdf/ADHOC-A_Turning_Point_Land_Housing_NRM_2012.pdf (accessed on 16 March 2015).

———— (2011) *The Report of Land and Housing Rights* (Phnom Penh: ADHOC), http://www.adhoc-cambodia.org/wp-content/uploads/2012/05/ADHOC-Report-on-Land-and-Housing-Rights-in-2011-English-version.pdf (accessed on 16 March 2015).

Allen, J. (2003) *Lost Geographies of Power* (New York: Wiley).

Amnesty International (2012) *Amnesty International Annual Report 2012, Cambodia* (London: Amnesty International), http://www.unhcr.org/refworld/docid/4fbe394a5f.html (accessed on 24 May 2012).

———— (2009) *Cambodia*, Briefing for the UN Committee on Economic Social and Cultural Rights (London: Amnesty International), http://www2.ohchr.org/english/bodies/cescr/docs/info-ngos/AI_Briefing_Cambodia_42.doc (accessed on 16 March 2015).

———— (2001) *Cambodia Urged to Drop Charges against Boeung Kak Lake Activists*, press release, http://www.amnesty.org/en/news/cambodia-urged-drop-charges-against-boeung-kak-lake-activists-2011-11-29 (accessed on 12 June 2014).

An-Na'im, A.A. (1990) 'Problems of Universal Cultural Legitimacy for Human Rights', in An-Na'im, A.A. and F.M. Deng (eds.) *Human Rights in Africa: Cross-cultural Perspectives* (Washington DC: Brookings Institution Press), pp. 331–367.

Arezki, R., K. Deininger and H. Selod (2012) 'The Global Land Rush' *Finance and Development*, March, pp. 46–49, http://www.imf.org/external/pubs/ft/fandd/2012/03/arezki.htm (accessed on 16 March 2015).

BABC (Bridges across Borders Cambodia) (2012) *Flooded Homes: Threat of Health Hazards Used to Evict Boeung Kok Residents*, press release, http://babcambodia.org/newsarchives/Threat%20of%20Health%20Hazards%20Used%20to%20Evict%20Boeung%20Kok.html (accessed on 23 May 2012).

——— (2010) *A Year in Review* (Phnom Penh: BABC), http://www.aisolution.biz/babc/Review2010.pdf (accessed on 23 May 2012).

Baxter, W. (2010) 'Boeung Kak Residents Appeal to UN for Help', *The Phnom Penh Post*, 22 October, http://www.phnompenhpost.com/national/boeung-kak-residents-appeal-un-help (accessed on 20 December 2013).

Borras Jr., S.M., R. Hall, I. Scoones, B. White and W. Wolford (2011) 'Towards a Better Understanding of Global Land Grabbing: an Editorial Introduction', *The Journal of Peasant Studies* 38(2), pp. 209–216, DOI: 10.1080/03066150.2011.559005.

CEDAW (Committee on the Elimination of Discrimination against Women) (2006) *Concluding Comments of the Committee on the Elimination of Discrimination against Women: Cambodia*, UN doc. CEDAW/C/KHM/CO/3, 25 January.

CESCR (Committee on Economic, Social and Cultural Rights) (2009) *Concluding Observations of the Committee on the Economic, Social and Cultural Rights: Cambodia*, UN doc. E/C.12/KHM/CO/1,12 June.

Chandler, D. (2007) *A History of Cambodia*, 4th ed. (Boulder: Westview Press).

Channyda, C. (2008) 'Boeung Kak Lake Residents Take Case to Supreme Court', *The Phnom Penh Post*, 29 December, http://www.phnompenhpost.com/national/boeung-kak-lake-residents-take-case-supreme-court (accessed on 20 December 2013).

Chayes, A. and A.H. Chayes (1995) *The New Sovereignty: Compliance with International Regulatory Agreements* (Cambridge, MA: Harvard University Press).

Cismas, I. (2013) *Legal Analysis of International Instruments Applicable to Large-Scale Land Acquisitions And Their Transposition In Domestic Law*, Working draft, SNIS project on 'Large-Scale Land Acquisitions in Southeast Asia: Rural Transformations between Global Agendas and Peoples' Right to Food', 9 February (on file with the authors).

COHRE (Centre on Housing Rights and Evictions) (2009) *Cambodia: COHRE Supports Communities in World Bank Inspection Panel Case*, press release, formerly available at http://www.cohre.org/news/press-releases/cambodia-cohre-supports-communities-in-world-bank-inspection-panel-case (accessed on 20 May 2013).

Cotula, L., S. Vermeulen, R. Leonard and J. Keeley (2009) *Land Grab or Development Opportunity? Agricultural Investment and International Land Deals in Africa* (London and Rome: IIED–FAO–IFAD).

CRC (Committee on the Rights of the Child) (2011) *Concluding Observations: Cambodia*, UN doc. CRC/C/KHM/CO/2, 20 June.

Cultivate Understanding Multimedia, and Digital Conservation Facility (2012) *The Reclamation and Development of Boeung Kak Lake in Phnom Penh*, http://www.cseas.niu.edu/cseas/conferences/cambodiaconf2012/boeung_kak_poster_std.pdf, (accessed on 16 March 2015).

De Schutter, O. (2011) 'How not to Think of Land-Grabbing: Three Critiques of Large-Scale Investments in Farmland', *Journal of Peasant Studies*, 38(2), pp. 249–279, DOI: 10.1080/03066150.2011.559008.

Derks, A. (2008) *Khmer Women on the Move: Exploring Work and Life in Urban Cambodia* (Honolulu: University of Hawaii Press).

FIDH (International Federation for Human Rights) (2012) 'Cambodia: A Mounting Human Rights Crisis,' *FIDH Briefing Notes*, https://www.fidh.org/IMG/pdf/fidh_briefing_note_-_cambodia_20.09.2012_final-2.pdf (accessed on 20 December 2013)

Franck, T.M. (1995) *Fairness in International Law and Institutions* (Oxford: Clarendon Press).

Gironde C., C. Golay and P. Messerli (2011) *Large Scale Land Acquisitions in Southeast Asia: Rural Transformations between Global Agendas and Peoples' Right to Food*, project proposal submitted to the Swiss Network for International Studies, http://www.snis.ch/project_large-scale-land-acquisitions-southeast-asia-rural-transformations-between-global-agendas (accessed on 16 March 2015).

Goodman, R. and D. Jinks (2013) *Socializing States: Promoting Human Rights Through International Law* (Oxford: Oxford University Press).

Golay, C. (2011) *Droit à l'alimentation et accès à la justice* (Bruxelles: Bruylant).

Golay, C. and I. Biglino (2013) 'Human Rights Responses to Land Grabbing: A Right to Food Perspective', *Third World Quarterly*, 34(9), pp. 1630–1650, DOI: 10.1080/01436597.2013.843853.

Golay, C. with contributions by I. Biglino and I. Cismas (2014) 'Large-Scale Land Acquisitions and Human Rights', in Gironde, C., Golay C., Messerli P., Peeters A. and Schönweger O., *Large-Scale Land Acquisitions in Southeast Asia: Rural Transformations between Global Agendas and Peoples*, Working Paper (Geneva: Swiss Network for International Studies), http://www.snis.ch/system/files/gironde_working_paper_lsla_southeast_asia_17.08.2014_0.pdf (accessed on 28 May 2015).

Heuveline, P. (1998) ' "Between One and Three Million": Towards the Demographic Reconstruction of a Decade of Cambodian History (1970–79)', *Population Studies*, 52(1), pp. 49–65, DOI: 10.1080/0032472031000150176.

House, S. and A. Billo (2011) *Cambodia's Land Reform and Boeung Kak Lake: Institutions, Politics, and Development*, Lee Kuan Yew School of Public Policy Case Study, http://lkyspp.nus.edu.sg/wp-content/uploads/2013/07/LKYSPPCaseStudy11-01_Cambodia_Land_Reform-Beoung_Kak_Lake.pdf (accessed on 20 December 2013).

Inspection Panel (2010) *Cambodia: Land Management and Administration Project* (*Credit No. 3650–KH*), report n. 58016, 23 November (Washington, D.C.: World Bank), http://www-wds.worldbank.org/external/default/WDSContentServer/WDSP/IB/ 2010/12/01/000334955_20101201025955/Rendered/PDF/580160INVR0INS1se00only191 0BOX353791.pdf (accessed on 20 December 2013).

IRIN (2013) 'Analysis: Why Land Rights Matter in Cambodia', *Irinnews*, 15 March, http://www.irinnews.org/report/97654/analysis-cambodian-land-rights-in-focus (accessed on 4 August 2014).

Kachika, T. (2010) *Land Grabbing in Africa: A Review of the Impacts and the Possible Policy Responses* (Oxford: Oxfam International), http://www.oxfamblogs.org/ eastafrica/wp-content/uploads/2010/11/Land-Grabbing-in-Africa.-Final.pdf (accessed on 16 March 2015).

Keck, M.E. and K. Sikkink (1998) *Activists beyond Borders: Advocacy Networks in International Politics* (Ithaca, N.Y.: Cornell University Press).

Khagram, S., J.V. Riker and K. Sikkink (2002) *Restructuring World Politics: Transnational Social Movements, Networks, and Norms* (Minneapolis: University of Minnesota Press).

Kingdom of Cambodia (2010[1993]) *Constitution of the Kingdom of Cambodia*, unofficial translation supervised by the Constitutional Council in March 2010, http:// www.ccc.gov.kh/english/CONSTITUTIONEng.pdf (accessed on 1 August 2014).

Leitner, H., E. Sheppard and K.M. Sziarto. (2008) 'The Spatialities of Contentious Politics', *Transactions of the Institute of British Geographers*, 33(2), pp. 157–72, DOI: 10.1111/j.1475–5661.2008.00293.x.

Levitt, P. and S. Merry (2009) 'Vernacularization on the Ground: Local Uses of Global Women's Rights in Peru, China, India and the United States', *Global Networks*, 9(4), pp. 441–461, DOI: 10.1111/j.1471–0374.2009.00263.x.

LICADHO (Cambodian League for the Defense of Human Rights) (2012) *Five Shooting Incidents at Land Dispute Protests in the Past Two Months Show Alarming Increase in Use of Lethal Force*, press release, http://www.licadho-cambodia.org/pressrelease. php?perm=269 (accesssed on 16 March 2015).

——— (2009) *Land Grabbing and Poverty in Cambodia: The Myth of Development* (Phnom Penh: LICADHO), http://www.licadho-cambodia.org/reports/files/134LIC ADHOREportMythofDevelopment2009Eng.pdf (accessed on 21 May 2012).

Marks, S.R. and A. Clapham (2005) *International Human Rights Lexicon* (Oxford: Oxford University Press).

McIntyre, K. (1996) 'Geography as Destiny: Cities, Villages and Khmer Rouge Orientalism', *Comparative Studies in Society and History*, 38(4), pp. 730–758, DOI: 10.1017/S001041750002051X.

Merry, S.E. (2009) *Human Rights and Gender Violence: Translating International Law into Local Justice* (Chicago: University of Chicago Press).

——— (2006) 'Transnational Human Rights and Local Activism: Mapping the Middle', *American Anthropologist*, 108(1), pp. 38–51, DOI: 10.1525/aa.2006.108.1.38.

Merry, S.E. and P. Levitt (2011) 'Making Women's Human Rights in the Vernacular: Navigating the Culture/Rights Divide' in Hodgson, D. (ed.) *Gender and Culture at the Limit of Rights* (Philadelphia: University of Pennsylvania Press), pp. 81–100.

Merry, S.E., P. Levitt, M.Ş. Rosen and D.H. Yoon (2010) 'Law From Below: Women's Human Rights and Social Movements in New York City', *Law & Society Review*, 44(1), pp. 101–128, DOI: 10.1111/j.1540–5893.2010.00397.x.

Moyo, S. and W. Chambati (eds.) (2013) *Land and Agrarian Reform in Zimbabwe: Beyond White-settler Capitalism* (Harare and Dakar: African Institute for Agrarian Studies–Codesria).

OHCHR (Office of the High Commissioner for Human Rights) (2014) *Development for Cambodia, but not at Any Price—UN Expert Calls For Oversight and Remedy on Land Concessions*, press release, http://www.ohchr.org/EN/NewsEvents/Pages/DisplayNews.aspx?NewsID=14845&LangID=E (accessed on 16 March 2015).

——— (2012) *Cambodia: "Human Rights Need to Be at the Heart of Land Concessions for Positive Impact"—UN Special Rapporteur*, press release, http://www.ohchr.org/en/NewsEvents/Pages/DisplayNews.aspx?NewsID=12147&LangID=E (accessed on 16 March 2015).

Osborne, M.E. (2008) *Phnom Penh: A Cultural and Literary History* (Oxford: Signal Books).

Peluso Lee, N. and C. Lund (2011) 'New Frontiers of Land Control: Introduction', *The Journal of Peasant Studies*, 38(4), pp. 667–681, DOI: 10.1080/03066150.2011.607692.

Phnom Penh Government (2011) *Lake Development Construction Officially Started*, press release, http://www.phnompenh.gov.kh/news-lake-development-construction-officially-started-1452.html (accessed on 2 August 2014).

RGC (Royal Government of Cambodia) (2005a) Sub-Decree on Economic Land Concession, No. 146 ANK/BK, 27 December, Phnom Penh, http://www.cambodia investment.gov.kh/sub-decree-146-on-economic-land-concessions_051227.html (accessed on 16 March 2015).

——— (2005b) Sub-Decree on State Land Management, No. 118 HNK/BC, 7 October, Phnom Penh, http://aglawfirm.asia/pdf/Intellectual/Social%20Land%20Concession/Sub-decree-on-State-Land-Management-E.pdf (accessed on 16 March 2015).

——— (2001) Land Law, No. NS/RKM/0801/14, 30 August, Phnom Penh.

Sar, S. (2010) *Land Reform in Cambodia*, paper presented at the International Federation of Surveyors Congress 2010, http://www.fig.net/pub/fig2010/papers/ts07j%5Cts07j_sovann_4633.pdf (accessed on 12 June 2014).

Sithan, P. (2012) *Land Conflict and Conflict Resolution through Cadastral Commission*, unpublished paper, http://www.forum-urban-futures.net/activities/papers/land-conflict-and-conflict-resolution-through-cadastral-commission (accessed on 11 June 2012).

Special Rapporteur on Cambodia (2013) *Report of the Special Rapporteur on the Situation of Human Rights in Cambodia, Surya P. Subedi*, UN doc. A/HRC/24/36, 5 August.

———— (2012) *A Human Rights Analysis of Economic and Other Land Concessions in Cambodia*, Addendum to the report of the Special Rapporteur on the situation of human rights in Cambodia, Surya P. Subedi, UN doc. A/HRC/21/63/Add.1/Rev.1, 11 October.

Special Rapporteur on Extreme Poverty (2012) *Report of the Special Rapporteur on Extreme Poverty and Human Rights, Magdalena Sepulveda Carmona*, UN doc. A/67/278, 9 August.

Special Representative on Cambodia (Special Representative of the Secretary-General on the Situation of Human Rights in Cambodia) (2007) *Economic Land Concessions in Cambodia: A Human Rights Perspective* (Phnom Penh: Cambodia Office of the High Commissioner for Human Rights).

Tonkiss, F. (2005) *Space, the City and Social Theory: Social Relations and Urban Forms* (London: Polity).

Tyner, J.A. (2009) *War, Violence, and Population: Making the Body Count* (New York: Guilford Press).

USAID (United States Agency for International Development) (2012) 'Cambodia: Property Rights and Resource Governance', *USAID Land Tenure*, http://usaidlandtenure.net/sites/default/files/country-profiles/full-reports/USAID_Land_Tenure_Cambodia_Profile.pdf (accessed on 17 April 2015).

White, B., S.M. Jr. Borras, R. Hall, I. Scoones and W. Wolford (2012)'The New Enclosures: Critical Perspectives on Corporate Land Deals', *The Journal of Peasant Studies*, 39 (3–4), pp. 619–647, DOI: 10.1080/03066150.2012.691879.

Conclusion

∵

CHAPTER 11

Large-Scale Land Acquisitions, Livelihoods and Human Rights in South-East Asia

Christophe Gironde and Christophe Golay

The various contributions to this volume show, first, that previous episodes of land acquisitions are crucial to an understanding of why, where and how the current wave is occurring; of how they are implemented and turned, or not, into production units; and of how and to what extent they affect livelihoods. Second, beyond the usual emphasis on foreign companies, historical analysis also allows us to take stock of the key role played by nation states, which put in place regulatory frameworks and public policies or adopted a laissez-faire approach that paved the way for current land deals and acquisition practices around land and natural resources. Third, this volume highlights the importance of economic and political dynamics at local, national and subregional levels, which prove in South-East Asia to be as powerful as the global forces typically foregrounded in writings on 'land grabbing'. This is observable in the (land deal) negotiation stage, during the implementation of deals, and throughout the process of the transformation of the livelihoods that such deals induce in the medium term. A processual approach, as used by Nooteboom et al. (this volume), goes hand in hand with historical analysis. The diversity found in the implementation of land acquisitions shows that land deals are more often the beginning of a process of transformation to new livelihoods than the end of former ones.

Overall, large-scale land acquisitions are a significant challenge for affected populations, but their consequences vary greatly between localities and among social groups. Dispossession, exclusion, disruption, etc. are undeniable. Extreme cases in which populations lost all, were displaced, and had to rebuild from zero (Cismas and Paramita, this volume) do exist. In other cases, some populations are left with some time and space for resistance, adaptation, opportunism, etc. Everywhere the processes of land acquisitions and their consequences are highly contingent on the particular contexts in which they occur.

The authors are extremely grateful to the anonymous reviewer for the comments and suggestions provided to the draft of this chapter.

In terms of human rights analysis, the gap is huge between the abuses and violations of human rights perpetrated against local populations and the human rights instruments that have been developed for protecting them. Although instruments and mechanisms exist at the international and national levels, they do not provide substantial protection to affected populations, as there is not much implementation on the ground.

1   Recurrence and Expansion of Large-Scale Land Acquisitions

The current wave of large-scale land acquisitions has often been addressed as a phenomenon caused by the 2007–08 'F-F-F crisis' (Food, Fossil, Financial). The food price surge and export restrictions undeniably triggered a reaction from importing countries, who attempted to secure provision of food by engaging—among other activities—in land investment (McMichael, 2012; Akram-Lodhi, 2012). The rush for land can also certainly be ascribed to agrofuel production, as illustrated by the case of sugar cane in Indonesia and the Philippines (Nooteboom et al., this volume), and to the fact that land has become a valuable financial asset (Smaller and Mann, 2009). Yet this short-term perspective is not sufficient for an understanding of the current dynamics of large-scale land acquisitions and the agrarian transformation they contribute to shaping (Zoomers and Kaag, 2014).

An argument has been made for 'analysing land grabbing historically', since the acquisitions 'tend to occur in cycles' and because each new cycle is somewhat related to the previous ones (Edelman and Leon, 2013, 1697–8). Roudart and Mazoyer (this volume) recall that large public estates, back to ancient times and the Old Kingdom of Egypt, have always existed—within or outside national or imperial boundaries—and are not unique to capitalism. Some, like those of the Roman State, were created for the purpose of funding wars and feeding armies; others, as was the case for Spanish and Portuguese estates in the Americas, for mercantile interests; others still to seize the opportunities presented by industrial demand and international trade (from wool in the sixteenth century to 'tropical' commodities in the nineteenth century), or to fund rapid industrialisation as in the 1930s in the USSR.

The need to look back into history is particularly valid in South-East Asia, which experienced not only the European colonisations and the opening up of 'previously inaccessible tracts of land' in the second half of the nineteenth century (Hayami, 2001), but also major territorial expansions from the 1960s in Thailand and the Philippines, then in Malaysia, Indonesia, and—lastly—in Vietnam from the 1990s on (De Koninck, 2003). Although most of the sites studied in this volume have experienced booms related to new crops, the sites' expansion is related to the role these crops played in previous decades and even centuries, as best illustrated by the case of sugar cane, which has been core to the economies and the societies of the Philippines and Indonesia since the middle of the nineteenth century (Hayami, 2001; Maurer, 1986). Until the mid-2000s, the extent of rubber exploitation remained very limited in south-eastern Laos and north-eastern Cambodia (Baird, 2011; Fortunel, 2014) and the crop was almost unknown to local populations. Yet, the development of rubber that began around 2005 has its origins in the rubber sector set up across Indochina (except in Laos, where the attempt failed) by the French early in the twentieth century. Following approximately three decades of disuse due to the effects of war and inefficient post-independence state structures (Aso, 2014; Pham and De Koninck, 2014), it has been revived from the 1990s on, beginning in Vietnam. The current dynamics of land acquisitions and crop booms in Champasak (Laos) and Ratanakiri (Cambodia)—the former involving not only rubber but also coffee—are for a substantial part the result of the cross-border territorial expansion of Vietnam's Central Highlands production area, in which there is no more frontier to open. For South-East Asia, these temporal dynamics suggest that the wave of land acquisitions that dates—or became visible—from the mid-2000s is somewhat a continuation of the territorial expansion witnessed from the 1960s on.

2 The Crucial Role of the State

In the same vein as Roudart and Mazoyer, Keulertz and Woertz (this volume) recall that in previous centuries states adopted laws and policies in order to set up production and trade regimes that best served their interests. In the nineteenth century, the abolition of protectionist laws enabled the cheap import of food—often grown a great distance away—to feed the growing industrial-urban working class. After the Second World War, production subsidies made North America and Western Europe into net grain exporters and enabled them to reverse trade flows by disposing of their surpluses in developing countries while at the same time replacing imported raw materials with domestically produced industrial or synthetic commodities. These state interventions also included, in the first half of the twentieth century, the introduction of regulations—most using quotas and taxes—to control food production, similar to the regulatory approach to controlling rubber adopted in Malaysia and Indonesia; and—in the second half of the century—assistance to smallholders, mostly provided via support for the diffusion of high-yield crop varieties and better chemical inputs (Bissonnette and De Koninck, 2015). In some cases, these interventions benefited large estates; in other cases they supported the expansion of smallholders; in all cases, they were of crucial importance.

The current wave of land acquisitions was preceded by legislative changes that established a state monopoly on land management and created insecurity in land tenure for local populations. This trend can be traced back to the land-related laws imposed on European empires' colonies and, as Merlet (2010) argues, to some extent to those imposed by the Roman Empire. States gained control over the land and left populations unable to claim their rights, typically due to the fact that customary laws were not registered by colonial authorities and later were not recognised by the states arising from the process of decolonisation. In cases where peoples' land rights were recognised, forest and fallow lands were not taken into account. From Indonesia and Malaysia at the time of the Dutch and the British presence to Cambodia and Laos from the 1990s on, there are striking resemblances among the processes of non-recognition of customary laws and of land takeover by the state. Furthermore, since the 1980s, states have received the support of international organisations that shape global development governance in this field; the most influential being the World Bank, the Food and Agriculture Organization (FAO), the United Nations Conference for Trade and Development (UNCTAD) and the Asian Development Bank, as well as major actors such as the European Union (EU) (Borras and Franco, 2011). These organisations have followed the path of land titling described by De Schutter (this volume), starting with Thailand in the 1980s (Burns, 2004; Hutchinson, 2008, quoted in Fortunel and Gironde, 2011; Verhaegen, 2013). They have provided substantial funding, guarantee schemes, technical expertise, and powerful legitimacy to the current land dynamics described in this volume. These interventions occurred in parallel with others that contributed to local populations' resettlement, and which were also supported by the same organisations, with the fallacious rhetoric that they were supporting 'voluntary resettlement' (Baird and Shoemaker, 2007).

De Schutter (this volume) reveals how the main outcome of the formalisation of land rights has been the creation of markets for such rights. This process, through which land titles have become commodities, has not only benefited the well-off groups within rural communities, but also opened the door to outsiders, local and national elites, and foreign buyers. The protective aim of land titling sounds like a fallacy when considering that titling can have powerful exclusionary consequences for certain types of actors (Hall et al., 2011; Dwyer, 2015). This can be found in the Lao villages studied by Senties Portilla (Gironde and Senties Portilla, this volume), where the policy of temporary use certificates for farmland and degraded forest was poorly implemented and later facilitated concessions instead. Similarly, Dwyer et al. (this volume) analyse how measures for regularising smallholder entitlements in Cambodia contributed, instead, to legitimising and enabling land concessions.

The ground for large-scale land deals was thus prepared by land laws and public policies that made them legal, as illustrated by the 'zoning policies' of Indonesia and Laos, and the creation of special categories of land use and permits in Indonesia and Cambodia. This process is the continuation of the trend to eradicate customary land laws and regulations, such as the various *adat* in newly independent Indonesia and Malaysia, which took hold across South-East Asia in the 1990s (Cleary and Eaton, 1996). This 'preparation' also involves an attempt to make land concessions legitimate by persuading local communities that they would benefit from the promised development of infrastructure and markets and from job creation. But such process has gone even further than that, as it was achieved through the progressive delegitimisation of former land rights, of the community institutions that governed them, and of prior land use. Village and population displacements in Laos—also called 'village consolidation' in the case of the smallest settlements in Laos and Cambodia—and the ban on rotational cultivation in Laos made the communities targeted for large-scale concessions vulnerable. In Ratanakiri, the Khmerisation policy further challenged indigenous peoples' livelihoods, as it led to the arrival of in-migrants who were better endowed in terms of financial, human, and social capital. Despite the emergence of certain opportunities, such as selling land plots to newcomers or the availability of jobs clearing those newcomers' plantations, all this increased the 'sentiment of surviving in a new insecure social environment' (Bourdier, 2009). It also created such a pervasive confusion regarding whom the land belonged to that it ultimately made the newcomers more acceptable. Thus, the drawing up and signing of land deals, although it can occur in a very short span of time, is rather the ultimate step in a longer process whereby land rights (property or use; individual or collective) have been contested by governments, weakened by public policies and legislation, and challenged by newcomers—mostly migrants and merchants.

3   Specificities and Diversities of Land Acquisition Trajectories

Among the factors that are striking about current land grabs is their suddenness—that is to say, the fact that many land deals are quickly agreed and signed (Neef et al., 2013), and that populations can thus be immediately dispossessed of their resources, discovering that their lands and natural resources have been enclosed overnight. Concepts such as 'rush' and 'boom' contribute to building a view whereby land deals trigger the full deployment of exclusion processes and spell the end of pre-existing livelihoods. Yet the signing of a land deal is also (just) the beginning of the story, as shown by the case of investors who were 'materially behind schedule or operating below capacity' (Zhan et al., this volume) and initial plans that were substantially negotiated and adapted before and during their implementation (Nooteboom et al., this volume). Although the process of implementation appears to be more monolithic and closer to original plans in the cases of Laos and Cambodia, it varies significantly depending on the types of investors and the corresponding reactions of populations (Gironde and Senties Portilla, this volume). 'Timing' also proves to be important in the power relations between former land users and new rights holders (Dwyer et al., this volume).

In contrast to the commonly held view of unstoppable land acquisitions and mono-crop plantation landscapes as an inevitable process, one must take into account cases where land deals remained mere intentions and plans on paper, as occurred in the context of the 1997–98 Asian crisis where Thai investors pulled out (Baird, 2011) or in the case of China in Africa (Brautigam, 2013). Where land deals do result in production, one must take into account the time it takes for the signing of the deal to lead to the effective occupation of land and production beginning, which definitively exclude former or other users. The conclusion of land deals is sometimes only the beginning of the story, because they may be contested on the ground; because investors may decide not to implement their proclaimed plan; because a plan as it appears on paper may not be the real plan—as in cases reported from Cambodia where companies, once they had logged precious trees, withdrew; or because investors may not be able to mobilise the capital needed to turn land into production. Thus, acquisitions are not always synonymous with immediate occupation—or with plantation/cultivation—and former users may have time, and space not yet occupied, in which to respond.

Moreover, one must not neglect the fact that the cropping systems that are currently being developed by large land estates may not last. This has already occured, for example, in the case of rain forest lands that were transformed to accommodate systems that quickly proved unsustainable (Dufumier, 2006). Keulertz and Woertz (this volume) also draw attention to the volatility of 'rushes' and to eventual reversals, illustrated by the case of Gulf countries' investments, which faded in the 1980s and 1990s only to return in 2008. This is of relevance in a context of global markets marked by high-volatility cycles, and of particular relevance in South-East Asia where the 'implementation gap has been particularly pronounced' (Keulertz and Woertz, this volume). This resonates with the cases of Bener Meriah (Aceh), where all large-scale investors pulled out; of Luzon, where the company changed its plan from growing on its large plantation to short-term lease contracts (Nooteboom et al., this volume); and of Ratanakiri, where large Vietnamese and Chinese companies have not all had the physical capital (machines, seedlings) necessary to rapidly transform all the land they were leased into tree plantations (Gironde and Senties Portilla, this volume).

Conversely, the beginning of the story may lead on to expansion and acceleration. Existing land deals and crop booms may lead to further ones, in the same way that pioneer migrants are followed by many others. Again following Edelman and Leon (2013), who call for a 'history of the present', one must add to links over time links across territories. The dynamics of rubber plantation in Cambodia and Laos are the result not only of Vietnamese-held land concessions but also of Vietnamese traders, who buy most of the liquid rubber and export it to Vietnam. Their presence is the strongest marker of the profitability of rubber for investors, companies, entrepreneurs, small peasants, brokers, etc. Similar spillover can also be seen for cassava, and—very recently—for pepper at the border between Ratanakiri and Vietnam. Another category of actors that link territories is the native population of Kampong Cham—the century-old rubber area of Cambodia—who play a crucial role in the boom taking place at the new frontier to which they migrate. Sturgeon (2012) highlights similar territorial connections between northern Laos and China, as Lao farmers have been able to benefit from 'sharecropping arrangements with relatives' from China who 'extended their rubber holdings across the border'. Short distance connections are more obvious, but there are also longer distance connections such as for northern Thailand, where farmers have been able to develop their own rubber farms after having learned tapping techniques in the south of the country where they were salaried workers (Sturgeon, 2012). These connections are found on a broader scale: the dynamics of industrial crops—including sugar cane and rubber, as well as palm oil, cocoa, and coffee—have been intertwined for several decades in South-East Asia, as illustrated by the changes in the comparative advantage and market shares held by the various countries (De Koninck and Rousseau, 2012).

4   Large-Scale Land Acquisitions and Livelihoods

The debate on the negative and positive impacts of large-scale land acquisitions on local populations is still very much open (Edelman et al., 2013).

The realisation that large-scale land acquisitions can have negative consequences for local populations is not new. Roudart and Mazoyer (this volume)
recall that tensions and violence have not been the exception; rather they
have been systemic features of the development of the large-scale domains
that have been forcibly set up, as illustrated by the examples of enclosures
in eighteenth and nineteenth century Britain, European colonial appropriations, and collectivisation in the former USSR. Local populations have been
severely dispossessed, and not only of their land; they also lost autonomy as
they were enslaved or were left with no other option than to accept poorly
paid salaried work from the new landholders; they were displaced, confined to
restricted areas (reserves for Native Americans), and/or—in the case of 'colonies of settlement'—exterminated. The same authors also highlight the fact
that when 'pro-poor' land laws have been passed, they have met with strong
resistance from large landowning elites.

Zhan et al. (this volume) conclude that the impact of large-scale land
acquisitions in terms of employment and income, land rights, and the environment, is largely dependent on decisions taken by governments and investors. Consultation with populations, at the pre-investment and initial stages
of acquisitions in particular, minimise the risk of land disputes. Messerli et
al. (this volume) see some positive changes occurring, with moves to replace
top-down, authoritarian processes of land allocation—which have further
marginalised vulnerable populations—with more inclusive implementation processes. They conclude that new policies are needed to support this
evolution and address the negative consequences of large-scale land acquisitions, including conflict, loss of pre-existing land use rights and access to
natural resources, the threat to livelihoods, and out-migration, which could
all drive new waves of poverty. They therefore propose a list of recommendations addressed to governments and investors, as well as to civil society
organisations; these include consulting and engaging with local populations,
formalising their tenure rights under a proper land registry system, monitoring adherence to environmental and water regulations, and undertaking social
and environmental impact assessments.

In-depth field research shows that the process and magnitude of dispossession vary significantly across communes and villages (Gironde and Senties
Portilla, this volume), and include, on the one hand, cases in which populations lost the vast majority of their lands without any compensation or opportunity to negotiate or even seek compensation ('severe dispossession'), and
on the other cases in which populations were left with enough land to satisfy
their basic needs ('partial dispossession'). In other cases, populations had to
rebuild livelihoods from zero after they lost all their assets when they were dis-

placed (Cismas and Paramita, this volume), a situation that the authors qualify as *extreme* dispossession (Gironde et al., 2014). The cases of 'better-practice' concessions in Cambodia analysed by Dwyer et al. (this volume) prove that concessions can be granted without evictions proving necessary and can represent a 'relatively good option compared to other local alternatives'. Yet the authors argue that there remain many challenges that must be overcome for these concessions to have a long-standing, positive impact on local populations, as such populations are left to depend on the benevolence of powerful actors. For Dwyer et al., models based on empowered communities with more secure forms of tenure are likely to work better for all parties involved.

Accounting for losses, typically of land, due to land acquisitions is actually a difficult exercise. In some cases, populations lose more land than indicated in the respective land deals themselves, as—in parallel—governments implement measures that additionally restrict people's access to natural resources, typically forest areas, or because large landholdings increase the distance people must travel to reach their plots and hamper activities such as animal grazing. In other cases, land losses were lower than indicated by an examination of land acquisitions areas alone, as not all land was immediately occupied by the new landholders, as explained above. Beyond the loss of land and access to natural resources, large-scale land acquisitions contribute to substantial transformations in local economies. The new socio-economic environment in which people have to reorganise their livelihoods is certainly more dynamic in terms of economic growth, diversification, and urban-rural linkages, but it also generates or exacerbates conflicts within local communities. Overall, the new opportunities do not benefit the majority of the population, who suffer from increasing competition over access to land and jobs. The benefits from crop booms and economic diversification are unevenly distributed and inequality is, overall, on the rise. The results of livelihood trajectory analysis (Gironde and Senties Portilla, this volume) echo the findings of supporters of large-scale land acquisitions, who have acknowledged that promises made are not kept and that land acquisitions are in some cases detrimental to a large proportion of the population (Deininger and Byerlee, 2011).

5   Human Rights Violations and Limited Responses

The negative consequences of large-scale land acquisitions for local populations can also be described as human rights violations (De Schutter, 2011a; De Schutter, 2011b; Künnemann and Monsalve Suárez, 2013). Golay and Biglino (2013) find that the rights that are most frequently violated as a consequence of large-scale land deals are the right to food, the rights of indigenous peoples to dispose of their lands and natural resources, the right to housing and the right not to be forcibly evicted, and the right to water. The authors show that violations of these rights tend, in turn, to trigger a wider pool of infringements such as lack of access to education and healthcare, and violations of cultural rights, and that procedural rights such as rights to participation and consultation; the right to give, or withhold, prior, free, and informed consent; and guaranteed access to effective remedies—including adequate relocation measures and compensation—are also threatened.

Analysing the jurisprudence of those United Nations mechanisms that have monitored the situation in South-East Asia, Golay (this volume) proposes a typology of the human rights violations that result from large-scale land deals. These violations include those linked to internal displacement and forced evictions, as also revealed by Cismas and Paramita (this volume), which often lead to drastic changes in livelihood opportunities; violations of the procedural rights of indigenous peoples, in particular their right to give, or to withhold, their free, prior, and informed consent to policies and activities that directly affect their land, territory, and livelihoods; and violations of the right to food of individuals and groups who are vulnerable to discrimination and marginalisation, including women, children, indigenous peoples, rural communities, and small-scale farmers.

New international instruments have been proposed in response to these violations. The former United Nations Special Rapporteur on the right to food, Olivier De Schutter, has presented a set of eleven human rights principles that should be respected by states, investors, and financial institutions when they negotiate and implement land deals (Special Rapporteur on the Right to Food, 2009). In 2012, the Committee on World Food Security adopted the Voluntary Guidelines on the Responsible Governance of Tenure of Land, Fisheries and Forests in the Context of National Food Security (Governance of Tenure Guidelines), with the aim of promoting secure tenure rights and equitable access to land, fisheries, and forests; of reducing poverty; and of realising the right to food. The guidelines specifically recommend that states provide safeguards to protect legitimate tenure rights, human rights, livelihoods, food security and the environment from the risks that could arise from large-scale land acquisitions, and that responsible investments should do no harm, should safeguard against the dispossession of legitimate tenure-right holders and against environmental damage, and should respect human rights.

While Gironde and Senties Portilla (this volume) are sceptical about the use of international guidelines at the local level, Monsalve Suárez (2013) shows that using such human rights instruments can have positive impacts on local populations, including 'the empowerment of oppressed groups to stand up for their rights, decreasing violence in land conflicts, changing the way conflicts over resources are framed, opening up space for policy dialogue centered on people's lives, fighting against agrarian legislation biased in favour of corporate interests and formulating alternative legal frameworks'. Monsalve Suárez also identifies a number of conditions that need to be in place for the application of these instruments to be effective. Awareness of rights and an ability to claim them are among these conditions, but she also stresses the importance of linkages with law professionals and advocacy networks and of pressure from below. Creative uses of different aspects of law become possible, especially when people have access to courts. Monsalve Suárez also recognises the limitations of using the human rights framework: it assumes that people know about human rights and have the resources to sustain political and legal action, and that the circumstances are such that they have access to justice, a condition that may be particularly circumscribed for women.

Golay (this volume) shows that these conditions, including access to justice—very often non-existent in cases of large-scale land acquisitions, are far from being fulfilled in South-East Asia, which could explain why human rights instruments have little influence in the cases studied. Cismas and Paramita (this volume) describe the extreme disparities that exist in Cambodia regarding the extent to which human rights instruments inform the acts and actions of the government in relation to land transactions, and regarding the strategies employed by affected communities. The authors suggest that rural-urban spatiality is relevant to explaining these disparities, with rural communities left with no information, consultation options, or access to justice, and urban dwellers having made extensive use of human rights language and mechanisms to challenge their own forced evictions with a certain success.

In the end, what counts from a human rights—and development—perspective is that the rights and needs of the local populations are respected, protected, and fulfilled. In the future, an argument more convincing than using the human rights framework to persuade states, investors, and financial institutions to ensure that large-scale land deals have a positive impact on local populations might be to demonstrate that land deals have less chance of being implemented if the rights of local populations are not respected. If the rapid and forceful acquisition of land exacerbates tensions between villagers and companies, prior consultations, negotiation, and conflict-resolution mechanisms could significantly mitigate these tensions and the negative consequences for local populations (Gironde et al., 2014). It is also important to note that informed, knowledgeable, and strong local leaders are often crucial in making the difference regarding whether, and—if so—under which terms, a land deal will be implemented (Gironde et al., 2014).

6   Beyond Current Land Dynamics in South-East Asia

Current land dynamics in South-East Asia bring to the fore a number of avenues for further research and policies that could better support local populations in their efforts to cope with, and benefit from, these dynamics. At least three of these avenues have been explored in detail in this volume.

First, this volume echoes the call by 'land grab' analysts to move beyond the initial picture and early-stage assumptions, a move reflected by the insistence on the need for historical analysis (see, for instance, White et al., 2012 for Asia; Baglioni and Gibbon, 2013 and Wily, 2012 for Africa; and Edelman and Leon, 2013 for Central America). The current wave of land acquisitions that became evident around a decade ago cannot simply be dated from that point in time. What has happened elsewhere, and before, is crucial to an understanding of the here and now (Edelman et al., 2013). The recurrence of large-scale land acquisitions and the formation of large estates under different contexts also call for an investigation of the cases and contexts of non-grabbing (Sikor, 2012) and raise the question of why there is not *more* land grabbing all over the globe.

Second, the importance of particular contexts in which land acquisitions occur calls for in-depth field research in order to make the link between particular contexts, processes, and outcomes of land acquisitions and the different trajectories of agrarian transition they contribute to shaping. Empirical material analysing how land deals are negotiated and then implemented across various governmental, administrative, and jurisdictional scales is crucial not only for the purposes of generalisation and out-scaling (Messerli et al., this volume), but also for the design of policies that correspond to realities on the ground.

Third, the outcomes of the current wave of land acquisitions can also been assessed from a human rights perspective. These outcomes have been addressed mostly in terms of dispossession, marginalisation, exclusion, disruption, etc. These analyses come mostly from the fields of political economy and political ecology and build on livelihood studies. Despite a great interest in the governance of large-scale land deals (Margulis et al., 2014) and the fact that many studies have shown that human rights violations can be one of their immediate consequences (De Schutter, 2011a; De Schutter, 2011b; Künnemann and Monsalve Suárez, 2013), a human rights perspective that would analyse the efficiency of using human rights instruments and monitoring mechanisms to mitigate these violations is still embryonic (Cotula, 2009; 2012; Monsalve Suárez, 2013; Narula, 2013; Clays and Vanloqueren, 2013; Golay and Biglino, 2013) and could also be developed further.

References

Akram-Lodhi, A.H. (2012) 'Contextualising Land Grabbing: Contemporary Land Deals, the Global Subsistence Crisis and the World Food System', *Canadian Journal of Development Studies/Revue canadienne d'études du développement*, 33(2), pp. 119–142, DOI: 10.1080/02255189.2012.690726.

Aso, M. (2014) 'Des plantations coloniales à la production socialiste la "vietnamisation" de l'hévéa (1956–1975)', in Fortunel, F. and C. Gironde (eds.) *L'Or Blanc, Petits et grands planteurs face au "boom" de l'hévéaculture (Viêt-nam-Cambodge)* (Bangkok: Institut de Recherche sur l'Asie du Sud-Est Contemporaine), pp. 65–82, http://www.irasec.com/ouvrage113 (accessed on 21 May 2015).

Baglioni, E. and P. Gibbon (2013) 'Land Grabbing, Large- and Small-Scale Farming: What Can Evidence and Policy from 20th Century Africa Contribute to the Debate?', *Third World Quarterly*, 34(9), pp. 1558–1581, DOI: 10.1080/01436597.2013.843838.

Baird, I. (2011) 'Turning Land into Capital, Turning People into Labour: Primitive Accumulation and the Arrival of Large-Scale Economic Land Concessions in the Lao People's Democratic Republic', *New Proposals: Journal of Marxism and Interdisciplinary Inquiry*, 5(1), pp. 10–26, http://ojs.library.ubc.ca/index.php/newproposals/article/view/2264 (accessed on 21 May 2015).

Baird, I. and B. Shoemaker (2007) 'Unsettling Experiences: Internal Resettlement and International Aid Agencies in Laos', *Development and Change*, 38(5), pp. 865–888, DOI: 10.1111/j.1467-7660.2007.00437.x.

Bissonnette, J-F. and R. De Koninck (2015) *Large Plantations versus Smallholdings in Southeast Asia: Historical and Contemporary Trends*, paper presented at the Conference on Land Grabbing, Conflict and Agrarian-Environmental Transformations: Perspective from East and Southeast Asia, 5–6 June, Chiang Mai University.

Borras, S.M.Jr. and J.C. Franco (2011) *Political Dynamics of Land-grabbing in Southeast Asia: Understanding Europe's Role* (Amsterdam: Transnational Institute), http://www.tni.org/report/political-dynamics-land-grabbing-southeast-asia-understanding-europes-role (accessed on 21 May 2015).

Bourdier, F. (2009) 'When the Margins Turn One's Step Toward an Object of Desir: Segregation and Exclusion of Indigenous Peoples in Northeast Cambodia', in Hammer, P.J. and M. Khmersiksa (eds.) *Living on the Margins: Minorities and Borderlines in Cambodia and Southeast Asia* (Phnom Penh: Center for Khmer Studies) pp. 177–185.

Brautigam, D. (2013) 'Chinese Engagement in African Agriculture: Fiction and Fact'. in Allan, J.A., M. Keulertz, S. Sojamo and J. Warner (eds.) *Handbook of Land and Water Grabs: Foreign Direct Investment and Food and Water Security* (Abingdon: Routledge).

Burns, A. (2004) *Thailand's 20 Year Program to Title Rural Land*, background paper for the World Development Report 2005, February 13, http://siteresources.worldbank. org/INTWDR2005/Resources/burns_thailand_land_titling.pdf (accessed on 21 May 2015).

Clays, P. and G. Vanloqueren (2013) 'The Minimum Human Rights Principles Applicable to Large-Scale Land Acquisitions or Leases', *Globalizations*, 10(1), pp. 193–198. DOI: 10.1080/14747731.2013.760940.

Cleary, M. and P. Eaton (1996) *Tradition and Reform, Land Tenure and Rural Development in South-East Asia* (New York: Oxford University Press).

Cotula, L. (2012) ' "Land Grabbing" in the Shadow of the Law: Legal Frameworks Regulating the Global Land Rush', in Rayfuse, R. and N. Weisfelt (eds.) *The Challenge of Food Security. International Policy and Regulatory Frameworks* (Cheltenham and Northampton: Edward Elgar) pp. 206–228.

———— (ed.) (2009) *The Right to Food and Access to Natural Resources. Using Human Rights Arguments and Mechanisms to Improve Resource Access for the Rural Poor* (Rome: Food and Agriculture Organization) http://pubs.iied.org/pdfs/G03065.pdf? (accessed on 21 May 2015).

De Koninck, R. (2003) 'Southeast Asian Agriculture post-1960: Economic and Territorial Expansion', in Chia Lin Sien (ed.) *Southeast Asia Transformed: A Geography of Change* (Singapore: Institute of Southeast Asian Studies) pp. 191–230.

De Koninck, R. and J.-F. Rousseau (2012) *Gambling with the Land. The Contemporary Evolution of Southeast Asian Agriculture 1960–2008* (Singapore: National University of Singapore Press).

De Schutter, O. (2011a) 'How not to Think of Land-Grabbing: Three Critiques of Large-Scale Investments in Farmland', *The Journal of Peasant Studies*, 38(2), pp. 249–279, DOI: 10.1080/03066150.2011.559008.

———— (2011b) 'The Green Rush: The Global Race for Farmland and the Rights of Land Users', *Harvard International Law Journal*, 52(2), pp. 504–559.

Deininger, K. and D. Byerlee (2011) *Rising Global Interest in Farmland: Can it Yield Sustainable and Equitable Benefits?* (Washington, D.C.: World Bank–International Bank for Reconstruction and Development).

Dufumier, M. (2006) 'Introduction: Slash-and-Burn, Intensification of Rice Production, Migratory Movements, and Pioneer Front Agriculture in Southeast Asia', *Moussons*, No. 9–10, pp. 7–31, http://moussons.revues.org/1979 (accessed on 21 May 2015).

Dwyer, M. (2015) 'The Formalization Fix? Land Titling, Land Concessions and the Politics of Spatial Transparency in Cambodia', *The Journal of Peasant Studies*, DOI: 10.1080/03066150.2014.994510.

Edelman M. and A. León (2013) 'Cycles of Land Grabbing in Central America: An Argument for History and a Case Study in the Bajo Aguán, Honduras', *Third World Quarterly*, 34(9), pp. 1697–1722, DOI: 10.1080/01436597.2013.843848.

Edelman, M., C. Oya and S.M.Jr. Borras (2013) 'Global Land Grabs: Historical Processes, Theoretical and Methodological Implications and Current Trajectories', *Third World Quarterly*, 34(9), pp. 1517–1531, DOI: 10.1080/01436597.2013.850190.

Fortunel, F. (2014) 'Kampong Cham et Ratanakiri, regards croisés sur l'évolution des grandes plantations cambodgiennes', in Fortunel, F. and C. Gironde (eds.) *L'Or Blanc, Petits et grands planteurs face au "boom" de l'hévéaculture (Viêt-nam-Cambodge)* (Bangkok: Institut de Recherche sur l'Asie du Sud-Est Contemporaine) pp. 123–142, http://www.irasec.com/ouvrage113 (accessed on 21 May 2015).

Fortunel, F. and C. Gironde (2011) 'Transitions agraires et recompositions sociales en Asie du Sud-Est', in Guibert, M. and Y. Jean (eds.) *Dynamiques des espaces ruraux dans le monde* (Paris: Armand Colin), pp. 215–235.

Gironde, C., C. Golay, P. Messerli, A. Peeters and O. Schönweger (2014) (with the contributions of I. Biglino, I. Cismas, C. Friis, P. Paramita, G. Senties Portilla and S. Seng) *Large-Scale Land Acquisitions in Southeast Asia: Rural Transformations between Global Agendas and Peoples' Right to Food'*, Working Paper (Geneva: Swiss Network for International Studies).

Golay, C. (2009) *The Right to Food and Access to Justice: Examples at the National, Regional and International Levels* (Rome: Food and Agriculture Organization).

Golay, C. and I. Biglino (2013) 'Human Rights Responses to Land Grabbing: a Right to Food Perspective', *Third World Quarterly*, 34(9), pp. 1630–1650, DOI: 10.1080/01436597.2013.843853.

Hall, D., P. Hirsch and T.M. Li (2011) *Powers of Exclusion: Land Dilemmas in Southeast Asia* (Singapore: National University of Singapore Press).

Hayami, Y. (2001) 'Ecology, History, and Development: A Perspective from Rural Southeast Asia', *The World Bank Research Observer*, 16(2), pp. 169–198, DOI: 10.1093/wbro/16.2.169.

Hutchinson, J. (2008) 'Land Titling and Poverty Reduction in Southeast Asia', *Australian Journal of International Affairs*, 62(3), pp. 332–334, DOI: 10.1080/10357710802286791.

Künnemann, R. and S. Monsalve Suárez (2013) 'International Human Rights and Governing Land Grabbing: A View from Global Civil Society', *Globalizations*, 10(1), pp. 123–139, DOI: 10.1080/14747731.2013.760933.

Margulis, M.E., N. McKeon and S.M.Jr. Borras (eds.) (2014) *Land Grabbing and Global Governance. Rethinking Globalizations* (London: Routledge).

Maurer, J.-L. (1986) *Modernisation agricole, développement économique et changement social. Le riz, la terre et l'homme à Java* (Paris: Presses Universitaires de France), http://books.openedition.org/iheid/4454 (accessed on 21 May 2015).

McMichael, P. (2012) 'The Land Grab and Corporate Food Regime Restructuring', *The Journal of Peasant Studies*, 39(3–4), pp. 681–701, DOI: 10.1080/03066150.2012.661369.

Merlet, M. (2010) 'Différents régimes d'accès à la terre dans le monde. Le cas de l'Amérique latine', *Mondes en développement*, 3(151), pp. 35–50, DOI: 10.3917/med.151.0035.

Monsalve Suárez, S. (2013) 'The Human Rights Framework in Contemporary Agrarian Struggles', *Journal of Peasant Studies*, 40(1), pp. 239–290, DOI: 10.1080/03066150.2011.652950.

Narula, S. (2013) 'The Global Land Rush: Markets, Rights, and the Politics of Food', *Standford Journal of International Law*, 49(1), pp. 101–175, http://ssrn.com/abstract=2294521 (accessed on 22 May 2015).

Neef, A., S. Touch and J. Chiengthong (2013) 'The Politics and Ethics of Land Concessions in Rural Cambodia', *Journal of Agricultural and Environmental Ethics*, 26(6), pp. 1085–1103, DOI: 10.1007/s10806–013–9446-y.

Pham, T.H. and R. De Koninck (2014) 'L'expansion de l'hévéaculture dans les hautes terres du Viêt Nam: l'endroit et l'envers', in Fortunel, F. and C. Gironde (eds.) *L'Or Blanc, Petits et grands planteurs face au "boom" de l'hévéaculture (Viêt-nam-Cambodge)* (Bangkok: Institut de Recherche sur l'Asie du Sud-Est Contemporaine) pp. 83–100.

Sikor, T. (2012) 'Tree Plantations, Politics of Possession and the Absence of Land Grabs in Vietnam', *The Journal of Peasant Studies*, 39(3–4), pp. 1077–1101, DOI: 10.1080/03066150.2012.674943.

Smaller, C. and H. Mann (2009) *A Thirst for Distant Lands: Foreign Investment in Agricultural Land and Water* (Winnipeg: International Institute for Sustainable Development).

Special Rapporteur on the Right to Food (2009) *Large-Scale Land Acquisitions and Leases: A Set of Minimum Principles and Measures to Address the Human Rights Challenge*, Annex to the Report of the Special Rapporteur on the right to food, Olivier De Schutter, UN doc. A/HRC/13/33/Add.2, 28 December.

Sturgeon, J. (2012) 'The Cultural Politics of Ethnic Identity in Xishuangbanna, China: Tea and Rubber as "Cash Crops" and "Commodities"', *Journal of Current Chinese Affairs*, 41(4), pp. 109–131, http://journals.sub.uni-hamburg.de/giga/jcca/article/view/576 (accessed on 22 May 2015).

Verhaegen, E. (2013) *La tragédie des communs revisitée. Les tenures collectives face aux politiques foncières en Asie du Sud-Est*, Etudes et documents du Groupe de Recherches Asie de l'Est et du Sud Est, No. 8 (Louvain la Neuve, Gembloux and Hanoi: UCL–ULG–CIRRD), http://www.gembloux.ulg.ac.be/eg/publications-cooperation-internationale/doc_download/421- (accessed on 22 May 2015).

White, B., S.M.Jr. Borras, R. Hall, I. Scoones and W. Wolford (2012) 'The New Enclosures: Critical Perspectives on Corporate Land Deals', *Journal of Peasant Studies*, 39(3–4), pp. 619–647, DOI: 10.1080/03066150.2012.691879.

Wily, L.A. (2012) 'Looking Back to See Forward: the Legal Niceties of Land Theft in Land Rushes', *The Journal of Peasant Studies*, 39(3–4), pp. 751–775, DOI: 10.1080/03066150.2012.674033.

Zoomers, A. and M. Kaag (2014) 'Conclusion: Beyond the Global Land Grab Hype— Ways Forward in Research and Action', in Kaag, M. and A. Zoomers (eds.) *The Global Land Grab—Beyond The Hype* (London and New York: Zed Books) pp. 201–216.

Index